Note

God Had a Question and

You Are the Answer

by Eric John, Celestine Wonderlun & Yes

Dedications

To the Angels

Abraham, Ann, Barbara, Becky, Ben, Bill, Billy, Bob, Brad, Burt, Camari, Camden, Capres, Carol, Christine, Cindy, Danny, Dave, David, Dorothy, Doug, Eric, Faith, Fatima, Gina, Glenn, Greg, Hazel, Herb, Herbert, Holly, Imogene, Ione, Jack, Jaiden, Janey, Janie, Jean, Jenesis, Jenny, Jill, Jim, JoAnn, Joe, Johnny, Juanita, Kelly, Knothead, Lindsey, Lisa, Lora, Lori, Madelyn, Mallary, Marsha, Martha, Matthew, Maxime, Michael, Mildred, Nancy, Note, Pat, Patricia, Patty, Ralph, Richard, Rodney, Rolan, Scott, Sharon, Sherri, Sherry, Smokey, Spencer, Stacie, Steve, Terri, Terry, Tim, Tom, Tristen, Troy, Tucker, Veronica, Waite, Warren, Wendy.

What is Note?

Josiah sat in his porch swing, swaying gently with the rhythm of the ticking grandfather clock just inside the screen door. He always found that sound. Joe was bird watching before his granddaughter arrived. Blue jays were building a nest in the thick of the old oak tree. A new family was moving in.

The smell of the fresh-cut lawn next door filled the air. *I wonder if the blue jays can smell that*, he thought. *Oh, they're probably too busy.*

Just then, his precious Breanna came walking up the sidewalk. Her ponytail swung from side to side as she strode confidently. She was on a mission and had things to do.

She walked up onto the porch and approached her Grandpa, who rose to greet her with a heartfelt hug. "I'm delighted to see you, Bree; please, sit, relax. It's a hot one today. Would you like a nice slice of cold watermelon to cool you off? We got a real sweet and juicy one."

"Maybe in a while. I need your help. Grandpa, I really appreciate this."

Bree was such joy to him, and he could only say yes to her. "Before we talk, I want to share how happy it makes me to see you smile when you first see me. I can tell you're not thinking about it; it just happens. It's very affirming, Bree, and I'm grateful. Thank you for that gift. I know you see the same on my face when we see each other. What are we talking about today?"

"I have a book report, Grandpa, on a book I kind of don't get. I mean, I get some of it, but not enough to make sense of it for my report. Have you read Note?"

"Yes, I have. I found a few pebbles for my pond in that one. What are you struggling with?"

"What is Note? What's it about?"

Josiah looked at her lovingly and proceeded. "Look at me closely and see me like it's the first time, all the many things about me you haven't noticed before. Take your time. Good. Now look past me.

"Everywhere you look, Bree, all you see is entirely unique from everything else. It will only be one time. Its existence is the first and the last, always. There is nothing in the complete Universe that isn't profoundly exclusive. The reason for that is, God asks a question: 'What am I?'"

Josiah paused to let Breanna chew on that.

"Wow, I don't get it. God asked a question...God!"

"I hear you, Bree; crazy, right? This is one of countless things beyond your Grandpa's comprehension. I don't know why God asked, but the Universe is the answer, or all of the Universes."

"Help me get there, Grandpa; I'm trying here."

"Take your book report. You read a book to write the report. You experience the book, discover what it means, and sum it all up. The outcome is that you know what the book is. God knows what will be but is discovering it. God knows what will happen but will experience it. God knows, and by discovering and experiencing all that is as it is, God gets the answer. The Universe was One and then evolved to be all of this. And it's just getting started. God discovers and experiences the answer as each moment comes and goes, with every unique everything occurring for the first and last time, everywhere. And consider this, Bree. Unlike us, God doesn't forget, and 'now' is not a new moment, but simply more of one. It's like a glass filling up with water, one unique something at a time for God to drink at the end, when the glass is full."

"I don't think I will put any of this in my book report, Grandpa. It's too big and I still don't get it. Back to my original question, what is Note?"

"Fair enough. When the Universe began, everything began. Song was born too. Think of the power of song in your life, Breanna, and how profound it is."

"You mean music?"

"Yes. Consider how it touches you and all those around you. Song may be a part of the word of God, and Note is part of Song. Music is like the air we breathe except it has a soul, an essence; don't you feel that?"

"Still deep here, Grandpa."

"Okay, the book. Note is about a part of Song that moves through the Universe from its beginning to its end, experiencing and discovering life through others' experiences of it. The book contends that humanity and the human spirit do, and will, play a large role in answering God's question. The stories in the book are through the human experience. There's a theme or a message in the book around humanity moving to the next level of community, so it can survive to impact the Universe favorably. In the end, Note serves as the solution for the Universe, which differs from the answering of God's question."

"All of that made sense until the last part. What do you mean, Note serves as the solution?"

"How much of the book have you read, Bree?"

"To be honest, Grandpa, not much; two chapters, that's all."

"Well, my delightful granddaughter, read the book and be open to it. There will be pebbles for your pond too. We can talk once you've read it. Fair?"

"Yes." Breanna paused. "Can I ask Grandpa, is it the same pebble for everyone?"

"No, I am confident that everyone who reads it will come away with something that's in there just for them."

"What's one pebble you picked up, Grandpa?"

"Though this wasn't spelled out in any of the chapters, Bree, reading Note brought this revelation to me: Love is the past and the present, like truth. That is to say, love is truth, and it's real. Hope is the future."

"Then love isn't the future?" she asked.

"Once it's not the future, it is."

. "I have to ask Grandpa, what about hate?"

"Great question, Bree. Think of a forest fire. The fire line burning through the forest is like hate. It destroys and presses forward. It's intense and short lived and dies once the fuel is gone. Behind it is life, where seedlings sprout and the new forest is born. That's love. Love is everywhere and long lived. Hate is short lived and passing. Hope is where love will be reborn."

"You got that pebble reading Note?"

"Yes."

Josiah watched Breanna stare at the pitcher of ice water sitting on the side table next to the swing. The heat and humidity were impossible to ignore on this day.

The glass pitcher had condensation on the outside with large drops of water rolling down its smooth surface to find the table, and she could almost hear the ice cracking in the nectar.

"I squeezed a lime in that water, Bree, and added some honey. It's really good. Do you want some of that?"

"Heck yeah," Breanna answered.

Note: The Foundations

Note is born right after the beginning of the Universe and lives throughout its entire existence. Song is one of God's angels; Note is part of Song.

Note joins a being to experience meaning or essence. The effect of joining beings elevates their clarity and awareness away from the chaos and the distractions of normal life. The impact on the soul Note joins is like the impact we feel when we fall in love. It overwhelms us while exciting us. We're hopeful and intoxicatingly immersed.

Note is untethered to time.

> The Universe is tethered to time and evolution. Consider a roller coaster where the cars leave the station for a wonderful experience around twists and turns, highs and lows. An amazing journey to be sure, but the cars are always tethered to the track.

> Time, evolution, and the Universe started together in the first moment when the Universe was in its purest form. And at its completion, when it is at its most complex, the Universe ends in the last moment. Note tethers to evolution and evolves with the Universe and all in it but is untethered to time. *Note can join, leave, and rejoin the roller coaster ride at any moment, while your—and my—experience is linear, tethered to time.*

Note is genderless. The pronoun for Note is note or we.

Note's evolution is over seemingly infinite time in countless experiences and souls. The fifty stories in this book are a slice of that. They dance with and around a theme of humanity moving to the next level of community. The symbol of a North Star to guide us is prevalent, as are paradigm changes in concepts like Reverence for Life.

Note's experience is throughout the Universe and across multiple galaxies on many worlds, but primarily in our Universe, Note's home Universe. The diversity of the Universe is unfathomable, and only some of its unique facets are on these few pages. In life, however, the essence of the human spirit is universal. From the beginning, everything has sought to go home, and human experiences are a beautiful representation of that. Even though the languages, inflections, and perspectives around one's experience are as diverse within the Universe as the Universe itself, this book depicts the human spirit in 21st Century American English, in cultures familiar to what we share around our blue world.

Primary characters are:

1. Note, part of the Song of God
2. Gray, an infinite soul with Christ consciousness
3. Grace, the breath of God
4. The Dream Maker, a tool of Grace in the dream realm

I hope there is a pebble in Note for your pond!

Note

for You

It's your birthday, and you hope your person bakes your favorite cake; you like the corners with the extra icing. Your person goes to the store and picks up the box of cake mix and the rich and yummy icing. Something good is about to happen for you.

The cake is the outcome, and you can taste all the love your person baked into it. The cake box with the cake mix has marketing fluff and a person smiling on the front. On the side of the box, you find nutrition data and those oddly named ingredients. You may just care about the baked cake with some candles. Or, you may care about all the ingredients in that fluffy, delicious cake.

Note, the book, is the whole package, with the marketing and smiling person on the front of the box, nutrition and ingredients on the side and the cake mix to whip up that birthday cake, just for you.

If you aren't interested in the ingredients, move past them in Note. If you just want to see if the flour in it is enriched or not, you'll find the answer. Still, if you want it all, it's all here.

Please consider reading only *one chapter a day after Chapter 3*. There's something in each story that may be for you. If you read this book to get it done and check the box, you may miss your pebble.

My hope is you have the best birthday ever, and each one from now on is better than the last. I hope the cake brings you joy in every bite, along with all those with whom you share it.

Table of Contents

The End

Note was in darkness for a profoundly long time. All the stars had lived their lives and died. The Universe was populated with trillions of worlds, all cold, still and dead now; the Universe was without light. So much time had passed that even the energy holding matter together was dissipating, and the matter was disintegrating. Note had faith that note too would dissolve and experience death and the ultimate peace. Note joined the last living being before the end.

With her head resting in his lap and her flowing hair laid over his leg, he lovingly stroked her head, feeling the warmth of her life, witnessing the profundity of it. Their eyes locked; there was nothing to say. It was done. Her mind floated into reliving their past together while bathing in the love of the beautiful moment. Adam heard her last breath leave her mouth, feeling it kiss his face.

Adam held his dear wife's body with loving reverence and sorrow. He was the last soul in the last living world, circling the final Star. He had entered a wormhole eons ago to get to this place—home—and Eve, arriving just centuries before this moment.

Note joined Adam and found the soul of Gray. Beyond words, they shared a sense of awe. There had been so much. The Universe was not infinite, yet it was incomprehensible.

And it all started with One!

Chapter One

God Spark

The Beginning

𝒜t wasn't day or night; neither existed yet.

It wasn't a moment in time, because time hadn't begun, nor was there promise of it.

There was no reason for it because everything existed already. Yet, somehow, could there be more?

God put a pebble into nowhere, and it became somewhere. The pebble was everything this Universe would become. Existence and space were born together along with time, truth, gravity, evolution, and singular existence.

Before the pebble, however, came a question, but not in words: What am I?

It started with a breath, the breath of God, Grace.

Essence charged Matter. Why and what combined, and space expanded endlessly. Essence would bear good and evil, while matter would bear positive and negative. The creation of the Universe combined matter and essence to create a singular existence, with each new participant distinct from one element to the other. Unbounded elemental births occurred as each moment succeeded the last. Time, truth, and gravity—along with matter and essence—are existence, seemingly infinite. The Universe is in perfect order. Chaos exists in perfect order.

In the very first moment, there was all of the sound that would ever be, altogether, the Song of the Universe. Note was born from Song. Pure essence and not constrained by time, Note would experience the lifeless Universe in all its glory and then life.

To experience "all" is to experience "all" from the beginning.

Order plus Chaos equals Evolution, and so it begins.

"The Big Bang did not occur as an explosion in the usual way one thinks about such things. The Universe did not expand into space, as the space within the Universe did not exist before the Universe. The Big Bang birthed the simultaneous appearance of space everywhere. The Universe has not expanded from any one spot since the Big Bang — instead, space itself has been stretching and carrying matter with it.

"Although the expansion of the Universe gradually slowed down as the matter in the Universe pulled on itself via gravity, about 5 or 6 billion years after the Big Bang, a mysterious force called dark energy began speeding up the expansion of the Universe again.

"During the first three minutes of the Universe, the light elements were born during a process known as Big Bang nucleosynthesis. Temperatures cooled from 100 nonillions (10^{32}) Kelvin to 1 billion (10^9) Kelvin, and protons and neutrons collided to make deuterium, an isotope of hydrogen. Most of the deuterium combined to make helium and trace amounts of lithium generated.

"For the first 380,000 years, the Universe was too hot for light to shine. The heat of creation smashed atoms together with enough force to break them up into a dense plasma, an opaque soup of protons, neutrons, and electrons that scattered light like fog.

"Roughly 380,000 years after the Big Bang, matter cooled enough for atoms to form during the era of recombination, resulting in a transparent, electrically neutral gas, setting loose the initial flash of light created during the Big Bang.

"The Universe was plunged back into the darkness since no stars or any other bright objects had formed yet. About 400 million years after the Big Bang, the Universe emerged from the cosmic dark ages during the epoch of reionization. During this time, which lasted more than a half-billion years, clumps of gas collapsed enough to form the first stars and galaxies, whose energetic ultraviolet light ionized and destroyed most of the neutral hydrogen."[1]

"The birth of stars the way we know them is because the temperature and density continued to increase until they reached what we call the 'flash point.' Until this moment, all the collisions between nuclei were like marbles bouncing off each other. Each nucleus, having a positive charge, would only get so close to another nucleus before being pushed away by the electrostatic repulsion between both nuclei. Reaching the flash point, some of these collisions occurred in a manner to allow the nuclei to get close enough to interact with each other. That allowed the strong nuclear force to bind these smaller nuclei together, forming a more massive nucleus, a process called FUSION. In the process of fusing nuclei, tremendous amounts of energy release, and this energy causes the star to shine.

"As the increase of temperatures and fusion continues, new and heavier elements form as their atomic size grows. The star has a central core of helium fusing into carbon, surrounded by a shell that has hydrogen turning into helium. As the carbon nuclei are produced, they are pulled toward the center, just as the helium nuclei were earlier, and a carbon core results. For an average-sized star, this is as far as it goes because of the mass of the star. There is not enough gravitational force (because of the lack of mass) in the star to allow the temperature and density to reach levels where carbon nuclei can fuse into more massive nuclei.

"If a star had sufficient mass, though, eventually enough carbon would accumulate so that the temperature and density reach a point where carbon nuclei could fuse into neon nuclei. This carbon burning core would be surrounded by two outer shells, the innermost burning helium, and the outermost burning hydrogen. This pattern of the central core collapsing and increasing temperature continues until a further round of fusion occurs, and more shells form. How many shells depend on the initial mass of the collapsing nebula. That is because the dominant force that produces conditions suitable for fusion to happen is gravity, and the mass of the star determines the force of gravity. If enough mass accumulates in a forming core, gravity will create enough force to raise the temperature and density to levels where the next series of fusion reactions can take place. The larger the mass of the Proto-Star, the greater is its ability to form more shells during the lifetime of the star. That will also reduce the lifetime of the star since the increases in temperature increase the fusion rates in the core and the surrounding shells, thus using up fuel even faster. Further cores/shells involve neon being converted to oxygen, oxygen fusing to silicon, and finally, silicon going to Ni (this product is radioactive and decays to form iron). Stars that reach this stage are red super giants.

"As the fusion process continues, the concentration of iron increases in the star's core, the core contracts, and the temperature increases again. When the temperature reaches a point where iron can undergo nuclear reactions, the resulting reactions are unique from the ones that have previously taken place. Iron nuclei are the most stable of all atomic nuclei. Because of this, when they undergo nuclear reactions, they don't release energy but absorb it. Therefore, there is no release of energy to balance the force of gravity. There is a decrease in the internal pressure that works with gravity to make the collapse of the core more intense. In this collapse, the iron nuclei in the central portion of the core break down into alpha particles, protons, and neutrons and compress even further. However, they cannot be infinitely compressed. Eventually, the outer layers of a material rebound off the compressed core and eject outward.

"This situation is like striking a rubber ball on the ground with a hammer. Initially, the hammer can compress the rubber ball because of its force. Still, eventually, it is stopped by the density and pressure of the rubber ball reaching its limit and is thrown back violently by the recoiling rubber ball, which itself will bounce off the surface because of this recoil. In the star, the outer layers of the core are like the hammer, and the core is the rubber ball. Following the collapse of the inner core, the outer layers of the star pull toward the center. That sets the stage for a tremendous collision between the recoiling core layers and the collapsing outermost layers. Under the extreme conditions of this collision, two things happen that lead to the formation of the heaviest elements. First, the temperature reaches levels that cannot be attained by even the most massive stars. That gives the nuclei present high kinetic energies, making them very reactive.

Second, because of the breaking apart of the iron nuclei in the central core, there is a high concentration of neutrons (called the neutron flux) that ejects from the core during the supernova. Surrounding nuclei capture these neutrons and then decay to a proton by emitting an electron and an antineutrino. Each captured neutron will cause the atomic number of that nucleus to go up by one upon its decay.

"With the large neutron flux created during a supernova, this neutron capture/decay sequence can repeat many times, adding protons to form increasingly more massive nuclei. These conditions exist for only a short time, but long enough to form the highest mass nuclei.

"Because of this 'rebound explosion,' all the outer layers of the star, enriched with the higher mass nuclei, are blown off into space. That material will later make its way into other nebulas to become incorporated into other stars (where the same cycle of events will repeat). Each cycle uses up more of the hydrogen and helium from the early Universe and creates more significant amounts of the higher mass elements.

"These are all the elements that make up the Universe today. It is what life is made of."[2]

Chapter Two

Earth Spark

A **little over nine billion** years after the Big Bang, within the Milky Way galaxy, a star system with the Sun was born. Humans later named the Sun, Sol. The star system was then known as the Solar system.

The first dawn, after fusion ignited the Sun, fell on a mammoth giant of a world, later named Jupiter by humanity. Jupiter's great mass would help decide the miracle of our solar system and the life it would yield. Jupiter's initial orbit around the Sun changed as though the breath of God blew it. It spiraled inward, closer and closer to the Sun, clearing massive amounts of debris from what we refer to as the asteroid belt. The result was only enough planet-building material to build worlds that were too small, having too little gravity to hold a light hydrogen atmosphere. The resulting conditions were perfect for a heavy atmosphere to evolve that would sustain carbon-based life. As grace would have it, and after millions of years, Jupiter returned to the outer solar system by its massive neighbor Saturn, leaving behind the environment for a cherished blue world.

Chapter Three

Love Spark

To experience "all" is to experience "all" from the beginning.

Note lived all the atomic combinations in every degree and physical circumstance but had yet to hear a word or feel love. To Note, time and truth were the same things since nothing was true until it happened, and each something only happened as time allowed.

Though Note would experience seemingly infinite happenings, there would be a first and a last for Note. Untethered to time, Note chose this soul to experience life for the first time and experience it from its beginning, conception.

***

Four billion six hundred million years after the birth of the solar system

Ankita and Anash sat quietly over a favorite vegan Indian potato chickpea stew. It was Ankita's night to make dinner; she prepared one of Anash's favorites with spiced potatoes, chickpeas, and carrots all simmered in a savory vegetable broth with spinach and raisins, plump and juicy. Toasted cashews and fresh lemon juice made it a meal with some crunch and freshness.

The smell of paint still lingered in the air; they had recently painted their dining-room windows and trim a vivid teal, which contrasted against the bright white walls. A redwood bench sat in front of the windows with two stacks of jewel-colored quilts. They each had a favorite that they regularly used when the windows were open and the air was chilly.

They owned a heavy antique teak dining table Ankita had inherited from her grandpa, and it commanded attention with its rich wood tone with a light stain applied decades before. Both the table and chairs adorned meticulous carvings and a simple color pallet. The front legs of the chairs were red with green accents, matching the table legs. Anash brought marigolds home today for Ankita to celebrate their love, and they were striking on the table, complemented by the chickpea stew. The wobbling ceiling fan above them caused the flower petals to sway, making the arrangement seem alive. The clean granite tile on the floor that he'd washed today was cool on the bottoms of their bare feet. The moment was special.

"Dinner is delicious," Anash shared. "Why are you so quiet? You aren't eating much either; what's going on? Share with me, Darling."

"Oh, Babu," she responded. "I'm sorry to be acting this way. I know I seem out of sorts or something, but yes, I must talk to you and tell you about my day. Please finish your stew. We can talk after."

He took another couple of bites.

"What is it, my love?"

Her mind appearing to be in another place, Ankita asked, "Have you ever stopped to think how remarkable all this is? We have a sun that's just a colossal explosion, and it's stable enough for our world to live as it does. As complex as all this is, Babu, it all works together in balance. Just being able to smell this stew, you know. I feel like I've just been skating on a frozen lake with no idea about all that's under the ice."

"Ankita," he said with a concerned voice, "What's wrong? Do we need to wait, Darling? What happened today?"

"Okay, I want to tell you," Ankita spoke pensively, "but first, I want to ask you a question. Do you believe in fate or chance?"

"What do you mean?"

"Do you believe that everything happens as it's supposed to, or do you think it is all just by chance, you know—what happens, happens?"

"That's a profound question." Anash donned a serious look. "Do you mind if I think about that a while? Does this have something to do with your day?"

"Yes. I want to tell you, Babu."

"My Love, you're frightening me," he said.

"Okay, I'm sorry for my hesitation."

Ankita's long, thick black hair curled around her beautiful reddish-brown face. Her dark eyes were marbled and intense, and her smile seemed to melt most who were fortunate enough to receive it.

"You know," she shared, "while I'm on vacation this week, I planned to go to Fort Kochi Beach one day after you left for work. Today was that day, and I was excited about going. I got to the beach during the sunrise. The colors of the sky were especially vivid today. I saw bright oranges and soft pinks reflecting off the sea, bouncing on the swells. It was stunning. I walked out to the water's edge and felt the water surging across my feet and through my toes. It was like it was the first time. I just can't explain it, Babu."

"We slept very well last night, Darling," he interjected.

"Yes, we did, but I was open to receiving it this morning. I heard laughing children, even that early, and it made me happy. I walked along the water for a while and then heard some acoustic guitar ahead. I felt compelled to find out where it was coming from. I found an older woman sitting on a log playing her guitar. I came up behind her. The closer I got, the more beautiful she became to me, but not in the usual way. I could tell as I got closer that the heartfelt music was coming out of one of the most worn guitars I've seen."

Ankita's eyes welled up. "When I got close, Babu, she stopped playing and turned around, and she too was stunned. She began weeping. I moved to hold her, and she dropped her guitar. She wrapped her arms around me and cried more intensely. We held each other for a while. When she regained herself, she pulled away just a little and asked if she could share something with me. 'Of course,' I said.

"She told me, 'When I was a little girl, I had the most vivid dream. In the dream, I was asleep and woke in total darkness, surrounded by the most beautiful music I had ever heard, or have yet to hear. I can best describe it as a song of angels. When I left the darkness in the dream, I found myself as an older woman on a beach, sitting on a log with a guitar, like I'm doing now. I knew it was a Tuesday as it is today.'

"'Of course,' she continued, 'I knew it was just a dream, but the memory of the music filled my soul. I drove myself to learn many instruments and base my life around teaching what I loved most: music. In every note I have ever played, I have strived to get to the song of the angels that filled my soul at that moment. I didn't know until just now that it wasn't a dream, but a glimpse.'

"'A glimpse?' I had to ask.

"'Yes. In my dream, a beautiful young girl walked up behind me, and when I turned to see her in my dream, I wept, and then she comforted and held me as you just did. In my dream, I knew her name was Ankita. What's your name?'

"'Ankita.'

"We both cried again, Babu. I can't explain how it felt, but the best word to describe it is perfect. I can't tell you any more than that right now. I need some more time, but there's more, and I'll tell you soon."

"Are you telling me she dreamed about meeting you on the beach today?" he asked with surprise.

"Yes. I can't eat anything. I'm sorry."

"I'm done, too, Ankita."

Anash had an idea, but then again, it may have been fate. "Let's put the dishes in the sink and then allow me to treat you to a soothing foot rub. You used to love those. I'm sorry I haven't done that for you in a while. I know it'll help you relax.

"I look forward to hearing more about your meeting with the woman whenever you're ready to share. What is her name?"

"Anjali. Her name is Anjali."

"I love that name," he said gently.

"Yes, I do too, Babu."

They had a long couch in their living room on the opposite wall of the bed. They would often sit there together, drinking tea and sharing their thoughts. Tonight, Anash got a soft towel and laid it on the couch; he then retrieved a bottle of her hand lotion. He took her pillow from the bed and brought it over, setting it on the end of the couch. She made her way to the couch and pulled her trousers off, laying them over a nearby chair.

"Okay," she said, "you take your pants off too. I'll light a candle."

Ankita laid down on the couch and raised her legs so he could sit down under her feet. He warmed up the lotion by working it in his hands before placing them on her. Anash lovingly rubbed her feet, toes, ankles, and calves. The warmth and softness of her skin took him aback as he felt overwhelmed with her lovely curves. He could see and feel her humanity in her delicate feet and considered how they carried her through her life.

While rubbing her right calf, he heard her weep softly.

Anash asked, "What's troubling you? Is it that it has been so long since I've done this? I'm sorry...I'll do it more. Is it your encounter with Anjali?"

Ankita paused and then asked him the same question she'd posed earlier. "Babu, tell me, have you thought more about fate and chance?"

"I haven't. What do you think?"

"Here is the rest of my story about Anjali. She told me about her dream, about the song, and meeting me on this day. She knew my name, Babu. She told me that after dinner, you would rub my feet, just like you are now, something you haven't done in a long time. She described the towel and the lotion.

"She told me we would make love tonight, and it would feel different, richer, more meaningful, and that I would be pregnant afterward. She told me that the song she dreamed of would live inside me. I believe all that Anjali said is true, Babu. Are you okay with becoming a father tonight?"

"Oh heavens," he said.

"I'm sorry!"

"Don't be sorry. I have wanted this for a long time, Ankita. If all you told me today is real, then I must believe in fate, and I do so want to have our children soon, you and me, and our family. As crazy as this sounds, I'm not surprised by this very bizarre happening. If there is fate, I may have known it would happen. All this should overwhelm me, but really, I'm happy."

"I want you inside me, Babu; be with me."

Ankita and Anash made love in the warmth of their home, with a light wind rustling through the bountiful tree branches outside their open window. The moment felt different, magical, and charged somehow with more meaning than ever before. They looked deep into each other's eyes as he raised his head, both knowing there would be a child now. The candle flame flickered. As the fire went out, Ankita conceived.

Note joined the female twin, later named Jeseana, when she was just a single cell but connected to her male twin and Ankita as well. As Note had experienced the birth and full development of the physical Universe, Note would experience the same in Jeseana.

Ankita felt filled with Song and knew the perfection Anjali had described. She told Anash immediately, and both were in awe that such a miracle could happen in their ordinary lives. Though it would be two weeks before they could test to confirm, they knew they were with child and Song. Ankita reached out to Anjali, now a treasured friend.

> "By the end of the first week, [the embryos had traveled] extensively, and multiplied from 1 cell to several hundred, dramatically [changed their] shape and complexity, and [begun] finding permanent housing.

> "Following implantation, maternal and embryonic tissues combined and [formed] the placenta. With the placental circulation in place, nutrients, oxygen, vitamins, and water in the bloodstream passed through the placenta and umbilical cord to the [embryos (and later the fetuses)].[3] Carbon dioxide and other waste [flowed back to Ankita].

> "The yolk sac [did its work,] another structure vitally important during early development. The highly vascular structure, surrounded by nutrient-rich fluid, absorbed the nutrients, and [delivered them for use by the embryos]. This method of nutrition continued while the placenta became more fully developed and began functioning. The yolk sac is also the site where the first blood cells formed and where reproductive cells, or germ cells, [originated]. A portion of the yolk sac [was to be drawn into the embryos, developing] the lining of the digestive tracts.

> "Only three weeks and one day after fertilization–the [twins' hearts began] to beat. By four weeks, [their hearts were beating] between 105 and 121 times per minute.

> "[Their brains continued] growing at an incredible rate. Between four and five weeks, the three primary vesicles divided into five secondary vesicles in each. During this time, the head made up about one-third of the

embryo's entire size. An early form of the cerebellum appeared by 4 to 4½ weeks; this area of the brain would later control muscle control and coordination.

"The respiratory system [continued] progressing as two primary lung buds form the beginning of the right and left lungs. By 4½ weeks, the right and left main-stem bronchi, the major airways to the right and left lungs respectively, were well established. They [began] dividing into the lobar pattern seen in the adult—three lobes on the right and two on the left.

"By five weeks, the embryo's livers were producing blood cells.

"Development of the stomach, esophagus, pancreas, and the small and large intestines [were] all underway.

"The permanent kidneys [appeared] at five weeks.

"Next to the kidneys, the gonads, or reproductive organs, [were] developing. [The twins were female and male.] These would eventually become ovaries in the female and testes in the male.

"The embryo's endocrine system [was] also developing. This system of glands [regulated] the release of hormones throughout [the twin's lives]. The pituitary gland [formed] at the base of their brains during week five and [began] secreting growth hormones and the hormone ACTH, which stimulated the further growth of the adrenal glands.

"The limb buds [continued] to grow, and by five weeks, the embryos [developed] hand plates.

"Cartilage formation [began] at 5½ weeks.

"By six weeks, a portion of the brain called the cerebral cortex [appeared]. Nerve cells, or neurons, in the spinal cord, now [developed] specialized connections. These connections, where neurons meet and communicate with one another, are called synapses."[4]

"[Though Ankita didn't feel movement] for at least another eight to ten weeks, the [embryos moved] between five and six weeks. The embryo's first movements [were] both spontaneous and reflexive. A light touch to the mouth area [caused the embryos] to reflexively withdraw [their] head, while the embryo's trunk I [twisted] spontaneously. [Such] movements are essential for the normal development of bones and joints.

"By 5½ weeks, nipples [appeared] near the embryo's underarms...

"The diaphragm, the primary muscle used in breathing, was primarily formed by six weeks.

"The 6-week [embryos measured] less than ¼ of an inch long from head to rump.

"The [embryos had] brainwaves by 6 weeks, 2 days!

"From 6 to 6½ weeks, the cerebral vesicles [doubled] in size. Individualized brainwaves recorded via electroencephalogram, or EEG, have been reported as early as six weeks, two days.

"Also, by seven weeks, cell groupings resembling taste buds [appeared on the tongues] and hiccups [began]. Nasal plugs [were] prominent at this time and [would] persist for another 6 weeks or so.

"By seven weeks, the [hearts had] four chambers.

"By 6½ weeks, the elbows [were] distinct and the [embryos began] moving both hands. The fingers [also started] to separate.

"The footplates and ankles also [emerged] while toes and metatarsal bones [began] to form in the feet. Joint development [was] underway, and the onset of primary muscle fiber formation [showed] the embryo's muscles [were] growing.

"[The babies continued] to fascinate themselves by moving their hands–an ability they [had] been practicing long before birth.

"The hands and [feet transformed] between six and seven weeks as separate fingers and toes [began] to emerge. At six weeks, the hand plates developed a subtle flattening between the digital rays. By six weeks, two days, the hand took on a polygon shape; prominent notches appeared between the digital rays by seven weeks, and individual fingers fully separated by 7½ weeks.

"Also, by seven weeks, the [embryos each moved their legs and exhibited] a startle response.

"The immune system [matured], evidenced by B-lymphocytes in the liver. After birth and relocation away from the protection of the womb, the lymphocytes [would] produce proteins called antibodies to fight infection.

"By seven weeks, the ovaries [appeared] in the female embryo. In the male embryo, a gene on the Y chromosome [produced] a substance causing the testes to begin to differentiate.

"From 7 to 7½ weeks, tendons [attached] leg muscles to bones, and knee joints appeared. Also, by 7½ weeks, the hands [were being] brought together, as [were] the feet and then out again. The [embryos each also kicked and jumped when] startled.

"Also, by 7 to 7½ weeks, nephrons, the basic filtration units in the kidneys, [began] to form.

"By eight weeks, [their brains were] highly developed and made up approximately 43 percent of the embryo's total weight. Growth continued at an extraordinary rate. One of the primary control centers for the body—the hypothalamus—[began] to take form. The hypothalamus eventually controls body temperature, heart rate, blood pressure, fluid balance, and the secretion of vitally important hormones by the pituitary gland.

"Slowly or rapidly, singularly, or repetitively, spontaneously, or reflexively, the [embryos continued] to practice the movements begun earlier and to move in new ways. Frequently, [their hands touched their face and head turned]. The many muscles of the face [were] largely well developed in preparation for the complex facial expressions to follow. Touching the [embryos produced] squinting, jaw movement, grasping motions, and toe pointing.

"The earliest sign of right- or left-handedness [began] around eight weeks...

"The diaphragm muscle wholly formed by eight weeks, and intermittent breathing motions [began for each]."[5]

"By eight weeks, the developing humans [measured] about a ½ inch from head to rump."[6]

Ankita downloaded an app she had heard about called "What to Expect."[7] The very cool app showed that her babies were the size of raspberries. She didn't know she had two raspberry-sized beings inside her.

"By the beginning of the fetal period, synapses, or connections between nerve cells, [were] found within the cerebral cortex. The fetal period [continued] until birth.

"By nine weeks, thumb sucking [began, and the fetuses could] swallow amniotic fluid. The fetuses could also grasp an object, move the head forward and back, open and close the jaw, move the tongue, sigh, and stretch...

"By nine weeks, the nerve receptors in the face, palms of the hands, and soles of the feet [would sense and respond to light touch from the other fetus]. Following a light touch on the sole of a foot [by their tummy mate], the fetus could bend the hip and knee and may curl the toes...

"The eyelids [fused] completely shut by nine weeks.

"The peristalsis previously restricted to the large intestine [began] in the small intestine.

"In the female fetus, the uterus is identifiable by nine weeks. Outside the body, the genitalia differentiate as male or female.

"The [fetuses experienced] a massive burst of growth between 9 and 10 weeks as weight increased by approximately 77%.

"The corpus callosum, which connects the left and right sides of the brain, [began] to develop at this time.

"Upon stimulation of the upper eyelid, the eyes [rolled] downward. That [marked] the first sign of eye movement for the twins. Vocal cords [were] developing. The [fetuses yawned, often opening and closing their jaws] as early as 9½ weeks. [Both fetuses] sucked their thumbs, usually preferring the right thumb.

"At the ends of the fingers and toes, nails [emerged, as did] fingerprints...

"By eleven weeks, the nose and lips [wholly form. The fetuses can now produce complex facial expressions and can smile]...

"Though gender [was] determined at fertilization, genitalia now [distinguished the] male from female.

"Between eleven and twelve weeks, a second massive burst of growth [occurred] as weight increased by roughly 58%...

"The taste bud cells that [appeared] by seven weeks matured into discrete taste buds but scattered throughout the mouth. By birth, the taste buds will [confine] to the tongue and palate or roof of the mouth.

"By 12 weeks, the arms grew to approximate their final proportion relative to body size. As usual, leg development [was] slower than arm development, and the legs still had not achieved their final proportion.

"The whole-body surface, except the top of the head and back, [responded to the light touch of the other fetus].

"The fourteen-week [fetuses each weighed about 2 ounces and measured] slightly less than 5 inches from head to heel.

"A division between the oral and nasal cavities [formed] this week as the opening in the roof of the mouths [fused] shut. [The fetuses often touched] their mouths, sometimes up to 50 times per hour. The jaws [opened] reflexively in response to pressure at the base of the thumb.

"Gender dependent developmental differences appeared for the first time starting at 14 weeks. [Jeseana exhibited] mouth movement more frequently than [her brother,] and this difference increased with advancing age. In contrast to the withdrawal response seen earlier, stimulation near the mouth now [evoked] a turn toward the stimulus while the fetus opens the mouth. These reflexes [mimicked] the rooting reflex, which would persist after birth to help the [newborns find Ankita's] nipple during breastfeeding."[8]

Ankita and Anash received the results back from an ultrasound procedure. They were the proud parents of twins, a girl, and a boy. They named their babies Jeseana and Gerrard.

After having a negative experience in the hospital and with the doctor during the ultrasound procedure, they did further research that seemed to support that childbirth in India in the medical system could be arduous. Ankita found outstanding outcomes through another venue.

BirthVillage was well known locally as a birthing facility with a Midwifery Model of Care, based around pregnancy and birth being normal life processes espousing a mother-centric model. It extended all the practices Ankita and Anash implemented to ensure the best potential outcome for the twins.

"By fifteen weeks, stem cells [arrived and multiplied] in the bone marrow. Most blood cell formation [would] eventually occur here. In the respiratory system, the bronchial tree [was] nearly complete. All airways [contained] smooth muscle and nerve bundles.

"The fetuses [could] feel pain! By sixteen weeks, the fetus produced many of the same hormones found in adults. Painful procedures [could have triggered] a hormonal stress response. As in newborns and adults, pain is followed by the release of cortisol, ß-endorphins, and norepinephrine into the bloodstream.

"The sixteen-week [fetuses each weighed] about 4 ounces and measured slightly less than 7 inches from head to heel. [Most of the neuron multiplication in the brain was complete by sixteen weeks].

"The eighteen-week fetuses weigh around 6 ounces and [measured] about 8 inches from head to heel.

"In the eye, the [retinas now had] discrete layers...In the teeth, enamel [developed] between sixteen and twenty weeks...A distinct motion in the fetal voice box or larynx like movements made during speaking [was coming into place].

"From eighteen to twenty weeks, fetal movement, breathing activity, and heart rate followed daily cycles called circadian rhythms, the same rhythms that characterized various biological activities throughout life.

"A protective white substance called vernix caseosa, now encased [each fetus], protecting the skin from exposure to amniotic fluid.

"By about nineteen weeks, the number of oogonia within the ovaries of [Jeseana peaked] at approximately 7 million. From that point, oogonia production ended forever, but their numbers decreased to about 2 million by [her] birth. Those oogonia would give rise to several thousand primary oocytes.

"The inner [ears], fully formed by twenty weeks, contributed to the body's ability to maintain balance.

"The cochlea is the frequency analyzer of the ear and converts sound waves of varying frequencies into electrical impulses, which are communicated to the brain. By twenty weeks, it [reached] adult size within the fully developed inner ear [for the twins]."

From then on, [Jeseana and Gerrard would] respond to a growing medley of sounds.

"[By nineteen weeks, over 20 million heartbeats had occurred in each].

"[The twenty-week fetuses weigh about 9 ounces and measured about 10 inches from head to heel].

"The twenty two-week [fetuses] each weighed slightly less than 1 pound and [measured] about 11 inches from head to heel.

"In the growing [fetuses], the two sides of the brain [began] to differentiate asymmetrically at 20 weeks.

"The structure of the fetal gastrointestinal tract [had] developed to approximate that of the newborn, although the full function is still weeks away [at this point].

"Rapid eye movement, or REM, [began between in week nineteen...]"[9]

Beginning at twenty-three weeks, Ankita and Anash started playing rich classical music in their environment to soothe the babies and stimulate them. Working with her midwife, Sharon, at BirthVillage, Ankita continued her yoga routines to stay fit but changed them to accommodate her new shape and condition. Warrior Two was her favorite pose.

Ankita and Anash started meditating together when the babies were conceived. They wanted to maintain good emotional well-being. They changed their lives to give their children the absolute best start in life.

> "By twenty-four weeks, the eyelids [reopened], and the [fetuses] exhibited a blink-startle response. The reaction to sudden, loud noises developed earlier in [Jeseana...]"[10]

During that week, Ankita and Anash hunkered down in a storm room while a massive thunderstorm passed. A lightning bolt hit the storage building in their backyard and shook the house.

> "[The loud noise caused the fetal heart rates to increase in the twins, as did the rate of movement.] Excessive fetal swallowing following the exposure to the loud noise could have led to a loss of amniotic fluid but did not. Possible long-term consequences for fetuses are the same as consequences for children and adults: hearing loss and deafness, [but neither occurred here].

> "[The twins at this stage also responded] to pressure, movement, pain, hot and cold, taste, and light.

> "The twenty-four-week [twins each weighed] about 1¼ pounds and measured about 12 inches from head to heel.

> "By twenty-four weeks, over 30 million heartbeats have occurred [in each].

> "[Jeseana and Gerrard had] impressive lung development as a primitive gas exchange now [became] possible in the event of premature birth. Terminal sacs [have appeared], which will eventually become alveoli. Alveoli [would be] the site for the oxygen/carbon dioxide exchange and is essential for survival outside of the womb.

> "By twenty-four weeks, the lung cells produced a substance called surfactant, a material necessary for successful gas exchange...

> "By twenty-five weeks, breathing motions [occurred] up to 44 times per minute.

"The twenty-six-week [fetuses each weighed] almost 2 pounds and [measured] about 14 inches from head to heel.

"[The two brains took off on a growth spurt of their] own. This brain growth consumed over 50 percent of the energy used by the [fetuses] and resulted in a brain weight increase between 400 and 500 percent.

"[Jeseana and Gerrard] developed a relatively plump, less wrinkled appearance because of increased deposits of body fat underneath their skin.

"Increasingly sensitive to different sound frequencies, [the twins could] hear many new noises with greater accuracy.

"A sweet substance was placed in the amniotic fluid and increased the rate of fetal swallowing. In contrast, decreased fetal swallowing followed the introduction of a bitter material. Altered facial expressions often [followed]…"[11]

Ankita's dietary intake would reach the fetuses rather quickly. When Ankita put garlic salt on her French rolls accompanying her favorite spaghetti and vegetable meatball dish, amniotic fluid assumed the odor of the garlic spices within 45 minutes of eating her double serving.

"By twenty-seven weeks, the thigh bones and the foot bones were each about two inches long (about 5 cm).

"By twenty-eight weeks, the sense of smell [functioned, and the eyes produced] tears.

"The twenty-eight-week fetuses [each weighed over] 2½ pounds and [measured] about 15 inches from head to heel.

"Each day, the adrenal glands [produced] large amounts of steroid products. The adrenal glands doubled in size since week twenty and would double again before the end of pregnancy.

"Breathing movements [became] more common, occurring 30-40% of the time in [each of the twins].

"The thirty-week [fetuses each weighed] about 3¼ pounds and measured about 16 inches from head to heel.

"By thirty-one weeks, over 40 million heartbeats had occurred [in each]. Wrinkles in the skin disappeared as more and more fat deposits formed.

"The thirty-two-week [fetuses weighed] about 4 pounds and [measured] about 17 inches from head to heel.

"Starting at thirty-two weeks, true alveoli, or air 'pocket' cells, [began] forming from alveolar ducts. [The development of alveoli continued] through birth and until about eight years of age...

"The thirty-four-week [fetuses weighed] about 5 pounds and [measured] approximately 18 inches from head to heel."[12]

The fetuses heard many sounds before birth, with Ankita's voice and heartbeat dominating other sounds. The newborns preferred the sound of Ankita's voice to any other.

"The newborns [would also] prefer female voices to male voices and familiar lullabies heard before birth to new songs after birth. [The twins could] distinguish prose passages heard during the last six weeks of pregnancy from further readings, providing additional evidence of in utero memory formation and learning.

"The digestive system further [developed] as the lower esophageal sphincter, a valve leading to the stomach, began functioning by thirty-two weeks.

"Blood-filtering groups of capillaries called glomeruli had completed their formation in the kidneys.

"At thirty-five weeks, the [fetuses] had a firm hand grasp.

"During the last eleven weeks of pregnancy, [the twins almost doubled] in overall weight, while brain weight doubled in the last nine weeks of pregnancy..."[13]

***

Ankita and Anash were touring the Kerala Museum in Kochi, India, 5.6 kilometers south of the BirthVillage.

"You know, Babu, you're just always right, you know that?"

"I know that isn't true, but why are you telling me that?" Anash asked playfully.

"Well," she answered with a grimace, "your idea to come to the museum, so close to the Village, and revisit the doll collection hit the mark. Darling, I think this is it; you'd better get me to the Village!"

"Oh my, oh my." Anash was excited. "Okay, we paid Ali to wait for us with the rickshaw; do we have enough time to take that?"

"With the taxi strike, we have no choice, Babu! Yes, I have plenty of time, I think. My contractions are just six minutes apart. I'm thrilled Ali's rickshaw has such a delightful padded seat, and we can remind him with great emphasis to stay away from the potholes. Yes, that will be best."

They awkwardly made their way out to the waiting rickshaw, and Ali helped Anash steady Ankita as she got up on the bright red seat.

"It's time, Ali," Anash stated stressfully. "The babies are coming. Please get us to the BirthVillage and avoid as many bumps as you can."

"Avoid all bumps," Ankita added.

"Yes, Mr. Silva, sir. Yes, Mrs. Silva," Ali said with a big smile on his dark round face. "I'll get you there quickly and as smoothly as if you're on a flying carpet."

Traffic was unusually light for midafternoon, and Ali kept his word and made it the smoothest 40-minute rickshaw ride ever. Anash got word to Anjali to meet them at BirthVillage.

With Ali's help, the parents-to-be made their way into the beautiful traditional home. The dimly lit space radiated with positivity, newborn photographs, incense, and even a cold pitcher of iced cucumber water with real glasses next to it.

Ankita wrote about the experience in her diary:

> Prizalu and Sharon met us with a calming smile and took us back to one of the birthing rooms, then quickly checked how dilated I was. To my surprise, I felt something odd. My water broke, and that's when something seemed to take over, something instinctive. I followed every request my helpers gave me. I heard one say, "Jump into the pool and push." I visualized that I would have several hours to reach the pushing phase, so I wasn't mentally

prepared to meet Jeseana and Gerrard so soon.

I could tell that Prizalu and Sharon were serious as they urged me to push, and I overcame the pain to do the best I could. I was very aware of both Anash and Anjali. Still, the most powerful thing was Song. It was as if this moment was all grace. The pain, the exhaustion, the opportunity...all grace.

I was so glad we'd chosen the water birth. The pool felt like home with the heated water comforting my back and muscles, and I knew this is where I wanted this miracle to happen. I committed all I had to push. Quickly, Gerrard's head appeared. It stunned me. It seemed like a very long time, but shortly, Gerrard completed his journey into his unknown world. Now, I had to increase my commitment to give every ounce of energy and will to push his sister into the world to join him, and before I knew it, Jeseana emerged. *She is beautiful*, I remember thinking.

We cut Gerrard's umbilical cord and then Jeseana's. When we cut Jeseana's, Song left me.

Anjali looked at me intensely; she knew Song was in Jeseana. My life profoundly changed. I would always long for the angels, as Anjali did.

The first day for the newborns would be traumatic, with new lights and sounds and chaos. Multiple hands would touch the babies, and each hand was different, some colder, some warmer, some softer, some more calloused. The sound of Ankita's mesmerizing heartbeat was gone, and the twin that had been right there up against the other for their entire formation was no longer there.

That was traumatic, but they had brains that were built to handle trauma. Over the first day, the twins' brains would limit the mass of sensations and concentrate on the basics of their new lives. They found their Mommy again in the unknown world throughout the day, taking in a new form of sustenance from her breast that met the needs of their tiny bodies. They would find each other and come to deal with the limitations.

Gerrard lost Note immediately after they cut his umbilical cord, so the trauma was more significant for him. Still, the beauty of his gestation inside his mother, along with Jeseana and Note, forged a person who would be an amazing man full of love, kindness, and compassion, with a mind that would discover meaningful things.

Note was with Jeseana for her entire first day, and Song allowed her brain to react to experience the foreign world much less traumatically. As a result, Jeseana lived a different life than most. She would experience an unusually broad awareness across many of the complexities within her human existence. Jeseana would grow up to be one of the most impactful leaders, not only for her country and her people but all nations and all people.

In feeling the great bond between Jeseana, Ankita and Gerrard, Note experienced the essence of a mother's love for the first time. The love Jeseana received on her first day from Ankita, Anash, Anjali, and the midwives introduced Note to the connection of separate beings and how it almost felt perfect, but just almost. It would always be almost from then on.

Over the life of the Universe, Note would join more than a trillion beings over trillions of years, spending a moment to a lifetime with each to experience the answer to God's question.

Note left Jeseana as she laid upon Ankita's chest, listening to her Mommy's familiar heartbeat.

In Between

Note discovered life was living matter where essence drives evolution. Life brought the dimension and dynamic that matter never could and was the path to answer God's question. The possibilities for essence were endless, leaving evolution unconstrained.

Note's experience of Jeseana's and Gerrard's gestation laid bare the intricacies, magnificence, and miracle of living beings. Living with Jeseana on her first day, before words, meanings, definitions, and understandings could bring order to the endless stimulus, Note discovered that life forms are built to get stimulated externally, to an extent leaving them almost oblivious to their inner kingdoms. Chaos could better reign in that space and, with it, make slow, steady and abundant progress.

Note, inspired by the human experience, sought next to experience humanity's future.

Chapter Four

Evolution of Humanity

Note joined Brek as he exited the elevator some 4000 feet below the surface in the Gator station. The station still had that fresh smell as the environmental conditioners were breaking in, and everything looked pristine.

"Welcome to Gator, Captain!" Brek looked over to find Bella standing off to his right. She was a droid in the likeness of a human woman within Brek's human edition.

"I'm Bella," the droid announced.

"Thank you, Bella. What's your position here?"

"I'm the Commander. I'm in command of the station."

"Thank you, Commander, very glad to be here."

"No, I'm Bella."

"Understood, Sir."

"Bella, just Bella."

"Thank you, Bella."

"You are a grateful human, Captain!"

"Brek. Please call me Brek."

"Good to have you, Brek; we've been looking forward to your visit."

"How are the base preparations and opening going?" he asked.

"There are just seven of us here now, including yourself. We only have the one ship that brought you in. Two more will arrive at the end of the month. We have good supplies, and the infrastructure down here is complete; it will house 483 when we have the furniture. For now, we're only ready for 30."

"Am I early, Bella?"

"We've had some delays in construction. We're ready for you, but just barely."

"Who else is aboard?" Brek asked.

"My staff, for now, numbering four, and Emma. She is Tartesian and is assigned to work with you."

"Tartesian? Interesting. I slept on the route until the transfer to your landing ship. I'm well-rested. I would like to see my quarters and meet Emma."

"Welcome, Captain." Brek heard a voice coming from behind him.

Brek turned around to find Emma approaching.

Emma, a Tartesian woman, was tall by human standards, standing at 86 inches. Her eyes were 25% larger than a human woman's eyes and were a vibrant oyster color. The rest of her attributes very much looked like those of a human woman.

Tartesians had bronze-colored skin which correctly insulated against anything but extreme temperatures and was impervious to puncture. Their protective skin and lack of modesty enabled them to manage without clothing. With long flowing silver hair, Emma's colors were striking, and her muscle tone called attention to itself. In intimacy, Tartesians would allow their skin to be more sensitive than human skin, and though it wasn't recorded, it was known that their bronze skin lightened a great deal when it was in the intimate mode.

Her magnificent presence overwhelmed Brek and left him almost speechless. Pulling himself together, he got out a polite introduction.

"You must be Emma. Good to meet you," he said, holding out his hand to shake hers.

Emma's hand was warm, and her handshake firm. His eyes met hers, and he stopped breathing.

"Breathe!" Bella spoke out. "Breathe, Brek."

"I'm sorry, I'm sorry to both of you. I was not ready to meet; I'm not prepared. I'm sorry."

"Nice to meet you, Captain; I'm looking forward to working with you. I've encountered other human men from your edition, and I know my appearance can be challenging. Your sexual instinct and drive are still high and primitive. Each species has primitive aspects, Captain, don't worry. You'll get used to my appearance, and your sexual attraction will calm." She smiled beautifully.

"No doubt about that. You can count on my professionalism. If you'll call me Captain, do you have something more appropriate for you than Emma?"

Brek knew she was dead on about his attraction to her, and he concluded it would help for him to accept her referring to him as Captain to keep their relationship by the book.

"Titles in my world are hard for humans to pronounce. It would be easy for Bella, but not you, so Emma is best."

"Another primitive feature of my kind?"

"Not at all, Captain. Your paradigms around language are entrenched in your minds, and they're effective."

She stopped there and studied him with a concentrated look. Emma wanted to leave the conversation there.

"Understood Emma, understood."

"Captain, I think we're getting off to an awkward start, and that's the last thing I want to do. Please, let's meet again in a few minutes and start this introduction process over. Are you hungry?"

"Why, yes, I am."

"Good. I think you may want to see your quarters and settle in. Why don't we meet in the mess hall in an hour and eat? We can get to know each other there and then get to work."

"I like it, Emma. I'll meet you in the mess hall in an hour."

"Good, Captain, see you then,"

Brek walked in to find Emma eating a Tartesian breakfast that resembled a kale salad. Having spent a good deal of time with humans, she had grown fond of green tea, and she had that to accompany her meal. Brek, a vegetarian, ordered the same thing from the computer but chose coffee instead of tea, black coffee.

"How is your breakfast?" he asked.

"Good, good. Your systems have come a long way in replicating Tartesian cuisine. It may be better than the real thing." Emma savored her salad.

After getting himself comfortable, he had some questions he was eager to ask, and some were appropriate enough to do so.

"Why are you here to work with me?"

She hesitated and put down her fork-like utensil. Emma answered carefully.

"I'm tasked with getting a better understanding of humanity, Captain. As you likely know, our species are different, and we want to better understand how humanity has survived and thrived, given your beliefs and the way you live your lives."

"Interesting. How can I help you better understand that? I'm not even of the most evolved editions of the race, and what you'll learn from me is of a much more, uh, what's that word you used earlier, uh, primitive nature."

"It is precisely your primitive aspects that can help me the most. Are you open to working with me?"

"Yes, I am, but I'm not quite satisfied with your answer."

"Oh?" She looked concerned.

"Why me, Emma? There is nothing special about me. You could learn more with another, I think."

"Why you? You got your bachelor's degree in atmospherics and were at the top of your graduating class. Then, you pursued and earned your master's in philosophy, serving as a teacher's aide to do so. Again, you finished at the top of your class. Philosophy! As far as I know from what I've discovered about you, you've had only one primary relationship, one that lasted four years until she went on to work on a starship. You haven't had a connection since. You had a dog named Buckles, and you worked odd jobs after you gained your master's, until Buckles died. Did you choose life with Buckles over your career, Brek?"

"I loved Buckles, but I just liked my career a lot. Simple choice."

Brek felt the loss of Elena and Buckles and was surprised to sense the grief he had buried several years earlier. His eyes watered.

"You then joined the Federation, and here you are. You are loyal, Brek, and loving, and philosophical. You work hard, hard enough to be the best at what you do. Why you? Because you are precisely the human I want to work with and learn from."

Brek recalled that Tartesians are known for their pursuit of details and studious nature. Keeping himself together, he said, "I hope I don't let you down, Emma."

"You haven't. You won't."

"You know that your nakedness and beauty are difficult for me, for my primitive side."

"I can appreciate that, yes. It's endearing. Please, if you need to stare, to get comfortable with me, please go ahead. My people are not self-conscious. We don't mind; I don't mind."

"You can permit me, Emma, but I shouldn't."

"I've studied humans, Captain, and this situation is interesting. Human women want you to stare and many times dress in a way to promote that, yet they don't want you to stare at them as a sexual object. They want to feel beautiful, and admiring their beauty with a stare is lovely, but they can't tell the difference between being stared at in that way or as an object unless they know you.

"Human men very much want to stare, and usually due to their animal desire. They know they shouldn't, so try not to get caught by the woman they are staring at. What I can tell you is both the man and the woman are trying to fill a cup that isn't full. For me, I am happy for you to stare, to fill your cup."

"I appreciate that, but though I very much want to stare, I can't. That's my nature. My people instill respect for others' privacy. I can't explain it, but I appreciate your openness to it. Perhaps as we work together, you will forgive some lapses in my concentration. I'll be trying to help you gather the information you need while I do my work."

"Thank you, Captain. I accept you," she said in a meaningful tone. "We're very intuitive. I know you're good, and I feel safe with you."

"Okay, then. Please call me Brek, not Captain."

"Brek. Very well. Tell me about your mission here."

"I'm a cloud maker. You probably know that from your research. Do you know about human world-building?"

"Yes, humanity is very well known for it, but please, tell me about it."

"I am happy to," he said, "but I can be more helpful to you if I fill in the things you don't know. Please, what can you tell me about it?"

"To be honest, Captain, I mean, Brek, from our point of view, humanity takes worlds and inflicts their will on them. What world-building is to you may be annihilation to the world you take. Humans change worlds, displacing the state of the world that existed before humans."

"Will our time together be hostile, Emma?"

"We are a candid people, Brek. Our time together will be, how do you say, yes, real."

"Frankly, Emma, I have considered that point of view many times. I am open to our conversation. Let me tell you how we view it."

Brek's kale breakfast arrived with his coffee.

"Tell me after you eat, Brek."

"Thank you, Emma. I'm taking the Viper out to look at the atmosphere more closely in an hour. Will you be going with me?"

"Yes, I would like that," she responded warmly.

"Do you need to do anything before we go?" he asked.

"Yes."

"How about I eat while you do that, and then you can meet me back here, Emma. We can talk a few minutes, then get to the Viper bay."

"Good. Be right back."

When Emma returned 20 minutes later, she found Brek enjoying his coffee.

"Hi, Emma. Have a seat. Let me tell you about our world-building. Oh, do you need more tea? Is that what you had?"

"I'm good, Brek. I want to hear your rendition."

"Very well. A long time ago, really, over a million years ago now, human science contemplated, studied, and achieved both policies and practices around finding dead worlds with certain attributes that could be converted, over time, to living worlds. Humans define a living world as one with a sustainable and stable environment. It could support one or all of the many life forms that we had identified."

"What's a dead world to humans, Brek?"

"I know the Tartesians are against the spreading of one's influence over others and inhibiting their unique path. It has always amazed me how well your society makes that happen. It's beyond me, in a good way, how you as one individual know where your influence ends and another's begins. To me, and I can only speak for myself, everything is connected, and everything influences everything around it. There are no dead worlds, scientifically. In the big picture, everything in the Universe is a combination of particles.

"That said, Emma, there are two classes of a dead world to us. We call one a 'Rock.' This planet was a Rock. Rocks have no life, living matter, living organisms, fossils, signs of water past or present, nothing. They are a piece of matter floating through space, but with incredible possibilities. With a Rock, we may change its size or content because that often requires changes all the way to the core of the Rock.

"We call the second a 'Lifeboat.' A Lifeboat has life of some kind somewhere below the surface. It could be from the past or present, but this is a world that knows life. We only add surface components to a Lifeboat, to leave whatever was and is below the surface alone. That is a rare world for us to find. Their surface, when we find them, is too inhospitable to support any of that existing life or any other."

"Interesting Brek. I was unaware of the Rock scenario you presented."

"This world is an example of that, as I mentioned. It had a toxic atmosphere with a surface temperature consistently around 400 degrees Celsius, no organic compounds, no water, and it showed that little had changed or evolved in eons. We found no plate tectonics or signs of life, present, or past.

"Yet, it had some real treasures. It orbits a Red Dwarf star that should be stable for a trillion years. It has a solid iron middle core with a liquid outer core that rotates in the opposite direction of the planet, which creates a powerful magnetosphere that can protect its atmosphere from solar radiation and solar winds. When our scientists found this world a great while ago, they found that the planet was very much like Earth's neighbor planet, Venus. It had a weighty atmosphere that was almost all carbon dioxide. Like Venus, it didn't have much tilt and had a prolonged rotation.

"Our scientists calculated the mass that would have to impact this world, its trajectory, and speed along with the chemical composition it needed to deliver, to remove the carbon dioxide from the atmosphere, reverse and increase the planetary spin while knocking it over to about a 25-degree tilt to allow for temperature movement. We found the asteroid we needed with significant amounts of calcium carbonate, and magnesium carbonate rock to help remove the carbon, along with the right additional characteristics. We shot the asteroid into the planet as calculated. The impact fractured the planet and increased the rotation of the outer shell of the planet while leaving the direction and speed of the turning inner core unchanged. One hundred thirty-seven thousand years later, after the planet healed and cooled, we delivered another asteroid to finish adjusting its rotation and spin momentum; this one was composed of ice, also bringing massive amounts of water to the world. The planet was again fractured but not as much, and now, some six hundred and fifty-two thousand years later, E29 glides through space, a planet almost ready for life."

"It almost sounds easy!" Emma exclaimed, showing that it impressed her.

"Difficult," he responded. "We were adding a third of the mass to the planet, changing the gravity, and altering the orbital path. The first asteroid elongated the orbit, which we corrected with the second. There are many details and calculations to consider, requiring months for the technology of the time to compute. Finding the perfect asteroids after finding the right candidate also took decades each time. Humanity took the long view, however, and took the time. And here we are today.

"We also need to get to work. Are you ready? We will have some downtime on the Viper. We can talk more then," Brek concluded.

Brek and Emma boarded and secured themselves in the Viper.

"Captain! Bella here."

"Brek here; yes, Bella?"

"Be careful out there, Captain. The Viper is all we have until the rest of our fleet gets here, and we don't have all the communication set up around E29 to help you if you get in trouble and you're out of range."

"Where is out of range, Commander?"

"We have communication spanning about 30% of the planet now, 15% on either side of the base."

"Good to know. I'm careful and have logged considerable time on the Viper design. Let's get going."

Brek and Emma began their ascent, slowly moving through two air chambers before finally being outside.

The Viper was a small and agile craft with excellent maneuverability. The ship could get to high speed in a short time if needed, but its primary purpose was for flying close to the ground of a planet with the ability to move around land features. The Viper was a spacecraft and could fly into space and any distance within an average star system. With no hibernation system, however, it was seldom used for any long haul. Engaging the autopilot and having the experiments running, Emma and Brek could rest and relax. They could enjoy the view and each other.

"You know you're stuck with me now, Brek."

"So sad!" Brek felt a rush of adrenaline through his body. *It just wasn't entirely fair,* he thought, but in a good way.

"I want to have some serious conversation; can we?" she asked softly.

"More about clouds?"

"You and I spoke about your edition, and your edition has some primitive aspects."

"Yes. So, you still want me to stare?"

"I'm happy for you to stare, but I want to ask you more about humanity's segregation of evolved states or editions as you call them."

"That's a pleasant conversation, to be sure. What do you think about it, Emma?"

"Do you mind telling me in your own words what humans did so we can converse from the same understanding?"

"Absolutely. Once humanity finally got past its conflict with itself and developed a genuine reverence for life and that reverence for life extended beyond just human life, it had the confidence that it could move forward, taking a long view. Our science progressed to a state that it could make worlds habitable while we also mastered being able to place humans into hibernation that could go on in perpetuity. The combination of all of that brought an opportunity for humanity to seed new worlds with humans at different stages of evolution. Each seeding had a primary task to concentrate on, in its society, over time and guidelines to help the populace work toward it."

"Can you elaborate more on that?" she asked.

"My world, for example. We're the world builders, though humanity has built worlds after us as it evolved. For us, the belief was that a planet might have to 'cook' for a million years after its initial modifications. Our edition, or generation, got sent to settle on a new world some 981,000 years ago...that was our travel time. Though protected and nourished over that time by our human caretakers, the entire population was asleep for 975,000 years. They woke us in waves, creating an environment and infrastructure for those that would awaken after, and within the first 250 years, everyone was awake and thriving on Sok. Over the last 6000 years, our planet and society have flourished and grown. We're proud of it. As world builders, building worlds has been the primary emphasis of our community throughout our society. For us, it's what we live for, and we've become very good at it. We build the worlds that were enhanced around a million years ago. Not all are ready, but some are, and it takes thousands of years to finish the job."

"What about the other editions, or generations?" Emma remained captivated.

"Let's settle on generations."

"Yes. Thank you, Brek."

"We don't mix with the other generations. They protect us, but we don't mix with them."

"Why?"

"I don't know. My belief is that with all of us being human, the earlier, more primitive"—Brek smiled—"generations may be jealous of the more current ones. My understanding is that humanity has evolved over the last million years to almost pure energy. It's more advanced than we can imagine. If it were another species, I and my fellow generations of humans might just be in awe, but they are humans, and somehow, that makes it seem, well, kind of unfair, but then I'm primitive."

Emma continued to try to understand. "So, they have seeded generations of humans on other worlds, over a million years, at different evolutionary levels, to develop specific skill sets and never meet each other? Is that what you are telling me?"

"Yes. In a nutshell. I will say, though, that we benefit from the work of the other generations, and their products may come into use. I am certain we will all meet at some point."

"What's a nutshell?" she asked inquisitively.

"It's a human response that means, that's what I'm telling you, yes."

"How did the early humans decide whom to segregate from the rest? Who determined what the segregated subjects would concentrate on?"

"Segregation. Interesting choice of words, Emma."

"It's not a natural process, Brek! On Tartesia, we very much value the natural process. For us, we don't think we're developed and knowledgeable enough to make decisions that could be an improvement over the natural process."

"Your race is amazing, Emma. The Tartesians are loved throughout our space neighborhood. That being said, and this isn't a judgment, but a question to ponder, how old is the Tartesian race?"

"1.3 million of your years."

"And here you and I sit, flying around in a ship, talking with a language after having limited thoughts chopped into words."

"It's not so bad," Emma interjected.

"I'm very much enjoying it, Emma, but humanity has evolved into beings of energy in less time than your 1.3-million-year history. One is not better than another, but is the human way a bad way? It seems to have worked out well."

"I'm, in human words, stumped," she admitted. "I can't argue with your point. It just makes little sense to me. Can we talk about intimacy for a moment?"

"You don't like to make things easy for me, do you, Emma? Humans don't talk about intimacy right after meeting someone. It's very personal to us. We have to gain trust with someone before we talk about it."

"I apologize. Tartesians don't know modesty, though we can appreciate it in others. I was using the topic to gain more clarification about you and humanity. We are objective and unemotional about it unless we are engaged in intimacy. Again, I apologize for causing you discomfort. I will find another subject."

"I'm okay with you talking about it. It's charged for humans because of the vulnerability that comes with it. I'm safe with you, and I know that. Please talk about intimacy."

Smiling, she continued. "When humans make love, they seem to want to achieve a result. Both the male and the female appear to want to satisfy their own needs first, selfishly. I know it's not always that way, but it appears to be so. Tartesians make love for hours, slowly and generously. Our connection is real and meaningful for both of us. Every curve, sensation, smell, taste, caress, squeeze, throb, each one is experienced by both together. Tartesians live now and experience each moment fully, completely. There is nothing beyond now; it is all right here, now, all the time. That seems much richer than your experience."

"I agree, Emma, it sounds beautiful, it does. My generation is much more short-sighted and disconnected, to be sure. Given human history, or the history I know of before my generation, let me share a conclusion I've reached. Human society has existed to evolve. The complexities and chaos of society create the need for answers and solutions. We need things that have never been conceived to solve problems that have never even been imagined. The journey begets evolution. At the end of evolution, there are answers to every question and a solution to every problem. The cup is full.

"My effort to fix your mistakes and mine makes me grow. If we don't make those mistakes or create that chaos, then we don't create a fresh problem to solve. I don't know for sure, but I don't think humanity exists to 'be.' Being as your people do sounds much more fulfilling, but if humans get satisfied, we aren't staying busy. Busy and selfish humans are problem solvers and evolve."

Emma looked perplexed. She thought she'd known the answer before asking the question, but the answer was different.

"Why did you bring up intimacy, Emma? Why did you select that avenue for your questions?"

"Connection, Brek. It's a common need for both our peoples. That's why humans evolved and why my people love. Intimacy is a good gauge to see how our races connect. I am sorry if it was insensitive."

"Thank you."

At that moment, the Viper took control. A chamber door directly behind the two occupants shut abruptly; the Viper turned toward space, and the engines fired full throttle. At the same time, the craft accelerated, and the words "incoming" came through Stella, the Viper computer. Brek and Emma felt the impact of a meteor behind the closed chamber door. The sound of the engines stopped, and most of the lighting went off.

"Stella! Status?"

"Puncture in the rear compartment, Captain. Full breach."

"Can we communicate with Gator?"

"Negative, out of range."

"Do we have navigation?"

"Negative, offline."

"Can you get it online?"

"Negative, control to navigation is severed."

"What do we have for life support?"

"This compartment will sustain your current oxygen consumption for 64 minutes. It houses one spacesuit that has five hours of life support. Heat is minimal, Captain."

"I don't see the planet, Stella. Where are we?"

"Viper took evasive action and got hit at full power in an undetected meteor shower. The Viper is two clicks from E29," Stella announced.

Brek looked at Emma with sadness in his eyes and caught the same in hers. There was enough light in the compartment for him to tell that her skin was getting lighter. "I'm deeply sorry, Emma. Things are bleak for us. We have one suit, and I want you to get into it. It will give you more time in case we get located, somehow."

"You're dear, Brek. I won't take it. You need to get into it."

"Damn it," he exclaimed. "I know your skin can protect you from the cold, but you still need to breathe."

"My skin would protect me from the cold, but it uses oxygen to enable that capacity. My skin will be as yours is soon to save oxygen,"

"That's why it's getting lighter, to use less oxygen?" he confirmed.

"Yes," she shared.

"Emma, it will get freezing in here before we run out of air. Damn it."

Brek began undressing. Emma sat silently, stunned at the circumstances.

Once undressed, he found an open place on the floor and sat down, leaning up against the wall. He opened his arms and asked Emma to come to lie against him. She moved down onto her knees and then turned in to place her back against his chest. Once against him, he covered them with the clothes he had removed. They felt each other's warmth.

"Why are you doing this, Brek?"

"If we're going to die, it will be together, and I want to cherish you and each moment until death comes."

Brek hummed.

"You're humming; how?"

"I can't explain it. I'm full of music somehow, and it's just kind of pouring out of me. I must tell you that your being in my arms, full of this Song, is nice. I can't imagine how that must sound to you."

"Yes," Emma responded, "it is very unusual to feel such a strong connection so quickly. But I feel connected with you, and it feels natural."

"Natural is the perfect word," he responded.

They could see their breath in the cold air at this point.

"I want to share something with you, Brek. I've heard about humans facing insurmountable situations with love. I didn't understand it until now. Your being willing to die with me is profound. I don't understand it. Tartesians don't make that decision."

"Would you say that everything Tartesians think or do or feel is based on reality and reality only?"

"Yes," she agreed.

"Do you believe that there is a reality you aren't aware of?"

"No. Reality is just what we're aware of. If we don't know it's there, it's not there."

"What about God, then?"

"For us, there is no God. God is abstract."

"What's love?"

"Love!" she answered.

"That is our biggest difference, Emma. For me and much of humanity, God is everything. It's everything we can't know, and infinitely bigger than we are. God is hope for us. I have hope now. Do Tartesians hope?"

At that moment, a breathtaking light came in the window, and a moment later, the Viper—along with Emma and Brek—was in the ship bay on Gator. Humanity saved one of their own.

"Captain, Bella, here. What's happening?"

Emma pulled away and got up on her hands and knees, facing back at Brek. Their gazes met. She was speechless while Brek was not.

"What word comes to mind, Precious One?" Brek asked.

Without hesitation, Emma responded. "Emancipation."

Note left Brek to resume the journey.

In Between

Note found humanity would be a large component in evolution, throughout the Universe, and over the ages. Note would also discover the human spirit in many species, on countless worlds.

Note was next to observe a being's awareness of the constraints that limited them.

Chapter Five

Words

Note joined Oz as he was receiving his first guest in months.

"Welcome, my friend, welcome." Oz opened his arms lovingly.

Oz and Turnlin embraced.

"I have a book for you, Oz."

"Oh, is it the one I asked you to get me?"

"Yes," Turnlin said proudly. "It's about captivity, but not the captivity that immediately comes to mind."

"Interesting, my old friend. Please come inside and have some wine and tell me about your journey and how things are at home."

Oz was part of humanity, generation b149kk3, the Librarians. They lived in a small green world in a remote star system. It was once a part of the Andromeda Galaxy before it collided and joined the Milky Way. The green world, named Frum, held a unique and scientifically unfathomable position between two red dwarf stars orbiting one another. A stable climate for eons enabled a lush and bountiful world with days that never ended. The population didn't know nighttime or star-filled skies.

Raised to be a scholar, Oz studied and internalized all the significant works of his civilization. His love for learning left little room for the emotions and chaos of his people. Books were his best friends. Over time, however, Oz found a longing, growing within, to find meaning in all the information. Facts and truths were abundant in the word, but what did it mean? Why did it matter?

Turnlin found Oz to be more fragile yet more inviting than the last time they'd been together. Oz's wrinkled face seemed an unlikely place for such deep, brilliant green eyes, complementing his boyish grin. The smell of fresh varnish filled the air, and Turnlin's eye caught a new dresser in the corner. Oz had become a stellar carpenter, creating furniture masterpieces sporting multiple wood species on each. Oz's creations were art but functional.

Oz opened the conversation. "Yes, I understand captivity; in fact, I live to be free from it."

"Tell me more, Oz."

"Please sit down, my friend. Let me get you that wine."

"Thank you, Oz. I am mesmerized by your dresser creation; it's remarkable."

"Thank you. I find beauty in the wood that's unmatched by anything else. To think it was alive once and now it's so beautiful as a dresser. I try to understand why we get such a resource as trees. They seem to sacrifice themselves so selflessly to us. They're captive, you know?"

"They are, Oz."

Oz handed his friend a generous goblet of red wine.

"Would you like some cheese with that?"

"No, thank you; this is fine. Please sit; tell me about captivity."

Oz sat in an exceptional rocker he'd built, and it seemed to embrace him.

"You see hundreds of books before you, Turnlin. Each was delivered to me by a person. Each person was like the book they delivered. All had a specific message in their being. Their distinctiveness is written on their life's page, like the words in the book they brought me. Each has a complex, unique and one of a kind persona, limited to their construct. I'm a book. You're a book, captive to our construct."

"Why have you asked for and collected these books, Oz?"

"Someone delivered each book, and each soul was special. Each book is special. I've sought a perfect truth inside each. It's very much like looking for the combination to the lock on the safe holding the greatest treasure. Gaining access to such a treasure requires knowing and exercising the right combination, in the right order, to unlock the door. The more blessings I know, the better are my chances to open the safe," he said, smiling.

"What is the treasure you believe to be inside the safe, Oz?"

"Freedom," he answered, raising his hands in the air. "I seek to be free from the page without ceasing to exist."

"Doesn't your existing in some conscious fashion tie you to the page?" Turnlin asked.

"That is part of the treasure, I think. I don't know. If my journey ends with my being nothing, so be it."

"You want freedom. Why?"

"That's the real question, isn't it? Why not just be good with the way things are? The answer is we are all limited by the words we deliver, the feelings we define, the sliver of the moment we experience. It's living in chunks. I want to be in the place of limitlessness."

He continued, "Let me share something with you that may provide a better picture."

"Please, yes, that will be welcome."

"You have heard me referred to as the eye man, have you not?"

Turnlin responded, "Yes, I know some call you that. I don't know the story, however."

"When I was a young man, an early teenager, I did a hallucinogenic drug with my best friend. I don't condone that now, I am wiser today, but we did it. In the middle of the trip, he and I locked eyes, and a box formed around them. Everything outside the box was blurry, but inside was crystal clear. It was the same for both of us. That was a profound experience for me, but just the beginning. From then on, I called it tunneling.

"Have you ever been around strangers and look toward one to have them turn to meet your stare? How do they sense that? I know you've been in a road machine and turned to look at someone you are passing, and they turn to look back. Is that right?"

"Yes, it is Oz. I have always been taken with that, but just accepted it. It appears there is some connection there."

Oz nodded. "When I was a young student at the university, a hypnotist came to show us his trade in our student union. I was passing by and saw the crowd. I joined them. They were passing out little sheets of paper for us to put our name on. I did so. They took them up and put them in a hat. He drew a few slips of paper and then called a name. He asked that person to concentrate on a brief question. He would tell them what he thought their question was and answer it.

"He was close to right on several people. Then he called my name. He said, 'Okay, Oz, now concentrate on your question.' Shortly, he stated, 'My, Oz, your concentration is strong. Your question is...' He was dead on, Turnlin, so I thought about that mental energy again, passing over a crowd.

"Not too long after, I was at my job, sitting with a coworker on a shift change. I was a genuine fan of this person, and she felt safe with me. We had previously enjoyed spiritual conversations. We sat across from each other, and I looked into her left eye with mine. We had a moment just out of this world. We both looked away, and I asked her if she'd experienced the moment. She confirmed it.

"That moment was full of our entire beings, past, present, and future, all in a moment. I had it happen one more time with another person years later. I decided after trying to make it happen with other people that the lightning bolt moment only happens between two welcoming people who are at the moment together. We can't be distracted or closed in any way. Some just aren't ready to be that open." Oz concluded, "That's why I'm the 'Eye Man.'"

Turnlin thought for a moment. "You call it tunneling?"

"Yes, it seems to fit, symbolically, don't you think?"

"How would you and I tunnel, Oz? It's compelling."

"Okay, Turnlin. Look straight into my left eye, yes, there you go. That's it. You feel our eyes locked into each other."

"Yes, this is powerful."

"Yes, and we are connected."

"Yes, I feel that," Turnlin said.

Oz then looked away and looked back. After that, they just looked normally toward each other. "It is very personal there, isn't it?"

"Yes, it's personal. It takes trust to do that, Oz."

"I agree, Turnlin. You'll find as you go through your days, you may pass someone and lock eyes, and you'll feel the power. It's okay for that moment because you are just passing by. No commitment."

"It is exciting, Oz, and powerful. But we didn't have the lightning bolt moment."

"No, we didn't. I don't think it is ours to have. It's a gift we're given—access to such a place."

"Thank you for this Oz, thank you." Turnlin put his flat hand over his heart.

"You're welcome, my friend! That lightning bolt moment is the freedom I spoke of earlier. There are no words there. There is no confinement. You are no longer a captive in a place."

After quietly sitting to digest these moments with Oz, Turnlin asked, "What do my visit and the book you requested provide, Oz?"

"You know me to be a voracious reader; I was a librarian, after all. I came to read books with great speed and diligence, almost as if my goal were to get a book and finish rather than find the meaning in it. Along the way, I heard about an ancient Earth book, called Note, and I searched a long time for it. I now know it was part of my journey. Fate, if you will. I remember much of it but will never forget the fourth chapter. It told the reader that Note was a book that must not be read in a hurry, that there were pebbles of meaning along the way to discover and add to the reader's life to help them on their journey. It used the analogy of a gourmet meal being slowly savored, to enjoy and experience, the many perfectly melded flavors.

"That changed my approach to reading, Turnlin, and I have savored every book and their person since, slowly, with an open heart. Those pebbles have built a precious path to what may be the freedom I seek. You and your book may be the finishing stone," he said, smiling.

"Do you recommend the book, Oz? Should I read it?"

"You should Turnlin, yes, because you and I are in it. The fourth chapter is about us, and this conversation."

"You say it's ancient; how can we be in it?" Turnlin asked with great surprise.

"Because it's all connected; we're all connected. I know now that I seek freedom because I'm connected to it." After a long silence, Oz spoke. "You won't be able to find the Note book. Can I give you my copy?"

Still stunned, Turnlin responded. "Please, Oz, I'm honored by your generosity." They savored their moments together.

Note left Oz.

In Between

Note found through Oz that freedom gets experienced through connection and the expansion of self beyond constraints. Constraints, like words, are authored. We seek freedom because we're connected to it. The experience in living beings is that each step into connection, no matter how small, is a step toward their greater being. Peace comes from connection.

Note experienced the full evolution of matter and recognized essence to be the platform to take evolution the distance. Note discovered the genius of life. Now, Note needed to meet Grace to know why Note existed.

Chapter Six

Meaning

The blood rushed into Jeff's head. As he bent over to tighten the final clasp of his heavy-duty ski boot, he felt his heart pounding and his face throbbing.

As he sat back up, Note joined Jeff, who then took a deep and satisfying breath through his nose. The air was cold and crisp. The sense of fresh air filling his lungs gave him goosebumps. *This is bliss*, he thought.

He considered the unknown journey he was about to take. Fear suddenly filled him, and frantic thoughts ensued. *I feel powerless, small, no control, wrong place at the wrong time. What am I doing?* That moment passed. Jeff chalked it up to the excitement of the unknown. "It's time to go," he told himself.

Jeff's thoughts slowed, and his inner voice quieted as he looked over the 84% incline in front of him. One of the greatest skiers of all time, he knew this slope was undoable. Skiing this slope was like jumping out of a plane without a parachute. But here, in this place, he walked with fate and destiny. Each choice is destined.

Having studied his path for months, Jeff leaned forward and began his descent.

He gained speed quickly, more so than he'd expected. The snow was good, surprisingly so. Perhaps this wasn't the dangerous track he had feared. *Why was this such a big deal? Why in the world will I be the first to tame this beast?*

Jeff reached the tree line moving over 100 miles per hour, with the sun glistening on the snow in front of him and powder flying from the back of his skis. His legs were busy absorbing the bumps and were strong and sure. He seldom used his poles; it was almost as if they were a nuisance along for the ride.

Suddenly ahead, and coming fast was a blind spot, could be a drop, but he had studied and surveyed this path, no drop.

Oh no, I needed to veer left back at the redwood...I didn't...oh my God; I don't know what's coming! The fear Jeff had at the top of the forbidding mountain was back and familiar. His legs felt weak and unsure. *Why am I here? I have so much life to live, death here will have no meaning, what have I done?*

Note could not ski for him but pierced the fear. Jeff concentrated.

He reached the blind spot, and it was a cliff. With no choice, Jeff skied over the cliff and flew. He tucked as was natural to do and looked ahead to his landing. He would land about 20 feet behind a giant granite boulder coming out of the mountain, some 30 feet wide and 15 feet tall. There would be no time to turn, and he would hit it at full speed. This was it.

His life passed before him in an instant. He remembered when he was five years old, and a car stopped at the corner in front of his house. They threw a cigarette out of the window and Jeff ran over to try it. He blew on it instead of inhaling. He remembered his mom picking him up at the airport in hot pants when that was a thing. Jeff remembered his first love and how they'd laughed. His kids came to mind, all those desserts, the campfires and holidays, early mornings sleeping late with her head on his shoulder. Fresh cookies, all the night shifts at the restaurant, chess games with Richard, kissing Kelly, his baby girl's perfect smile with her first shiny white tooth, hash browns. All of that and all that would have been. Done.

Then, suddenly, a high gust of wind caught him and changed his trajectory. Jeff landed solidly with the granite boulder passing by his left side only four feet away. With no time to react, he was in and through a stand of trees before coming out into a clearing he recognized as his original planned path.

His legs were sturdy again, with mega adrenaline speeding all his reactions and thought processes. Jeff made it to the bottom of the deadly mountain, alive, but by the Grace of God. Every moment now would be a gift, one to earn.

After indulging in a hot shower, Jeff laid down on his soft, well-used lodge bed and fell asleep. He didn't dream. He just slept hard.

At 5:00 PM, the phone rang.

"Hey, buddy!" Chan announced.

"Oh hi, Chan, I must have fallen asleep. What time is it?"

"Time for you to come down to the lounge, Brother, come on down."

"Okay, see you shortly."

***

Jeff walked into the earthy lounge to find Chan sitting at a table over in the corner. The room was rugged and comforting with high timber ceilings, thick log walls, and old pictures with the generations of people that lived in this remote place. With only 12 tables and none of them large, it was clear this was not a family resort, but one more geared toward regulars or lifers—those with this magnificent mountain range in their blood. Jeff started coming here with his father and grandfather and had now passed his love for this place to his only child, Patricia. Knowing he was taking on the forbidden part of the mountain this trip, he came alone, planning to meet up with his best friend, Chan, afterward.

Chan, a writer, was an idealist who knew there was a book in him he could share to make a difference. Like seeking one's only true love, he sought the message within him that would mean something profound to someone somewhere. Being introspective, he had done the math on what he had consumed during his life. Chan considered all the cows killed to make up the countless hamburgers and steaks he had eaten, and remembered the many moments he'd shared with others where he made it about himself and didn't hear or "see" the other person. Why did the cow die to feed him? Why did she cry deeply for his smallness? What was so important about Chan's existence that his two children would live their young lives not knowing if their father loved them, or even recognized something special about them because of his dedication to his work?

Yes, Chan's math impacted him in such a way that he wanted to make up for his life and earn it. He was clear that his path was finding that incisive message that might impact even one person in a good way. It could come any time, in any way. He was open to it and invited it.

Jeff and Chan met each other halfway and embraced. "I love you, man," Chan said.

The two made their way back to the table. After easing into their scratched leather chairs with frosty mugs of beer in hand, they talked.

"You're sitting here with me, Jeff. That means you did it. Did you do it?"

"I did it, Chan, but I was stupid to try. I shouldn't have done it. I shouldn't be here and don't want to talk about it right now. Okay?"

"Sure, Buddy, I hope you can share at some point. I care about you, Jeff."

"Thank you. I know you do. So, tell me, Channy, what are you writing now?"

Smiling, Chan replied. "It's called 'Three Questions.' The premise is that we're all surrounded by answers; we have only to ask the question. To ask a question, you must have determined a need. Perhaps something is missing somewhere, something only the right answer can complete. It's at the top of your mind, so it must be your highest need at the time. That's an answer in itself. Finally, you must figure out how you might get the answer and what the conditions need to be to ask the question. A question is a big deal, Jeffrey. An answer is a tremendous deal. If answers surround us, then we have only to ask the questions."

"I like it, nice, Chan, I hear you, it feels right. So why three questions?"

"Keep in mind that I am inferring three meaningful questions. We're only human, Jeff, and we stay away from meaning most of the time," Chan said, still smiling. "Three meaningful questions that get useful answers would be quite a haul. You don't have to stop with three."

Chan's eyes darted over toward a figure sitting in front of the fireplace. He quit talking for a moment. Jeff followed to see what was drawing Chan's attention. It was easy to understand.

There, in front of the oversized fireplace with crackling logs burning and sizzling, was a mesmerizing figure. The old man with long and flowing silver hair, draped in a deep blood red honeycomb knit cardigan, sat gazing into the fire from the oversized Queen Anne leather chair. Jeff couldn't take his eyes off him.

"You know Jeff, he's remarkable, isn't he? I'll bet he has some answers."

Jeff turned back around, and his eyes met Chan's. "Yes, let's go ask him three questions. We have to." Jeff could feel Note strongly.

Chan took a deep breath and got up from the table. Jeff followed. Both made their way over to the old man.

Upon their arrival, the old man looked away from the fire and up at Chan. His skin was a deep olive, but what surprised both young men immediately was how blue the old man's eyes were. Both Chan and Jeff lost a breath.

"Pardon me, Sir," Chan said when the old man spoke out.

"Hello Chan, you have three questions for me!"

Stunned, Chan said, "How do you know my name and about the three questions?"

"A question for you, why wouldn't I?" the old man replied. "Answer to your question, I know you, and you know I know you."

The old man looked over into Jeff's eyes. Jeff/Note relived the gust of wind that had saved his life, and a message came to them: "Grace is the breath of God."

Chan readied for an additional question when Jeff grabbed Chan's shoulder and announced, "That was your first question, just two more!"

"Wait," Jeff blurted, "I want to ask a question, though you probably already know what it is, but for Chan's sake. Are you God?"

The old man responded to Jeff's question. "Does a mule appreciate the breadth, sophistication, and capacity of a human being? Does an ant understand the intellect of a mule? If an amoeba could be impressed, how impressed would it be with the amazing ant?

"We can each only comprehend what we can appreciate and quantify, Jeff. I know my knowing you and Chan is impressive to you, but there is more than you can comprehend about me. As it is for you, Jeff, so it is for me. There is more than I can comprehend!

"Accept that one thing is no better than another, so an ant is not better or more than an amoeba, and so on. Just know that this Universe comprises all of us, Jeff. Every particle has a place. Know that all of us, each particle, is required.

"To answer your question, Jeff, I'm an old man."

Chan asked his second question.

"What is the most critical thing in the Universe?"

Turning his attention to Chan, the old man answered. "Reverence for Life, all Life."

Jeff had a fleeting thought. *Isn't everything alive, somehow?*

A smile came to the old man's face and then, turning back to Jeff, he proceeded. "Everything is alive, so Reverence for Life is revering everything. For humankind, you must make progress with reverence. Humans may revere humans because they can appreciate those like themselves. A white person may revere other white people, but not black, brown, yellow, or red people. Some may revere wildlife, but not cattle. To move forward, and get to tomorrow, humankind must make progress toward revering life more every day, every moment. Take it in steps. First, get to where if it has a heart that beats, it's alive, it's life. Revere it. From there, come to realize that if it grows, it lives. Then if it changes, it lives and finally, if it exists, it lives.

"The journey to this place will answer all your many questions, and remarkably so. Revere all Life. It is what you are—I revere you."

"I am a writer, and I know you know that." After another deep breath, Chan asked his third question.

"What do I write?"

"Life starts and ends in the same place, but it goes everywhere in between. Write about the journey and let your heart be your guide. It's not what you say that matters, but what you mean. Find the meaning, write something that means something. Be something that means something!"

With that, the old man looked toward Jeff and then into his eyes. His blue eyes pierced through every barrier, straight to Note.

Now, go! Find the meaning.

Note left Jeff at that moment, on a certain path. Note had been in the presence of Grace personified.

In Between

Note knew Grace to be everything but more available than God. There is only one power more, "Awesome." Meaning is the North Star and Note's contribution to the answer. The Universe was born from a question. Answering the question is the journey and meanings build the answer.

Note's experience of the Universe to this point substantiated that the Universe evolved in directions and waves, much like the wind blowing over a desert and pulling rain clouds in, eventually. Grace was one current and Note felt there must be preordained souls that impacted large swaths of life. Note felt drawn to this moment, this being, this soul.

Chapter Seven

Polar World

Sky was a bright and beautiful woman in this world with dark ebony skin and hazel eyes that beamed brilliantly. Her long flowing black hair laid over the front of her shoulders. She sat peacefully as the craft flew smoothly through the air. Sky smelled the coffee aroma in the cabin. She remembered the many times she had enjoyed the smell of coffee in her life. Whenever she smelled coffee, something good was happening, family and friends were close, and rest was at hand, ease. At twenty years of age, Sky had finally achieved what so many of her peers yearned for. She was independent.

Note joined Sky and felt the sensation of ease. Note's journey had been an excessively long one this time and over a great distance, passing hundreds of galaxies. Note continued to experience awe over the distinctiveness of the Universe. Each piece and part of it had some special and meaningful attributes all its own. Note was immediately aware of Sky's uniqueness too. At that moment, everything changed.

The engines went quiet, and the craft descended. The mood in the cabin quickly became frantic and fear-filled. In what seemed like only seconds, Sky felt everything come to an immediate stop when they hit the water. The screams stopped, and pain passed throughout her body as her leg bones snapped. She felt her nose leave her face. Sky couldn't take a breath. Note's connection with Sky at that moment gave her a wave of peace.

She felt the sensation of ascension as her seat lifted her through the sea toward the surface. Suddenly, she felt a jolt, as a large piece of buoyant debris came up under her, raising her into the air with her crippled body still strapped to her seat. Sky was miraculously adrift on a wing section, buoyed up by an intact but empty fuel tank. She was one of three survivors, but each drifted off in slightly different directions. Being unconscious after impact, they each drifted too far apart to get back to one another.

After regaining consciousness, Sky's next task was to withstand both the magnitude of the event, along with the intense pain she again felt in a broken body. She couldn't and slipped back into unconsciousness.

In Sky's next lucid moment, she heard voices, and then one voice more than the others. "You're safe, girl, you're safe." The pain took command, and Sky slipped into unconsciousness once again. When she awoke, she felt a soft and consuming mattress below her, surrounding her while her head rested on something firm. The pain was minimal now. They covered her face with a dressing, and she could feel her legs, but they felt encased and immovable. Oddly, even with the bandage, she noticed the smell of coffee. And then Sky remembered the craft. She felt a moment of terror, then turned her attention to the softness of the sheets beneath her.

Julian spoke. "Hello, Girl. I'm Julian. You'll be okay." He looked into her beautiful eyes and recognized that they were looking past him. "How do you feel?"

"What happened?" Sky asked. "Where am I? What's happened to me?"

"We found you floating in the sea," Julian responded softly. "You've been in an accident and have severe injuries." Her eyes continued to lazily look past him as he spoke. "What's your name?"

"Sky. I'm Sky. Where am I?"

"You're on Rambus, and you're welcome here." Worried about the lack of eye movement, he asked, "How is your vision, Sky?"

"I'm blind since birth. Julian, the bandage on my face is flat over my nose. Is my nose okay?"

"Your nose is different now, Sky. Your nose was gone when we found you, and our doctors worked to give you a new one, as best we can with our limited facilities. It will be adorable, I'm sure."

"As a blind woman, I don't know what ugly is Julian, though I've heard about it. I must be hideous," Sky said and wept.

"You are beautiful," he said kindly, "though you are wrapped like a birthday present, certainly very beautiful, though." Julian laid his hands on her arm.

Sky's mind was full of chaos and questions about this insane moment and what was to come, but she felt the warmth of Julian's hands on her arm and knew a blessing was happening.

"Thank you, Julian," she said sheepishly. "I'm sure you're pretty too! I'm very grateful to you and your people for saving me and caring for me. Have you been able to reach my family to let them know where I am and that I'm okay?"

"We don't have the technology to reach out to your people, Sky, and we are very secluded here with no means to transport you back home. You may be here for quite some time, Sky, but I'm confident they are looking for you and will find you."

With Note in her being, Sky knew this was as it was supposed to be and knew she was safe here. This was her family now, for a while.

"I don't want to be a bother, Julian. I will be forever in your and your people's debt. Thank you again! Please express my gratitude to the others."

"I will, and you're welcome."

"Your dialect is unique, Julian, almost hard to decipher."

"We are a long way from anyone here, and we talk how we talk." She heard some mischief in his voice but could tell he wasn't offended.

Over the next thirteen weeks, Julian and Sky spent hours and hours together each day. Julian supported Sky through arduous therapy sessions, and they grew closer by the moment. Sky helped Julian to get in touch with his senses beyond sight and discover parts of himself beyond the obvious and easy. Sky and Julian fell in love.

One night, the two sat in front of a plump campfire. Laying back against Julian's chest, she was excited by all of the sensations. She was aware of the sound of the crackling fire and of the wind blowing through the trees, sounding tall and solid. She could hear the surf petting the beach and the sound of Julian's breathing. His breathing harmonics were so familiar to her she could tell him from all others.

She smelled burning wood on the fire, mixed with the mildew of the forest. Someone was baking downwind, and Sky could tell it had just come out of the oven. The delicious aroma expanded beyond the kitchen and through the open window. She could smell the oils the therapist had rubbed into her skin earlier and the natural fragrance of her Julian, again unique to only him.

Sky could feel the heat of the fire against her face. She was aware of the breeze blowing gently against her and causing a sensation of cooling as it collided with the light sweat in her eyebrows. Sky could feel the pressure of Julian's arms wrapped around her and pressing her breasts lightly together. She could feel his heart beating and was mesmerized by the rhythm of his breathing. Her body still hurt from the damage and all the efforts she had endured to get whole again, but at this moment, Sky felt the strongest desire she had ever known to unite, to connect, to merge with her extended self, Julian.

"Make love to me, Julian, take me somewhere where we can be alone forever, just us. I want you with all that I am. Take me. I ache for you."

Julian, feeling the same, led her to a beautiful experience together. Gray was conceived that night, conceived in love, in the presence of Note, surrounded with grace. It profoundly changed the Universe as it was meant to be.

Note joined Sky on a world that was the forgotten experiment of an ancient race that had cultivated this part of the galaxy hundreds of thousands of years before. This world, known as Jote to its population, had only two races, the Blacks, and the Whites, each genetically engineered to be one or the other. The experiment was to find out if the important characteristic of skin color itself impacted the evolution of a species. When Jote was populated, the Blacks and the Whites were far apart and divided by vast seas. Neither had the technology to move great distances to meet the alter inhabitants of Jote, so the experiment stayed pure and evidence gathered indefinitely without contamination. In the event that the Jotes evolved long enough, the "makers" built in a genetic attribute to force the races to come together after a great while, or they would die.

After eons, the Whites and Blacks discovered one another but, not knowing they would have to work together to save the other and themselves, jointly decided to maintain two separate societies. As a result, significant percentages of Jotes were dying, and each generation became more and more susceptible to the genetic time bomb.

The Blacks developed an aggressive society with more emphasis on science and technology than the Whites. The Blacks had an evolving space program. The Whites made spirituality more of a priority, which was clear in their wisdom. The Blacks concluded that their technological advantages proved their genetic superiority. The Whites were aware of their military disadvantages and feared the Blacks.

Eight more weeks passed. Sky and Julian were inseparable and bonded with each other on many meaningful levels. Their immense and rare love was apparent to all those around them.

The bacon was crispy this morning and salty.

"I just love the cheese your mom puts on the eggs, Love," Sky said, licking her lips, "and I salivate over how crispy the bottoms of her biscuits are. The butter lingers on my tongue with every bite I take. You are so thin for a man who eats so well."

He giggled and looked at his beautiful Sky, thinking how blessed he was to get to look at this amazing woman and feel her against him too. He leaned over, whispering, "You taste better!"

Sky snorted. "And sorry to go on and on, but your mom's egg salad sandwich with cheese is to die for. Every crispy bite, I can taste the butter along with the nuts in the bread. The mild cheese is rich, oh my, yummy. I am surprised how good it all smells too. I thought without my nose, I would miss out on all of this, but it's fantastic."

Julian's mom, Donnah, said with a smile in her voice, "You sure like food, Sky, and butter for sure. You have quite the appetite!"

At that moment, Julian's father rushed into the room.

"Her people are coming, Julian," he shouted. "We have to get her to the beach and hide."

"What? WHAT?" Julian and Sky both wailed out.

Julian's two uncles burst into the kitchen. "Spaggie," Jant called out, "the Blacks are coming; we have to get Sky to the beach!"

"NO, NO, NO!" Julian yelled out.

"What's happening?" Sky pleaded, "What's wrong? What's happening, Julian? Hold me, what's happening?"

At that moment, Julian's uncles grabbed Julian while Julian's Dad, Spaggie, wrapped his arms around Sky, gently but firmly to control her. They carried Julian away, yelling, screaming, pleading.

"I love you, Sky. I LOVE YOU BABY, and I'll LOVE YOU FOREVER!" The sound of his voice receded as they carried him farther and farther away.

Sky was alone without her Julian. In the grasp of this powerful man, crying and dazed, she became limp.

Spaggie lifted her and hurriedly made his way toward the beach. Sky could hear both the sound of the surf and the large and powerful boat motor getting closer. She heard a man hollering, "That White has her. Do I shoot it, Captain?"

Spaggie yelled out, "No, I'm bringing her to you. We saved her. NO."

Another voice shouted, "Stand down, Sargent. We can kill it in a minute if we need to."

Spaggie laid Sky down on the sand. "We love you, Sky." She felt his arms quickly pull away from her and heard him running as fast as she had ever heard anyone run.

"Do I kill it?" the Sargent asked again, hoping for an affirmative.

"No," the Captain responded, "let's get to the beach and get the girl."

Dazed and bewildered, Sky felt the soldiers pick her up and move her into a small craft. The engine roared as it hopped across the swells out to the ship. Rachel was assigned to care for Sky and made the trip to the beach to get her.

Holding her, Rachel asked softly, "Did they hurt you?"

"Who do you mean? My family, the ones you took me from. No, they saved me. Please take me back."

Surprised at Sky's response, Rachel's voice changed, becoming stern and impatient. "Family? The Whites, your family? That's ridiculous."

Sky remembered what she'd been told about the Whites who lived in another part of their world, back when she was a little girl.

"What do you mean, Whites?" Sky barked. "My love's name is Julian. Take me back and meet him; he isn't a White. He's everything: kind, smart, deep, loving. He does not differ from you and me. Take me back!"

Rachel recalled from her file that Sky was blind. "Were you and Julian in love?"

"Yes! He is my forever love. Take me back!"

"Is your name Sky Dalton? We think you are Sky Dalton, from the crash?"

Sky broke into gut-wrenching crying. "Please take me back. Why are you doing this? I beg you, take me back!"

Not knowing to whom she was talking, Rachel filled in the blanks. "One of our crafts was lost in this area almost six months ago. We found two survivors among this chain of islands, so we have continued to move through them, looking for other survivors; we believe you're one because you're Black, and this island chain is occupied by one of the lesser advanced populations of Whites. Please, what is your name?"

"I am Sky Dalton."

Rachel picked up her phone. "We have Sky Dalton here."

At that moment, the motor stopped laboring, and the boat slowed, level in the water. The rescue team reached the ship. As they moved to the vessel, Sky heard Rachel tell someone, "They raped her. Find out if she is with child." Sky's legs gave way as she left consciousness. She was four months pregnant with her blessing, which would be known forevermore as Gray.

***

Sky and her mother Barbara were reunited after their time apart. Barbara loved having Sky back. She had raised her alone after her husband died when Sky was 13.

Several months after returning home, Sky gave birth to a loved gray-skinned baby. Sky named her Gray. Barbara told her that Gray had deep blue eyes, and Barbara could sense something incredibly special about her.

They allowed Sky to keep Gray because of Rule 41. The Blacks thought themselves to be a generous and open thinking people with great compassion, and rules such as Rule 41 helped them believe that. According to the rule, a White raped Sky, resulting in a child. Gray's birth was not Sky's fault, and society did not hold her responsible. Rule 41 supported Sky's pregnancy with government support and help along with maternity leave until Rule 57 engaged.

Barbara, Sky, and Gray were remarkable together; devoted, loving, encouraging, thriving, inseparable. Sky's maternity leave allowed her to be with Gray around the clock. Along with being her mom, Sky was Gray's best friend. Gray didn't realize how unusual her life was. She never saw or played with other children. Other than an occasional doctor or government worker, she never encountered another person outside her mom and grandma. When she was in the ground vehicle with Sky or Barbara, she sat low in the seat wearing a hooded garment, hiding her from the world around her.

Sky read to Gray every day and started discussing the meanings of life, thought, and relationships as soon and as much as her little girl could listen, hear, and review. Sky was amazed at Gray's evolution and the depth of her innate understanding of all they shared. She was a miracle to Sky and, unbeknownst to her, a miracle on a near-infinite scale.

On the night of Gray's fifth birthday, while in a deep sleep, Gray had a dream, a profound vision that would change her life when she later understood it, one of divine inspiration. In the dream, it was the eve of her next birthday, when she would turn six years old and Rule 57 would be in effect.

Note moved from Sky to Gray, and Sky felt a great sense of loss but associated it with the next loss she would experience. Note was immersed in blue and knew without knowing that this was an infinite soul note joined. Gray was boundless, calm, connected, profound. This soul, unlike Note, however, was in a being and was limited to the experiences of that being. She experienced the existence unique to only Gray. Her personality was not in full connection with her beautiful essence.

As Gray's sixth birthday approached, Sky and Gray sat down on the bed where they often did to talk and read. "Baby," Sky said with a quivering voice, "I have a lot to talk to you about tonight." Her eyes watered.

"What's wrong, Mommy?" Gray's voice was high pitched and soft. She was a little girl who did not understand what was coming. She reached out and put her hands onto Sky's knees. "What's wrong, Mommy?"

Sky then covered Gray's little innocent trembling hands with her own. "Something terrible is about to happen, Baby. I don't know how to find the words. I can't believe it's true; I don't know how to start."

Gray spoke out first. "I've been having horrible dreams, Mommy! In one of them, we are sitting here on the bed, just like this, and you tell me I will have to go away with other people. In my dream, it happens; I'm ripped from you. They hit you to make you let go. Then they take me away. I can't bear the thought of it. I can barely tell you about the dreams."

Sky's stomach fell, and her mouth was suddenly dry. She couldn't see her little girl, but she could feel her and hear her weeping voice. Gray was a piece of her and was her very favorite part, the most wonderful, beautiful, and amazing morsel of life she'd ever known.

She pulled Gray onto her lap and back against her chest, wrapping her arms around tightly around her daughter.

"You are the most special, remarkable person I know. There are no words to express all that you are to me, Precious Daughter. Nana and I will always love you with all our hearts, and you will forever live inside me, Gray. I am Black, and Nana is Black, everyone here is Black, except you Baby. Tomorrow, on your sixth birthday, they will come to get you and take you away."

"No, Mommy, NO NO NO." Gray's head shook wildly.

"I don't know when I'll get to see you again, Baby," Sky broke down, "but I will always be with you, forever, it can never be lost."

"No, Mommy, NO NO NO!" Gray hollered.

Barbara came into the room, and the three held each other and cried and screamed from time to time, desperately, for hours and hours.

It was 9:00 on the morning of Gray's sixth birthday, and the door buzzer sounded. Barbara, Sky, and Gray didn't move and held each other even tighter. After the buzzer sounded several more times, the door gave way to a battering ram and violently flew open. Four officers with weapons drawn made their way over to the frantic family and ripped Barbara away, forcefully hurling her across the small room. Gray and Sky clung desperately to each other, hollering for mercy with tears and slobber flying. Finally, a gun butt smashed into Sky's face, and her unconscious body fell to the floor. Gray's little arms couldn't hold on any longer, and she was in the hands of the bastards. A bag went over her head and a tie was pulled taut around her little neck.

The last sound Gray heard from her family was her Nana crying out after her.

Rule 57 was the Blacks' way of showing compassion in the rare case when a Gray was born in the Black world as a result of rape. So long as the Gray skins were never seen in the community, and no one other than the government knew of their existence, they could live with their Black mothers, but only until the age of six. The government would then take the Gray skinned child and transport them to Yarne, a prison island far out to sea. Few Gray skins were known to exist in any community in the Black world. There was no tolerance.

***

There was no kindness for a long time. Gray had known only love, compassion, respect, hope, and joy until her sixth birthday. Note's presence in her was Grace, and that was enough to keep her tethered to good in the Universe when everything around her had become so dark.

Yarne was a large landmass in the vast Titan Ocean. Jote was such a massive world that it had great masses of land that were still unmapped. Jote had a population of 11 billion Black and White Jotens, but only 30% of the area had been colonized, even sparsely. With more significant technology, the Blacks had identified and mapped all their lands, but large amounts of land in the White portion of Jote remained yet to be discovered. Such expansive land reserves were one reason the Blacks and Whites never confronted each other. Both had more space and resources than they could address or exploit.

With two magnificent mountain ranges and three large inland freshwater seas, Yarne too was relatively virgin territory. It had been 300 years since the Blacks designated Yarne as their prison island, and its population grew over time to just under 10 million Jotes. Most of the society on Yarne was in the south, underneath the extensive Saiden mountain range, with several peaks over 40,000 feet. This part of Yarne was close to the Jote equator. The high mountain range prevented rain from getting to the other side, so most of northern Yarne was desert. Storms were immense on the south side, where the population lived, and hydroelectric power supplied Yarne communities in the south with all the electricity they needed. The Saiden range served as a protector for the Joten inhabitants.

As the vessel Sarnex approached the shores of Yarne, toward the city of Duman, military boats approached it. The boats confirmed its identity along with its cargo and allowed it to come onto shore. The naval ship Spifitzs joined it to protect her as it came into port. The horn sounded, and warning cannon shots rang out, letting the Jotens onshore know they needed to clear the area around the dock until the Sarnex could drop off Gray. The Spifitzs had sharpshooters and gunners on deck to address any infraction.

The Sarnex docked for just five minutes. In that time, they moved Gray and her little bag of belongings to shore. They removed her hood; they spoke no words. The cold water off the coast made this a cool place compared to the mainland, and the wind coming in off the water caused Gray to shiver. She heard the engines of the Sarnex rev up and looked to see the craft pulling away. Gray was all alone, but not for long.

Living cargo, like Gray, did not come to Yarne often, and when it did, it didn't live long unless the Yarne authorities got to it first. The civilization on Yarne had developed laws for its inhabitants to lessen chaos and disorder, but Yarne was a land full of prisoners, and some of them, quite a few, were evil.

Grace was close to this poor child today. Once the Sarnex and Spifitzs were out of range, five of the Yarne militia ran up to get her. Olden picked up Gray to carry her, and the other four soldiers surrounded them while they quickly made their way off the dock and up toward the Fortress. Gray couldn't be sure if this was kindness or not, but it felt like it, and the first such kindness since being in her Momma's arms.

Behind walls constructed two centuries before, the Fortress was a community within a community. It was a holy place. The hefty gates opened as the six souls approached and closed once they were inside. Olden didn't set Gray down but carried her toward a stone house, knocking on the door once they arrived.

The door creaked as it opened, and an older man with a gentle smile was there to greet them.

"Hello, little one," Sparen whispered. He looked at Gray, and their eyes met. "Oh my, you have blue eyes, yes, you do. Any trouble, Olden?"

"No, sir, oddly, there was no one around, at least that we could see."

Sparen looked back at Gray and back into her eyes. "Yes, that is odd. Please leave her with me."

Olden set Gray down and then said something unexpected to all, himself included. "Thank you, little girl."

Sparen held out his hand to Gray, and she raised hers to take his. "Come in, little one."

It was a dark and dusty room with thick stone walls and very few windows. It smelled of tree logs, and there was a stack of them in the corner. A smoldering fire crackled in the oversized fireplace.

"What's your name, little one?"

"I am Gray."

"Well, Gray, you must be hungry and thirsty after your trip. Do you need to use the loo?"

"What is your name, sir?" Gray asked with authority.

"Sparen. I'm Sparen," he smiled.

"I need the loo, sir. Can I trouble you for some water? I'm very thirsty."

"The loo is over there. I'll get you some food and drink. Meet me at the table over there when you come back."

"Yes, sir!"

Gray returned to find Sparen sitting in a thick wooden chair at the table. She quickly focused on

 a metal plate with dense bread and jam, next to an oversized cup of water.

"Please, sit. Eat."

Sparen sat quietly, watching his guest eat the bread and jam and drink most of the water.

"Would you like more, Gray?"

"No, thank you, I'm full," she said as she grinned.

"How can you grin after what you've been through?"

"You are kind, sir; it is your kindness I respond to."

"Please, call me Sparen and come sit with me. I want to hear more about you."

They made their way over to the billowy sofa covered with smelly brown hides.

"Tell me, why is your skin gray?"

"My momma is black, and my daddy is white! Momma told me that's why I'm gray."

"I have never seen blue eyes, Gray; how do you come by those?"

"I don't know."

"I see. Where's your daddy?"

"He lives with the Whites. Momma was in a crash, and Whites found her. She told me they saved her. Momma and Daddy made me. They love each other."

"You seem very calm to me, Gray. I know those people who brought you are not kind people, some maybe, but as a whole, not kind. How did they find you? Is it that rule?"

"Yes, rule 57." Gray's eyes watered, and her nose started to run.

"Were you calmly ready for them to retrieve you, Little One?"

"No!" Gray became angry and gritted her little crooked teeth, but then just as soon, she became calm again.

"I am happy you are here safely. What do you know about this place?"

"No one said anything to me, Sparen. I don't know where I am, but I know I'm with you, and you are kind. I like you."

Her next statement surprised Sparen. "I don't know what lies before me, but I know I will choose my path, as I'm doing now."

"Forgive me, Gray," Sparen inquired curiously, "but how does a six-year-old know her path, and how could a six-year-old get asked that question? How can I be asking that question of you?"

Gray grinned again. "Why am I here with you, Sparen? Do you welcome everyone that comes here?"

"No, I don't," he responded. "I think I know who you may be, Little One. I had a dream that you may come here. The Dream Maker visited me. I didn't know about it until the dream. I didn't see your face, but I saw those eyes, your deep blue eyes. It was the most real dream I've had, Gray; I have forgotten none of it in years. I had it before you were born.

"Tell me, do you hate the Blacks that took you from your Momma and brought you here?"

Gray thought for a moment and then replied crisply and with no softness. "I am not happy with them, not happy at all. It's like being bit by a dog. It hurts, really hurts bad," and then her voice softened, "but it doesn't mean it's a nasty dog because it did a bad thing. No, I don't hate the Blacks or anyone. I'm not happy with them, though."

Sparen was astonished. *She is much older than six,* he thought.

"Forgive me, Gray, but it is rare for such a young Joten to talk this way. Why don't you hate them when they took you from your momma, your home?"

"I had a dream, too, Sparen. When I turned five, I met the Dream Maker. It comes to me every day. Would you like to hear about it?"

"Please!"

"I was walking along a path in my dream; I've never seen such a path, I admit. It was amazing. I saw animals and plants and bugs of every imaginable shape, size, and color. I learned about them in books Momma and Nana shared with me. Along the way, I am confident I smelled every smell. Like all the living things, some were beautiful to behold while others were hideous to me. The smells went from pungent to a bouquet."

Sparen's left eye raised as he thought, *Bouquet. Big word for a six-year-old.*

"I read a lot," she responded.

Did she read my mind? he wondered.

"I heard beautiful sounds on the path that melted me, while also hearing sounds along the way that made me cover my ears. I was barefooted on my walk and without clothes. The path was sometimes flat and bare, but other times covered with tall grass. I experienced painful heat and unbelievable cold that I didn't know I could survive. The path and the grasses would be smooth and soft and then harsh and prickly. I grew thirsty along the way, often I might add, and found drink, some of which made me want to vomit when I took it in my mouth and other drinks that were quenching and delicious."

Sparen's eyes opened wider, and his heartbeat picked up as he considered what Gray was sharing with him.

"I experienced all the extremes I relayed to you, Sparen, but everything in the middle too. Honestly, I don't know how I could experience all of that, in one dream, in one night, but I did."

"How did you feel Gray, do you remember?"

"Yes. I am young, you can appreciate that, Sparen, and there is a good deal of life I haven't lived and emotions I have yet to discover. That said, I felt every emotion I can think of from dislike to love, fear to security, everything."

"That is a fantastic dream to be sure, Gray."

"That's not all."

"Oh, please, go on."

"At the end of my journey on the path, I saw a fork before me. One way was beautiful and light, full of life, and felt happy and, well, good. The other path was ugly and dark, foreboding, repulsive. It made me sad and depressed when I looked at it. It was bad. I knew I had to move forward in my dream, and I had to choose, and it was easy for me. I chose the righteous path.

"I see that path every moment, Sparen, in my mind. I see you on that path. I'll stay on that path."

Sparen sat in silence, knowing who was before him. She was, well, beyond definition.

She looked squarely at him, locking eyes, and said with a voice that sounded ageless: "I don't hate!"

"I don't know what to say, little one. How can I help you?"

"Answer this question, Sparen!"

"Yes, Gray."

Gray knew questions bring answers that are sometimes unknown and undiscovered before the question to find them is asked. She made sure she had full left eye contact with Sparen and then posed the question. "What does my dream mean?"

Sparen felt himself inhale for the first time in a while. The breath felt cool against his throat, and his lungs rejoiced at their opportunity to do their work. Locked into Gray's left eye, his eyes watered.

"You dreamed of life on the path. The path you were on before the fork is everything in this existence...good, bad, and everything in between. You described all your senses, Gray: sight, sound, smell, taste, and touch, along with your feelings and emotions, and in each, you seemed to experience each in their entire range. I agree that it is profound that you could dream of all of that in one dream because to live all of it may take a soul an eternity to do."

"Yes," Gray responded. She reached her little hands out and took his old and worn hand in hers. Their eyes stayed linked.

Sparen continued. "That path, before the fork, is like all life, a Universe in balance, whole and complete, good to bad and everything in between.

"But you came to a fork, Gray, as we all do, but your fork was very pronounced, good versus bad. To choose one over the other was to leave balance and lose everything on the unchosen path. As you have chosen the righteous path, another somewhere has chosen the bad, and the Universe stays in balance. That's what it means, Gray."

"Yes, yes, that's what happened to me."

He closed his eyes for a moment to regroup.

"Come back, Sparen, come back."

He squeezed her hands and opened his eyes to connect with hers again. "Where does all this come from Gray, your kindness, your wisdom, the way you talk to me?"

"It is not mine, Sparen. I'm a vessel, a messenger. I carry the message. I'm not the message. May I continue?"

"Please," he said in awe.

"On a night before I turned six, something came to me, joined me."

"What is it, little one?"

"I can't put words to it. It's vibrations, wonderful vibrations. I sensed them along the path in the dream. They are all working together in harmony. I think of our people, the Whites and the Blacks and me, a Gray skin. We should all be together, Sparen, in harmony."

Sparen shared, "That was my dream, Gray, that a little girl would come to shore in a boat, she would be gray with your eyes and would speak or share a language that would unite all the peoples of our world. I had a sister that was gray skinned like you, and they destroyed her. I know they don't know what they're doing. Gray, I think you are that little girl and will save them from themselves."

"I will help all I can, Sparen; that is the path I have chosen. My words, thoughts, this body, bind me and limit me. I live in chunks; each moment is separate from the last or the next. I must walk this good path through these chunks and in a world of chunks. Do you understand?"

"Yes," he responded. "Each thought is separate and distinct from the last, a chunk. Unlike your dream, the one that was complete and whole and eternal, your life in this realm is in chunks. Your walk along the path is in steps, and even if you know what's coming, you can't see it until it's the moment or the chunk you're in. Does that sound right, Gray?"

"Yes." She paused and then continued. "Sparen, why do you think I had the dream?"

He looked back into her eyes deeply and felt himself melt. "Because, Little One, you are the dream."

At that instant, Note felt that the doorway had just opened to the meaning of the Universe—the purpose of existence—but the truth was more than Note could take in, and the next moment came, as did the closing doorway.

Over the next six years, Gray and Sparen discussed and contemplated many things while she shared time with each of the others in his group, all expanding each other's awareness and understanding of the surrounding reality. Though it lacked the nurturing she experienced with her momma, Gray's life felt enriched. She thought of them daily, and Sky and Barbara felt her love across the distance.

On Gray's 13th birthday, she and Sparen sat again on the billowy sofa to have the conversation he had told her would come.

"Our time together has been immeasurably profound, Gray, and I feel honored to have shared it with you. The goal we have is mutual, and it's freeing the peoples of this world from their smallness and intolerance for those different from them. We know that beneath the surface, we're all much the same," he said, smiling.

"Yes!"

"You know, too, that we have to get you back to the mainland to share your message. It has to start there."

"Yes, I understand."

"We have protected you from the world out there while evolving together behind these walls. You'll need to spend the next year out there. We have two contacts that you'll start with, but you will need to survive the year before you go back to the mainland. If you survive, and I am confident you will, you'll be much more prepared for what you'll encounter."

"When do I go out there?" Gray could not hide the concern on her face.

"We will spend the next two days educating you on the specifics of what you'll encounter. You will have to make decisions and choices. We'll give you the knowledge to help you do that. Get with Polan in the morning to begin your preparation."

When morning came, the light above the clouds came through enough to illuminate the heavy rain coming down, almost in torrents. Gray had become very accustomed to the large volume of water that fell from the sky here. She often wondered how anyone on Yarne accomplished anything with the constant deluge. The rain continued to erode the beautiful countryside, along with the Joten attempts at drainage control. Gray just learned to love being wet.

Polan entered her small room with hot tea and bread for breakfast and carried several rolls of paper. After enjoying the bread and tea, Polan pulled out one roll and opened it on the ground in the middle of the room. He spoke.

"There are four primary populations on Yarne, Gray."

"What divides them, Polan?"

"Their minds," he responded.

Polan continued. "Most of the people here live south of the Saiden Mountains. Only a few live in the desert in the North. The group in the North is the worst of the lot. They are lawless, mostly, the survival of the fittest and all that—and are cannibals. They eat each other, prisoners, the weak and the old. We call this group the Teeks. Unfortunately, a community of Teeks has come to the South and have mixed among the other groups. They are responsible for many of the missing. You'll see them traveling in pairs and with no hoods. The rest of the population moves around in groups for protection against the Teeks.

"The Teeks seek lighter-skinned Blacks and any Grays or Whites here. There are a good number of lighter-skinned Blacks, and there is a population of Whites. Not sure how they got here. They keep to themselves, however, out there, somewhere. The authorities mandate that all who move around outside their dwelling do so with full robes with large cowls. The population complies for their safety."

"What's a cowl, Polan?"

"A large hood. It's what we wear, Gray."

"Thank you."

"We have friends out there you can stay with at night, but you must go out into the streets during the day. It's a year for you to discover more about yourself and the breadth of Jotanity beyond these walls. The evil out there will surprise you, but there are heroes too."

"What do you recommend for food, Polan?"

"The jungles are full of fruits. Just never go into them alone. You'll have a family too and eat with them. Do you have questions?"

"No. Thank you again, Polan. I will learn about my family when I meet them. I'll miss you."

"And I'll miss you, Gray. Our friends will come to get you in the morning."

Gray woke while it was still dark and looked around her room. She admired the surrounding stone and reveled in the thick wood above her. She often thought about how they were formed and born. The stone was eons old. Perhaps it was once sand on a beach that was then covered with layers and layers of new sand. *What was that like?* she wondered. *Did the temperature change much? Do rocks feel anything? Is there any life in a rock?*

The wood was just a seed once, perhaps a burr that fell from a noble tree in the forest. It was lucky enough to take root and grow over decades or centuries to become a magnificent tree itself, letting go of burrs under its high canopy. What birds sat in its branches? What squirrels ran around it and bugs burrowed into it? How many animals lived beneath it for protection? How many rains and sunsets and early Jotens had it seen? What story could this old wood tell?

There was a pronounced chill in the air this morning. Gray felt some anxiety but was confident she would do well on her next journey. She reminded herself that whatever happened to her each day, she already knew her path: the righteous one.

Gray sensed it was almost time to leave. She put on her robe and sat on the ground meditating and centering for nearly two hours before she heard a knock at the door. She rose and opened it to find Polan and Sparen along with over a dozen of her friends and neighbors standing outside her door, lining up and down the hall.

Walking into the group, she felt their hands patting and squeezing her back and shoulders. "Good luck Gray, we love you, Gray, be safe, come home soon." She remembered Barbara and her momma and knew they loved her, and she loved back. That's why she was surrounded. The entire group made their way to the gate along with her, where two individuals, both men, greeted her in dark robes with cowls.

"Gray," Sparen said, "these are our friends, Joelen and Parday. You will stay with them and their families. We wish you well, Gray. You are a light!"

"Thank you, Sparen. This will always be my home, and you will always be my family." Her eyes watered, and she reached out to hug her adopted father. They never embraced here, but the entire group surrounded Sparen and Gray, and all hugged the little angel in the middle.

After a few moments, they pulled away with heads down. Gray pulled her hood over her head and turned to her new friends, Joelen and Parday, and moved over by them. They pulled the large creaking gate open, and they made their way outside. Tears rolled down her cheeks.

"Keep your head down, Gray," Joelen ordered. "Learn to see before you without raising your head too much. Grays don't survive out here; keep your head down."

The smells were different outside the walls and beyond the gate. Sewage was open here but stayed clear because of the abundant rainfall. It wasn't raining now, and the light warmed their backs.

There were many sounds out here too: young ones, animals, street vendors, the sound of carts on the stone streets. Gray continued to look down until she got to her new quarters. She would spend the rest of the day there to acclimate and adjust and get a good night's sleep before she would venture out the next day. Her daily companions that she had yet to meet were her age, both male and both spiritualists, though not from her former community.

The new day arrived amidst a significant rain. Gray joined Gute and Ronan at the table for porridge and ate until she was full. They spoke few words until it was time to go.

"What do we do out there?" Gray asked.

Gute looked at her gently. "We serve."

"We serve," she mused. "What does that look like?"

"There are endless needs out there. We are open to seeing them; we help. Ronan and I are serving you. You need help, right?"

"Yes. You are both very Black. Do you have to wear hoods?"

"Yes," Gute responded, "we wear them as do most, to protect those that aren't so Black."

"I remember Polan telling me about that. Why do we go out in the rain when it is raining hard like this?" Gray asked.

"It is often raining hard like this, Gray."

"Right, it is!"

Using large leaves from the rainforest, the Jotens engineered umbrellas to shield themselves from the rain. They layered the leaves over a platform that lowered over their heads to sit on their shoulders. The platform had a brace going down the back. They attached each blade to the platform at a slight angle to shift the weight backward. The mountains shielded the wind in this part of the small continent, so the rain leaves worked flawlessly here. The lack of wind also allowed the rain to fall almost straight down, another plus for allowing one to remain relatively dry on the top two-thirds of one's body.

Open sewage and insanely wet conditions led to open sores on the population's wet feet, making them susceptible to the bacteria. Sandals were a must for the team. They were thick, soft, and squishy.

Gray, Gute, and Ronan were out and moving slowly on the streets. They came upon a woman moving alone, a dangerous act.

"Woman," Gute spoke out. "It's Gute." They knew Gute well in the area as a kind soul.

"Thank goodness it's you, Gute. My father fell ill during the night. He can't move. I need to get to the doctor and ask for his help."

"How far away is your father?" Gute asked seriously.

"Seven streets that way." She pointed north.

"These are my friends, Ronan and Gray. Please take them to your father. I will get a doctor."

"You will be alone," Ronan spoke out.

"The doctor is just up there; he and I will be two," Gute noted.

"Thank you, Gute, thank you. Come, please." Leading Ronan and Gray, she moved at a quick pace. Arriving at the abode, she called out. "Father, father, I have help, and the doctor will be here soon."

Bete and her father Shin lived alone. Her mother had disappeared many years ago. Shin laid on a pile of hay in the corner of the little room. A small fire burned in a pit on the opposite wall. His eyes were dazed, and his skin was cool and clammy. Bete fell to his side and took his arm. "Father, help is coming!"

Gray kneeled next to Bete and next to Shin's head. She put her hand on his forehead, and he let out a groan. His eyes cleared and looked up to meet hers.

"Woman, what is your name?" Gray asked gently as she kept eye contact with Shin.

"Bete."

"What is his name?"

"Shin," Bete answered.

"Shin," Gray spoke, stroking his forehead. "You have been a good man, and I sense that. You are loved; I know that. You will never be lost, Shin."

Ronan looked down with astonishment at what was happening. Gray's voice differed from that of the young girl he had just met.

Shin's mouth tried to smile. He looked at his Bete, their eyes met, and then he passed.

"Father, father!" She wailed and laid her head on his chest.

"Bete, you can't be here alone," Ronan spoke out. "Do you have another family?"

"No."

"You'll need to come with us after your father's body gets picked up."

"No."

"Yes, you must," Ronan pleaded.

"I don't care!" Bete was empty.

Gray set her hand on Bete's arm, and she raised her head back up.

"Your life matters," Gray told her meaningfully, "and there is great joy ahead for you. Everything is dark now, but there is joy ahead. Trust me! We want you to come with us. Say yes and do so." Bete felt Gray's love, and it melted her in her deep sadness.

"Yes, I trust you. I will go."

Ronan looked over at Gray again with surprise. Over the next couple of hours, Gute and the doctor arrived. Soon after, the gravediggers came to remove Shin's body. Gute, Ronan, Gray, and Bete then made their way back to the cottage where the rest of the family welcomed her. Bete stayed with them for a few days while they identified her new home.

It was early afternoon; the rain stopped, and Gute, Ronan, and Gray left the cottage once again to serve. It wasn't long before they came upon a couple under a porch; she was giving birth, which was a desperate and vulnerable situation to be in with the Teeks looking for such opportunities.

"Ronan, keep your eyes open for trouble." Gute kneeled and scooted under the porch. "Hello, I'm Gute. I'm here to help. How close are you?"

"My contractions are coming every three minutes, lasting about 45 seconds. I'm awfully close, I think...I don't know...it's my first, oh, here comes another one, oh!"

Gray and Ronan kneeled next to the man.

"What are your names?" Ronan asked.

"I am Stuling. This is Marah."

"You don't have to be afraid, Stuling," Gray said calmly. Stuling looked over to find the source of the voice and caught her eye.

"Your skin is gray, and your eyes." He could see into the hood.

"Yes, I am. Breathe, Stuling."

She then reached out and put her hand on Marah's tummy, "It's time," Gray said. "Push, Marah!"

Marah let out a scream and then pushed. Stuling's hands were crippled, so Gray moved over to receive the infant. Gute watched with surprise.

"Push," Gray said so softly it drew the angels' gaze. "Push."

As a crowd was gathering, Gray once again put her hand on Marah's tummy, and Marah seemed to calm some. The fragile little soul came out into the world, under the porch. Gray put her hands under the head as it emerged and then the body.

Ronan pulled a knife from his robe and cut the cord. Gray kissed the infant, and it took in its first breath, and then another, and another.

"You have a girl," Gute said as Gray laid Marah's daughter on her momma's chest. A woman in the crowd brought forth a garment and handed it to Gray. She put it over the baby.

"Marah, do you have a place to go?" Gute asked.

"Yes, my parents will allow us to stay with them for a short time. We thought we had more time before the baby came."

"Can you walk?"

"No."

"I can carry her," Stuling spoke, "but not both her and the baby."

Gray smiled. "I will carry the child."

Later, as it got dark, Gute, Ronan, and Gray left the home of Marah's parents.

"We have to get back to our home," Gute remarked.

The three made their way back in good time; they spoke no words.

Gute, Ronan and Gray continued to go out to serve each day, and it wasn't long until they knew of Gray around the community and beyond. Within half a year, she no longer wore her hood to hide her skin color. She was still in some danger, however.

The massive island had a rare week of sunshine with no rain. It was startling to the population, but appreciated. Gute, Ronan and Gray were at the northern edge of the community when they saw a large group of men without hoods surrounding a figure. Was this an attack, or had one of their own fallen, the three wondered?

Gute spoke quietly. "They are Teeks; we need to stay clear! There are many."

"It is odd to be sure; we need to get out of here quickly," Ronan added.

"No," Gray said. "You go. I'll stay."

"No, Gray, that's not a good idea. We must leave together now." Gute was emphatic.

"You go, I'll stay," she repeated.

Gray started walking toward the group of Teeks. Gute and Ronan followed. As they neared the men, they separated to allow the three to enter. In the middle laid a Black man, Kog, leader of the Teeks. His son was next to him, a stunning figure with dark black skin and oddly red eyes.

"You're Gray, the healer. I've heard of you; we've heard of you. Your eyes are as they said."

"What is your name?" Gray asked calmly.

"Jent. I am Jent, son of Kog. This is Kog." He looked down at his unconscious father.

"I need my brothers here to be safe, yes?" Gray stated powerfully.

"Yes," Jent agreed.

Gray had developed the ability to feel energy and, in a small way, impact it. She didn't know, but Kog had a brain tumor in his frontal lobe that was causing seizures to come more regularly as his condition deteriorated. He regained consciousness as she placed her hand on the side of his head.

Kog's eyes watered as he looked back at Gray and into her deep blue eyes.

"You are the Gray child. I see you are special, aren't you?"

"We're all special, Kog. What do you see when you look at me?"

"Peace. I see peace."

"Other than peace, what do you see, Kog? Tell me."

"Gray. I see gray skin."

"What does it feel like when you see gray skin?"

"I feel like a master. I feel like I have to take you and control you." The surrounding Teeks grumbled with agreement.

"That makes no sense, Kog. Here we are, and you are lying on your back while I'm not. How are you a master, and I'm not?"

"You are gray-skinned! Now, what's wrong with me?"

"I can't see it with my eyes Kog, but I feel it when I touch your face. You have something in your head, and it's alive."

"Can you fix it, Gray One?"

"No, Kog."

"Then what must I do?"

"The thing in your head matches the hate in your belly, Kog. You can't fix what's in your head, but you can fix what's in your belly, and that will heal you much more."

Kog could sit up now and then stand.

He held his hand out to Gray to help her up; he towered above her and was the largest of the Teeks.

"You talk in circles, Gray!"

"Listen more closely then, Kog." He looked around as his team muttered at her seeming—and potentially—misplaced courage. "I'm happy to make more sense for your benefit. You look at me and see gray skin. You look at the people in this community and see food. Everywhere you go, there's fear. Here and now, all fear you. You're surrounded by a very high wall, tight around you. Your existence is limited and fruitless, yet you have the most significant opportunity of your life, right here, right now."

"Go ahead, Gray."

"Come, walk with me alone; do you feel up to it, Kog?"

"Jent will join us; he will assist me if needed."

Jent motioned to the men to disperse.

Gray turned to Ronan and Gute. "I will see you back at our home," she said.

"Gray, no, you can't go with them! We may never see you again," Gute implored.

Jent turned on them aggressively, and Kog spoke out. "Let them go, son. Monks, she will come back to you."

Kog, Jent, and Gray started up the street. Everyone cleared off the surrounding road.

"You see, Kog? The fear, the poison?" she reaffirmed.

"So, you will talk to me about poison?"

"I just wish to ask you questions. What do I call you, Kog?"

"Everyone but Jent calls me Sire. He calls me Father. No one calls me Kog; call me Kog."

"Have you lived here your entire life, Kog?"

"No, I arrived here as a child with my mother and father. They were imprisoned here for helping a Gray like you. My mother didn't live long here. The Teeks took my father and me as slaves. He was a professor back on the continent and was skilled in engineering, and the Teeks soon came to revere him. He was a natural leader too and soon was Sire. When he passed, I became Sire."

"Do you read, Kog?"

"Yes. My father procured books from the population, though few."

"Do you eat people, Kog, kill them, and eat them?"

"Yes."

"How can you do that?"

"They are just meat, Gray. Can we sit under that tree? I am feeling weak."

They made their way over to a large tree with an expansive but flat canopy. Each branch was magnificent. After sitting and getting comfortable, Gray started questioning again.

"Kog, please, can you tell me what prejudice means to you?"

"Prejudgment," he answered.

"And you, Jent, what does prejudice mean to you?"

"It means nothing to me, Gray. It doesn't matter."

"Why doesn't it matter?"

"Because getting what I want, what I need, that's what matters. How I judge anything doesn't matter."

"Is that right, Kog? Is Jent, right?"

"He is young, and it's right to him."

"Is it right to you?"

"No." He answered slowly, softly, "It matters."

"Do you want to see what I see, Kog?"

He looked back at her and knew he had a choice to make. The doorway was before him.

"Yes, how?"

The Jotens had never heard a note. They had never listened to a song or watched a band come together to bring a song to life. Gray was with Note. She was full of Song. It would be the platform to unite this world as music lives through all essence. Music is essence.

Gray reached out and put her hand on his face and looked into his left eye with hers. They tunneled. It all happened in just an instant, a moment. At that moment, both experienced an astounding number of unique distinctions, but each in harmony with the rest, all in harmony and moving forward, not moving forward visually but moving forward energetically. Both reveled in Note and Song and the peace of it. They both blinked their eyes and were back under the tree with Jent.

"What do you know now, Kog?"

"Prejudice is the opposite of appreciation. Judgment is the stifling of recognition and realization. Moving forward is recognizing distinction and being grateful for it, all of it. It all moves forward, together, harmoniously. Every part matters, each piece. That is what I know now, Gray," Kog conceded.

"Yes, I get that too, Kog. This is a substantial gift, and I thank you."

"Those words—and that message—are not mine Gray, but I will own them. What was that sound that fills you?"

"The sound we shared is the way home for our people. I have much to learn, but I believe it's the way home, the way forward, away from prejudice. Each sound is essential in the whole sound."

"What happened to you two?" Jent asked. "I have never heard you talk that way, Father!"

"We have much to talk about, Son. Let's get back to camp. Gray, come see me often; you will always be safe."

"Kog, I have two last questions, but I ask for only one answer."

He nodded.

"This question is for you to answer to yourself, and I hope you do. It is, how do good people do bad things? And I want you to answer my second question. If the village brings the Teeks food, will you quit eating the people?"

Kog smiled. "Yes, if you can find someone brave enough to bring food regularly, we will quit eating everyone. We don't eat that many, anyway."

"To start, I'll bring it," Gray said lightly.

Kog rose to his feet and leaned some on Jent as they started moving back onto the street. As they moved farther away, the people started coming back out on the street, astonished by what they had witnessed from their hiding places. The legend of Gray was expanding.

Over the next couple of months, Gray would go out to serve by herself. She also delivered foodstuffs to the Teeks. They were no longer a threat to her. One of them usually accompanied her as she moved around the community. The Teeks changed, and no longer removed people. They would eventually serve as the protectors for all their fellow islanders. Fear was subsiding, and more laughter heard.

Back at their home, Ronan said, "Gute, I need to take Gray to see Ann. You've seen all that I've seen. She's the One; she has to be."

Later in the evening, Ronan sat with Gray, watching the sunset in the south. Both delighted in witnessing the magnificent sky that night. He told her about Ann in the forest and how he wanted to take Gray to meet her. They agreed to set out the next morning.

The next morning came as a flood. It was raining hard, and the sky stayed dark even though the day was arriving. Great torrents of water were running through the streets, leaving the drainage system overwhelmed. Rains like this didn't come often and were feared; in fact, several would lose their lives today. Gray entered the primary room to find many of the family sitting and sharing warm tea made of the rich sippa leaves. Ronan looked up and smiled at his good friend.

"Good day to you, Gray. Please join us for tea, and I will get you some fruit."

"Thank you, Ronan, but I must start on my way."

"Oh no, Gray, we have a Jappa rain out there; no one's out. I know we talked about a trip today, but I can't take you now."

"Thank you, Ronan. Yes, it's a Jappa rain, but I'm to see your friend today."

"I can't take you out in this; I cannot."

"I know where she is. I'll be fine. We are to meet today. I'm going alone." She looked over and caught his eye. And, at that moment, he knew Gray knew where Ann was, and he knew too she would get there safely.

"I understand, but you must stay dry. Come, let's talk a moment."

Ronan moved away from their friends. They walked to a quiet area. He spoke to Gray like a big brother. "When you get to where she lives, you'll find Ann is on the other side of a deep ravine, a treacherous one. It'll have raging water in it today. There's a bridge that goes over the abyss to her hut. In all the time I've lived, Gray, only Sparen has crossed over the bridge to see Ann. I've never met her myself. Even though they have never seen her, there's a group here that takes care of her needs. They leave food in the middle of the bridge, and she comes to get it. I know somehow that she will receive you, Gray, and I have talked to Sparen about this moment. I am excited and honored to be here with you now, and to have you in my life."

Gray's eyes softened. She held her hand out and set it on Ronan's arm. "You are the dear one, Ronan. I love you; you know that, don't you?"

"Yes, I know," he said, humbly smiling.

"I must go now and float to Ann's!"

Gray wrapped herself in warm clothes, and then she wrapped huge Junnet leaves around herself to keep the water out. Topped with a Junnet leaf bonnet, Gray set out on her journey.

As there was no wind again this morning, the water fell straight down. Keeping her eyes on the muddy ground to keep her footing, Gray slowly made her way toward the forest. There was no path to Ann's house as only the caretakers and Sparen were welcome. The trek was arduous, and it took her many hours to make it to the ravine. The rain continued to wash the fresh blood from Gray's scraped, scratched, and punctured arms and legs, a toll the thick brush and thorns were taking on her body. The Junnet leaf had also mostly torn away. She felt utterly wet all the way through.

As she reached the ravine, the rain stopped, and sunlight peeked through the canopy. Gray could see the long and rickety rope bridge from where she stood. She made her way toward it until she stood in front of it. On the other side, some 400 feet away, Gray saw the hut, nestled back in the forest. Holding her hands out and grabbing the drenched hand ropes, she made her way across the lively bridge, noting its musky smell and humbled by the power of the surging waters below.

The door to Ann's hut was on the left side, and Gray found it open. She approached and slowly entered. The hut was embracingly warm. She saw an old woman bent over, crying in a large rocking chair in front of a smoldering fire, and then heard the weeping voice softly speak out. "Shut the door, Child, and get out of those clothes. You'll find a blanket on the bed. Wrap yourself and lay your clothes out to dry."

"I am bleeding, Mother," Gray said.

"We all bleed, Child, even you. Pay no mind."

Ann continued to weep as Gray disrobed and wrapped the soft, quilted blanket around herself. She made her way over to Ann and stood beside her, putting her hand on her white hair.

"Why do you cry, Mother?"

"Because you call me Mother," Ann answered. "Sit, please."

Gray sat down in a simple chair across from Ann.

"Why else do you cry, Mother?"

"I cry because you've come. I've lived my entire life alone, seeking a pure existence of goodness, trying to live each moment as fully as I could. I've tried to listen to every single word of this life, as all of this around me spoke. I've grown old but never doubted that there was something more. I have done the best I could do." Ann's voice buckled, and her crying intensified. "All of that, dear child, with just faith, no proof. Now you're here. You are the proof. I hurt with joy, so much joy. Thank you!"

"I am here, Mother, but I'm just Gray, a young girl, a Joten like you. However, I'm not alone; there is another with me."

"Yes, I sense that. You are Gray, but like everything, you are not 'just' Gray. I have discovered," Ann continued, "that everything reveals itself only as we can perceive it. Though it all exists, always, it only appears to us when we perceive it, affirm it. You just know what you can perceive, Gray, and you don't perceive all that you are, all that this is."

"Okay, I don't know what I don't know."

"Yes," Ann answered easily.

Ann's weeping subsided. She leaned back with her eyes fixed on Gray.

Gray sat back too. She couldn't appreciate what others saw in her because her perspective was through her eyes, with her mind. To Gray, she was just Gray. *Why did Sparen, Ann, and others treat her with such reverence?* She wondered. *I try hard, I care, I love, but what's the fuss?* she thought.

"Tell me, Mother, who do you think I am?"

"I know who you are. You're the One, the carrier, the turning point for our world."

"I am just Gray, Mother."

"You say you aren't alone, and there is another with you. Please tell me more, Child."

"There's an order within me, a blending of sounds, a rhythm, and I love it. It moves me, Mother, to my very core. I fall into it and think it is another soul. Do you know what it is?"

"Can you look deeply into my eyes, Gray, and share with me?"

Gray looked over into Ann's bright green eyes and then focused on the left eye. Ann's old wrinkled face nestled her amazing and vibrant eyes within her dark black canvas. Gray and Ann began tunneling; both met Note. After some enlightening moments, Ann turned away. Both knew they had been joined.

"We will call it Song," Ann said as she started weeping again.

"It's heavenly, isn't it, Mother?" Gray said, smiling softly. "What do you think Song is?"

"A messenger from the source, the word of God maybe. Would you ever be complete without it now, Child?"

"No, never. It's a wind carrying my soul. As you suggest, Mother, it may be the word of God; it's like being surrounded and enveloped by God."

"Yes, though yours, Gray, is a special relationship with God, yes, I feel the same with Song."

"I don't know what you mean about God and me, Mother. I'm just Gray."

"There is something this Universe wants, Gray, a reason for this Universe. You are one possibility for it to find its answer. As for now, you are the answer to this world, our world. After, only God knows," Ann said, smiling.

"What answer, Mother?"

"All things, all want to go home. The more we connect, the closer we get. Song is connection. You are connection, Gray!"

"Yes, Song is the connection, Mother. It is an infinite number of sounds existing distinctly but in unison with each other, all moving together in a rhythm that carries my soul, our souls."

"Yes, Child. And you will bring our world together with it, the Whites and Blacks, distinct but in unison with each other."

"What is my path, Mother?"

"There is technology on our island to record sounds. You will introduce Song to some of our people and find inspiration to record Song. When you sleep, your dreams and a friend within you will introduce you to tools to produce Song out here, beyond our minds. You will record it and take it back to the Blacks. It will make its way to the Whites, and in time our world will come together."

"Yes, yes."

"We won't meet again in this realm, Child, but we will always be together. Your visit has completed me. I am finished here. Leave me now and go with my love."

"You will never be alone, Mother. I know to share that with you."

Ann began again to weep. "Go, Child. Thank you!"

Gray made her way out of the hut and back across the bridge, working her way back through the dense forest to make her way home. In the months to come, the Dream Maker visited in her sleep, introducing her to various crude musical instruments and the way to play them to share Song.

Gray's family sought islanders and fellow prisoners who would experience music and be changed by it, learning the various instruments and the language of music she presented to them. She made her way to the different colonies on Yarne to find her musicians and faced many challenges as she encountered deep-seated prejudices amongst the competing clans. In the end, she had a five-piece assembly, with a White, two Grays, and two Blacks. They made music together and recorded it on the elementary recording devices they had available, both audio and video.

Before leaving Yarne, Gray wanted to meet with Sparen.

To Gray, it felt like the day she first entered the compound. The vegetation had flourished even more since then. As she approached Sparen's quarters, she locked her eyes on the one-of-a-kind wood door on the front. How had she missed it the first time? It looked to be hundreds of years old. She hadn't seen many doors in her life, but how could any other door have this much character with the grooves and knots and sheer heft? It looked as if they had changed the hardware on it many times over the years. Appearance did not mean much on Yarne; performance did.

The door swung open to a melted, smiling face, and the joy was mutual.

"Welcome home, Gray. You honor me with your return!" They shared a warm hug.

Gray took a deep breath and felt welcome in the dark and dusty room with the thick stone walls she remembered. It still smelled of the tree logs that were still stacked in the corner. A smoldering fire spit sparked in the oversized fireplace as it had the first time she was there.

"Please sit with me and tell me about your experiences. Leave nothing out."

They talked for hours and hours until finally, it was time for them to part.

"Thank you for sharing all of that and all of you, Gray. I have been saving my most important question until the last."

She studied him with a concentrated look, and her blue eyes deepened, almost as if she knew the question.

"What is the most important thing you've learned, Dear One?"

Without hesitation or doubt in her teenage voice, Gray answered, "I've learned that everyone and everything is trying to get home."

"Home?" Sparen knew what she meant but had to process, so his question and puzzled look gave him some time to take in her answer wholly.

"You know, home, Sparen."

"Yes, you are our home, Gray. I know that. What is home for you?"

"There are several for me," she said softly and slowly. "Here with you is home, and there is the home that is too big to put into words, chunks. My home is with my mother and grandmother. Ann, she is home. My family here is home. Really though, the home we all seek is that big one."

"The one you can't put into chunks?"

"Yes, that one, Sparen, my friend."

"I have never forgotten your chunks, Gray. In the north and south of our great world, there are massive ice caps, and the surrounding sea is littered with ice chunks of all sizes. I always think of that when I remember your talk with me about chunks when I first met you, and it helps me make sense of this reality. We navigate around all the chunks and must focus on each as it could impact us negatively. Because we focus on the chunks, we forget about the destination—forget about home, perhaps," Sparen said with a falling voice.

"I'm glad our prison island isn't in the far north or south, Sparen," she quipped.

"I hope, Gray, that in time I can come to understand more of what you know of home."

"My good, good friend. I know I'll see you there. I will see you when we get home." Gray spoke with profound softness. It was almost wordless.

"Thank you, thank you for the gift you are."

"You are so kind to me, Sparen."

"Finally, Child, let's talk of your journey back to the mainland."

***

Years after they had brought her to Yarne to spend her life, Gray prepared to be smuggled back to the mainland with her musical recordings sewn into her robe. Gray's robe covered her completely, leaving no evidence of her skin color. All those that heard Song knew it was a miracle for the future of their world.

The plan was for the smugglers to deliver Gray back to the mainland, where Sparen had connections that would get her to a safe house to live while they determined how to get her music to the media. Gray arrived on the mainland, but no one met her. She quickly found herself on her own in the hostile land with no means to find her mother or any other friendly soul.

***

Several months had passed. The weather was finally starting to warm during the day, and Gray had hope that the brutally wintry nights would soon find the warmth as well. She had watched many fellow homeless Jotens fall victim to the cold over the previous months. The season of rejuvenation was at hand. The trees were budding, and the brown grass before her started showing sprouts of green. Hope was afoot with the change of seasons.

It was midafternoon on the same day when Gray heard the squealing of tires followed by a thunderous crash nearby. Compelled, she made her way toward the sound. Exiting the forest, she saw a vehicle turned over on the quiet road ahead. Suddenly, it burst into flames. She felt a jolt of heat. The flames were on top of the vehicle. Below, in the passenger section of the overturned vehicle, she saw an unconscious woman and child. Gray ran toward the car, almost tripping over her robe, feeling the heat getting more and more extreme as she approached. As she reached the side of the vehicle where the child was, flames came into the vehicle cockpit from above, plummeting toward the two imperiled souls. Gray reached in through the small opening in the crushed window; the flames surrounded her.

Genevieve, the eleven-year-old girl, opened her eyes just as Gray's burning hood fell off. Before Genevieve was a Gray angel. Their eyes locked, with Genevieve feeling both Gray and Note. During that moment, she became oblivious to the intense heat. Lost in Gray's blue eyes, she felt hope!

With much of the top of her robe burned off, Gray took hold of Genevieve through the opening and pulled Genevieve into her body. Gray surrounded her while she rolled away from the vehicle.

The pain was more significant than anything Gray had ever physically experienced. Now that she and Genevieve were away from the fire, she relived the feeling of her skin melting away in the intense fire and barely remained conscious. The pain raged. She was now deaf in one ear.

Genevieve was burned severely above her shoulders with facial damage. Both of her legs had snapped as the car overturned in the accident. She was mercifully unconscious again.

Gray heard approaching emergency vehicles and followed her instincts. She placed her burned hand over Genevieve's heart; love poured through her and into this little girl. Gray then limped quickly into the woods, fearing what would happen if they discovered her. The bottom of her robe was intact along with the music disk, but she wouldn't realize that for some time. For now, she felt the fear of dying or being captured while also feeling despair for the damaged child she had just saved.

Note was a solace to Gray amid the pain, a pain she would endure for several months as her newly deformed body healed and survived. Her head's appearance was now hideous to those who saw her, but her head was no longer recognizably gray.

Later, as the cold season returned, Gray met true evil for the first time. This evil was not that of ignorance, but evil with no care or compassion for anything beyond itself. Walking down a path, Gray was attacked and violently raped by three men. Leaving her cruelly damaged, she again survived and discovered that she was pregnant.

Over the next seven months, Gray continued living on the streets, eating out of trash cans. Even with the hardship, she finally had hope that she would have someone to love who loved her back. Gray's maternal instincts kicked in. She was homeless but did everything possible to have a healthy baby and give her baby a better life than she'd had. She remembered her momma and grandma and had big hopes of finding them someday. She remembered many of their happy moments together; they were part of her. Gray was hopeful!

It was early on a warm and cozy day. The sky was the clearest Gray had seen in a long while, and the bluest too. Note comforted her and filled her with Song. She felt the baby moving briskly, but something was different today. The excited mother-to-be realized her precious bundle was ready to enter the world. Because she knew it was too early, fear swept through her.

The fire, streets, and the attack had crippled Gray, and her small daily diet out of garbage cans left her severely malnourished with soft bones, a condition called osteomalacia[14]. Knowing she needed help, Gray made her way slowly and painfully toward a nearby hospital. She lived in the area just to be close to a hospital in case she needed help with her precious baby.

Gray came staggering toward the front of the hospital, covered from head to toe with another robe she'd rescued from one of her street buddies who had died. Gray, Note, Little Bit—Gray's name for her unborn baby—and the video approached the entrance when orderlies came out to assist her. They quickly saw her disfigured face and blue eyes but could not quickly tell that she wasn't Black because of the scarring.

Once inside, Johnest brought a wheelchair and wheeled it in behind her. They gently lowered her on to the seat as her pain surged. Little Bit's movement slowed.

"My baby," she cried out. "Something's wrong with my baby!"

Dr. Sanda approached quickly to assist. "Get her into 7, stat!"

Gray was on a gurney in 7 within 20 seconds, surrounded by Dr. Sanda, Johnest, and two nurses. "Get that off of her," Dr. Sanda barked. Ronnette cut the robe to get it off. Gray's skin was visible.

"Doctor, she's Gray skinned. What do we do?" Johnest asked anxiously.

"Clear out, everyone, clear out!" Dr. Sanda barked.

"No, no!" Gray screamed. "Help my baby, NO, don't leave us, help us!"

Gray heard the door close and lock. Her water broke at that moment, and Little Bit started coming. Minutes later, Gray sat up to hold her dead beloved Little Bit in her arms.

At that moment, Gray lost all will to live. The despair surrounded Note in unknown darkness. All was still for a moment, and everything stopped, as did Gray's heart. The One was gone.

When the light returned to Note, Note's journey started anew.

***

Sometime later...

"Madam President, thank you for taking my question. My sources tell me our security services have something, something from another world. Can you comment?"

"Yes. That's the reason for this press conference. I have the most profound message to share; it isn't from another world, but from our own. You know the story of my mother's death in the vehicle accident when I was eleven. What wasn't shared was how I survived it. I've always thought an angel saved me, and I believe that today more than ever.

"I was trapped in the burning overturned vehicle with the fire quickly forming around me. She entered through a small opening next to the ground. I opened my eyes to see her gray skin melting off her head in front of me, surrounded by flames. My eyes were drawn to hers; they were a deep blue. I heard a new language at that moment. It was life-altering."

Gasps went through the room.

"You react negatively to my story, but that's the gift she brought us. A Gray with blue eyes pulled me from the fire, allowing me to be here today. But there's more.

"Months later, security was summoned to a hospital close to where she saved me. She had been savagely raped and became pregnant. Her baby was coming prematurely as the Gray was sick, weak, and malnourished. She went to the hospital for help, and they locked her in a room by herself, with no help. No one stood with her because she was a Gray. The woman that will end up saving our world died holding her dead baby in her arms, all alone, locked in a room, waiting for security. Now gasp!

"When security arrived, they found a video in her clothes with a new language on it, one with tools to make it and voices to speak it. The language itself has profound effects on those who hear it. The Gray was on the video with another Gray, a White, and two of us. They all spoke the language together, harmoniously. We have teams that have mastered recreating the language and reached out to the Whites on Lontusious and shared it with them. We found it to be profound and universal between both sides."

The faces in the room softened.

"The connection brought our security forces together, along with our medical resources. We found the cause of many of our unnatural deaths. It inflicts both the Whites and Blacks with the same condition, but Grays don't have it. The cure for our affliction is to join with the Whites, on every level. Our prejudice and feelings of superiority must become history. The language, left to us by the Gray with blue eyes, is a miracle."

"Madam President?"

"Yes, Dala!"

"Was the Gray with blue eyes of this world?"

"Yes, she was born here under Rule 41 and stayed secluded. Our medical team noted the blue eyes, a first on our world, and tested her a great deal but found nothing to cause it. They noted it as an environmental perversion perhaps, genetic in her White father. She was, and is, in fact, one of us."

Through grace, a timid voice from the back of the room, speaking softly, asked an odd question.

"What word comes to your mind?"

Genevieve choked up and swallowed hard. "Forgiveness. Forgiveness is the word, for we know not what we do." She then looked to focus on where the question came from when another came from the same area.

"Did she have a name, Madam President?"

"Her name was Gray! Her name was Gray."

At that moment, Genevieve found the woman asking the two questions in the quiet room. She had black glasses to cover her blind eyes, and a face wet with tears. "Ma'am, you're Sky, aren't you?"

Gray introduced Jote to Music, and the epiphany of harmony saved a world.

In Between

Note discovered that each race had different tools, some had music, some didn't. The conflicts and challenges each race faced, however, had many similarities. Note perceived an inner desire and drive in living beings to move beyond the conflict to a more peaceful state. Peace has attributes that are profoundly compelling in the Universe and shine like the light to the moth.

Gray is divine.

Note felt impacted by one of the significant questions within intelligent life. Is everything destined to be as it becomes, or is it all by random chance?

Chapter Eight

Fate Scribes

The capsule slowed as it approached Bamblin. Its lone occupant was unaware that she was nearing her destination. Bamblin, a spherical ship the size of the Earth-Moon, was the home of the Jerisians, a master race that had the unique honor of knowing the destiny of all—the fate of the Universe.

The Jerisian race had existed over 834 million years. Their DNA limited the Jerisian's evolution to a sentient life form at an advanced but still physical level. Their star inevitably consumed their world, going into a Red Giant phase. They survived after building this massive ship over thousands of years and leaving their heating world behind.

Both a reality with fate and without fate exists. For the Universe of destiny, the Jerisians were the scribes, and even though a degree of what they could share was more evolved than they could comprehend, they had it to share with any being who asked. Knowing fate made no difference as it was fate itself.

Soren's capsule had carried her hibernating body some 234 light-years from her world. As Fate Scribes, the Jerisians knew of Soren's journey and arrival down to the moment and had prepared for it. Bamblin tractor beams locked on the vessel and disengaged its navigation and propulsion systems, bringing it safely into the ship and landing it on the nest.

Bamblin Control provided signals to the capsule to compel it to wake up its occupant. The process began. Soren opened her eyes after 13 minutes of resuscitation. Note joined Soren as her eyes opened to see the capsule lid rising swiftly. Her eyes focused for the first time in almost 500 years. Only a moment before, she was lying down in the capsule back on Franin, her home world, seeing the smiling faces of the lab technician, program director, and her mom and dad.

Her first breaths were painful. "Welcome, Soren! I'm Tabar; welcome to our world. Please lay still for a few minutes to give your body time to activate entirely." Soren felt a mist spray land on her skin. "That spray is gzangrins. It will help you recover quickly," Tabar reassured her.

Quickly overcoming her surprise at his appearance, she spoke, "Thank you, Tabar, yes, I'm feeling tingly. Not in a bad way, but tingly. How do you know my name?"

"Gzangrins are nanobots, Soren, and they are moving through your system, diagnosing, and repairing any damage your body may have sustained during your journey. You were in hibernation for 487 of your years. You should be able to move normally now. Please try to sit up. We know your name because we knew you were coming. You'll hear more about that soon."

She sat up carefully and slowly looked around at this world beyond the nest where the capsule laid. She felt stunned but refreshed at the same time. Soren viewed a silver realm. Her home world of Franin had blue-green waters, light blue skies, and vivid green vegetation. Franin was primarily a blue world, like many planets that developed humanoid life.

Bamblin was a silver world with a gray sky and no clouds. Soren didn't know she was inside a massive ship as she could see a horizon. From her vantage point, she could see abundant vegetation, but the foliage was a deep burgundy red, which perplexed her. She knew that the green plants of Franin are green because they contain a pigment called chlorophyll that absorbs light in the red (long wavelength) and the blue (short wavelength) regions of the visible light spectrum. The green light isn't absorbed but reflected, making the plant appear green.[15]

What would cause such rich burgundy foliage? she thought for a moment.

She turned back quickly and looked at Tabar. "Where am I?" Soren asked.

"You're on Bamblin. We're the Fate Scribes that you journeyed to find. You have arrived successfully. Please, if you're ready, come with me," Tabar requested.

The surface she stepped down on was squishy but dry. Though she saw no lilacs, the air smelled of them. It occurred to her that there were no sounds, and no bugs, birds, or wind. No leaves were blowing, and no sound at all other than music in her mind.

How odd this is, and the music, I don't recognize it, but it seems familiar, Soren thought. *I know this music. It will come to me; it's familiar. I almost have it.*

Her concentration returned to her journey with Tabar as they approached a rock wall that they walked through effortlessly. *These people or things are very advanced,* she thought.

A ship full of systems and beings working them were inside the wall. The Jerisians were tall and thin. Some were ten feet tall and only a foot wide at any point, except for their heads, which made up some 20% of their height. They had no eyes but seemed to have ports that may have been for hearing. Sound also seemed to come from the port when Tabar spoke to her.

Initially, Soren thought Tabar had no arms, but as she walked, she saw long thin links of his body separate and extend to take some action and then return to merge with the body. She saw up to four such arms extended at one time, all returning to rejoin Tabar's torso.

Their skin or surface was a dark and golden brown that looked moist but not wet, as if they did some rigorous exercise that brought about a good sweat. Soren found the Jerisians to be odd looking, but exquisite. She wondered if all of them had a voice as soothing and harmonic as Tabar's.

The area they were in was vast and highly automated. Oddly, there were no corners anywhere. Everything was rounded and flowing, and many containers held fluids, which reminded Soren of aquariums back home; the fluids were dark and saturated colors and moving inside their containers. Several were being attended to by the long, thin, beautiful brown Jerisians with the large heads with a single port in them. Arms were coming and going. All was well on Bamblin.

They came to another wall and walked through into a smaller room. A woman who reminded Soren of her best friend from young adulthood joined there.

"Welcome, Soren. I'm Mayen."

Soren felt taken aback. "Mayen...how is that possible?"

"I'm Mayen. I'm not the Mayen you knew, but I am like her in many ways. I'm an artificial life for your visit. We on Bamblin know all things that have been already, that are now, and that will be. We know too of the limited number of visitors we will have over time, so we prepare for each. We made me for you."

"Do you know every thought I'll have?" Soren asked.

"No, we don't know what's inside the minds of anyone, ever. The fate we know is the happenings throughout time. Though that is limited, happenings are infinite and are so numerous for each distinction in the Universe that we can surmise the thoughts and motivations behind an action, but it's only a supposition. The fate we scribe is all fate around happenings."

"You knew of my mission to come here and my journey, Mayen?"

"Yes, we knew you were coming. We knew why you were coming because of the conversations that happened in your world before you came. We understand why you are here, that we would have this conversation and every word and inflection in it, and all that will happen after."

"And you are Mayen because Mayen happened?" It captivated Soren.

"Yes, and your love for her happened." Mayen shared.

"I'll always love Mayen; she was—and is—very dear to me. Then you know I will ask this?"

"Yes, Soren."

"Why am I here?"

"Joseline Render, on your world some 1682 of your years ago, received a visitor from Bamblin. It was a life form like me we patterned after Joseline's late grandfather. Joseline was one of the philosophers and physicists on your world at that time and who prophesied that there were multiple realities within this Universe and various Universes. Amongst the many truths she spoke of were two distinct paths, one of fate and one without, or chance as we call it.

"You exist in fate, Soren, as does your world and all you know. The paths of fate and chance can cross in time but never join—let me emphasize that! They can never join. There too is only one way for a soul to leave the path of fate to that of chance, and that is to be purely good or bad. On every tangent within the Universe, bad destroys itself, and good is creation. Only within pure creation or destruction is fate voided. We will speak no more of destruction around this truth."

"I'm not sure I understand, Mayen. That isn't the way I think. I'm a grounded and pragmatic individual, and what you are sharing is very lofty to me. I sense how important it is, and I hope you'll be patient with me. I want to understand. Will you be patient with me?"

"We knew you would speak every word you just spoke and have known for a notably long time. There is nothing for us to be patient about. The Universe is made for the way you think, Soren. Everything in the Universe divides from everything else. The Universe has boundaries, and everything within it has them. You and I have our outer boundaries. The same is so for every particle that makes up each thing that exists. Even existence has limits as it is distinct from nonexistence.

"The only boundless reality in all creation is creation itself, and creation is pure good. Pure good is attainable for a living being but is exceedingly rare as it requires no ego, and no sense of self, which is, in fact, a sense of distinction. Pure good requires no judgment, living totally in the moment while expanding awareness with no motivation of reward. For most, it is unattainable."

"Are you able to attain it, pure goodness, Mayen?"

"I'm not a living being with a soul like you have, Soren. All living beings have a soul, and that is the conduit to creation."

"Please continue telling me about Joseline and the visitor like you," Soren requested.

"Mark joined Joseline in her retreat and introduced himself, his origins, and his reason for appearing to her. Though we can see all the happenings until the end, we don't share all truth with any seeker. Mark did not share all truth with Joseline. What we didn't share and will confirm with you is that your world will get destroyed in your year 6239 by the impact of a planet-killing asteroid measuring 583 miles in size. There was and is time to change the path of the dwarf planet, but not if a miracle doesn't occur. That's because fate has the asteroid slamming into your world, and your civilization ending as a result."

"I have to sit down." They'd overwhelmed Soren with their message.

Mayen and Tabar quickly responded to Soren's distress and helped her ease down to sit. Mayen sat down with her while Tabar continued to stand. Tabar's port moved down its body, however, to be level with Soren's head.

"And why do you share this end with me, Mayen?" Soren continued.

"You may be part of the miracle, and that is unclear to us, unusually so. Though it was clear until you arrived, something has changed. The only way we can quantify it is that there is Song in you, and it's pure goodness. That isn't part of our fate, Soren. The future of your world is now unclear to us.

"We have produced an experience for you, Soren, that will make you happy. We know you need nourishment. Are you feeling okay now?"

"Yes, thank you."

"Please follow me," she suggested.

Soren followed Mayen toward a regular-looking door. She opened the door and gestured for Soren to enter.

Suddenly, she was in her elementary school cafeteria and looked to her right. She saw her childhood friend, Johnny, at the end of the cafeteria line. He was motioning for Soren to come over. As she was on her way to Johnny, her other good friends surrounded her. They didn't seem to notice that she was grown up.

"I have a hard booger, Serrie," Johnny told her. "Do you want it?"

"No, you're gross!" Soren responded with a disgusted look, but smiling.

"Okay, I'll keep it in the oven for you," Johnny assured.

Rachel joined in. "You're so gross, Johnny Bootwormer!"

The three laughed and made their way along the line.

"Hiya, Soren!"

"Hello, Mrs. Wemblon," she said with a big smile, almost losing her breath.

Mrs. Wemblon always worked the vegetables and rolls in the cafeteria. A large woman, her apron usually had flour and generous spillage on it. "How's little Jeepers?" she asked.

Soren remembered her puppy at home, Jeepers. The thought melted her. "Her little teeth are still real sharp, Mrs. Wemblon, and she wags her tail so fast I can't see it."

Mrs. Wemblon smiled back, and Soren's grin got bigger.

"Are you having your usual, Little Angel?"

"Yes, please." Soren heard her tummy growl. It had only been 487 years.

Mrs. Wemblon put a big helping of over-buttered broccoli on the plate and ladled liquid cheese over the top. Then she added the jewel: one of the famous cafeteria rolls. Those cafeteria rolls were and still are celebrated throughout the Universe. She handed the plate to her right to Mr. Poppets.

Soren moved along in the line. "It's been so good to see you again, Mrs.

Wemblon!"

Donna Wemblon seemed surprised at Soren's comment. "Thanks, Sweetie. See you tomorrow."

"Hi, Mr. Poppets."

"Do you want the roast beef, Girlie?"

"No, Sir, can I have the cheese pizza, please?"

"Heavens, yes, excellent choice." The cheese pizza got cooked on a sheet pan but was prepared with too much cheese today. That happened sometimes. Mr. Poppet needed to lift the pizza 24 inches before the cheese separated from the pizza below. He wore plastic gloves and used his ever-present spatula; it hooked on his belt when he wasn't in the line.

"We have your favorite ice cream cups, Girlie," he added.

"Strawberry?" Soren's face lit up.

"Yep! Here you go." Mr. Poppets handed her the delicious lunch, and oh, it smelled devilishly good.

Rachel leaned over to Soren, "I hate strawberry, you know, but I'll get one and give it to you."

"You are my very best friend, Rachel," Soren volunteered.

Johnny looked back with a hurt face.

"My very best *girl* friend," Soren stated so that both could hear it.

Johnny healed right away and reached out to grab his half-pint of chocolate milk.

The trio made it over to a table and got to work on their lunches. Johnny finished in no time and started talking about his pet frog.

"I got to see Chucky poop yesterday."

"Shut up, Johnny, that's gross," Rachel blurted out.

Soren had forgotten the extent to which she loved her friends and the cafeteria workers. She'd completely forgotten how good the food was. Soren picked at it and savored every bite as though she was having a second chance, and she was. No bell rang either—more time with her friends and the food.

Mayen walked up to Soren as she finished and found her giggling almost uncontrollably with Rachel and Johnny. As Rachel continued to tease Johnny about his frog, Soren knew quickly that she was on Bamblin.

She looked over at Johnny and then Rachel. "I love you guys so much. You are my best friends ever!"

Soren's sincerity and serious tone gave the children pause.

"Can you play after school, Soren?" Rachel asked.

"Yes, see you then," Soren responded solemnly, looking back at Mayen.

Her eyes teared as she got up from the table and carried her tray over to the dishwasher window.

After setting her tray down, she turned and took a minute to look over this room and all those she loved in it. She heard Mrs. Wemblon and Mr. Poppets talking to students in the line. She licked her lips and tasted the strawberry ice cream. She then remembered her lifelong habit of licking her lips after dinner and knew it had started here, in this place, because of the strawberry ice cream.

She looked to her left and saw Mayen waiting for her. Soren made her way over toward her and then looked at her friends one last time as she made her way across the room. Johnny was throwing some kind of goo at Rachel. Soren laughed and then turned back toward Mayen.

They made their way out of the cafeteria and started walking down another hall toward another door.

"Where are we going now?"

"Next, you will be back on your world, or it will seem that you are back on it. You will be in a setting on Franin that will happen on fate's course. It's destiny."

"Unless there is a miracle, right?"

"Yes, Soren, unless there is a miracle," Mayen agreed.

The door opened, and Soren walked into an amusement park that was long in the future from anything she had seen.

"Okay, Darling, do you want to start with a ride or your cotton candy?"

It was Soren, but in another body, her body but not her body. She was with her daddy.

She remembered her old life on Franin and how she grew up without her dad after his death in a machine accident. She recalled how sad she'd been for such a long time. She would sit in her room that her dad had painted Soren's favorite color, surrounded by all the stuffed animals he'd given her. Soren and her dad had named them and given each of them a personality and a voice. He'd kept one of them in his room, a little blue monkey with a tad of a dark character like his. She had named it Sammy. Sammy was a little saucy with some attitude but had an enormous heart, like his. She loved her dad so much and never lost her sense of him.

"Here he is. My daddy!" Soren felt delighted.

"You okay, Tad Bit?"

"Yes, Daddy, I'm just kind of happy!"

His soft and puffy face supported a light shading of whiskers and a mighty chin. His awaiting eyes contacted hers, and Soren felt timelessness. It was Daddy.

He took her hand; it was soft here. In her other life, she remembered her dad's hands being rough and calloused because of his work. But here, his hand was welcoming and warm.

"Let's start with the cotton candy; just don't overeat this time, okay?" he said playfully.

"All right, Daddy, I'll control my ravaging love for that webby sugar."

His entire face was a smile.

They made their way over and got their cotton candy.

This is yummy, she thought.

"Daddy!"

"Yes, Tad Bit."

"I know you want to tell me something. What?"

He looked at Soren, and his face changed; it wasn't a smile anymore. After looking around to make sure they could talk privately, his chin wobbled as he began.

"We can't be sure, may know today, but we think we've found a planet killer asteroid on course to hit our planet."

She wanted no more cotton candy. Here, in this place, at this moment, Soren knew her father was a planetary scientist at the Space Center, and she understood all he was sharing.

"What are you hoping for, Daddy? What's the best case?"

"That it will miss us, Tad Bit, but if it does, it won't be by much, and our planet will still get a significant dose of gravity that will move the seas in catastrophic ways for all of our cities close to the coasts. The water will move toward the killer rock and then rush back to equilibrium after the killer has passed. It will destroy all our coastal cities globally, and there's more. If it passes by us, we will still draw in many of its larger trailers, and we can't see those right now. We don't know what we may get. It will negatively impact our atmosphere, but we aren't sure to what degree. That is all the best case."

"How much time do we have, Daddy?"

"Whatever will happen is just over six months off. We'll know if we're spared the complete annihilation that will come from a direct hit—or if announcing any of this is pointless—in the next couple of days."

"Is there anything we can do?"

"I'm afraid not. It's a beast, a bona fide planet killer. The planetary defense was a priority several hundred years ago, before the Chank took power and plundered our society and resources. We just never regained our footing enough to put the resources into such an endeavor at the expense of rebuilding our civilization. Now, things are good, but we don't have the means to protect ourselves from the magnitude of this threat."

Soren lived with her family over the next 26 weeks until the planet killer arrived and hit Franin directly, breaking the planet's crust apart and killing all life in the world. The government messaged the upcoming catastrophe to the population with a week to go, giving everyone the chance to make peace with their reality.

Soren spent her last moments leaning into her mom and dad, surrounded by the rest of her family. They each held one another. At the time that the heat from the blast arrived, Soren found herself back on Bamblin with Mayen, sitting in a white room.

Soren felt emotionally crushed. "Was that real?"

"It hasn't happened yet. But it will. It's fate," Mayen answered gently.

"Unless there is a miracle?" Soren was almost pleading.

"Yes, Soren. Unless there is a miracle."

It stunned Note as well at a depth of the love felt over the months, all ending so abruptly.

"That's what my world sent me here to find out?"

"Yes. Your visit is odd to us, Soren. Fate is everything to us and everything around us. Destiny is absolute, yet in your case, we sense the possibility for a miracle. As I told you before, there is Song in you, absolute goodness. As fate, we knew you would carry it. Because of it and the possibility of moving into chance, we can't see if you will bring a miracle to your people and change the fate of your world."

"What's next, Mayen?"

"We built a ship for your return, Soren, much more advanced than what you arrived in. You will take it back to Franin. That is all we can see at this moment."

"I'm ready. Send me home, Mayen."

Two Jerisians entered the room.

"Come with us, Soren."

The four made their way to the Nest where a chrome-colored cylinder sat. It had no doors, but Soren knew it would receive her. Her time on Bamblin was magnificent, and her presence on the world of fate impacted it too.

Mayen put her arms out to hug Soren, and Soren stepped into it. "We love you, Soren; we're with you." The two Jerisians nodded affirmatively. Mayen extended her arm toward the ship, and Soren followed the lead and stepped toward it. It received her.

She laid down in the reclined seat. The ship seemed to shrink around her. A bold and vibrant purple atmosphere surrounded her and then, as she looked forward, the ship's skin became clear. She could see all her surroundings. The ship lifted off the nest. Mayen and the Jerisians lifted their arms and waved. The ship turned and started heading toward the exterior of Bamblin and then left the world.

The abundant Universe surrounded Soren. Stars were everywhere; it was stunning. She felt sleepy. When Soren awoke, she was approaching Franin.

It wasn't blue and green like when she'd left. A gray cloud shrouded it. The ship descended into it. Soren could deduce that the atmosphere was full of smoke and ash. In the centuries she'd been gone, her world had been through a nuclear war. It was now under the control of the Chank. The nuclear winter was subsiding, but considerable damage had occurred on Franin.

At that moment, Note was pulled from Soren by another power. That was the first, last, and only time a higher power would intercede with Note. It was as if fate would not allow Note to intervene. The deck of destiny stacked in fate's favor. Soren felt the loss of Note and experienced meaningful fear, almost panic. At that moment, the ship landed.

"Commander, the vessel has landed."

"Fire on it. Destroy it!"

The batteries pummeled the small craft with escalating munitions. Nothing would destroy it. Seeing the onslaught, Soren continued to lie in the ship until the attack—and her terror—subsided.

"We've hit with everything we have, Sir. No impact."

"Then we have no choice but to see what they want; the next move is theirs."

Soren didn't know if the protection the ship offered would extend to protecting her person. She rationalized that she had not responded with any defense or offensive counterattack, so perhaps the Franish warriors may realize she was there in peace. Regardless, Soren knew that she needed to leave the ship to tell her story and, having made that decision, sat up. The ship expanded to give her room, and then as she stood up, her upper body left the confines of the ship.

"Roaden, give me your long-range rifle."

"Yes, Commander."

Commander Yanif raised the rifle, getting Soren's head in his sights.

Soren yelled out. "Please, I'm here to help! I come in peace! Please, I'm here to help!"

Yanif pulled the trigger.

Centuries later, Franin was destroyed.

In Between

Note found part of the answer about destiny but could only comprehend some of it. Fate plays a major role in evolution, but that brought more questions to bear. With chaos being rampant, is it destined too?

Chance appears much less prominently. What does chance do to destiny after chance?

A message reigned in Note's being that may have been a message from home:

I know what will happen, yet I still must discover it.

Note was perplexed with understanding destiny and was so for an exceedingly long while, to the point of tickling madness. Note needed to find structures in the Universe's fabric to tether to and rely on, to give sanity a foundation.

Chapter Nine

Fifth Dimension, Mercy of Time

All living beings have the security of being tethered to time. This moment comes, is experienced, and passes to the next. The bliss or devastation of a moment will come and go. The constraint to a timeline offers protection to all because it allows for hope for what may come. Time is a gift to the living.

What was about to happen would only happen one time in this Universe, like everything else. Shania would physically go wherever her mind landed. When she thought of a place or a moment, she would physically go there in her reality. It was only possible when untethered to the timeline (as Note is naturally) while existing in the multiverse where "the other choice" is made, and "the other thing" happens. This would be Note's first experience with the multiverse.

***

Shania was a lost soul.

She was both a spiritualist and physicist on Drote. The Drote theorized that a soul in the Fifth Dimension wouldn't tether to a timeline. With all things attached to their own timelines, time travel wasn't possible in a dimension where a timeline is absolute. Time is a constant in the first four dimensions. Note was of the Fifth dimension.

Shania pondered the Fifth Dimension as a means of undoing or redoing instances in her past that haunted her. The life-changing choice she'd made centered on abandoning her child to be with the man she loved.

Before bed, Shania remembered trying to connect with her son earlier in the day.

Teddy, why won't you respond to my texts? I'm your mom, and I love you. You're a grown man, for heaven's sake. Why won't you forgive me and let me be your mom now? Everyone needs a mom!

Shania didn't consciously realize that Note was coming to join her, at least not yet; Note was on her future timeline. She had a premonition, however, of Note's being and arrival, and sensed that when Note arrived, she could leave her timeline and move freely in the Fifth Dimension. Note joined her while she was sleeping and dreaming about her Brian. They entered the Fifth Dimension and were free from her timeline while entering the multiverse in that instant.

***

Shania opened her eyes and turned to see Brian next to her. It was sadly familiar. She knew a miracle had happened. Shania was back with Brian and had an opportunity to save their marriage by working hard to act differently and win his love again.

He opened his eyes and glanced over at her with an empty look. Their many fights had broken his spirit, and depression found him.

"Good morning, Darling," she said. "I'm so sorry for all I've put you through. I had a dream last night that changed me, Brian. You can trust me now. You can have hope again; I want to take care of you and be the woman you fell in love with years ago. Can I touch you?"

A brief glimmer was back in his eyes. Shania had not talked to him like that—so softly and gently—in years.

"Yes, I would love for you to touch me," Brian answered as he continued to melt.

They pulled each other close, and he felt her hungry arms and hands appreciate him fully. She had her Brian back, and it felt remarkable. Soon, he was inside her, and she thought, *I don't deserve such joy, to get forgiven like this.* She thought of Teddy. And at that moment, untethered to the timeline, she was with her baby boy.

Teddy was nine years old now and sitting in front of Shania. "Don't you love me anymore, Mommy? Why are you leaving me?" He wrapped his little arms around her and cried, "Don't leave me, Mommy, don't leave me. I'm so sorry, Mommy. I will do better. Please, please, don't leave. What did I do? Why are you leaving?" Snot ran down his face and mixed with his tears. The look on his face was desperate.

Shania felt crushed. Her biggest mistake in life was relived in person, all over again, but with the clarity of knowing how bad it really was and knowing all the damage that would result from it. She remembered that she left Teddy and her husband Rex for selfish reasons. Shania felt happy and alive with Brian.

Suddenly, she was with Rex, telling him twelve years of marriage was over. "I'm sorry, Rex. I love you; I will always love you, but I want more."

"I've given you all of me, Shania," Rex said, pleading. "All of me! What don't you have here with Teddy and me?"

Shania was back with Teddy, reading him a bedtime story and watching the delight on his face as she read each word. His face was bright and full of hope. Teddy was secure, loved, and thriving. She read about the little train that could and then moved on to Mr. Bubble. Teddy laughed and giggled. *Such joy I see in his face. I feel fulfilled, bringing this joy to him,* Shania thought. *This was one of the best moments of my life! How could I have left my Teddy and broken his little world?* Her mind went back to him, pleading for her to stay.

Suddenly she was there again, but now with even more pain and anguish because she knew what she was doing. She thought of Brian and how good she felt with him.

Shania was then with Brian. She loved the way he smelled and how he held her. "I love you so much, Darling," he told her as he looked into her eyes and then leaned forward to kiss her deeply. When their lips touched, she remembered Rex and their first kiss.

Shania was back in time with Rex having their first kiss and feeling the same high she felt later with Brian. Shania melted with what the future held with Rex. At that moment, she thought of Teddy being born and how, as soon as Teddy entered the world, she felt she understood her life's true meaning.

She was in the birthing room with Teddy nuzzling on her breast. Flowers surrounded them, and Rex was asleep in the recliner in the corner. Shania's mom, Charlotte, carried two coffees into the room. The smell was magical, and it was the best coffee Shania ever enjoyed. She remembered the hazel flavor with extra half and half, sweetened with brown sugar. Charlotte sat down on the bed. When their eyes met, Shania thought about how disappointed her mother was with her years later when she told her about Brian.

Shania was in her mom's kitchen, having coffee, hazel flavor with extra half and half, sweetened with brown sugar. "What's on your mind, Little One? I can tell something troubles you. What is it?"

"I met someone," Shania offered. Charlotte's face transformed. "I know, Mom, it's a mess! I didn't mean for it to happen, but I found the love of my life. It's my one chance to be happy. I want to divorce Rex."

"What about Teddy?" It exasperated her Mom.

"Rex will fight for Teddy, and I can't blame him. He's a wonderful father, and I'm leaving him for another man. It doesn't look good."

"How can you leave your baby?" Charlotte was in disbelief. *I don't know this person,* she thought.

"Teddy is nine now, Mom, not a baby anymore. To be honest, Mom, he's a little shit ass often."

Charlotte felt incensed. "Do you remember when you were 17 and dated both Bob and Munette and how you tricked each of them into believing you were their 'One?'"

Instantly, Shania was at Munette's funeral. She remembered how crushed he was when she told him about Bob.

Then Shania was with Munette, broken before her, on his knees. Shania was his first and only. For months he wrote her a card every day, expressing his love for her. Munette was Shania's biggest fan and continually praised her. Drool was dripping from his mouth as he wept before her. Munette was a destroyed young man; he felt utterly betrayed by the one he held most dear.

Shania thought about when she visited his grave, and then she was there. *It's a beautiful tombstone,* she thought. *He was a remarkable young man; I did this, and now Brian and I are broken.*

Suddenly, she was with Brian. "I feel like I am in prison here with you!" Shania shouted angrily. "I can't escape. It's hopeless!"

Brian's face hardened even more. "How can we bear this stress?" Brian pleaded. "My heart is racing again. That can't be good for me."

Shania was losing her sanity as each trail of thoughts found more guilt in her past, which she instantly relived in reality. Shania remembered that she came from the Third Dimension for a moment. Then she remembered her first experience in the Fifth Dimension, and she returned to that moment.

"Good morning, Darling," she said to him. "I'm so sorry for all I have put you through. I had a dream last night that changed me, Brian. You can trust me now.

You can have hope again; I want to take care of you and be the woman you fell in love with years ago. Can I touch you?"

A brief spark was back in his eyes. Shania had not talked to him like this in years, so softly and gently. "Yes, I would love for you to touch me." She immediately recognized the cost of this moment and knew that to become happy with Brian would not undo all the carnage or erase the guilt. There was no place to be oblivious here. She was fading fast now.

"What's wrong, Shania?" Brian asked. "What's wrong?" It echoed in her mind.

***

Note intervened and brought her to the thought of her favorite swimming hole, where she often went alone in the Third Dimension. The water was cool, but perfectly so, and the air was crisp. Shania was aware of her entire skin in this blanket of sensations, and such focus gave her a moment of peace, a cessation of thought.

Note rarely took action to save a soul, as each experience was a profound one to have. Note was not to judge the course a soul took. But, for Shania, Note felt moved to save her and perhaps save Note too from the madness. Shania could hear a faint Song slowly growing louder and more engrossing and attracting her essence to merge back to who and what Shania was. Faith Hill's powerful voice singing, "If I Fall Behind,"[16] brought Shania back to the moment on her timeline when she thought of that Song as she drifted off to sleep on the night of their journey, the moment right before thinking of Brian. Note shot sharp sounds through Shania's mind. Shania woke up. She opened her eyes for a moment and thought, *Oh, thank goodness, it was just a nightmare. I love being here, right here, in my bed.*

Shania was back and tethered on her timeline and, with clarity, returned reconnected to the last moment she remembered before her journey, lying next to Brian, watching him sleep. Shania was home. Both she and Note knew meaning and order again.

Though Shania thought she had experienced a nightmare, it was so real and intense that it changed her path. Shania came to realize and appreciate that living on a set timeline in the Third Dimension gave her the freedom that comes from being a captive to time, with hope for the future. Shania was free from the burden of the endless choices, and infinite values, timelessness awarded. On a timeline, Shania could revel in the successes built from the previous moments and suffer for the mistakes. Being a prisoner of time was a gift. Note left Shania.

In Between

Note comprehended that the Universe has guardrails to keep everything safe and on the path. Time is a primary control, with the past, present, and future giving each soul sanctuary on the journey. Hope lives in that place.

Note experienced the concept of tunneling with Oz as a doorway into a higher realm of connection. Next, Note was to uncover another doorway.

Chapter Ten

Doorway

Note passed a great gas giant, Polegan, in the Soroan galaxy. Note approached a blue moon, with vast deep seas and one substantial landmass, green and mountainous. The gravity of Polegan was massive and pulled the tides of the seas to 200-foot swells. The coasts were all cliffs because of the attack of the water against the land, and the population centers were well inland. The gravity was such that the colonists lived under domes with controlled gravity, pressurized to suit the humanoids.

Drexdon was the smallest community in a secluded area on this moon, Honan. Drexdon was a scientific camp with scientists studying the impact of gravity on the evolution of living organisms, hoping to determine if there is a measure of gravity that makes life impossible, much like the timberline on a mountain beyond which trees cannot grow. The average tree on Honan was 1000 feet high with a root system as deep.

The rotation of Honan was on its side, so the same face was always toward Polegan. The molten inner core, along with the water, moved toward Polegan, leaving Honan with an elliptical shape. Volcanic activity wasn't rare.

***

Christon was barely past middle age and could best be described as a spiritualist. His mother and father were each geothermal scientists when they accepted their assignments on Honan. He was born there and knew no other world. He was an unplanned addition to his parents' family, and though they accepted responsibility for his being, they lacked the full commitment in raising him. His sense of self and confidence suffered.

Christon learned more in life by making mistakes than from guidance. He married four times, seeking his person. The years of trying and failing made him a wise man for his age, and through grace, he finally came home, to Adola, his precious, better half.

Adola was much the opposite of Christon, having an upbringing with committed and doting parents. With unbridled attention, she learned to listen and hear the wisdom of others. She avoided making many of the mistakes he had.

Adola was married before Christon to a wonderful man, an engineer from Earth she'd met as a young woman. They enjoyed a deep and abiding love that grew until his untimely death after 27 years together. She felt crushed emotionally for years and never expected to love another, and then Christon entered her life.

Christon differed from her late husband, Jobe. Jobe was cerebral and sure, while Christon was passionate and insecure. Jobe was a genius of sorts and could explain most everything scientifically. Christon was a dreamer and thought big beyond science. Jobe was beautiful to look at and always took Adola's breath away when she saw him. Christon was an average-looking man with odd facial features that included a right eye that was noticeably higher than his left. They were a deep blue and stunning on his odd face. The two men were dear to Adola, and her heart was large enough to love them both.

Note joined Christon as the couple sat together, leg against leg, on the couch drinking coffee and looking out their oversized back window at the horizon with the black sky background. The ground was light because Polegan was always above them and filled 25% of the sky. The reflection of its Star, Sansus, off Polegan's surface, reflected back toward the elliptical moon. The light was not enough to diffuse in the atmosphere, so space and the stars in it were almost always visible.

"Darling, I don't know how to bring this up. You are everything to me, and our life together is beyond anything I could have hoped for, but there is something I, well, I just want to talk with you about," Christon said.

"Sure, Baby, though you know when you start out like that, you scare me a little," Adola responded.

In the early years of their marriage, Christon's insecurity caused him to ask her many questions about the depth of her love for Jobe, something he never felt he could compete with. Christon didn't feel like enough. Adola's love seemed like mercy to him, and she was way more than he deserved.

"Well," he continued, "it's not one of my insecure conversations like in the past, but it's about something significant."

"That's a great setup, Christon. Okay, I am sitting down and holding on for dear life; what do you need to share?"

"You know I've been a dreamer my entire life, and always believed the doorway to the next level of existence is right next to us, we just don't see it. I crave going to that place and going there with you."

"Okay, yes, I know you are a dreamer. I love that about you; go on."

"I know that my need to make love with you every light period is a burden on you. I owe it to you to make sure I understand the burden because I can sense it now sometimes."

"Oh, the lovemaking, yes. I have been sensitive about that. I know you remember it impacted me when we were talking about getting married, and you shared that you 'required' lovemaking every light period. I love you so much, Christon. I've been happy to give you that over the years as much as has been possible, but yes, I resent it sometimes. I feel like a tool to help you climax. I don't have your drive, and I don't understand that drive. I adore you, and you're dear to me. But on some level, that 'requirement' just doesn't seem good, doesn't fit the picture. Does that make sense?"

Christon heard her words. He appreciated them.

"Yes. I've realized some things recently that I want to share. But first, you must know, with every fiber of your being that there is no way, none, that you are possibly a tool. First, I idolize you. I would be *your* tool, not the other way around.

"Not long after meeting you and making love with you, I melted. I hadn't melted before. When I climaxed, and you pulled my cheek against yours, every time, I felt you and your love. Your generosity and all of that filled all the spaces that I could connect within that moment. You melted me, Adola. I am melted."

They looked into each other's eyes and locked in.

"You have never been, nor could you be a tool. I need you more than you can know, however, and not to make me climax. I am intoxicated by you. I can't take my eyes off of you when you're in the room. When I see the beauty in this life, and it touches me, I think of you. I am addicted to you, Adola. I need you to know that."

Adola smiled and knew that all she was hearing was true. She responded. "Yes, I know, Darling, and I am so glad. It's hard for me to grasp what you're describing, but I know it's true. Life with you, Christon, fills me up. I'm yours, and I want to help you find the peace you seek. I know our lovemaking is more a part of that journey for you, and I want nothing more than to walk with you down your path." She leaned over and kissed him gently, and they embraced.

"Thanks for talking to me about this. Can I share some of my recent progress with you?"

"Please. I'm your person. I want to hear about it."

"Over the last 70-day periods, each time we made love while I climaxed, I tried to open my consciousness to discover the next realm. I need you to know how much a part of every moment you are, and that's all our love together that runs through me, not just that moment of orgasm. I believe, however, that the pinnacle moment of the orgasm is so overwhelming that at that moment, we can move forward beyond this space. For me, as I have told you before, the climax is a spiritual moment as much or more than a physical one."

"Christon, you are such a dreamer. I still can't understand what you're talking about. Lovemaking is something that feels exceptionally good, and being loved by you feels wonderful, reassuring, and, well, I feel needed and wanted by you while we love one another. When I climax with you, it feels profoundly good, and I too want to share it with you, which is why I hold you or lay on your chest after. I don't need to go there all the time as you do, but I know you know that already," she said, smiling.

Leaning back against the couch and squeezing her thigh, Christon asked her a question.

"Why do you think we're together, now, here, at this moment, drawn to have this conversation?"

"Because we love each other," she answered. "Why do you think we're here now?"

"To connect. We're drawn to one another to connect, to be bigger than we are alone. Our connection enables us to go beyond our boundaries and live more. My appreciation for all of you makes me bigger and more appreciative of everything else. My craving for you is my craving for our connection. My addiction for you is my addiction for us, which is more than I am. All evolution seems to take all things toward merging and connecting.

"It is like a moth trying to fly into a light source, drawn to its death as a moth, but drawn to something more."

"Thank you for sharing this with me," Adola said lovingly. "I am in awe of our closeness."

Note left Christon.

In Between

Note reflected on Adola and Christon's love and how, as two distinct people on many levels, they gravitated toward each other to connect. As a dreamer, Christon sensed a doorway to the next realm while Adola felt a connection in their love. Connection on any level was a step toward home. Everything from the first hydrogen atom was driven to get home.

Note had not experienced the multiverse yet, but was keen to live the journey after, "the other choice." There was a path to do so in this Universe.

Chapter Eleven

Prison Walker, the Other Choice

"Good Morning, Sally!"

"Good Morning to you, sir, how can I help you?"

"I'm Jesse Farnwick, Assistant Chaplain for Z Floor, for the execution today."

"Your paperwork?"

"Here you go."

Sally was a portly lady with distinguishing dimples. Her uniform was a size too small, but her beautiful face and smile grabbed your attention before you could notice. Her friends and peers always teased Sally for the one untied shoe she inevitably wore. The deep red fingernail polish accentuated her soft skin. Sally was a joy to behold.

In her deep voice, she asked, "How do you know my name, Mr. Farnwick? Have we met?"

"Well, yes, we met a very long time ago, but I can't recall where."

Although she felt comfortable with him, Jesse and his calm manner gave Sally pause.

"It smells delightful here, Sally!"

"Vanilla, it's vanilla you smell," she replied.

Note joined Jesse and knew right away that Jesse was a Prison Walker.

Prison Walkers were unique souls throughout the Universe that visit the guilty souls to experience the alternate life they would have lived if they had made a different choice in a key moment. It was as if the prisoner walked up to a fork in the road. They chose the left path the first time, and it brought them to this moment. With a Prison Walker, they experience the result of the other choice, the other pathway.

"Brad, Orlando's dinner guest is here, the Assistant Chaplain. Okay, I'll tell him," she said.

Sally gestured to Jesse. "Please have a seat, Mr. Farnwick. Brad will be down to get you shortly."

Jesse sat on the old lumpy cushion on a tired purple chair. The walls were pewter with lavender shells. The wallpaper was worn where people put their heads back on the wall as they waited. Though smoking had been prohibited many years before, the old carpet still told the tale of a time gone by.

As Brad approached, Jesse observed that he was twirling two jade Baoding balls in his left hand. *Hmmm, I think he is left-handed. He's very good with those,* he thought.

"Mr. Farnwick?" Brad extended his hand. "What can we call you other than Mr. Farnwick?"

"Please call me Jesse. Did Sally have anything to do with the wallpaper with the lavender shells? The environment is soft for a prison."

"Yes. Sally has been here for 22 years and gets what she wants. This prison is a hard place, and she wanted this room a little soft. Okay, Jesse, let's get to Z."

"Bye, Sally, very nice to see you again," Jesse remarked as they passed by her desk.

Sally smiled big. She still couldn't remember meeting Jesse Farnwick before, but he felt familiar. "Have a great day, Jesse. Thanks, Brad!"

Z Floor held the death row inmates.

"You're here to sit with Orlando Innedez for his last meal. Have you read up on him?"

"I have," Jesse responded. "He was found guilty of committing a savage crime against a young child some 32 years ago."

"That's right. I've been around some bad ones, and Orlando doesn't seem like one of them, but what he did, it was bad."

The two walked through the halls and a series of locked doors until they reached the death watch area. The death watch cells were close to the execution chamber and under 24-hour surveillance.

"We're briefing the team on what will happen today, Jesse, in 15 minutes. This is good timing for you."

Jesse made his way around all the individuals in the watch area and introduced himself. At 0900, they met in the conference room. Ralph Walters, the associate warden, ran the meeting.

"Welcome team, I hear you're the dinner date," he said, looking over at Jesse. "Welcome to you. Okay, team, let's go over how it'll go down today."

"We've already tested the closed-circuit television and audio system to broadcast the execution. We will broadcast to witnesses within the prison only.

"At 11:00 AM, the execution support team will retrieve the lethal injection chemicals from the secure area. The three drugs will be midazolam, vecuronium bromide, and potassium chloride. They will get enough drugs to fill two sets of nine syringes. We will use green labeling on one set and orange on the second. They supervise the process.

"At 3:00 PM, Orlando's last meal will get delivered to him in his cell. He has requested a taco, chile dog with cheese, a bag of Fritos, and Diet Dr. Pepper. He's asked to have his meal with someone in the cell with him. That's Mr. Farnwick here.

"At 5:00 PM, the execution team will arrive and occupy the executioner waiting area. We will safeguard their identities by exposing them to as few people as possible."[17]

"Orlando will get dressed for his execution.

"Our lethal injection recorder, tasked with monitoring the lethal injection process, will go to the execution chamber with a medical technician to prepare. The phones in the chamber will get tested and approved.

"A member of the medical examiner and a doctor will get to the capital punishment garage.

"At 6:45 PM, they will gather the family members of the victim and official witnesses in a waiting area.

"At 7:00 PM, a prison extraction team will go to Orlando's cell. He will approach the door, put his hands out, and get handcuffed. He will be told to go to the back of the cell. Once there, the team will enter.

"He will get escorted to a gurney. He can move there on his own, or we will move him. He will get restrained and moved to the execution chamber. Once in the chamber, the IV Team will establish and intravenous fluid line in both of Orlando's arms.

"A representative for our Attorney General will remain in the chamber during this IV procedure along with Orlando's attorney.

"With the IVs secured, Orlando's hand will get taped, palms up to the gurney arms. The representative for our Attorney General and Orlando's attorney will then move to the witness room. The witnesses will be confirmed to be in place, and the closed-circuit television and audio system will get turned on.

"At 7:10 PM, we open the blinds between the witness room and the execution chamber.

"I will contact the Department of Correction commissioner to confirm there's no last-minute stay or clemency.

"If we're to proceed, I will allow Orlando to make a final statement. After that, we execute.

"After my signal, the executioner takes the first syringe, and inserts it into an extension line, then applying a slow, steady pressure.

"The first two syringes are 100 cubic centimeters of midazolam, followed by a saline flush. The procedure will continue with this line using the green syringes so long as there are no issues with flow through this tube, in this arm. If there is any issue, they will complete the process in the other arm.

"After they have administered the midazolam, I will determine if Orlando is conscious. I will brush the back of my hand over his eyelashes and call out loudly to Orlando while I shake Orlando's shoulder. A witness will document this procedure.

"If Orlando is unresponsive, I will direct the executioner to administer the second and third drugs. If Orlando is responsive, I will ask the executioner to use the backup set of midazolam in the second arm and IV.

"When unresponsive, the executioner will insert two syringes of vecuronium bromide followed by a saline flush. This drug is to stop Orlando's lungs.

"They then insert the final two syringes of potassium chloride to stop Orlando's heart.

"Five minutes after completing the execution process, the blinds to the witness room are closed, and the television turned off.

"The doctor will enter the execution chamber to check Orlando's body. He will confirm his death or otherwise.

"When dead, I will address the witnesses and state, 'The sentence of Orlando Innedez has been carried out, please exit.'

"Witnesses will be escorted out of the prison, and the proper authorities notified of the successful execution.

"We will remove Orlando's body, and place it in the medical examiner's vehicle.

"We know Orlando's request for funeral arrangements. He has no family; I will arrange a pauper's burial."[18]

"Questions?"

"Why the Diet Dr. Pepper Warden, what difference does it make?"

"It tastes different from regular, Sargent. Any other comments?"

"No, Sir," Brad spoke up for the team.

"I have one, Sir," Jesse said.

"Yes, Mr. Farnwick."

"My question is, why do you refer to him as Orlando instead of his last name, Innedez?"

"Well Jesse, we see a lot of bad in here, and what Orlando did was as bad as it gets, but there's something human about the man, something kind. I respect that. He deserves what he's getting. I believe that too."

"Thank you, Sir."

"You're dismissed." Mr. Walters announced.

Jesse stayed back with Brad as the last to exit.

"Jesse, some words about being with Orlando this afternoon while he has his dinner. He must be cuffed while you are in there, Jesse. I don't know your background, but I'm confident you have a good one or wouldn't be here today. It won't be pleasant."

Looking into Brad's hazel eyes, Jesse responded, "I'll be fine, tough times for all."

"His chow will arrive at 2:30," Brad confirmed.

"I'll be ready," Jesse affirmed.

"Lieutenant," Brad called out, "Jesse is in tow with you."

"Yes, sir. Come on, Jesse. I'm going on break."

Jesse followed Lieutenant Baker toward the break room. She turned toward him. "I'm Rebecca, Rebecca Baker."

"Nice to meet you, Rebecca, I'm Jesse."

She waited for the last name. It didn't come.

"Jesseeeee what?" Rebecca asked. She remembered Mr. Walters had called Jesse Mr. Farnwick, but she had little confidence remembering names, so she didn't risk it.

"Just Jesse," he looked at her, smiling.

"Okay, Mr. Jesse, I'll eat my sandwich. Vending machines are on the other side of that wall, coffee too."

"Thank you, Rebecca. Where are you sitting?"

"Corner, over there." She pointed to the little two-topper in the corner.

They met about the same time, and he pulled out her chair.

"Oh, now, Mr. Jesse, you don't have to be doing that stuff."

"It's a law where I come from Rebecca, and I'm not breaking any laws, not here."

She smiled.

Rebecca was blessed with dark brown skin and dark brown eyes with a magnificent smile and bright white teeth that yelled out, I am full of joy here. Join me. *An angel complexion*, Jesse thought to himself.

"How far along are you?"

"That's very personal, Mr. Jesse."

"Why, thank you. Yes, it is." He agreed.

She felt at ease with this man. "Eighteen weeks."

Sipping his coffee, then looking over his cup into her eyes, he asked, "Are you excited? Is this your first?"

"It's my first, yes, and the daddy is running around on me, so maybe my first and last."

"I'm sorry, Rebecca."

After two good sized bites, chased by her TAB soft drink, she confided, "I'm scared for my baby. Working here, I've seen a lot of dudes that caught some bad breaks and made grave decisions. They throw their lives away, you know. I'm a Black woman and might be a single mom. I'm just frightened for my baby, you know?"

"Little Barton will be just fine, Rebecca."

Her mouth dropped open. "How did you know about that name?"

"Common name," Jesse answered, "you know."

She was still struck, and set her sandwich down, but felt peace.

"Your son will be a doctor, Rebecca, a neurologist. Barton Baker will find some enzymes in the human brain that impact age. You will be immensely proud of him."

Her heart rate slowed. Looking into his eyes, she asked, "How do you know that, Mr. Jesse?"

"I see choices, Rebecca. All the men in this place made a series of decisions that brought them here. You make choices. Barton will make choices. Yours and his will take him there."

"I hope you're right, Mr. Jesse. I don't know how you could be, but it feels right, and I don't understand that either."

"Tell you what, Rebecca. Do this for me. Look at your hands, and study them closely, their shape, color, the way they look when they're relaxed, then look at the table beneath them. Remember this moment. Then take a deep breath and pay attention to how it feels, filling your lungs, and remember, don't forget it."

She took a deep breath.

"Now, look around you and see how the floor trim meets the wall. Do you see the tile next to the trim? You can see from the change in the grout's darkness how the tile gets mopped. Remember that, and the tile and the trim. Now look up and around the room and see the microwave. Can you see the brand, and how many buttons are on it? And the paper towels next to the sink. They have flowers on the edges. Remember, take note.

"Now look at me and see my face, the pores in my skin, the wetness in my eyes. Look down and see my heartbeat in my throat. Take me in. Remember me.

"Now, remember all of it and concentrate. You can always look back and remember the moment I told you about Barton. You'll cherish it, Rebecca, I promise."

"Wow, this is crazy. Do you have anything else for me?"

"Sure. Listen to the sounds in this room, this environment. Let me be quiet so you can hear it."

"Yeah, I can hear the refrigerator motor and air conditioner. Yeah. Should I remember this too?"

"No need, this one's for fun. The sound you hear from the refrigerator and air conditioner are impacted by the walls and floor and shape of the room, not to mention the size and number of people in here at a given time. Every environment has its unique sound. That's what I have for you, Rebecca. Like each of us has our own voice, every environment has its own sound, and every single one is unique, like us."

"That's kind of cool. I like that. It may not seem like much, but it reminds me of how much there is. I can't even comprehend it. And you're cool, too. Thank you, Mr. Jesse, whatever your last name is!"

"Your welcome, Rebecca. It's good to see you."

She sat there still, looking into his eyes.

"Just Jesse, is that right?"

"Yes, just Jesse."

Jesse arrived at the chow hall at 2:30 to pick up Orlando's last meal. They presented a tray with a taco, chile dog with cheese, a bag of Fritos, and Diet Dr. Pepper, along with a napkin and glass of ice, no silverware. Everything was on paper plates on a round tray.

Rebecca and another corrections officer led Jesse and the meal through the maze to the death watch area and the cell holding Orlando. Looking through the top window, Sam called out. "We need your hands, Orlando."

Orlando approached the door and extended his hands through the slot. Sam put on the handcuffs, and Orlando moved back.

"Turn to the back wall, Orlando, and put your hands up against it," Sam ordered.

Orlando did so.

Rebecca unlocked the door while Sam watched Orlando. With the door open, Jesse entered with the tray and heard the door shut behind him and lock. Sam called in, "Enjoy your taco, Orlando."

Orlando slowly turned around, and when he saw Jesse, he broke into a genuine smile. He was a small man with an accentuated forehead and large ears, drooping eyes, and eyebrows that had never been trimmed in his 51 years of life.

"The reason I asked to have someone sit with me for my last meal was that I had a dream it would be you. Your name is Jesse, right?"

"Hello, Orlando. A dream, a vivid dream that was clear as day?"

"Yes. Do you know about it?"

"Dream Maker, my old friend," Jesse shared and smiled back. He set the food down on the little table.

"Sit, Orlando. Please."

Once both Jesse and Orlando sat, Jesse looked up toward Orlando, and their eyes locked. They spoke no more words aloud.

"Remember what you did, Orlando?"

"I can never forget it. It was savage, terrible, unforgivable. It was wrong, as wrong as anything can be. I'd give my life for Chuckie if I could or would have if I could keep that day from happening. I deserve what will happen to me tonight. It just won't make it right, Jesse."

"Go back with me to the choice that brought you here, Orlando, go back. What do you see?"

"I'm with my Grandma. She's telling me about my daddy and gramps and his father and how they each became alcoholics and made choices that ruined each of their lives. She told me it was a curse on the family and that their fate got written when they took their first drink. Grandma cried when she said that. She squeezed my hand hard. 'Make a different choice,' she said, 'and don't go down that road.'"

"My life was hard, or at least I took it hard. I gave myself an excuse to make that choice, and once I started drinking, my life just got worse until finally, I did what I did."

"Orlando, do you remember when you made that choice to take that first drink?"

"Yes."

"Remember that," Jesse instructed.

"Yes."

"Good, Orlando. This is the life you would have had if you'd made the other decision, the other choice."

The vision filled Orlando's mind. He shut his eyes and experienced decades of moments in perfect order, all leading to this moment in time. Orlando arrived at his small house close to the beach next to the Pacific Ocean in Northern California. He was a carpenter and boat maker, well known in the community for his work. His wife, Natalia, was a nurse in the local clinic and his daughter, a microbiologist. His favorite pie was pumpkin with whipped cream, and he loved iced coffee, making his own batches for him and Natalia to share.

His victim in his current life was not his victim in his other but was his senator and gaining fame within his party. Everything felt different, rich, complete, full, hopeful. Orlando could see good in so many. At that moment, Orlando felt his true essence. Each can make choices of one kind or another if disconnected from themselves, and Orlando made such a choice.

Suddenly, Orlando came back to his moment in his cell with his last meal and Jesse.

"Thank you, Jesse, but why do you do this, why for me after I did such an unforgivable thing to Chuckie? Do you do it for everyone?"

"You and I were destined to meet in this way, Orlando. We're the product of our choices, and your choices brought you here. What you did was the worst, but you know that, which is light. To love Chuckie as you do was another choice you made over all these years. I'm here because of your light. Now eat."

Orlando spoke aloud.

"Do you like marshmallows, Jesse?"

"Love 'em," he answered.

Note left Jesse as Orlando ate his last meal.

In Between

Note appreciated that choices are profoundly impactful. Every step is the first step of a new and certain path.

Note now wanted to explore the truth.

Chapter Twelve

Pinocchio is a Bitch

Note joined Russ as he sarcastically said to his mother, "Hell, no, Mom! Leave me the *f*alone!"

Russ, short for Russell, was an 18-year-old Caucasian American young man with budding facial hair, the same dark brown color as the long hair draping over his shoulders. His deep and magnificent green eyes peered over his flat-tipped nose. Braces years earlier gave Russ a near-perfect smile, but a lack of care left him with yellow teeth.

Note experienced the turmoil and chaos in Russell's mind. He lacked a direction and self-confidence, very much disliking himself.

"You waste both of our time. You know nothing about me, leave me alone!" Russ blurted.

"Russ, we have to talk. Jolene is not welcome here if we don't talk."

"I'm 18, Mom. I'm an adult. I can have anyone here I want."

"This is your home Russ, but it's my house, and until or unless you are paying the bills, it's my rules."

Russ realized his mom owned the power here. Though he yelled a good game, he knew he depended on his mother's patience and generosity.

"Okay, what do you want?"

Beth, short for Elizabeth, had been a struggling single mother for almost a decade. An elementary school teacher, she was forced to work two jobs, which left Russ alone most of the time, playing the video game Apex Legends.

"I want to sit down and have a conversation."

"Okay, sit down."

"Where? There's no place to sit in your room. Piles are everywhere, and it stinks too. Do you ever do laundry?"

"Is this the conversation you want to have?"

"Clear me some space, Russ, or let's go into the family room to visit."

"Here's good, Mom. Let me make some space for you."

Russ moved some clothes off a beanbag in the corner of his room, then plopped back onto his bed, where he spent most of his time. Beth sat down and worked to get comfortable in the beanbag. He thought about what was going down. *I hate having to deal with her, but I'd be on the street without her, I guess. I can take her shit for 30 minutes, I hope. I need to act like I care, yeah.*

"I need your advice, Son."

Russ hadn't heard his mom start a conversation this way, and it piqued his interest.

"On what?"

"I'm lost on how to help you, Son. My fundamental need now is to talk to you about Jolene coming over, but I feel like we need to talk about more than that, and more than talk, Russ. I want us to connect here. I'm not your enemy."

"I know. I don't mean to be difficult for you. I never tell you, but I know you take care of everything, and I feel guilty about it, I do, and then I'm mean to you too. I really kind of hate myself."

"Oh, Bubba, don't do that. It's a tough time for you."

I like it when she calls me that, he thought.

"Yeah, but look at you, Mom, you struggle every day. You work your ass off. Nobody loves you, except me, that's sad, and you have me for a son."

Beth's eyes watered. *He's right,* she thought. *What's the use?*

"You're right. It's tough for me, too, and sometimes, I wonder what's it for. I hear ya. But call it love, I want to fight for you. My life may still get to a sunny place, maybe not. But I want to see you happy. I've been happy, I know it's out there, and I want to see you have it."

"Jolene makes me happy, Mom, and my games; they make me happy."

"Why do you think that is?"

"With Jolene, I make her laugh, and smile, I love her smile. You probably don't know this, Mom, but I rub her shoulders a lot, and she moans when I do it. She is pretty uptight, Mom. I feel important to her. I like that. With the games, well, my mind gets clear when I play them. I know most of what to expect, and I get it, it makes sense."

"What I'm hearing Russ is that doing something kind for another person and seeing the result makes you happy. I hear that you're happy when there's order in your world. Is that right, is that what you're saying?"

"That feels right."

"Do you feel good about talking to me now? I genuinely appreciate it; can you see that in my face?" she asked.

"I can, Mom, now that you ask, yes, I can. Okay, I don't want to ruin all this pleasant stuff, but you wanted to talk about Jolene being over here, right?"

"I do, Russ. May I ask you some questions, please?"

Russ grunted, "Sure."

"What would happen if Jolene got pregnant?"

"She won't."

"What if she did?"

"I use a condom, Mom."

"They are only 85% effective, leaving a 15% chance it won't be effective. What would happen if she got pregnant?"

"I'd have to support her and the kid."

"So, you would have to have a job and work hard enough and long enough to support Jolene and the baby?"

"Yes."

"You've never worked a job, Son. I'm not digging on you, but you haven't done that yet. I know you will, but you haven't yet."

"Right."

"Where would you live?"

"Um, I don't know, Mom."

"We haven't had this conversation Russ, but I don't want to support or raise your child. No offense, but I'm kind of done with that. I sure don't mind babysitting from time to time, but I don't want to be responsible for your child."

"Okay, right," he responded.

"Would Jolene marry you?"

"I don't think so. She told me she would only marry a college grad. I'm in love with her, but she 'just' loves me. I don't think she would marry me."

"Even if you had a baby together?"

"Right, I don't think so, Mom." He looked down, and his chin wobbled.

"I'm sorry, Son. Well, then you would pay child support for 18 years, like your Uncle Don did. Is all that worth it?"

"Not really, no. But Jolene wouldn't get pregnant, anyway."

"How do you figure?"

"Well, because I don't cum, Mom?"

"What?"

"I don't cum. I want Jolene's happiness over mine."

"Do you wear the rubber then if you know you aren't going to cum?"

"No? I'm not going to cum!"

"You leak son, to clear the way for when you do, so the sperm is good to swim to the egg. If you are inside anyone for any time at all, you need to wear a condom. Look it up, Bubba, on the internet. They call it pre-cum."

"This is weird, Mom; this is a weird conversation."

"That's why I have issues with her being over here, Russ. If I support that, then I support you and Jolene having sex and potentially having a baby. I can't do that. I just can't."

"Okay."

"I can't stay away from her, Mom."

"Then let me talk to her about making sure you don't get her pregnant."

"Uh, no, can't do that."

"It's worth a little embarrassment, Bubba, really, it is."

"Then will you talk to all my girlfriends going forward? I won't have any then."

"You need to learn what to do and talk to your partner too."

"Was I planned Mom, or was I a mistake?"

"Oh, Russ. I'm glad to have you."

"Was I planned?"

"No. As you can see from our being alone now, your dad was not the right guy for me, but we had sex, and here you are."

"So, he pays child support?"

"He has, but mostly he doesn't. He owes it, and the law is after him on it, but that's another conversation."

"Now it's a downer again, Mom."

"Sorry, Bubba. Let's try to fix something."

"Okay, what?"

"Well, first, let me tell you I'm always impressed when we talk. You're growing up and are a smart dude. Your thoughts about why Jolene and games make you happy impressed me. How about we build off that?"

"Okay, how?"

"You said you're happy when you play games because it clears your mind, you know what to expect. If you ask me, we're fairly limited in this world. To communicate, we mostly have to talk. We must sleep every day, eat regularly, and even use the bathroom frequently. In this world, those are accepted givens."

"Right!" Russ agreed.

"A job is almost on that level. To survive, you must pay for shelter and food. You need to be safe, and often that has an expense to it that a job pays for."

"So, you are pressing me again to get a job."

"No, I'm pressing you to take a step toward happiness. A job gives you hope, and things you can expect and rely on. That's big stuff. You still don't drive and haven't taken action to drive. If you decide you'll go to work, you may decide you need to drive. More success, more structure, more happiness."

"And more independence!" Russ added.

"Yes, more of that too."

"I agree, Mom, I do. I've been struggling with something else—the truth."

"Please, tell me more."

"Well, you and I kind of agree with what you said about working, I hear what you're saying. I think I can hear the truth in it. But the truth is complicated, or it seems to be. I still don't agree with you about Jolene. Our truth is different. How can truth be different on the same subject, Mom?"

"That's fricken deep, Russ. I don't know that I can answer that. So, you think about stuff like this?"

"I like the way you say fricken Mom; you're kinda cool. Yes, I think about this stuff, though it seems a little clearer to me right now and my head is full of music too, more than usual."

"Tell me more, Russ."

"It's like the truth is really what we accept. Two people can see the same event and see it in two different ways, so aren't they both true?"

"Hmmm," Beth was thinking. "Well, the event happened. That's the truth, it seems. The color commentary or perception may be different, but the event happened; that's the truth."

"Very cool, Mom, very cool. I hear you on that. The event is the truth. Then what happened in the past, in each moment, was the truth. How it was interpreted can be different, though, and not the truth. The event being interpreted was the truth."

"I think that sounds right, Son; this is so deep. Tell me more."

"Okay, look, I'm holding this sock up off the bed. If I let it go, we both believe it'll fall back on to my bed, but we really don't know until it has happened."

"Wow, Son, I hear what you're saying. We can both base our predictions on the truth around gravity, but still, it's not true until it happens. Wow!"

"And dig this. If I were to drop the sock, only I know the truth of why I dropped it. That's my personal truth. You know, Mom, I wish the truth were real, like a real bitch. If you know the truth and lie, then you're up against the bitch, and the bitch always wins. I wish it were absolute so we could all work from it. I mean, today, anyone can say anything and call it the truth. Has it always been like this?"

Beth answered. "When I was young, we held the truth in high regard. Everyone didn't abide by the same truth, but at least we sought it and punished those that didn't abide by the accepted truth."

"It's a free for all now, Mom. I wish Pinocchio were real or could be for all of us. That would give us each some form of personal integrity because we all know our truth or the truth about our actions or activities. If we lied about our truth, our nose would grow. Yes, bring that on Mom! The truth would be a bitch or our best friend."

"I didn't know, Russell. I'm so much more confident about you and your future, and that's the truth." Their eyes met in joy. Note left Russ.

In Between

Note learned that the truth becomes clear in a calm place. Peace seems to energize the clarity with which one observes the truth. *Peace comes from connection,* which also means the greater the peace, the higher the power of clarity, the more truth is apparent.

Next, Note was compelled to discover the strength of truth. Is it ever present?

Chapter Thirteen

What is Truth?

"Rachel, did you get that?"

"Sorry, Neil, yes, I have it, thank you."

Rachel's day was finally over. She closed her laptop, put it in her bag, and sat back in her chair for a moment to organize her thoughts.

"Are you okay, Rachel? You made it through another week!"

Neil was a good boss and had worked with Rachel for a long time. They were close. He was unaware that Rachel learned she had cervical cancer and accepted the offer for another job just two days before.

Note joined Rachel as she responded.

"I'm good, Neil. But we need to talk on Monday; there's something I need to share with you."

"Is now a good time for you, Rachel?"

"No, I need to grab Melvie and deliver him to theater practice. They're doing Les Misérables this year, and Melvie gets to play Jean Valjean, the male lead. He's developed so much, Neil. I'm proud of him." Rachel's eyes watered and Note felt the gush of a mother's love. In truth, Melvie was over at his friend's house for a sleepover, but he would practice on Saturday. Rachel just wanted to put off the heavy conversation with Neil.

"Helen and I want to come to watch him, Rachel; let me know when."

Rachel wondered if her resignation would change his mind.

"Thank you, Neil. I'm out of here; see you Monday!"

She felt less than herself and was afraid, feeling lost. Rachel didn't feel tethered to anything in herself that she could count on for the upcoming storm. She made her way to church.

Rachel walked in and saw Father Sullivan. She had reached out to him on her way to make sure they could talk. "Thank you for seeing me, Father. I'm lost and don't know what to do."

"Talk to me, Rachel. How are you lost?"

"I can't seem to find the truth, Father, and I sense that without it, I won't make it. It's like I'm just floating deeper into the abyss."

"What do you mean?"

"I learned last week I have cervical cancer, and I'm scared to death. They discovered it during a routine exam two weeks ago. I looked for another job during that time because I must drive so far to my current place, and the money just isn't enough to make ends meet. Along with that, Melvie will graduate this year, and I have nothing saved for his college, nothing. I was successful in my search, Father, and received a job offer for a position that will pay me over 25% more a year, and it's much closer to where we live. I accepted the offer but didn't tell them about my cancer. It worried me they might not hire me, but now, I'll take the job, and they'll find out they hired a woman with cervical cancer who will need medical treatment to potentially save her life. I just seem to be making decisions I'm not proud of.

"It's just not the way I thought life would be. No husband, not enough money, nothing for my treasured son in the bank, lying or at least hiding the truth from a new employer that trusts me to help them be successful. You see the politicians lying on the news. Women and children are dying all over the world because of men fighting to control someplace, product, or idiom. The Earth is in peril. We hunt the wild kingdom to extinction. What gives, Father? What's the use of it all?"

"Yes, Rachel, why do we endure, and why do some decide not to? How much time do you have, Child?"

Rachel didn't expect the question and repeated it. "How much time do I have? What do you mean?"

"I mean, do you have two hours to spend right now? I'm hungry and would like us to go across the street to Alfredo's. I love their lasagna, and I want to talk to you about your question and your situation. Maybe, once your tummy is full, you may not be as lost!"

"Okay, Father, I have three hours, that's better than two. Can we get you lasagna and figure all this out in three hours?"

"Yes, Rachel, I think we can. Let's go."

Father Sullivan and Rachel made their way through the impressive sanctuary and out the 20-foot-tall mahogany doors at the front of the church. Father Sullivan had a thing about jaywalking, so they walked down to the corner to wait for the walk light to make their way across to Alfredo's. Upon entering, Sidney, the host, approached them. "Good afternoon, Father. Good to see you, Sir."

"Good to see you, Sidney. How's your momma?"

"She's doing well, Father; today is a good day."

"I'll be making my way to see Clara on Thursday afternoon; she's a kind soul."

"Thank you, Father. Is the booth in the corner all right?"

"Yes, I love that booth," he responded happily.

"Follow me!"

Sidney led them down the side of the dark restaurant toward the booth in the far-left corner. The carpet was worn but held up because of its quality. The original vibrant design had faded over the years, leaving subtle coloring. Alfredo's opened in the 1950s and was built with dark hardwoods and lavish fixtures to attract the highest level of clientele in the day. Alfredo's was well taken care of over the years, seemed fresh, and still posh. But its patrons' economic status continued to decline as the wealth of the city moved north, away from the area.

Rachel and Father Sullivan slid into the booth. She looked at the menu and immediately looked to see what she could afford, maybe a small dinner salad.

"Do you like lasagna, Rachel?"

"Yes, I love it; it's one of my favorites." Knowing she couldn't afford to pay for the lasagna tonight, however, she told the priest, "I had a late lunch, so I don't have much of an appetite. I think I'll just get a small salad; that's all I have room for."

Arriving at the table, their waiter Donovan did the standard intro.

"Good afternoon, Father and Ma'am. I'll be taking care of you today. Do you need more time to decide?"

"Hello Donnie, how's Sally doing?"

"Good, Father, started a new job today. She's excited about it."

"I'm happy to hear that, Donnie. I'd love to see you both at Mass on Saturday."

"Thank you, Father. What are you having?" Donovan asked.

Before Rachel could answer, Father Sullivan smiled big and said, "Donnie, lasagna for two, with extra cheese and an extra side of garlic rolls, please." He looked over at Rachel and asked, "Do you want a salad to start?"

"Yes, Father, Donnie, Donovan, yes, a house salad with ranch on the side, extra croutons, and extra tomatoes, please."

"I'll have a small Caesar, Donnie!"

"What are you drinking, Rachel?"

"Water with lemon, please."

"Yes, for me too!" Father looked up at Donnie and locked into his eye for a moment, smiling an impressive smile. It was clear that just that moment had a positive impact on Donovan. It impressed Rachel.

"Thank you!" Donovan left the table.

"So, let's talk, Rachel."

They both sat back against the full leather seatbacks. Their breathing slowed.

"Let's talk about truth. What do you think the truth is?"

Rachel felt Note, and a door inside of her opened.

"That's a hard question. I'd have to think about how to answer that."

He leaned forward and rested his arms on the dark hardwood table. He smiled at her and left her space to search for the truth.

"I think the truth is obvious, Father, and we all recognize the same truth because it's pure. That's a hard one to answer, really hard, but I think that's what truth is." Rachel was silent and looked back at Father Sullivan, looking to see if he approved of her answer. Right then, Donovan showed up with the water and salads, leaving after he set them down.

"Yes, Rachel, truth seems hard to grasp. It's wonderful that you feel it as you do. I know you said recognize, but maybe it's something you feel."

"Why are you asking me about truth, Father? Do you think I've been dishonest with you?"

"No, I don't ask for that reason. You mentioned it back in the church. These salads look delicious."

They both dove into their salads. The Romaine lettuce was fresh and cold. "Their croutons are magical, doesn't even seem like bread, oh my!" Rachel said while so enjoying the moment and the salad.

"You know, Rachel, you are diving into that salad, almost like you're famished."

Being lost in the delight, she responded, "Yes, yes, I'm ravenous, and this is delicious." She quickly remembered that she'd told him about her lack of hunger because of a late lunch. She looked up at him with a blush on her face and caught his penetrating but gentle gray eyes, meeting her look.

"Rachel, the truth can be complicated, or seems to be. Do you read?"

"Yes, I love reading; it delivers me to places I've never been. I love it."

"How much of what you read is fiction?"

"Most of it. I love to escape. I know that doesn't sound good, but that's the truth."

"It sounds fine to me," he said, smiling. "While we wait for our lasagna, let's talk about the truth. Is that okay with you?"

"Yes, Father."

"I've thought a lot about the truth. It occurs to me that we can only base the truth on what has happened or is happening and can be substantiated or proven. It's not anything else. That's saying it's not belief, opinion, or speculation."

"Wait, Father. You believe in God, isn't that true?"

"I absolutely believe in God, I can substantiate that, but it may or may not be true that God exists unless it can be substantiated or proven."

"That's hard to get my arms around. Why would you limit the truth like that, Father?"

"The truth carries significant weight, do you agree?"

"Yes."

"Then, that which carries substantial weight with us should be accurate. If the truth is just what I can substantiate or prove, I've relieved some of my burdens, and my life is better."

"But the truth, I mean, it's like you have God, then you have the truth. It's big! Your thoughts on it seem to lessen it," she added.

"Just the opposite, Rachel. The truth is reality. All reality is the truth. That's big, right?"

"Wow!"

At that moment, Donnie arrived with an assistant. While Donnie held the steaming and generous portions of lasagna, his assistant cleared away the salad plates. Setting the lasagna down gently with pride, he asked, "Care for shredded cheese?"

"Please, Donnie," Father Sullivan responded. Rachel's eyes were twinkling. Donnie grated ample portions of cheese on the top of the already cheesy lasagna. It melted right away.

The sauce was intensely flavored, and the meat was in just the right amounts and more of a decoration. The wheat pasta wasn't over or undercooked and shared a flavor of its own that just added to the dish. It was hard to tell what all kinds of cheese were on and in the lasagna, but each was creamy and delicious. The marinated taste of olive oil, red onions, minced garlic, pepper, red wine, and Italian tomatoes was the best ever.

"Oh my God, Father, this is fantastic!"

"Please, Dear, Lord's name in vain."

"Sorry, Father. Forgive me, Lord. This is SO GOOD!"

They both got quiet, overcome with the delightful bounty. After a few bites, Rachel's mind processed Father's thoughts about the truth.

"Okay, Father, so the truth is reality; all reality is the truth. I may be able to work with that. Then, what's a lie?"

Father Sullivan set his fork down, finished his mouthful, and wiped his mouth with his napkin. She had never paid attention to the character of his hand or the large class ring that adorned it, but did so now.

"A lie is a statement or a response that one makes that they know isn't true."

"What if it's kind of automatic? Like when we sat down, and I told you I wasn't that hungry. I just didn't want to order anything I couldn't afford, and I also didn't want to burden you with paying for my meal. What's that?"

"It's a lie. Why not just tell me you needed to order what you could afford? Then I have the option to offer to buy your meal or not."

"Okay, what about the potential new employer? I didn't tell them I have cancer, but they didn't ask."

"You ask because you know. If you ask, you know. You know a prospective employer is not adding you to their company to pay your medical bills while you work through cancer. You know that."

"Yes. And if I tell my prospective employer I just got a cancer prognosis, they may rescind the offer."

"They may, but it's based on truth, and the truth is good."

"But I need the money, Father. I need it badly."

"What you need is to heal, Rachel. And I must tell you. The truth has always enjoyed a remarkably close friend; I have seen them together often."

"The truth has a friend?" she asked.

"Absolutely. Grace. They are often together, and when you're friends with both of them, Rachel, life is like this lasagna."

They smiled at one another and then, like synchronous swimmers, both picked up their forks and dove back in. Their intake slowed, and Rachel stopped first.

"Why do people lie, Father? Why do I lie?"

"Really, it's why did you lie, because now you won't? You know now. You weren't sure before. Truth and Grace were with us today, but fortunately for us, they don't eat food."

"Thank you. Why did I lie? Why do others lie?"

"Some people are not good, Rachel. They know they're lying and know it damages; they simply choose to do it. They're not good. Their essence is not good. You want to watch for and stay clear of those people. Others like you are good people that don't know what you know now. They justify the lies and usually for good reasons. That's what makes it confusing."

"I'm terrified, Father."

"You have cancer, Rachel. You have cancer in the most advanced time for humankind in a country with the most advanced medical capabilities. I take it you have insurance with your current employer."

"Yes."

"And see, you have insurance. You also have the truth and grace, and me for a friend. You're blessed with Melvie and your current boss. Is his name Neil?"

"Yes, Neil."

"You have all that. That's a lot. And your cancer may have brought you here to Alfredo's. Have you ever eaten lasagna this good, Dear Girl?"

"Never!"

"Life is good. I don't think you need to be scared, and I'll pray for you. Good to be you, Rachel."

"Yes, it is, Father."

"Do you think we feel the truth, Father, feel reality?"

"We're real. We feel ourselves, mostly. Yes, we feel the truth."

Note left Rachel.

In Between

Note realized truth simply is. The perceived importance of it in the life experience is fluid.

Note next needed to explore the darkness of fear.

Chapter Fourteen

The Guardian

Her mother, Tamra, screamed, "**You** aren't even a man! A man would take care of Jaselle and me and make sure we're safe and secure in our own home. All I get from you is beatings and pain while you take your selfish ass out to spend what little money I make and get laid. What about us?"

"You're the one who got herself knocked up. I never wanted any of this! You wanted your baby and now you have her, and this ain't my problem."

"She's *our* baby and she deserves a real daddy who acts like a man. My daddy was a man. I know what a real man is, and you ain't it!"

From her crib in the next room, Jaselle heard the slap and then the groan as his punch landed in her mother's stomach. Tamra cried out, "Get out! We're better off without you!"

Another thud, crying, and groans, and then Tamra said defiantly, "You can't hurt me, you're too pathetic."

Jaselle heard heavy footsteps pass by her door and then back the other way as Arnold went to their bedroom and returned to the living room.

"Arnold," her mother screamed, "NO!"

The gunshot was deafening. The thin mobile home walls muffled nothing. After a couple of minutes, the door slammed, and everything was silent.

Jaselle stood in her crib looking toward the door, waiting for her momma to come in as she always did. All the yelling was familiar, and all Jaselle had ever known, but Tamra had been a loving mother and they were especially close. This time something was different; it was quiet, and Tamra didn't come.

Note joined Jaselle and felt fear for the first time. Note found darkness, and no sense of safety. Jaselle was too young to know things Note found inside her—the loneliness and isolation she felt as she drew in from her world to protect herself. Note recognized Jaselle's sense of self and knew that she wanted to live.

Smoke entered from under the door, and as the temperature rose, Jaselle's little body was sweating. Something was very wrong here, Jaselle knew. "Mommy! MOMMY!" she hollered.

Flames burst through the door, and panic arrived instantly. The air grew dark and deadly. The ultimate fear filled Jaselle, as she was at the mercy of a moment that didn't care. Note felt overcome with Jaselle's physical pain and gut-wrenching fear that drowned out everything good.

At that moment, the Guardian stood before Jaselle with outstretched arms, and her fear and pain disappeared. Their eyes locked, and their hearts were one as Jaselle felt the love and belonging she hadn't found before. The moment was delicious; the flames were beautiful.

As Jaselle left with the Guardian, Note's journey resumed, forever changed. Note knew torment, fear, helplessness, and despair and what came from darkness and evil. Note knew the Guardian, too, and that there was mercy in the Universe.

In Between

Note recognizes that the Universe is whole with the best and the worst and everything in between. In matter, Note's experience of destruction was that it resulted from, or resulted in, creation. In life, the same is true, but with meaning. Evil impacts life's meaning, creating suffering. This is hard.

Note next explored how life forms can follow another life form into the darkness, mindlessly.

Chapter Fifteen

Of One's Own Mind

It was as if they *were mindless, like I'm mindless!*

Rolan walked up behind SS-Standarten Führer Hans Schneider just as Hans uttered those words.

"Good day, Colonel. An SS Colonel rarely wants to get interviewed by an American journalist. Why did you ask for me?"

"Well, I know I have little time before I go to trial, and I have things I want to share, I have to share. I can't make up for what I've done, but I can share, and that's why you're here. What's your name?"

"Rolan, sir. Rolan Meltzer."

"Jewish?"

"Yes, sir."

"Perfect," Hans stated.

"I will answer a few of your questions, then tell you what I want to share. Since you're a Jew, only one question about Jews, just one."

"I understand," Rolan agreed. "First question. The war turned against you when Germany invaded the Soviet Union. Why did the Führer make that decision?"

"Good question, Rolan. I should prepare you. My view is German and isn't popular now. With that in mind, it happened for two reasons. Territorially, as of March 1918, Germany had control of Poland, Lithuania, Estonia, Latvia, Finland, and other areas. We lost all of that under the Paris Peace Conference of 1919 at Versailles, which humiliated us and needed to get rectified. The Führer wanted that territory back.

"More importantly, however, the Führer believed the Bolshevik Revolution put the Jews in power over the mass of Slavs, who were, in his opinion, incapable of ruling themselves and were instead being ruled by Jewish masters. The Nazi leadership saw the war against the Soviet Union as a struggle between the ideologies of Nazism and Jewish Bolshevism. Most of our soldiers considered the Soviet enemy to be subhuman. The Führer referred to the war in radical terms, calling it a 'war of annihilation.'"[19]

Rolan posed an additional question. "Were you one of those that believed the Soviets to be subhuman?"

"Yes," Hans responded.

"What did your superiors share with you about Germany's war strategy in the East?"

"Germany's war in the East was based on the Führer's long-standing view that Jews were the great enemy of the German people and that Germany's empire needed territory to expand into the East. Our generals under the Führer's direction focused attention on Eastern Europe, aiming to defeat Poland and the Soviet Union. After the occupation of Poland in 1939, all Jews living in the General Government area were to be confined to ghettos, and those who were physically fit were to be required to perform compulsory labor. In 1941, the Führer decided to eradicate the Polish nation; within 15 to 20 years, the General Government was to be cleared of ethnic Poles and resettled by German colonists. About 3.8 to 4 million Poles would remain as slaves, part of a slave labor force of 14 million we intended to create using citizens of conquered nations.

"Besides eliminating Jews, we planned to reduce the population of the conquered territories by 30 million people. These figures did not account for the Soviet Union conquest."

"We know what happened, but what was the plan, Colonel? How would you reduce the population?"

Hans answered, "Through starvation in an action called the Hunger Plan. It would divert food supplies to the German army and German civilians. Cities would be razed, and the land allowed to return to forest or resettled by German colonists."

"Here is my one Jewish question. Why did Nazis hate and annihilate the Jewish people?"

"I will concede, Rolan, that it was Nazi racism and hate. In the hierarchy of Nazi racism, the Aryans were the superior race, destined to rule the world after the destruction of the Jews. The lesser races over whom the Germans would rule included the Slavs—Poles, Russians, and Ukrainians."[20]

Hans continued, "The hate for the Jews ran deep within our society. The Führer expressed his support for race theories and more territory for the German people. The German race had to strive for mastery in Europe or face annihilation."

"What about the undesirables, Colonel, the less fortunate?"

"People with disabilities, or divergent sexual orientation or of a different race needed to be removed from the population."

"To be honest, Colonel, I don't know why I'm here, talking to you after what you and your country have done. My guess is you hate me, even now, because I'm a Jew."

"I do hate you, Rolan, but I wish I didn't. With all the power a man could hold in his hands, the Führer drove our country forward to make this craziness a reality. Remove the hate before all this started, and there would have been no war. I can't express that to you enough. I don't want to hate you."

"How was it possible to kill people like roaches, Colonel?"

Hans looked over the North Sea from the dock in Bremerhaven. On the evening of September 18th, 1944, 206 Lancaster bombers of the Royal Air Force attacked the center of the town and destroyed it within 20 minutes. 618 dead, 1193 wounded, and 30,000 homeless were the result. Two of the dead were Hans' mother and father.

"You have the same question I do, Rolan. I pose this question and have a goal," the Colonel said. "Why do people follow blindly and obliviously, thinking and doing bad things while following bad people or ideas? That's my question. My goal is to pose this question to you and your readers before I get executed for my atrocities and I know you will answer it. I can't undo what I did, but we must answer this question, Rolan. The Great War was horrific, and this war was much worse. Will the next one be survivable? These wars can't happen without followers obliviously and blindly following some measure of insanity."

"Okay, Colonel, I hear you. You have my full attention. How should we proceed?"

"Here is a little of my story, Rolan. I was one of the officers on Kristallnacht, the Night of Broken Glass, in November 1938. I shot my first Jew in the back of the head as he turned to comfort his wife and little girl. It felt great, and I liked it. He was a rat to me.

"That was the beginning of the end for the Jews. At that point, we started arresting the Jewish men and sending them to death camps. We enslaved others for farming and destroyed their synagogues, businesses, homes, and schools. The man I shot was just one of 100 that got murdered over those two days.

"I remember distinctly being in the cafeteria at our headquarters and having a life-changing event, one that would haunt me from then to now. Something entered my head and my soul, really, it was like a Song. From that moment on, I was conscious of what was happening, and I've never forgotten the blood coming out of that Jew's head after I shot him. I learned his name was Abram. I can't get Abram's wife's horrified face out of my mind either, or her little girl with her hands over her mouth; she had small red gloves on.

"Yes, I felt nothing more than exhilaration and power when I did it, Rolan, but since the music entered my head, my soul, I've never stopped feeling the deserved guilt I carry for it.

"As an SS officer, I was under great scrutiny and always under a watchful eye. We were to report anything odd we noticed about our peers to our superiors; I had no friends. We were to trust the Führer and his guidance and direction. I only killed two Jews after that, Rolan, but I also took part in tragic events. And during all of it, I was cursed and blessed and probably because of the Song, always the Song."

"How were you cursed and blessed, Colonel?"

"They would open up and start talking to me, Rolan. I'd be with a Jew on their way to die, and they would just open up to me like they were a family member. I could see they were surprised by it too. It was like they just started sharing what they were with me. That's the blessing. The curse is they're gone now, and I didn't stop it."

"Can you tell me about one of them?"

"Yes. I'll get to it. It's part of what I mean to share."

***

"They assigned me to the town of Odessa, initially part of Ukraine, but taken by Romania, our ally. Odessa was under Romanian control. I commanded a regiment of 500 troops. Though I didn't pull the trigger, I commanded troops to do so.

"It's now called the Odessa massacre. After a two-month siege, we, along with

Romanian troops, captured the city of Odessa. By the time we took control, Odessa had around 80,000 to 90,000 Jews."

"Do you remember the approximate time, Colonel?"

"Mid-October, 1941," Hans answered.

Hans continued. "Four days after we seized the city, a time-delayed bomb placed by the Soviets before they evacuated the city detonated in the Romanian headquarters. The Romanian commander, four German naval officers, and 63 other people died in the explosion. The day after, I received orders to kill 5000 to 10000 of the hostages we held. Many of them were Jews.

"Many of my troops were involved in the action and they followed my orders. Two days after the bombing of the headquarters, we gathered about 5000 Jews near the outpost of Dalnik. We took the first 50 Jews to an anti-tank ditch. They were personally shot by the commander of the 10th machine-gun battalion, Lieutenant-Colonel Nikolai Delian. We then herded a group of Jews into four barracks that we prefilled with gasoline and put holes in the exterior walls so we could shoot those inside with machine gun fire. We shot them, then lighted the barracks on fire that afternoon. Those that couldn't fit in the barracks to murder, we shot the next day.

"Those who weren't in the first group that went to the anti-tank ditch, or the barracks, or shot the next day that had arrived in Dalnik, were pronounced forgiven. We required them to register so we could kill them later. After registering, they went back home to find we had occupied their houses and plundered their property.

"Less than two weeks later, we issued an order obliging all male Jews from 18 to 50 years old to appear in a city prison or risk death on the spot. From that day through the end of February 1942, we sent the entire Jewish population of the city to various concentration camps, organized by Romanians in the countryside. By the middle of December, about 55,000 Jews were gathered in Bogdanovka. We murdered all of them over the next 30 days. My troops and others did the task, including additional Einsatzgruppe SS, Romanian soldiers, Ukrainian police, and local German colonists.

"A month later, other officers organized a death march for 10,000 Jews in three concentration camps in Gault. Around the same time, still in January, we evicted the last 40,000 Jews from Odessa, mainly women, children, and old men to a ghetto in Slobodka. We designed it to kill them over time through starvation, exposure, and disease.

"We finally deported the remaining 19,000 Jews to the Bereza district. Most would soon die from hunger, cold, or bullets."

The details stunned Rolan.

"Do you need a few minutes, Rolan, to gather yourself?"

"How do you recall such details, Hans?"

"I can't forget any of it. Like countless others, I complied mindlessly. We are what made the insanity possible because we did what they ordered us to do. I can't forget any of it."

"Hans, you told me a Jew would walk next to you, on their way to die, and they would just open up to you like you were a family member."

"Yes, even though I commanded the troops doing these unspeakable things to them, the Jews didn't know. I often walked with my troops to show leadership; I knew what I asked my men to do was difficult for most of them. Yes, many times, the Jews would open up to me. I remember all of them, every one of them."

"Is there one that haunts you more than the others?"

"Yes. Brigita, a young mother in her twenties with a 4-year-old son and a 6-month-old baby in her arms. She'd met her husband Luca in the orchestra in school. He was a cellist, and she played the viola. Their dream was to earn their way on to the Vienna Philharmonic Orchestra. She told me Luca brushed her long black hair every night. Brigita's favorite color was purple. She had a purple tie holding back her matted hair. Brigita loved to knit. Her son wore socks she'd knit for him. His name was Alexander.

"They'd shot her husband in front of her the day before. On this day, in the march, her little boy could barely keep up and struggled fiercely to do so as long as he could. He finally fell to the ground and got trampled as we forced the procession to move forward. Soon, the weight of her baby became too much. Brigita stayed with her baby and was shot next to the road rather than set her baby down and proceed.

"She shared many things with me before the end. Brigita talked, I listened. She was precious, Rolan, and her children were cherished, and I am positive Luca was too. I will never forget the sound of her voice or how it changed as she lost her son, and her hope ran out as she stepped out of line to die."

"What did you do?" Rolan asked.

"I shot her in the back of the head. Brigita and her baby were the only other Jews I killed myself."

Rolan's mouth gaped, and he sat quietly. His breathing stopped for a moment.

"The soldier behind me took pleasure in killing the children in front of their mothers and then killing them during their deepest anguish.

"I prevented that. Brigita never saw my gun rise, or the trigger pulled. She died holding her living baby. I shot the baby immediately."

"Mercy?" Rolan asked.

"There was not much mercy in this war, if any. It was all I could do in such a travesty."

"Can you answer your question, let me look at my notes? Here it is. Your question Colonel is, why do people follow blindly and obliviously, thinking and doing bad things while following bad people or ideas?"

"I think everyone wants to matter, Rolan, and if they accept you in a community, you feel you matter more. It's okay until the community goes off course, and then it's too late. In our case, fear and weak minds—without societal values based on good things to lock on—dominated our community. Likely a result of the poverty after the Great War. The Führer had a well-organized but evil path out of chaos. The masses fell for and followed the orderliness, and all felt like they mattered in the thriving community.

"That's what we must not do. We, as a society, community, humans, must adhere to values, not order. Doing so will provide both order and the future. If every person, everywhere, has a North Star that they all put first above all else, then one could only follow good, or not follow at all."

"And the North Star, Colonel?"

"Reverence for Life, every life. No compromises, no excuses to do anything else. Teach every human from their beginning and through their development to revere life, every life. It'll take generations, but it will keep this from ever happening again, and if one reveres life, every life, we would consider the condition of such a life and seek to make it the best it can be. It must be the North Star, above all else.

"Many factors cause us to follow another, but we usually follow things on the outside. We need to discover ourselves within. The Song has taught me that. There is something profound inside each of us, and if we listen, we will hear!"

"Would you still hate me, Colonel, but revere my life?"

"No, Rolan. I would love you." Note left Hans.

In Between

Note became more aware of the importance of order and how creative or destructive herds can be. Humanity during this time had an almost unlimited track to run, from evil to good, and every lane was full. Note knew humanity would survive this period, but the suffering was unbearable. Focusing on a North Star, like reverence for life, would cause more good and less bad. Such a North Star lacks human frailties, weaknesses, or charisma and is safer to pursue for soul's yearning for home.

Note sought to discover prejudice further while experiencing one of humanity's compelling events.

Chapter Sixteen

The Trench, We Are Not Alone

Jada finished her run around the small track on the deck of the repurposed US Navy Guided Missile Frigate, Kong, a ship initially commissioned back in 2020. The track surrounded the old heliport which housed the revamped Deep Submergence Vehicle *Limiting Factor 2*, renamed Valcrom. The sea was active today, and the rocking of the ship made her run more interesting as it toyed with her balance. Gray skies felt ominous to her, but still much lighter than where she would be a day from now.

After getting cleaned up, she met Alex in the briefing room. Note joined Jada.

Alex addressed her. "Good Morning Sir! Lieutenant Alex Wyatt here, Sir."

"At ease, Lieutenant. Call me Jada."

"Thank you, Jada. This is irregular, Sir," he added.

"I'm a people person, Alex, especially today." Jada felt immersed in Note's depth, without knowing Note was another being within hers.

The briefing room used all the latest technology and a table that would seat 15. A coffee station was always well-stocked at the side of the room. They made their way to it while they waited for Captain Quet to arrive with her aides.

Jada was African American, 34 years old, brilliant, muscular, determined, and driven. She practiced judo and painted landscapes to unwind. Jada didn't straighten her hair and wore it only an inch in length. Her speech was to the point, and she didn't hesitate to use the fluent vocabulary she'd gained as an avid reader. Jada specialized in deep-sea research, with an emphasis on the ecosystem.

Alex was a gifted Mexican American, 29 years old, and was attracted to philosophy. He loved music and played several instruments well, including guitar, bass, drums, and piano. His material was represented on Spotify and boasted a minimal following. Alex had married once, but it didn't last, after multiple deployments to different campaigns. Alex was a geologist.

"You're not who I was expecting to go down with, Alex."

"They pulled Matt; I don't know the story. I'm well qualified and can attest to that. I've studied the Mariana Trench for years and know it quite well."

"We'll be good, Alex; I have full confidence."

They made their way to the table with their hot coffee, sitting across from one another. Looking up at him, Jada asked, "Are you a book reader or movie watcher?"

"Most definitely a book reader. While a movie presents someone else's vision, reading allows me as the reader to build the entire set. It makes it much more personal because the image in my head is friendly to me, with my perspectives and preferences."

"Nice, Alex. It's almost so simple and obvious that it's profound. I've never recognized that."

At that moment, Captain Quet and her aides arrived. Everyone stood and saluted.

"Please sit," the Captain stated.

Once comfortable, the Captain spoke to the team. "I don't know what you know, so let me just start at the beginning and catch you up.

"A week ago, on the thirteenth at 0927, we almost lost the Helicopter Destroyer Alexandria Ocasio-Cortez over the Mariana when something extraordinary happened. A giant bubble originating at the bottom of the ocean in the trench rose under her. The AOC was in precisely the wrong place when it came up, being halfway on and halfway off of it. The front of the ship rose with the elevating water, the bubble pushed up, and when the bubble burst, the vessel got hit with a high-velocity jet of water spurting down into the sea, trying to push the AOC under with it. It's a miracle they survived, and I know you heard about the casualties.

"We've sent down drone subs to find where that damn bubble came from, but we don't see it. We need eyes down there; we need your eyes," the Captain shared.

"What do you and your team think we're looking for?" Jada asked.

"Lieutenant?" The Captain looked over at Alex.

"We think we're looking for a hole, Sir. The bubble was massive, and we don't believe a methane bubble from the floor could have been that big. We think there was an air pocket down there somehow, and it was compromised. We've looked for the hole, Sir, haven't found it."

The conversation continued around the details of the mission, including the time frame. They would launch at 0530 the following morning. The meeting adjourned.

On the way out of the meeting room, Alex asked, "I'm booked except during the dinner hour. Would you care to get together to discuss the mission?"

"Thank you, Alex. I can meet you at 0400 in the morning but already have dinner plans for tonight," she answered.

"Very well, Colonel. I'll meet you in the mess hall at 0400. Have a good evening, Sir."

"Thank you, Lieutenant."

Jada arrived at the mess to meet her good friend Rayhana at 1900. She'd already arrived and was holding a table.

"Hi, Jada! I'm so happy to have you join me tonight," Rayhana said with genuine joy on her face.

"I'm delighted to see you, Rayhana. Not only a friendly face, but the kind face of a friend. Thanks for finding me and reaching out. How long are you here?"

"I'm just on board for the week, and I know how busy you are."

Jada and Rayhana put their caps on the table and headed over to the mess line.

"Do you know what's good here, Jada?"

"Well, to be honest, I'm a vegetarian through and through, but the fried chicken on this ship is famous and deservedly so. I'm getting that with corn on the cob and fried taters. I'll feel so guilty but will find some way to justify it. What are you in the mood for?" Jada asked.

"I haven't eaten meat for 12 years. Let's call it a science project to see if it makes me sick, not to mention the grease, but if you're in, I'm in—same damn thing."

"Well said, Rayhana, well said!"

They gathered their plates with whole wheat rolls with butter along with iced teas and made their way back to the table. Seated, they dove in. Rayhana took the first bite of chicken, a thigh.

"Oh, my word Jada, this is delicious." Juice ran down her chin, and she made her exclamation with a full mouth. "Poor bird, so sorry, forgive me, Lord. Wow, this is good!"

Jada followed suit and picked up a fried chicken leg. She looked at it for a moment, then up at Rayhana's joyful face and then back at the chicken. She took a big bite.

"Oh shit, this is good. This is delicious, girl!"

Jada and Rayhana savored almost every bite until they were full. They forgot to talk. The meal took all the energy they had. They finished in about eleven minutes. Their eyes met, and they both broke into guilty smiles.

"Oh my," Rayhana said.

"It's a secret, right?" Jada assured. "Give me your pinky." The women exchanged a pinky promise.

Pushing their trays away and leaning forward, Rayhana asked the first question.

"How are you and Georgio doing, Jada?"

Her face turned serious. "We ended it. He's not the one."

"I'm sorry. What happened that made you feel that way?"

"Nothing happened. I enjoyed Georgio. We had a lot of fun together, and he was awesome to me. I love him; I always will. He's just not the one, and I can't find my person if I have Georgio in my arms."

"How did you know for sure, Jada?"

"When I kissed him, it wasn't home. I thought about how I was kissing him, objectively. I think I will melt when I find my person, and we kiss."

"I never took you for an idealist. It sounds like you were great together."

"Is Rome the one, Rayhana?"

"He's perfect for me but doesn't fill me up. I don't know what 'the one' means. I learned about relationships with men from my mom. She talked to me about all the things you need to do to make a marriage work, and that's what I do. Fortunately, our husbands must meet us halfway these days, so Rome has worked to make the marriage good too."

"Has worked... interesting choice of words," Jada recognized. "If you lost him, what would that do to you?"

"I know I'd be sad for a long time, but I would be okay. Why do you ask?"

Jada answered. "I am sad too, losing Georgio. What I want is to so connect with my person that my life can never be the same without them."

Rayhana looked at Jada with a concentrated look, still processing what her friend had just described. "I hope you find that; I do."

"I'm sorry. I know Rome is your person, and no one could be closer. I am just expressing what I hope for."

"You sound like you're at a time of inner reflection, Jada, some self-discovery going on."

"It's true, but I don't just want to talk about me. What's important to you right now?"

Rayhana's eyes watered, and she looked down.

"What's wrong?" Jada asked compassionately.

"I can't talk here. Let's go out on the deck and find a quiet place."

The friends made their way through the narrow passageways of the ship out to the deck. They went to the bow to stand by the railing. The ship was quiet in the water with the upcoming mission the next day at that site, and the wind off the sea was gentle. It was a cloudy evening, and the sun would appear from time to time to bounce off the calm waves. The days were long this time of year.

Jada squeezed Rayhana's arm and invited the conversation. "Talk to me."

"I'm full of crap. Rome is having an affair, and it's killing me. He doesn't know I found out. She's a friend of his sister, and I think he loves her. I talk big, but I don't know what I'll do here."

"You're going to cope. It'll hurt like hell; you'll get through it, but for now, you will cope."

"I guess he's not the one," Rayhana said meekly.

"No, probably not,"

"Because if he were, I would be enough, right?"

"Yes," Jada affirmed.

"How do I cope? Do you know much about coping?"

Jada stopped leaning on the rail and stood up tall, turning to her. Rayhana responded in kind. Jada asked a question firmly and passionately.

"What color am I?"

Rayhana was taken aback by the question and regained her wits to respond. "Black."

"My people know about coping," Jada stated seriously, but with a reassuring smile.

"Yes, you know about coping."

Jada turned back to look over the water and leaned against the railing again. Rayhana did the same. At that moment, Jada saw a magnificent dolphin rising from the water. It stayed in a steady position just under the women and raised its head gently out of the water. The sun came out from behind a cloud at that moment, and sunshine bathed the dolphin's wet skin, and then they saw the sun parking on one of the magnificent animal's blue eyes.

"Oh, Jada, look at its beautiful blue eye. I've never seen one like that," Rayhana paused. "I'm sorry, Jada, please talk to me about what you cope with being black."

Jada seemed lost in her own world. She felt connected with the dolphin and sensed it was looking at her. Note was strong. She continued to lean against the rail, looking at her new friend in the water.

"I learned a great deal about the Black experience from my father. He shared one thing with me I will never forget. Let me try to get this right.

"He said, 'Jada, imagine you're a man with your hands tied behind your back by your captors. You're in their court surrounded by them. The audience has several people that feel compassion for you but say nothing. You're innocent, and even the judge knows it and doesn't want to have to try you. But others in the room press for your trial and conviction because you are different, and they don't understand or cherish you. Their rage is real because they're full of hate built on lies and misperceptions. Yes, you're going down, and you know it, even though you're a good soul who has done many good things and is loved by those who genuinely know you. The system isn't broken, Jada. It's designed this way.'"

Jada remained with eyes fixed on the placid dolphin.

"I wanted to confirm that my father was talking about how a Black man suffers in the broken system."

The dolphin dove under the water, and Jada stood back up off the rail and turned back to Rayhana.

"I said to him, it sounds all too familiar to what we've gone through Pop, the persecution of the innocent in ignorance."

"'Yes, Jada,' he said, 'the trial I speak of is all too familiar for our people, but I was describing the trial of Jesus Christ.'"

Rayhana held her breath for a moment.

"Tell me more, Jada."

"It's hard for me to wrap my arms around, but when I think of what humankind did to the son of God, and I see what we do to each other today, it looks remarkably similar.

"Most times, we value money more than life and men more than women, and white skin over brown skin, and power over justice. Those who have the power own the loudest voice, and the rules adjust to their benefit. We idolize people who are shiny objects and follow them to empty places.

"From my observation, Rayhana, it's all the things Jesus and his teaching promoted that we *do not do*."

Rayhana spoke. "It's almost magical that we are having this conversation. I just finished studying the teachings of Jesus Christ. Jesus was asked which commandment was the greatest, the basic principle that begat all the others, and he replied, 'Thou shalt love the Lord thy God with all thy heart, and with all thy soul, and with all thy mind.' (Matthew 22:37–38).

"Two things stand out to me about this, Jada. First is, the fundamental motivation behind all morality must be love, and second, that God lives in all of us, so to love God with all our heart and soul, is to love each other that way, everyone."

Jada responded, "I completely agree. One of my beliefs is, if you don't know something, maybe you get a pass if bad things happen. On the other hand, if you *know something*, you must take action to make it good, or you'll pay the price in our Universe. That's a simple belief, but my analogy is if you see a nail in the road, you'd better pick it up, or you'll end up getting a flat tire soon. Well, we know it's messed up, so now we better fix it."

"What do you think the theme is here?" Rayhana asked.

After considering the question for a few moments, Jada answered.

"Mostly, we've spent the first 2000 years after Jesus being grateful for God's forgiveness. We've done that without changing our conduct to differ from those that persecuted him, and we know it too. Now, it's time for humankind to spend the next 2000 years living as Jesus taught us and loving each other fully. In my mind, Rayhana, it starts with revering every human life and helping each one to be all it can be. That will be glorious," Jada said, smiling.

"We started, however, talking about being Black and your experience of that but then moved to the persecution of Jesus Christ. Are those the same to you?" Rayhana asked.

Jada answered, "We've done the same thing to countless others over time that we did to Jesus. I bring up my father's story about the trial of Jesus because we all revere Jesus. Jesus is the son of God. He was loved. Yet, people did the same things to him we do to each other. If individuals recognize that they can be so ignorant that they can persecute and murder the son of God, that may be a wakeup call to our smallness. Waking up, opening our eyes, seeing, and comprehending can take us to the next level together. That's what occurs to me, Rayhana."

"I have to say, Jada, you're fortunate to have had a father who talked like that with you. I'm sorry I don't know this, but is your father still alive, and can you share his name with me?"

"I'm sad to say he is no longer with us. His name was Malachiah."

"I'm sorry he's gone. His name is one of my favorites. Do you know what it means?"

"No, I don't."

"Malachiah means Messenger of God," Rayhana shared.

"Ah yes, you're a writer. You and words are good friends. I love that about you," Jada remarked. "The meaning of Pop's name is fitting. I hope you write about what we talked about. You'll find the right words."

"Things are better now, Jada, right?"

"Yes, they are better, and I'm proud of how most people found their better angels and stayed engaged to confront the injustice."

"I didn't expect such a conversation, Jada. I am inspired to pick up the pen. Thank you for that," Rayhana shared.

They made their way over to a place to sit on the deck. They sat quietly together as the sun finally decided to set, leaving a vivid color burst petting the wave tops.

"Dearest Rayhana. We talked about coping, but no more about your painful reality. I so want to be there for you while you get through this ordeal with Rome. Something good will come, but we must get to it. You are not alone. Let me be there for you, please."

When it was time to part, they stood up and embraced. "I love you, Rayhana," Jada said. "Call me for sure."

"I love you more, Jada. And what about that dolphin? WOW." They smiled and parted company.

***

The next morning, Jada met Alex early to discuss the mission plan and then made their way to the DSV, Valcrom. They worked their way into their positions in the DSV and checked the systems for launch. With everything in order, they hoisted the ship over the side of the Kong and lowered it into the water. After checking batteries, life support, and propulsion, the tether released, and the Valcrom set out on its own.

"Kong, all systems go here. Permission to descend?"

"Permission granted. Safe travels, Colonel, see you back soon," the bridge responded.

At that moment, Jada felt she needed to look out the small round window between her feet. She did and saw the deep blue eye of the dolphin looking in at her. Her left eye locked in with the dolphin's and Note grew strong within her. Alex heard Jada let out a deep and relaxed breath.

"What do you see, Jada?" he asked.

Jada fought to hide a tear running down her face. In a quivering voice, she answered. "Grace."

Alex spoke out. "You're going spiritual on me."

"Always," she replied. "Do you want to drive?"

"Please," he responded.

The Valcrom descended steadily, moving through the sunlight and twilight zones, quickly reaching the midnight zone where they were bathed in total darkness for the rest of their descent. Just past 3300 feet, they had only 32,737 feet left to go.

"I studied your file last night, Alex, and I noted your interest in philosophy. We'll be descending for a while, and the Valcrom is monitoring itself. Talk to me about philosophy."

"What do you want to know?"

"What draws you to philosophy? That's what I'm asking."

Alex didn't know Jada yet and felt averse to opening up to give her the meaningful answer he had to offer. Full of Song, Jada sensed his hesitance.

"Please look at me, Alex."

Her request surprised him, but he complied without apprehension.

Their eyes met, and he knew he was with a friend. They would share. "I am drawn to philosophy like I'm attracted to this trench we're moving into. There is more than can be seen, heard, touched, tasted, smelled, felt, or known. I can't help but wonder. I couldn't access your file, but I asked around, Jada. You're an artist. I've often wondered, how does someone create from nothing?"

"You're not through telling me what draws you to philosophy, Lieutenant. I'll answer your question after you finish answering mine."

"That's fair. I have a strong sense that most everything matters. It's not clear why it all matters, and that's more than just intriguing to me. I'm attracted to finding the answer to that. It's a philosophical question. Now, please answer my question."

Jada answered. "My answer to how someone creates from nothing extends your answer to me. It's because there's more. With every stroke, I discover things running through me. I feel like a conduit. It's somewhere, and it comes through me to the canvas. Does that make sense?"

"Completely. You are a philosopher with a brush," he said, smiling.

"I doubt that we'll figure it all out today, but what is something interesting you contemplate, Alex?"

He pondered the question for a few moments—or about a thousand feet of decline into the sea. "We're like chameleons, Jada, in that we change depending on the audience. My mom and I shared a particular type of cadence and communication while my dad and I had another. It was the same for each of them with me too. When the three of us were together, it was different. I could go from my mom to my dad to the three of us all being together in a span of fifteen minutes and watch myself change from one person to another and back during that time. I found myself to be different with each of my friends. You and I have developed a connection, and I will probably always come back to this mode if you and I meet alone again."

"I understand what you're talking about, Alex, and we are chameleons. But how do we know how to change our skin color so easily? That's a treasure to find for sure, Lieutenant," she said with a soft smile that he saw out of the corner of his eye.

"We only have a limited amount of time and peace here, Jada, but I hope you can share something you contemplate."

"Yes, I can," she responded. "It's this saying: It's always darkest before dawn. I say I contemplate that one, but I believe I may have just realized what it means to me. I think it's the time just before we wake up to the truth or understanding. It's like the last moment the door is closed, right before it opens, and the light shines in."

"I love that, Jada. Okay, we are 100 feet from the bottom. Let's get to work."

"Full floods on," she called out.

The Valcrom hovered over the bottom while its crew, having no clue, decided which way to go.

"Okay, it's a big sea floor, and we're a long way down here, looking for a hole we're guessing might be in the area. What does your gut tell you for which direction we should go, Lieutenant?"

"I studied the sea currents in the area and looked at what was happening on the surface when the bubble came up under the AOC. My calculations tell me it moved west from where it occurred on its journey up. That tells me it likely came from the trench wall we know to be two miles to our east. That would also explain why we can't find the hole with our systems up top."

"Agreed. Let's go east."

"Roger that."

"You're very relaxed down here, Alex, considering the environment outside," she observed.

"It's my sixth time down here, Jada, and our technology is thankfully strong now to enable this. We have little of a reason to send people to the ocean floor, but we can more easily when we need to. What do you know about our craft?"

"I know the capabilities, Alex, but not the craft itself. What stands out to you about it?"

"The Valcrom is the most maneuverable configuration we've used to explore in, but the part that impresses me is the sphere we're inside. We are at around 16,000 atmospheres at 35,000 feet down, but they rate this sphere for 30,000 atmospheres. We just came up with this high strength, low weight material two years ago and reinforced the existing submersible. The Valcrom is the first deep-diving submarine to use it, and it opens up many exploration capabilities down here."

"How does she maneuver?"

"If there's trouble down here, Jada, it won't get us away from it, but it scoots nice."

"What do you think we may find today or down the road?" she asked.

"I don't know, but my guess is we'll be astonished. It was a massive bubble!"

Alex continued, "It's surprisingly barren down here; I am always amazed by that. When I was a kid, I lived in Colorado in a small town not too far from Denver. There was a park across the street and a pond in the park. Now and then, the pond would dry up, and when it did, all of us could see hundreds if not thousands of crawdad holes on the bottom. Even as a little tyke, I loved to find crawdads and bring them home as pets. I found a mommy crawdad once with eggs under her tail. The bottom here reminds me of the bottom of that pond, flat.

"I hope the hole we find doesn't look like a crawdad hole. You can always tell when something digs a hole from the outside because the dirt mounds up around the hole. I hope we don't find that," he shared.

"I agree with you on that one. Yes, I do. Kong, this is Valcrom," Jada messaged to the ship. "We are moving east to the wall; do you have our position?"

"Yes, Valcrom. Telemetry shows good, all systems go. Your heart rate is slow, Colonel. We thought you might be asleep."

"Thanks, Kong, wide awake here. Valcrom out."

Alex guided the Valcrom forward toward the east, keeping the craft some 100 feet above the bottom to keep from stirring up the silt. The front floodlights were on, and sensors sent pings in all directions looking for something irregular. He was easy with the joystick. Jada looked away from the screens to notice the bottom of a tattoo coming out of his right sleeve.

"I feel compelled to ask you about your tattoo."

"Now is an odd time to do that," he responded.

"I get compelled at odd times," she replied with a smile while looking over at him.

Keeping his right hand on the joystick and reaching across with his left hand, he unbuttoned his right sleeve around his wrist and rolled it up while keeping his concentration on driving the Valcrom.

Jada kept from watching his progress, waiting to look down to see it all at once. Once his left hand went back to working the Valcrom controls, Jada looked down at his arm.

"It's beautiful, Alex. I have no words. Can you tell me about it?"

The tattoo on his forearm was a doorway. On this side of the portal, it was dark, depicted with multiple dark shades of purple on his light brown skin. The door frame was dark blue with no door attached. Through the door was a naked baby curled up in a ball, lying on its side, with its back toward the opening. It rested on a pile of large and vibrant green leaves. Light blues seemed to come from the other side of the baby's head as if it was born with blue lights for eyes, looking into the distance. The baby's arm rested on its side, with the hand lying on its bottom. The fingers were distinct and detailed. A light came up from the other side of the baby; rays from the light came through the doorway onto the purples. The sky on the other side showed additional blue with big puffy white and grayish clouds. A little green frog sat on the doorway threshold, looking over at a fly on the other side, again with transcendent detail and color. Thriving grass was all around the leaves under the baby.

"I'm happy you like it, Jada."

Before he could continue, she told him, "I love it!"

Her words softened him. He continued, "I was driving in my pickup years ago, and a car passed me. Their rear window was down while the front was closed. A little hand rested on the sill. I saw those precious fingers on that little hand and thought about how that small person trusted the people in the front seat to keep her safe. I envisioned her being a little girl. I thought about how she believed that big vehicle speeding down the road would protect her. I was enjoying music in my truck, one of my favorite Pink Floyd songs, and I was just melted by how delicate she was and how she trusted her world.

"That's why my tattoo shows the hand as it does. The doorway comes from my spiritual being. I feel like we are always close to that place if we'll just see it. The baby is a combination of humanity and God to me, lying on the leaves which symbolize abundant life. I can't tell you why I feel so strongly about all the blue and variations of it, including the purple on the outside, but blue is meaningful to me, somehow. That's the reason I work in the oceans as much as I can. If I were to sum it up, Jada, I would say the tattoo is of grace." His eyes watered, and Jada's did too. She looked up at him and genuinely saw his humanity. She reached her right hand over her waist and squeezed his forearm.

"Thank you for sharing, Alex."

"You're not going to ask about the frog and the fly, Jada?"

She sat quietly, waiting for the answer.

"It symbolizes the food chain, yet in the doorway, even that basic need gets overcome with grace. I have a question for you. What's your favorite ice cream flavor?"

"Rocky road," she replied.

"We're coming up on the wall, Jada. Which way?"

"Your tattoo is on your right arm. Right, go right."

"Right it is." Alex guided the Valcrom to the right, along the cliff wall.

"Our dive teams haven't been over here," he shared.

Moving steadily for several minutes, Alex and Jada concentrated on the screens where they saw the best view of what was around them. Staying 100 feet off the bottom, the Valcrom moved up and down as it came to small hills on the floor. As the Valcrom went over the top of another hill, they found the hole.

"Oh my, look at that," Jada said with excitement.

"Kong to Valcrom. Your heart rate jumped, Colonel, as did yours, Lieutenant. What's your status?"

"We found a hole. We need to get Captain Quet and the team on the horn."

"We're here, Colonel," Quet responded. "What do you see?"

"It's big, Captain. We stopped forward progress. We can't see the back of it at this angle. The Valcrom is next to the opening, not in front of it."

"Describe the hole, Colonel."

"It looks like 300 feet in circumference, and it's vertical in the wall like a cave. There's no rock on the outside of the hole, so if the face gave way, it gave way inside and fell inside. It's clean outside, completely void of rubble—the silt on the outside ends at the entrance. We can see that."

"Do your instruments show water flow going into the hole, Colonel? Could you get pulled inside?"

"Negative, Captain," Alex responded.

"How do you two feel about moving in front of the hole and shining the floods in? We have all your sensor information here and are monitoring that closely."

Jada answered, "We're good with looking in the opening, Captain." She looked over at Alex with a disarming smile. He tapped the joystick and pushed it gently forward. The Valcrom moved in front of the hole and turned its lights into it. Darkness was all they saw.

"We see nothing other than darkness, Captain," Jada stated.

"Okay, Colonel. Drop a beacon and come on back up. We'll figure out our next move."

"Captain," Jada responded, "request permission to enter the hole." Jada was full of Song and felt no danger. Alex's concern was obvious; she looked back over at him and moved her lips to say, "We'll be okay!"

"We'll lose radio with you, Colonel, and probably telemetry. I don't like it."

"We're here, Captain, and there isn't much that could be a problem for us at this depth. We won't go in too far."

"Okay, Colonel. Drop a beacon before you go in. Just come back safely," the Captain agreed.

"Beacon deployed, here we go. Take us in, Lieutenant," Jada said with the audience in mind.

Radio contact severed once they entered the opening. The Valcrom sensors showed they were coming up on a wall 1200 feet ahead. At 500 feet from the wall, they saw the hole turn downward. The circumference grew to 400 feet.

"How far down can we go, Alex?"

"I would feel safe to 45,000 feet, Jada, but are you sure about this?"

"Yes. Take us down."

The Valcrom descended to 42,118 feet when sensors showed them entering a massive cavern. Below them was a vast pile of rock and rubble, but no silt. They viewed no sediment anywhere in the cavern.

"That's likely the rock that gave way to open the hole, Jada. The air pocket must have been in this cavern. There's no silt in here, so this isn't natural."

"What do you mean, Alex, not natural?"

"Something beyond nature made it, Jada. It may have been an exceedingly long time ago when the plate tectonics moved this closer to the surface, but something created this cavern. I think we should leave another beacon and get out, Jada."

"Move past the pile, Alex. I want to see what's on the other side."

Alex nudged the joystick, and the Valcrom moved forward. As it moved away from the rock, they again saw darkness going down. The cavern didn't appear to have a floor.

"Alex, I want to go down a little more. How do you feel about that?"

"I don't like it, Jada. I admire your courage, but we're no match for anything down here."

"Just a thousand feet, that's it. Okay?" she asked.

He took a deep breath and exhaled. The scrubbers were working extra hard.

"You outrank me, Colonel; you don't have to ask."

"I can see your concern, Alex. I can't tell you why I'm not afraid, but I'm not. To tell you the truth, my head is full of music. It's crazy. All that said, I won't take your concern lightly or disregard it."

"Roger, 1000 feet," he agreed.

Alex used his left hand to manipulate the thrusters to ease the Valcrom down. At almost 43,000 feet, they saw the bottom of the cavern and immediately spotted three sizeable holes on the north wall.

"Colonel," Alex spoke excitedly. "Look below the holes. The piles of stone are small and uniform. It looks like crawdad holes. Something made those, and we should withdraw."

"Full stop, Lieutenant, and kill the lights. Do it!"

The Valcrom's motion stopped, and it maintained its position. Alex shut off all external lights. In the darkness, Jada and Alex could see a dim light coming from the three holes. At that moment, the light in the middle tunnel started getting brighter. Something was coming toward the mouth of the hole.

"Shit," Alex said with resigned excitement.

"Full floods, Lieutenant," she ordered.

Alex turned on all the external lights and adjusted them toward the middle hole.

The light from the hole continued to get brighter over the next few seconds. Alex spoke out excitedly.

"Look, Jada, what's that? Impossible!"

The large dolphin that had kept Rayhana and Jada company the night before moved easily past the Valcrom toward the mouth of the middle hole.

"A dolphin, Jada! They can't survive this depth. This is impossible."

The light in the hole stopped getting brighter as the dolphin maintained its place. The light dimmed, receding until the hole was dark again.

Both Jada and Alex were in tears. They looked to each other and then down at the tattoo. They then looked back at the screen, seeing the dolphin in front of the hole.

"I'll drop a beacon," Jada said. "Take us home."

Jada and Alex eased their way back out into the open sea, seven miles below the surface, and began their journey back up to meet the Kong. They failed to turn on cameras to record the event and agreed with each other not to communicate anything about the dolphin.

With communication reestablished, Jada reported back. "Captain, we're not alone."

Humanity found that intelligent life beyond our world exists. It was a good thing. Jada and Alex found each other with the help of fate, grace, and alien life. His kiss was home to her. Abraham was born to them five years later. That, too, was a good thing.

Note left Jada.

In Between

Note delighted in how the opportunity to progress surrounds humanity and how challenges and significant events get placed at humanity's doorstep because they fight and struggle to rise beyond their limitations. Note determined humanity is heroic.

Note was next to join a messenger nudging human society to the next level.

Chapter Seventeen

Town Hall

"Thank you, Ms. Wallace, for joining us this evening for this town hall event. As the audience knows, you're the only candidate running without executive experience, and you are not well known outside economic circles, yet you are showing a solid rise in the polls."

"Thank you, Anderson and the citizens of New Hampshire, for inviting me into your state and your homes tonight. With a government as broad and robust as ours, it's essential for a leader to have the right characteristics and attributes. I hope my qualifications, characteristics, and attributes are the reason my campaign is gaining support." She smiled as the audience applauded their agreement.

"Let's get started, because I know we have a lot of ground to cover tonight," Anderson said. "How would you describe a couple of your most important qualifications, beyond your strengths in economics?"

"First and foremost," she said, stepping forward to address the audience, "I see every person I meet or encounter as someone who matters. That's a North Star for me, and it colors every policy and life judgment I make. We all like to feel like we matter, and we all do, whoever and wherever we are."

Note joined Michelle at that moment.

Anderson said, "I've heard others describe you as an original, Ms. Wallace, and say that the things you share are not what we normally hear from a person running for president."

"Please call me Michelle," she interjected with a smile.

"Okay, Michelle, thank you. Are Americans finally ready for not only a woman, but a Black woman to be their president?"

"Kamala Harris opened the door for us, after others opened the door for her, so I think so. I hope that, as Americans, we can move toward finding our common ground and to love each other while seeing and cherishing our differences, whether that be color, gender, race, religion, or sexual identity. You know

Anderson, this is the stage of my life to take this on, and I'm a Black woman, so here we go."

"I like to ask candidates I talk with to share something funny. Do you have something funny you can share with us, something we probably don't know?"

"Why, yes, I can. As you can see, I have an unusually big nose. Can everyone see it? Of course you can. It's an enormous nose." The audience laughed uneasily.

"It's a beautiful nose, Ms. Wallace."

"It's Michelle, Anderson, and my nose is a whopper. Okay, so I have this giant nose, but I can't smell anything. I have a rare condition called anosmia. Mine was caused after birth by a cerebral vascular accident, commonly referred to as a stroke. Our brains are immensely complicated, not just in what they can do but also in how they work. I experienced an arteriovenous malformation that damaged parts of my brain, and that left me without a sense of smell."

"You had a stroke?"

"Yes, I had a stroke. I'm a Black woman with a colossal nose who had a stroke and is running for president, Anderson. Are my poll numbers climbing into the heavens as we stand here?" The audience laughed easily and applauded.

Anderson smiled, but turned serious. "What's the likelihood of another stroke in your case? Is it more likely than for me, for instance?"

"My brain is well analyzed, probably more than yours, and I'm in good shape. My VP will be smarter and more qualified than I am, so if something happens to me, you'll be in excellent hands."

"What's it like to live life without the sense of smell, Michelle?"

"Smell, like many other aspects of our bodies, is a miracle, one we take for granted. Smell integrates with our ability to taste and impacts our memories, and it protects us from dangers like smoke and spoiled food. I challenge everyone in this room and listening to the town hall to take a few moments over the next week to google your sense of smell. You'll find how profound it is. Once you've done that, you can better understand how profound you are, each one of you. Then consider your other senses and how profound they are. Please, even if you don't donate $5 to my campaign, go out and research your sense of smell. It will amaze you; I promise."

"Not to press on this one, Michelle, but can you elaborate a little more on what you've missed?"

"My grandmom was Indian and lived in the state of Kerala in Southern India."

"Wait, Michelle, I'm sorry to interrupt, but you're African American with an Indian grandmother?"

"They adopted me, Anderson. That's another story, but I was most fortunate.

"Okay, back to my nose. Grandmom was a magical cook, or so I'm told by those who could smell. I remember watching her make what I'm sure are delicious dessert treats called jalebi. That's fermented batter, deep-fried, and then soaked in sugar syrup for a few minutes. Though I can't speak to the taste of them wholeheartedly because I can't smell, I know them to be crispy, golden, syrupy, and juicy. I've seen people's eyes water with joy when they put her jalebi in their mouths. Not me.

"When those people shed tears because of their delight, they made a memory. They then associated it with the taste and smell of the jalebi in the presence of my grandmom. I don't have those. I've needed to make myself eat over the years because I don't have the same appetite that those with all their senses have.

"If something is burning on the stove, I have to see the smoke because I don't smell it. If the cream in the refrigerator is bad, I don't smell it, so I need to go by the dates on the box. I don't smell foul food. That's dangerous. The sense of smell, like all our other senses, is a magnificent gift, Anderson. I hope you will cherish yours."

"I will more so from now on, Michelle, thank you."

"My pleasure, Anderson. Sorry, that ended up not being that funny."

He smiled. "Okay, let's get started. We usually begin with questions from the audience, but my producers tell me you have a request."

"I do. I want to have a few moments to present my view, because it'll be from that view that all my answers come. Is that acceptable?"

"Yes, please go ahead."

Turning toward the audience, Michelle paused a moment to collect the audience's attention. "Thank you again for having me here. I feel honored to be in your presence, and I know that our time together tonight will make a difference. This is my starting position: Things are not as difficult as we make them. Suitable answers are close at hand to most challenges. Many of the problems we face are significant, and some are life limiting, but the answers are more substantial and life-promoting. So, let's talk, and share, and think and do. Let's do big, good things!

"Specifically, these are the things I want to address as president:

"Income inequality. A society with 'have nots' can't meet its positive potential. I know we'll discuss that later.

"Everyone needs an avenue to attain self-actualization. We will measure the success of our society by the number of citizens who have the means to achieve it.

"An appreciation for our differences, concentrating on inclusion over exclusion.

"Reverence for life. Every life matters! We need to make decisions that promote life and consider the good of all over the good of one.

"Reverence for dignity. Recognize it to revere it, and we will.

"Expansive educational opportunities to supply and increase knowledge, while helping every human individual find what brings them the most joy and enables them to be most productive for themselves and their family.

"And finally, we must promote a moral community. There are some arguments about what's moral, arguments about issues like abortion, but we can agree on 90% of what's moral while we debate the rest.

"Those topics are a heck of a start for us. When we achieve them, our lives will be much better. So now: what's on your mind?"

Anderson said, "Before I invite the first question from our audience, politicians have always made bold pronouncements like what you just listed. They all sound good, but it's too big and too grand and ends up just being talk. How can you help our voters know that there is meat on this bone?"

"I'm delighted with your question, though I'm a vegetarian." Michelle smiled, and the audience laughed. "Do me a favor, all of you. Talk to me tonight and then decide if I'm just talking or if you think I'll work with every fiber of my being to address what I just shared. Fair?"

"Fair." Anderson looked out to the audience. "Fair?" The audience affirmed.

"Okay, our first questioner is Ted Jabbet, the owner of a plumbing business with seven employees in Lincoln, New Hampshire. He has a question about economic philosophies. Ted?"

"Yes, thank you for taking my question. I don't know any other way to ask this, but do you lean toward socialism over capitalism?"

"Thank you, Ted. That is right in my economic wheelhouse. Capitalism or socialism? We need capitalism on steroids.

"First, capitalism best fits the primary tenet of the US Constitution that each of us, as equals, should be able to have life, liberty, and the pursuit of happiness. To maximize capitalism, each life must matter as a producer and consumer.

"From an economic perspective, each life is an asset that must get maximized. As the producer and consumer, YOU are an essential asset for capitalism. We can leave no one behind! A maximized life must have maximized opportunities for one's abilities. Every dignified way of life matters. Every dream and aspiration matters. Every family, every culture, every journey toward God, matters.

"I see capitalism on steroids as a three-legged stool. We just talked about the first leg, self-actualization. The second leg, democracy, is essential to maximize capitalism and bring us together.

"Officials elected by the people to represent them must work to unbridle the population from the undue influence of the powerful, because that influence naturally results in economic inefficiencies and propagates excessive income inequality. In a pure democracy, every citizen must be able to vote and with no form of manipulation. An educated and rational voter will maximize capitalism and the living standard of the population.

"Finally, the third leg is social responsibility. For capitalism on steroids to work, social responsibility sets the standard for how everyone achieves their self-actualization. The Preamble of the US Constitution states:

> "'We the People of the United States, in Order to form a more perfect Union, establish Justice, insure domestic Tranquility, provide for the common defense, promote the general Welfare, and secure the Blessings of Liberty to ourselves and our Posterity, do ordain and establish this

Constitution for the United States of America.'"

Anderson interrupted and said, "I think, and Ted, correct me if I'm wrong here, but I think what many like Ted want to understand is, what do you think the role of government should be?"

"Summarily," Michelle said, "the Preamble outlined the role of government! Importantly for our capitalism on steroids, the government's role in promoting the general welfare is best achieved by eradicating poverty and the cost of poverty, mandating, and working tirelessly for education, and supporting healthcare for all Americans on every level."

"Many of your opponents are calling for Medicare for All again, getting insurance companies out of healthcare, beyond cosmetic medicine perhaps," Anderson said. "Do you support Medicare for All and removing insurance companies from the healthcare equation?"

"That's what I call a symptom question, not the root question. Let me tell you what I believe to be the root question and answer that.

"First, I think we can all agree that our well-being is our priority. If each of us can get the best healthcare from whom we want, and providers and doctors get rewarded reasonably for all their hard work, commitment, and investment, we would have the bases covered, yes?"

"Yes, I can agree with that," Anderson confidently stated.

"Okay. The root question is about jobs. Most of us put food on the table and a roof over our heads through earning a paycheck and having a job. How do we make sure everyone has a job in our capitalistic system?"

"I'm sure Elizabeth Warren would have a plan for that, Michelle. Do you?"

"I'm sure she does, and here's what I think. We have abundant resources, numerous opportunities, and challenges, along with the genius and wealth needed to meet them. My plan is that we look ahead to what we will need, under the auspices of each individual having the opportunity to reach their potential. That is our list to fill. We check that list against what we must do it with, and go acquire, design, or build the rest. We reevaluate regularly. And as a world community, we must concentrate on maximizing global resources and the worldwide creation of real *long-term* value and production," Michelle said.

Anderson smiled again. "That's an ambitious plan and vision, and it sounds like you have thought about it at great depth. Now, I want to ask you about one of the hot topics going around today: reparations to Black Americans for slavery. What are your thoughts on that?"

"There is more here than I have time to talk about but let me start like this. Four years ago, Harvey Weinstein got convicted for sexual crimes against women, and it was big news because of how powerful he was and frankly, for how long men like that had gotten away with such despicable conduct. What does this have to do with reparations? Well, I'll make you wait on that for a few.

"I'd like to talk to the folks in this room to find out some of their experiences. It will help me frame my answer on reparations. Can I ask the audience a few questions?" Michelle looked out to the audience to get their response.

The audience showed Michelle they trusted her with light applause.

Michelle continued. "Is there anyone here who has held a position of power and allowed that power to get the best of you? I know this is a tough question, and if you raise your hand, I may ask you to share, so please don't, if you don't want to share."

The audience sat quietly, looking around. A man in his late fifties stood up and spoke out, "I can speak to that."

"Thank you, sir," Anderson addressed him. "Can you share your name?"

"Thomas. I'm Thomas." He looked over at Michelle, and his eyes locked onto hers. His breathing slowed, and he relaxed.

"Thank you for standing, Thomas. I don't want you to share anything you don't want America to know. We're on national television!"

"I'm happy to share; it's important. When I was younger, my then-wife and I started a business that ended up being highly successful. I managed the business mostly, and my wife took more of a support role. For the first time, I experienced power in a big way. I made the big decisions; I was important and felt that way. My crew treated me like I was special, even though it was just because I signed their checks. My powerful position allowed me to ask some personal questions I would not have otherwise been able to ask, and I ended up in an affair that ruined two marriages. It's hard to forgive my conduct." Thomas cleared his throat and looked at his feet.

"Thank you, Thomas; I sense you have a message for us."

"Yes, I do. Power is intoxicating, and we can get lost in it. I didn't even know I was lost, and I think that is more normal than not. Every person must learn how to have power and do good with it rather than bad. That's my message."

"Thank you, Thomas. It's an honor to have you here."

Thomas sat back down, and the audience stayed quiet.

"Michelle," Anderson said, "what are your thoughts on power?"

"I agree with Thomas. I think it is one of the most important aspects of life we need to know and understand. We all get it and use it and we have it used on or against us, and we are all impacted by it. Nations are born and die because of it. Power is like air, Anderson. It's all around us. Pay attention to it; it matters."

Turning toward the audience, Michelle said, "I promise I haven't forgotten about reparations. Now, how many women in the audience have experienced gender discrimination? Please, just raise your hands. I won't call on you, I promise."

"Only half are raising their hands, Michelle. I'm surprised there aren't more," Anderson said. "I know I asked you about a Black American being elected, but do you think we can elect a woman president?"

"You saw the primary in Michigan in 2020, right?"

"Yes."

"Biden won handily over Sanders, a double-digit win. Four years earlier, Sanders won over Hillary Clinton. Same state, same Bernie, well-known Hillary Clinton, but she lost. What's different? She's a woman."

"Many often-accused Secretary Clinton of having likability issues, wouldn't you agree?" he asked.

"Let me pose an additional question to the audience, Anderson, if I may. How many of you have heard Secretary Clinton's speech addressing the United Nations for the World Conference on Women in Beijing, China, on September 5, 1995? I'm talking about her well known and impassioned 'human rights are women's rights, and women's rights are human rights' speech. Raise your hand if you've heard it."

Hands went up around the hushed room.

"If you haven't heard it, I encourage you to seek it out; it's easily found on the internet. Those words came from Hillary's heart. You can see and hear who she is in those words, and she's done the work in countless ways to back up those words. That work of Hillary's is profound to me. It speaks to how human society is, most times, oblivious to the value of each of its members, and how power in the wrong vein divides and compromises us. We, politicians, like to express our conclusions, but I just want to ask you, all of you. How do we light a young girl on fire and burn her to death because her dowry is too small? How?

"Death by a thousand cuts, that's how.

"Self-demise from a thousand compromises.

"Now add the burden of oppression and prejudice to that. We need to live from a place of light so we can see." Michelle turned to face Anderson.

"The question initially posed was about reparations to Black Americans for the atrocity of slavery in the United States. Reparations to make up for the injustice imposed on a race of people over a long time, a wrong that continues today on many levels. That injustice has cost millions of lives.

"Okay, reparations. Though I'm ready to answer that because I need to, Anderson, I'm not excited about how we may all feel after I do. It's like when you know something's wrong with the structure of your house, and you've seen signs of mold. You have professionals out to inspect, and they hand you the results. You don't want to look, but you know you must. You read about all the damage the mold caused and the expense to fix it. It's well over anything you allowed yourself to imagine."

Michelle looked out to the audience. "Do we go there? Are you ready before the house gets condemned?"

Three audience members clapped, and then slowly, a majority clapped supportively.

"I guess we go there, Michelle," Anderson said.

"Thank you, everyone." Michelle opened her arms to the audience and then proceeded. "Being a Black American, raised in our community, I am well versed in what discrimination feels like and is. I've given a great deal of thought to it. At the end, I'll look to Anderson and say, 'Anderson, what's the answer to all of this?' He'll know and tell us, in a word."

Anderson was clearly surprised but nodded.

"I'm writing a word on a piece of paper—Anderson, turn around—and I'm asking this gentleman in the audience to hold it." She walked to a man sitting in the front row and said, "Will you please hold this until I ask you to open it and read the word?"

He smiled and agreed, and Michelle turned back to Anderson. "Please open your eyes now, Anderson." She made her way back up on stage and then turned to the audience.

Michelle asked, "Can anyone in the room speak to the Panic of 1837?"

After a couple of moments, a Black American man raised his hand. "Yes, ma'am, I can. My name is Joseph Washington."

Joseph stood and took the microphone and began speaking. "I think most of us remember the great recession of 2008 when the financial system almost collapsed. An eight trillion-dollar housing bubble burst due primarily to subprime mortgages. The entire house of cards fell, giving us the most prolonged recession since the Great Depression.

"In 1837, a remarkably similar situation was exploited in the same way, with the same result. Instead of housing and housing prices being the fuel, it was cotton. Instead of home loans being the collateral, it was Black people who were enslaved. Most times, the same enslaved American was used as collateral on many instruments, multiplying their value far beyond true book value. America produced more cotton than the world could consume, and the price of cotton crashed. When it did, the value of the enslaved Black Americans fell too, and indentured-human-secured instruments became almost worthless. States refused to back them even though they were obligated to do so, and the wealthy plantation owners—protected by their states who created them—were also not held responsible. All the investors took a bath, and that cascaded through the economy."[21]

"So, Black people weren't only enslaved, but used as collateral!" Michelle interjected.

She continued, "This collateral began arriving in our country in 1619. The first 20 enslaved Africans arrived in Jamestown, Virginia. They seized the twenty human beings from a Portuguese ship where they survived the tortuous journey shackled in the bowels of the boat, lying in their own feces. From 1525 to 1866, force took some 12.5 million Africans to the New World, which included North America, the Caribbean, and South America. Nearly 11 million survived the journey, and roughly 26 percent of the human cargo were children. That's 1.5 million human lives lost, each one precious.

"It's no secret that the very existence of America, and America's wealth, was built on the backs of slaves. Our country's greatest export—and the source of the extraordinary wealth of all the millionaires in the Mississippi Valley and New Orleans—was cotton. And the only way that the cotton boom could happen was by enslaving non-white people and forcing them to work, even if it required violence against them."

Members of the audience became restless, shifting in their seats and glancing around the room at each other in unease.

"Consider the Civil War," she continued. "A large segment of the nation determined that slavery was so valuable—and such a crucial part of its nature—that it was willing to secede and risk many of its men's lives to safeguard it. Slavery was more than an institution in the South; it was the foundation of their way of life. Free labor whipped out of enslaved Black human beings set the stage for much of the abundance many of us enjoy today."

Michelle paused to let her words sink in. "Here's what Black people and families have received after being torn from their homes and being enslaved to give America part of its economic miracle. Today, the typical Black household has 6% of the wealth of the average White home. The median White household has more than $110,000 in wealth holdings compared to less than $10,000 for Black households. 73% of White families own a home compared to 45% of Black families, and the average value of white homes is 70% higher than those of Blacks. We own less than 10% of the wealth. Some 35% of young White Americans get a college degree, while only 20% of young Black Americans do. Black Americans earn lower wages than White Americans for the same job. Blacks are the first to be laid off when the economy has issues, and the last to get rehired with the economy comes back. White-owned businesses create 55 million jobs, with annual revenues of 12.9 trillion dollars compared to the 1 million jobs created by Black-owned companies and 188 billion dollars in revenue. A Black person's life expectancy is shorter, with less access to good healthcare. We are all acutely aware of the justice system in America and how it impacts our communities of color.[22]

"Anderson, this is such an important reality that the more facts and data we have, the better. We know there are compelling racial wealth studies and I recommend we each examine this issue and work together to resolve it. I came across an Axios story that drove me to consider things more clearly, and I'd recommend you check out '10 myths about the racial wealth gap.'[23]

"Today, Black Americans don't feel wanted or appreciated in our country. I know I often feel that way. We are many times outnumbered, like in this audience today, and many of you have grown up in a system that looks down at those of us with this skin color.

"All of that is why there is a question about reparations. All we want is real equality. It's true. Anderson, that brings me to what I consider being the most important message I can convey. Can we go to a commercial break first?"

"Sure, but why, Michelle?"

"I want everyone in the television audience to have their children leave the room. I don't see any in here. I need about four minutes with just you adults. Kids shouldn't hear what I am about to share. That's why we need the break, Anderson."

"Are we good?" Anderson spoke out to his producer, waiting for the response through his earpiece.

"We'll be right back," Anderson said as he looked into the cameras.

Both Anderson and Michelle left the stage to freshen up and returned right before going live.

"Welcome back to our Town Hall with Michelle Wallace. When we broke, you were talking about reparations for the Black community in America, Michelle. Please continue."

"Thank you, Anderson." Michelle then turned to the audience. "Out of all we've talked about tonight, this is the most important part to me. It is what I fear the most that can derail us. Our willingness to enslave people, to let human beings starve, to allow the helpless to get murdered, or drop barrel bombs on communities, scares me and shows how precarious human existence may be."

Michelle continued. "Before I go on, I want to say that I have seen extraordinarily good and encouraging things in people. I have more hope than fear, but everything can get derailed unless we devise a system where a calamity isn't possible. Again, this is the most important message I'll deliver tonight."

The room was quiet, waiting for Michelle's next comments.

"I want to discuss three different versions of reality with you.

"Reality one.

"Your day starts as you wake up with 'your person.' The world is eager to have you, and you're excited to be in it. It's a world without prejudice, inequality, or inequity. You'll encounter no homeless people when you go out. Everyone you see will genuinely acknowledge you, and you will respond to them with a nod, wink, or wave. Whatever the weather is, it's natural and unaltered by human activities.

"Crime doesn't exist, and your doors can stay unlocked. You love your home and neighborhood and know it will be just as good or better 30 years from now. Your children are healthy, happy, and are prospering while discovering more about themselves and their gifts each day. You don't have to worry about finances, healthcare, or security, and you are amazed by how you, your best self, produce for your community, and it for you.

"Now, reality two.

"You live in the small town your parents lived in, and their parents before them. Everyone knows everyone and helps each other when challenges come. You are happy there and see a future for yourself and your children. Suddenly, one of your neighbors finds gold nuggets down in the creek, and it becomes apparent that your little town is close to a big vein of the precious metal. The folks in the big city up the road hear about the bounty in your creek and descend on your community. They expel you and your family from your home and take it over, along with all your possessions. The same happens to your neighbors. Before you can get away, they capture you to enslave you to mine for gold at their behest. You're separated from your spouse and children, but not before you witness, or experience, female members of your family being raped and abused.

"You work endless hours, mining for gold from sun up to sun down without enough to eat. Some of your former neighbors who work next to you die of starvation or get executed for low performance. You know it is just a matter of time for you. You constantly think of your family, wondering where they are, how they are.

"The first is the reality we want and would like to deserve. The second reality is the one we have. Society is holding up today, but what if the have-nots finally decide injustice isn't acceptable anymore? The have-nots have risen to displace the haves several times in human history. Were the haves at an event in an auditorium listening to a politician the night before the crisis? If society falls apart, how safe are your children? How much are your investments worth? If the gas stations don't have gas, how well does your car work? When's the last time your power went out for a few hours at your home? How was that? What about climate change?"

"Michelle, I feel like I need to jump in here," Anderson stated. "There's a lot of wrongs in today's world, but I don't know that I agree that the second reality you speak to is the one we have."

She responded. "I think you have to look at human nature. In just the last 500 years, not counting the many horrendous events of World War II, we've conducted some 80 genocides, resulting in the deaths of millions of innocent human beings, each precious, like all of you. The near-complete extermination or subjugation of all the native and indigenous peoples of the Americas, North, South, and Central are just two of those 80 genocides. Please, look around the room tonight; how many Native Americans do you see?

"The travesty has been conducted by tyrants and populations of multiple skin colors and religious denominations. The millions of casualties died from a combination of factors including starvation, direct violence, and disease. Slavery is a terrible blight on this country, but enslaving conquered populations have been a staple of economic reality for centuries, worldwide, and it exists today.

"Today we have four major conflicts on Earth, five lesser conflicts, and 17 minor conflicts. Thirty-nine of every 1,000 children born will die before they are five years old. Twenty-three percent of the human population on our planet are multi-dimensionally poor.

"To your point, Anderson, only some of humanity is entirely under reality number two at this moment, and for some of us, it is in our histories. None of us have the first reality. Most of us are in a hybrid of one and two; that's the third reality I mentioned. The danger with this reality is that it's not sustainable long term. It is a reality that will end, and either on good terms or bad.

"With that in mind, we must prevent two things. The first thing is to prevent bad on any level to take hold in our communities, and we know what bad is. The second thing to prevent is the acceptance and tolerance of bad, on any level. Failing such prevention can release the poison pill, as it has multiple times at the expense of millions of lives."

"I hear you, Michelle, but realistically, how do we protect ourselves from ourselves?" Anderson asked.

"We do it with order, institutions, a North Star, and controls. The North Star must be reverence for life and reverence for dignity. Our institutions must support the pursuit of the North Star. Democracy supports institutions and the controls they devise. Order toward living a more rewarding life prevails. That's what I see."

"And how do you tie all that back to reparations?"

"So, reparations to me means that every single person alive at this moment gets a chance to live the fullest and most wonderful life they can hope for, with all of us working together to make that happen. Honestly, we have to open our eyes to a new reality and paradigm where we revere every life." Michelle turned back toward Anderson. "And how do we do that, Anderson?"

Anderson answered quickly. "Love. That's what comes to me, Michelle."

Michelle turned away from Anderson and looked at the man holding the piece of paper. "Sir, please tell me the word written on that piece of paper."

The man pulled the paper out of his pocket and opened it. "The word on the paper is love."

Michelle looked out to the audience. "When I asked Anderson that question, how many of you received the word 'love' before he said it?"

Most of the audience raised their hands.

Michelle spoke with tears in her eyes. "I call that a Grace spark. Grace is in and all around us, and when we listen, we hear it. Many of us were listening.

"You've heard about systemic injustice," she continued. "We have to move to the system of valuing each other without qualifications. We are all unique and special. Let's cherish that. I love each one of you. I'm a Black woman who genuinely cherishes my life, but I would give mine for yours. All of you matter to me.

"My Black brothers and sisters have endured injustice for over four centuries, and

I not only want all of us, all of you, to fix it, but I expect it. There can never be another genocide, or another unarmed Black man killed by the police. We can't forget anyone, because we all matter."

"You say we all matter, Michelle. Are you out of step with the Black Lives Matter movement?"

"When I leave here tonight, Anderson, and walk to my car, there will be someone who watches me approach my vehicle while thinking, 'How can she afford a car like that? I wonder how much welfare she gets?'

"I drive a Camry, but it's nice and I keep it clean.

"My point is that the negative energy we harbor toward one another is real and is a habit. It feels natural as we limit each other. In my opinion, and I think the evidence will bear it out, America's Black population is the most persecuted and abused segment in our society. For me, Black Lives Matter is a movement to state the obvious, unequivocally, with the intention to right the wrong.

"The reality is that all of us have to take one step at a time to go from where we've been and where we are to where we're going. It's a process and a journey. In bringing justice to the most persecuted segment in our society, we raise all people. The result of our victory together, as Americans, is a beacon for other nations and all of humanity to stamp out the persecution of all other races, genders, doctrines, and orientations around our world."

"The producers want me to lighten things up," Anderson told her softly. "Parents, your kids can come back in the room now."

Michelle looked at him warmly.

"I have a question," Anderson said. "It's a little off the wall, but pertinent here."

"Sure, go."

"Well, all of us in this room are opening up and sharing freely. Why isn't it like that more often? Do you have any thoughts on that?"

"Something compelling to me, Anderson, is how people seem to shield themselves from each other. You know, like no one wants advice unless they ask for it, and even then, they just want a little of it. It could be too that we all realize on a deep level that only we understand our individual experiences. But here is what's cool.

"We seem to trust and be open to the written word. You can read a book or a passage from a book that can change your life. You're open to it, and you receive it. I hope we all continue to read, Anderson, and help everyone be able to do so. It is a special medium; one we seem to trust." Michelle smiled.

"Thank you, Michelle. We have a foreign affairs question from the audience. Let's move to Sanya Heterloper from Enfield, New Hampshire, a councilwoman for the city."

"Thank you, Ms. Wallace, and I apologize; this may not be a simple question for the time you have to answer. How would you handle the North Korean nuclear conundrum? I can't imagine anything good coming from how things are going with North Korea."

"Okay folks," Michelle said, "you are an audience that doesn't mess around. Thank you for your confidence in me."

The crowd laughed.

"Until the last few years, we enjoyed a world order of sorts. Bookmark that thought. Let's consider a world where these things are unacceptable:

"Nuclear weapons. We may need atomic power for future space transport, but nuclear weapons, unacceptable;

"Starvation;

"Genocide;

"Guns in the hands of angry people;

"Government corruption;

"Prejudice, along with the social and economic impact it generates;

"Gender inequality;

"Slavery and exploitation of any kind; and

"Climate change.

"These things are unacceptable. It's not a wish list. The answer to North Korea and all unacceptable things is the same. The world, as one, unites against the intolerable things. It will require a world body such as the United Nations that we set up differently than it is today, with a new set of goals. The new world body must promote—and force, when needed—the movement toward a better world where every life matters and gets maximized. Here we go again…the same theme. Every life must be revered, anywhere in the world, and all must have the opportunity to be all they can be.

"Take North Korea. They have, in the past, allowed millions of their people to starve to death, and we, the world, have tried to help but have not stopped it. In the world order I envision, the world body would move into the northern half of North Korea, take it over, and take care of the population. We would feed them at first and then help to promote their well-being beyond that over time by assisting them to contribute to their world in ways that bring them satisfaction and fulfillment. If a despot wants to allow their people to starve, we move in. That is an extreme example, but it draws a picture. It's like you're taking care of everyone in your home. You just do it."

"Just to be clear, Michelle," Anderson asked, "are you talking about a world government?"

"Yes and no. The USA would be the USA, but the USA wants to be a nation in a world of nations that promotes the well-being of every one of its people, and it wants to be a nation on a planet that is not getting warmer every year, and it doesn't want to be a nation that worries about having its population vaporized by nuclear weapons. So, the US would take part as it does now in the world order, but the world order would be more proactive and have a plan. Again, the better the pieces, the better the whole."

"North Korea will not let the world community come in and take over part of its land, not without a fight."

"True, Anderson. In the long run, a bully will not take on an entire neighborhood if they want to survive. It may not be easy the first time, but the community will prevail."

"Interesting, Michelle. Before closing, is there anything else you want to leave us with tonight?" Anderson asked.

"Yes. I have a picture I want to plant in your minds. Think of yourself as a syringe. A syringe can deliver a substance when the plunger is pushed or take something in if it's pulled. A syringe is a tool that holds the substance being delivered or retrieved.

"If I'm a syringe, what do I want to deliver? The answer that comes to me right now is a vaccine that heals and saves. It helps you protect yourself from things that'll do you harm.

"Now, consider a syringe of heroin. It provides a short period of thrill that takes you out of your reality. You may get addicted, fight to get more of it at great expense to you, and that addiction may ruin your existence or even cost you your life. We all know people, politicians, false leaders who are syringes of heroin.

"Like a syringe, you can fill yourself with whatever you choose, and that's what you will deliver."

Michelle stood silent after that. It was clear she had made her point.

"What do we concentrate on Michelle?"

"That's the most important question tonight, Anderson. Take the long view. Figure out the cause and fix that, not the result. Short term, address the painful results while always working the cause, long term."

"We just have a couple more minutes. Do you have anything you want to say in closing?" Anderson asked.

"Yes! We have experienced some wonderful things together tonight," she said, turning back toward the audience. "It's very complex out here, with real ramifications. In selecting your next president, you want someone who can lead you up the mountain. They need to show you they see the top and the way to get there. They need to show you how they will include you on the journey. Follow that person and follow yourself. The answer is in you.

"Over 50 years ago, Martin Luther King woke up on the day he would deliver his 'I have a dream' speech to the world. He didn't know how magical it would be then and still be today. Moments like that are coming, and it's for that reason I have hope. I believe grace is with us, amazing grace."

She received a standing ovation.

After an hour of shaking hands and taking selfies with the members of the audience, Michelle made her way backstage, where she came across Anderson waiting for her. He had removed his electronics and changed into a casual shirt with slacks. He wanted to share a quiet conversation between the two of them.

"Michelle, I feel honored that we could spend this time together. I have one question that I didn't ask out there if I may."

"Please."

"I know you are an economist, and that's a science. For you, where does faith come into play, if it does?"

"God is everything to me, Anderson. What I'll say to you is that the miraculous splendor God is playing out is way ahead of our ability and willingness to appreciate it. I so hope we get far enough along the road to appreciate it. That's my hope and life's work, and why I take part."

"How does one get to faith in your mind?"

"I believe commitment is the conduit to faith. The more committed we are, the more faith we have. Faith is the place beyond yourself. Do you feel that?"

"Yes, I do," Anderson said. "I believe you will find many voters who will be comfortable with you."

"Bless you, Anderson, and I mean that." Michelle held out her hand to shake his.

"I believe you can win," Anderson said with a smile.

"I'll be dropping out soon. When I was thirteen, I was trout fishing with my grandpa. He was a trout whisperer, and it mesmerized me watching him fish. I remember that day so vividly. It moved me so much to watch him, I finally needed to ask. 'Grandpa, how did you get so good at this?' His answer was surprising, but reasonable enough. He said, 'This is what I've always wanted to do.' I asked, 'Be a fisherman?' He said, 'No, Michelle. Be your grandpa!'

"It wasn't his fishing skills that mesmerized me so, Anderson. It was his love. Grandpa asked me what I wanted to be. I told him I wanted to be President of the United States. He told me, 'You're a messenger.' That's all he said. I've witnessed messengers in this world, Anderson."

"I'm sorry, I still don't get why you are dropping out."

Michelle explained. "Evolution happens in tiny increments, purposely unnoticeable. The country wants to get to what we have talked about tonight, but over time. They will choose a candidate to get them there incrementally.

Messengers speak of profound change. Mandela is one of the few messengers to take power."

"I understand. What do we do next?"

"Reverence for every life, Anderson, that's the answer." Michelle paused, then asked, "I have one last question for you. What's your favorite word?"

"My favorite word?" Anderson's mind got quiet so he could hear his word. "Transcendence. That is my favorite word at this moment."

"Thank you, Anderson!"

Note left Michelle Wallace to renew discovery.

In Between

Note recognized Michelle to be a change agent. Was she part of fate?

Note witnessed countless worlds twirling in space, inhabited by beings that relied entirely on the health and hospitable nature of their planet. Each of their lives depended on environmental stability and a social order that worked to the good of the whole over time. Note would experience a similar reality on a boat.

Chapter Eighteen

The Boat in the Sky

Note joined Sebastian at the end of his school day. Sebby, as they fondly called him, was a skinny seventeen-year-old with freckles on his light pink skin and voluminous amber eyes under unusually bushy brown eyebrows. Without thought, Sebby put his books and computing device in his satchel; he was preoccupied with getting out on the deck to watch the approaching storm come in.

Sebby was aboard the Orion, a sea-going vessel on the planet Youton in the Carabatese galaxy in a solar system close to its center. Youton was extraordinarily massive compared to the size of Sebby's race, leaving the journey for the Orion to span sixty years to get from their home continent to Jupin, on the other side of the vast sea. By Earth's standards, Youton's size equaled the size of Jupiter, while Sebby's race was microscopic compared to humans.

Youton's seas offered barely any current and no waves to speak of. The star that warmed the planet was insanely hot and bright while equally being far, far away. All of Youton's moons had collided with the great planet long ago, leaving little to stir up anything on the mighty world. Youton's core consisted of iron that was almost cool. The planet quietly floated through space much closer to its death than its birth. Sebby's race would fulfill its destiny before Youton would, however.

The sixty-year voyage meant the Orion must be a fully self-sufficient vessel, able to sustain itself autonomously through the decades. Every challenge, need, and opportunity had to be met or harvested aboard the Orion by its complement of 5291 souls.

Sebby's species never discovered radio frequencies and hadn't found or developed communications outside of direct personal interaction or signals within eye view. Just as the Orion conducted no communications with anyone off the ship, there was no connection with each other on the boat outside of addressing in-person or via delivered messages.

Sebby was a future captain prospect and, after working his way up through the various functions of the crew, was expected to be ready to assume the role in about fourteen years. At seventeen years of age, he was mindful of the expectations around him and accepted them without question. It was what he was to do.

Jasmine joined her best bud as he leaned against the rail, looking off in the distance at the darker skies.

"I just love storms, Jasmine! I wish we could see more of them."

Youton wielded no jet stream, resulting in a mild and calm climate in the center of a giant world where temperatures held steady and weather patterns became predictable. Storms were minor and rare on Youton.

"Tomorrow's the big day, Sebby. Are you excited?"

"Yes, I am. I've wondered many times how we make all this work out here in the middle of the sea and, though they have shared how it's done in class, seeing it done is what'll drive it home for me. I need to understand it, to ensure it continues to go smoothly and unfailingly. I appreciate that everything connects to everything else here on the Orion."

The next morning arrived, and Sebby reported to Chemicals.

"Good morning Sebastian, welcome to Chemicals. I'm Major Yuesepien; you can call me Feodor."

"Good Morning, Feodor. I go by Sebby."

"Fair enough, Sebby. What do you know about Chemicals?"

"Well, I know and appreciate that what we have on board the Orion is all we have, and that it has to last for our entire voyage. I know there used to be natural life in the sea ages ago that we could have used, but no longer. The sea's chemical makeup is now toxic to our people, while it keeps the planet livable with a significant contribution to our atmosphere and climate moderation. We float across certain death if the Orion is compromised or if we can't provide for ourselves on this vessel. I know the Chemicals specialty helps us use and reuse our limited resources."

"Very good, Sebby. Yes, that's Chem in a nutshell, though it's immensely complicated. Please sit. Let's talk about it. Would you like some tea?"

"Thank you, Feodor; I'd love some tea."

"The Orion set out twenty-three years ago, Sebby. We left with a year's worth of fuel, eight months' worth of food, and two months of water. The Orion would keep us warm when it was cold and cool when it was hot outside and protect us from the toxic sea. It knows where it's going so long as we keep it running and fueled to run. You're seventeen, right?"

"Yes, I'm seventeen."

"So, the Orion set out six years before you were born. The ship has limited space, so the population can't grow in an uncontrolled way. There was a death onboard that made room for your conception. People get old here. They will die. Others die of natural causes as time goes on. Everyone onboard has a purpose here, and those activities must get done, so when one of us can't do our job, others need to. Babies can't do much work very well, so we have to plan for the need for fresh resources along the journey.

"Chem is primarily responsible for using chemistry to help us raise food, clean our water, provide medicines, and assist our medical staff. Our clothes come from Chem processes, as does our fuel and the materials to construct or replace material items. Sebby, we couldn't be out here without Chem.

"Of what I just talked about, what is most interesting to you?"

"Food. Food and water, Feodor."

"We know what nutrients our bodies need to survive and thrive, Sebby. All this is possible because of the basics. How long will we have together to learn Chem?"

"I'm with you for three months, Feodor, and delighted."

"Are you wide awake?"

"Yes, Sir!"

"Okay, let's talk about the basics." Feodor explained the chemical building blocks of living things and went into some detail about the ways living things get and use nutrients from food.[24][25]

"That's the nuts and bolts of it. What we do in Chem is to manipulate molecules to fill our many needs for nutrition, energy, hydration, and so on. You'll love this, Sebby. Chem is a blast. The thing I love about it is that knowing how it works ties everything together for me. We're chemicals, Sebby. Are you ready?"

"Let's chem, Feodor!"

He stayed with Feodor for seven months instead of three and didn't want to leave when it was time to move on.

"Sebby, I can't tell you how much I've enjoyed working with you, and your smoothie invention will bring joy to generations. I hope I will see you often here in Chem. I know you will be busy, but I hope to see you."

"Count on it, Feodor."

They started with a cordial handshake that turned in to a hug.

Sebastian's next practice was governing society, and his mentor in this practice was the old woman, Sarah.

"Good day to you, Sebastian. I've heard excellent things about you from Major Yuesepien."

"Thank you. I go by Sebby."

"Thank you, Sebby; I go by Sarah. Let's sit down and visit."

"Tell me, what impressed you most about Chemicals?"

"It surprised me how intricate and balanced it is. Everything on the Orion is uniquely complicated but works well together. I didn't comprehend all that goes into our life out here."

"Sebby, that's a great setup for Governance. It, too, is complicated and must be flexible to adapt to needs as they change and evolve. I heard from the Major that you loved Chem. I hope you feel the same about Governance when we're done."

Sarah was one of the original officers on the Orion. She held the position of second in command on the ship. Now, in her seventies, she was looking forward to retirement but had yet to groom her replacement. There was some concern onboard around the impact on the mission if Sarah was to become unable to perform her duties. As a future captain, Sebby would need to know how to step into the role for a short period, if required.

"I'm excited to learn about Governance but want to start with a question. There's some concern on the Orion that you are close to retiring without an heir apparent. Can I ask why, Sarah?"

"Yes, I'm glad you asked, and I'm happy to answer. Governance is the glue that keeps everything together on the Orion. It's more than policies, procedures, and enforcement. It's the framework for society and must be successful.

"The head of Governance has to take on a broad view to recognize the complexity. To be honest, given our limited number of prospects, it has taken all this time to identify the right person. She's in your class, Sebby."

"Can I take a guess, Sarah?"

"Please."

"Monique."

"Yes. Why do you think Monique's the one?"

"Monique is a natural leader and works to build consensus in our class. She's always impressed me with how she can see and appreciate multiple points of view. I've sought advice from her many times. I'm almost surprised she is not the prospect for Captain."

"We aren't surprised by that, Sebby. You have unique qualities that make you the one for that role. I'm excited too for Monique to take over for me. You two will work together for the rest of the journey. One of my most significant considerations must be who will run things when the Orion gets to the other side. As Captain, you will continue to lead this family until or unless you assimilate in a large community there. My replacement will have to govern. The governance we have here is much more limited than the role of a broader government on land. On land, a government does everything we do, and it earns or takes in money and spends it. Here, each person trades their skills and capabilities for passage on the Orion. That's much different.

"What have you learned about Governance in class, Sebby?"

"I've studied how governments govern in normal circumstances and all the parts of society the government impacts. I know that here, on the Orion, you and your team dictate an acceptable framework to give order to our existence. I can appreciate the 'acceptable' part in that you work to get the buy-in of our community. What's your biggest challenge, Sarah?"

"Enforcement. Enforcing means something or someone got to the line. That's not good. In our circumstances, I spend most of my effort governing in such a way that we motivate no one to push beyond the accepted norm. It's funny, but that's where governments on land usually fail. First, they fail because they don't understand how their population feels and the extent to which they may be resisting. Second, because they don't know, they respond in a way that's too extreme, which causes more resentment.

"What I've learned about good governance, Sebby, is it's at its best when it's 'aware' of its impact and careful to make and keep that impact positive. The other trick is that we must set boundaries we can deliver within successfully. So long as we provide what we say we will, the restrictions are acceptable. That has been my biggest challenge."

"That is most intriguing, Sarah. You have my undivided attention and support."

Over the next decade, Sebastian would immerse himself in disciplines around the Orion including:

- Economics and finance
- Arts and literature
- Cultural heritage
- Music
- Construction
- Science
- Navigation
- Spirituality
- Relationships
- Family development

During Sebastian's 24th year, Jasmine and Sebastian married. Two years later, their daughter Fawn was born. Sebby began his final mentoring practice in Religion with Mother Roan.

"Welcome, Sebby; I've looked forward to mentoring you for some time. I hear you are progressing well and will be an outstanding captain soon. Oh, and happy birthday, belated. I believe you are 28 now. Congratulations!"

"Thank you, Mother Roan; I'm delighted to be with you. I want to admit to you upfront that I don't have the religious inclination of many others on the Orion. I know, as our Mother, you are a leader of the religious experience here, so I want you to know where I stand."

"Thank you, Sebby; I appreciate your candor. I lead all the many religious factions here on the Orion and find God in each of them. Religions are crucial in that they help people to aspire to more than what they see. It gives people hope.

"Being people, each of us can just perceive and understand a few things, so no religious experience or dogma is complete. I see your position as another religious experience, Sebby. If you held no hope in your heart, you wouldn't get out of bed, and since you have hope, you aspire. Enough said. I hear you, and I get it."

"Thank you, Mother. At my age, I realize that I think I know more than I do and know more than I think. That's a mouthful to say and a brain full to contemplate. I'm open to learning what I don't know and further discovering that which I do."

"I love the way you think, Sebby; you are already wise and will be a wonderful leader for us. Please ask me a question."

"Okay, Mother, I have a question no one will answer. I've asked it many times."

"Ah, yes, I've heard about this question you have been asking, one of two items you ask. My guess on one of the two you want to ask me is, why are we on this voyage?"

"Yes, Mother, I have that question. This voyage is no small thing, and its success is not guaranteed. We must cross the sea for some grand reason. Do you know why?"

"I do. Only the Captain and I can answer that question. We're the only ones who know. Because you will be Captain before we complete our journey and will probably be the Captain when we reach our destination, you must know why. I've taken time to consider your question, Sebby, and have kept tabs on your development to determine the right time to give you the answer. I know you're ready now.

"Our world is old, as you know, and it's dying. Our civilization is finding it challenging to make up for what the planet isn't doing anymore. We can survive this journey, for example, but just barely, and there's little room for error. There's little balance now between the needs for living things and the environment on Youton.

"Our teachings back home tell us that the most developed pockets of our civilization exist over the sea on the Jodian continent. Sebby, this is a mission of faith as we have no contemporary contacts from Jodian, nor have any ships like the Orion come from Jodian to our continent. We put all our best technology on the Orion with the best minds we could bring together. When we left port, we calculated a 15% chance of lasting three years out here, and we've made it for 34 years now. Our odds of getting to Jodian now are better than 50% if we don't find an obstacle we can't address. The reason we're on this voyage is the survival of our civilization. What is your other question?"

"Please give me a moment to process what you shared, Mother. I know our journey is important, but it's more than that, I see now."

After a few moments passed, Sebby asked his other question. "What am I here to learn from you?"

"As Captain, you will have the most considerable burden to bear on the Orion. You now know that you don't realize how things will turn out. You, our current Captain, and I are the only ones that know our potential peril. You'll learn faith from me, Sebby."

"That's a tall order, Mother. Faith is abstract to me. Do you know what faith is?"

"Yes. Faith is the surrender of self."

"Respectfully, Mother, why do I need to know that?"

"These people and those born to them will look to you to lead them through anything that may put them in peril. That level of leadership will require you to be bigger than you can be. You must have faith to 'be' from that place."

"I think I understand, Mother."

Note left Sebby. Note appreciated that, as a vessel on a toxic sea on an uncertain journey where survival depended on every crew member, the Orion was very like a civilization on a planet floating in space. While survival was uncertain, it was likely if the inhabitants worked together as a family.

In Between

Note found inspiration in how everyone on the boat worked together with the North Star of surviving the voyage to find a home on the other side of the sea. Their collaboration overcame many opportunities to fail. Trust was an unspoken pillar on the Orion.

Chapter Nineteen

Grandpa, Either Way, the Cancer Dies

The Earth year is 2062 on a Tuesday. Note joined Samuel as he sat quietly on the foot of Rhodonna's hospital bed and watched her sleep. She'd accepted an artificial spinal cord implant and was the first to survive the surgery. They would release her from the hospital in a few days to return home, with months of physical therapy ahead.

As an intense rainstorm blew against the window, Sam thought about what a blessing Rhodonna was in his life. They shared everything and enjoyed being with their children and grandchildren. Sam thought about the great courage that Rhodonna showed when she agreed to undergo this risky surgery, after the accident that left her a quadriplegic. He felt lucky to have been able to care for her and their family over the past ten years and looked forward to the possibility of a return to their previous life of activity and shared experiences.

Rhodonna shifted slightly in her sleep and Sam smiled. *When she wakes up*, he thought, *I'll tell her our favorite story about Grandpa. She always loves hearing it.* He thought about the day that he'd spent with his grandpa, the day that changed his life.

Sam's grandpa was his favorite grown-up, and just being around him seemed to make everything make sense. He was gentle, and a superb listener. He didn't offer much advice, but he listened to Sam, and that made him want to talk to Grandpa.

When he'd visit his grandparents each summer, they always watched Mister Rogers' Neighborhood together. His grandpa reminded him a lot of Mister Rogers; both men always smiled, and when they talked, it mattered.

When he was a little kid, Sam was deeply afraid of spiders—all those eyeballs and little hairs—but now he revered them, after his grandpa told him a story. He and Grandmom lived in a house with a two-way fireplace, one side in their bedroom and the other in their bathroom. One day he saw a web hanging off the fireplace handle in his bathroom. When he saw that spider hanging there, he just wanted to let it live there in the middle of a beautiful bathroom, and die with dignity, and without fear. That story made a powerful impression on Sam.

He thought about the special day he and his grandpa went fishing, and he remembered it like it was a minute ago.

***

"Grab two poles," Grandpa said. He pointed across the small shed. "They're over there behind the shovels."

"Got them, Grandpa! Do we need anything else? Do you want a blanket to sit on?"

"Cushions would be nice, Sammy. Thanks for thinking of my tender keister."

They loaded up Grandpa's old Silverado and were off to his favorite place on the little river. As Sam rolled down his window to feel the warm air, the Song from the heavens came into his being.

"Radio is all yours, Sammy. Let's rock."

Grandpa is so cool, Sam thought. *How did I get so lucky to have him for my very own grandpa?* He moved the channel to classic rock and one of their favorites came on, "Once in a Lifetime" by The Talking Heads.

"Hey Sammy, do you want some Fritos?"

"Are you having some, Grandpa?"

"Nope," he responded. "I just started a new stick of gum."

Their fishing spot was back in the woods, a good hike from the truck and through a dense forest. Though animals traversed it regularly, they never saw signs of people, or trash, or even walking paths. It smelled of wet dirt and worm heaven, along with masses of vegetation. It was spring, and all the greens were so vibrant with new leaves replacing old ones, and flowering plants and trees opening their arms to the busy bees that lived for the great harvest. There were plenty of thorns, too, and vines growing up on the trees as thick as Sam's wrists.

They finally arrived at their spot, and Sam pulled two icy waters out of the cooler he'd carried. Grandpa set the cushions down where they could lean back against Elwood, the grandest of grand live oak trees in the forest. They figured that Elwood grew there for 400 years to give them a place to rest and fish next to that crystal-clear stream all this time later. They'd found the spot five years earlier, after

Grandmom died.

"Want me to bait your pole, Grandpa?"

"Yes, I'd love that," he responded.

Sam loved to watch his grandpa cast. He was an accomplished backhand caster, and he taught the skill to Sam. The stream was only 20 feet wide and slow-moving. With their lines in the water, they leaned back against Elwood.

"When we come out here, I usually do most of the talking and you listen," Sam said. "I'm as thirsty to hear what you have to share as I am for this cold water; more so, in fact." Sam looked at Grandpa expectantly.

"I'm just filled with gratitude today, Sammy. I learned many things being a biologist and then kept studying all this after I retired," he said, gesturing around the spot. "Since retirement, I've studied the physical cosmology of the Universe, and that branched off in many directions. After all, I've learned, I'm immensely grateful for this life, this chance. Are you sure you want to hear what's on my mind?"

"I'm entirely sure I want to hear everything you can share," Sam said with a smile as he settled against the tree to listen.

"Okay. Since we can see the moon barely outlined in the sky—see it up there?" he said, pointing to the sky, "let's start by talking about the moon and its relationship to the Earth, sound good?"

Sammy nodded and listened intently as Grandpa described the egg-shaped moon and its elliptical orbit, and how it affects the tides. When he told Sammy how the unusually high tide in 1912 was because of the closeness of the moon which also causes higher winds, and how the high tide caused many icebergs to float out to sea, and how all that combined to create the setting for the Titanic's sinking, Sammy was excited.

"That *is* compelling, Grandpa! I think I know inherently how connected things are, but most of it isn't obvious. I wonder if scientists knew all that stuff back then about the moon, tides, and ice and stuff. You always say that once you know something, you must do something with what you know. I love that one!"

After a thoughtful moment, Sammy said, "Tell me a little about this world, instead of the moon. It seems busier here."

"You sure, Sammy? I was a biologist, you remember."

"If you can," Sam said as he winked at him.

Grandpa leaned back; this was a topic he loved to talk about and could discuss in detail, which he did. He talked about fungi, nematodes, and roundworms, and that led him to tell Sammy more about the stratification of species and ecosystems than Sammy already knew.

"Earth is the only planet known that has a biosphere," Grandpa continued. "I know you know that's a pretty word for the parts of a world such as the surface, atmosphere, and potentially hydrosphere, that are occupied by what we consider living organisms."

"Hydrosphere? What's that, oceans and stuff?"

"Exactly right, Sammy. The Earth alone can maintain the exact environment we need to stay alive. The balance is critical, and we all depend on each other. If all of an organism disappeared from our biosphere, our environment would shift to a radically new state. It may seem to happen gradually, but the balance changes. If a layer of organisms in the soil disappeared, the molecules of the soil or streambed would become smaller and more straightforward. The ratios of oxygen, carbon dioxide, and other gases in the air would change. A new equilibrium would be approached, at which the resulting environment might appear as an alien world would today."

"Seriously? Wow! Everything is related and tied together that strongly? I mean, I knew everything was connected, but I didn't know it was *that* important." Sam took a swig of cold water and exhaled in happiness. He had everything he wanted.

"Yes, that's very much it. I cannot be your grandpa without your being my grandson. This lifetime we have is such a miracle, but we stand on a mountaintop, and if the mountain below our feet disappears, we fall." Grandpa paused for a moment to check the fishing pole, then returned and sat next to Sam.

"Sammy, I need to give you one topic that I want you to incorporate into your being. It is one of the best gifts I can give you. I don't want to talk about it today. I just want to give it to you and then move on. Deal?"

"Sure, I'm down with that, Grandpa."

"Balance."

Sam waited for Grandpa to say more, and when he remained silent, said, "Okay.

Let me ask you a question, Grandpa. I was watching the news with Pop last week and saw the injustice happening in Yemen, with all the people starving, children, babies. To them, this life is not a miracle because of their great suffering."

Sam noticed his grandpa raising his left eyebrow, which always showed that he was ruminating. Sam loved that.

"Great point, Sammy! One of the greatest missing elements I see in humankind is that we don't have the reverence for life that's essential. Every one of those suffering people, and all suffering people, deserves to experience the blessing of this miracle." Grandpa looked up at the sky for a minute and Sam waited patiently, because he learned that these pauses meant Grandpa would say something important.

"I think of this world, and what humankind is doing to our environment and ourselves, and I liken it to cancer. Cancer is alive and strives to live at the expense of the host. It doesn't honor itself or the future, but thrusts itself forward in chaos. As a species, we have an opportunity to be like a white blood cell that protects the host from a cancer cell. Cancer kills the host if we don't kill the cancer. Either way, the cancer dies."

"I get it, Grandpa. If we want to live, we can't be cancer. If humanity protects and reveres life, it lives. If it doesn't, it dies."

Sam and Grandpa leaned back and looked up through the thick and green canopy. Big, fluffy clouds floated past in two layers, each moving a different direction, but slowly. Elwood's tree bark was uniquely pronounced and stuck slightly into Sam's back, but he liked it. The rains of the last week caused the water to rush quickly and some dead trees floated past. They jumped up to grab their poles and keep them from being dragged downstream.

They sat back in their spot, leaning against Elwood, and Sam said, "I have a question I've wanted to ask you. We've caught no fish here. We haven't even gotten a nibble. What's the deal? Where are the fish?"

Smiling, Grandpa responded, "Well, Sammy, there are no fish here to catch, at least not where we throw our lines. And our bait isn't right for what's in these waters, anyway."

It flabbergasted Sam. "What? Then why do we come here to fish?"

"We're not fishing, since there are no fish here that will attack our bait. We're here to 'be' together. Hasn't it been the best?"

It really has been the best, Sam thought, and that reminded him of another question. "Oh! What are you most grateful for, Grandpa?"

"I'm most thankful for the opportunity. The opportunity is everything, Sammy, everything. My question to you, my amazing grandson, is what are you going to do with *your* opportunity?"

***

Rhodonna woke up and saw Sam's eyes filled with tears. "What is it, honey? What's wrong?"

"I was just remembering that special day I shared with my grandpa, and about how I wanted to tell you the story again. Do you mind?"

At the end of the story, Sam and Rhodonna sat in lovely and reflective silence, smiling at each other. Rhodonna reached for Sam's hand and said, "I don't understand the Song you've talked so much about that fills you, but I am delighted by it. It may have saved us. I didn't know until now how dark a place I was in, trapped in my broken body. You sang to me all the time and kept music around me so I could be here with you now, alive with hope! I'm the first to survive this surgery, and I only had a 30% chance of doing so. Yet, here I am with you. Your Song may have saved me, Sam!"

Sam lowered his head in gratitude for the Song, for his grandpa and his wise lessons, and for Rhodonna.

"Tell me though," she said, "what do you think your opportunity was, the one your grandpa alluded to?"

Sam moved closer to Rhodonna and said, "You."

Note left Samuel.

In Between

Note loved this dear family and was loved by them. The essence of the family was one of being part of the solution, not the problem. Sam, Rhodonna, and Grandpa were all servers, and their truth was beautiful.

Note wished now to understand better how society creates itself.

Chapter Twenty

Where Goodness Comes From

Jody woke up to the speeding siren passing below her open apartment window. She thought about Rodge for a moment, and then her eyes became affixed on the cockroach standing defiantly on the far wall of her apartment, above her dresser. The shadow created by the nightlight more than doubled its perceived size in her sleepy eyes.

It's a life, she thought. *Every life is valuable; every life is important.*

Jody pushed off her heavy quilt to find the fresh morning air filling her apartment. Shivering, she found her panties from the day before next to the bed, thought better of it, and made her way toward the dresser. The cockroach gave up its defiance and scurried down the wall and under the base trim with enough speed and determination to make the lint and hairball move a tad.

Jody threw on some jeans and a knit top, deciding against a bra on her slight frame in exchange for some quick warmth. Temporarily protected from more goosebumps, she darted over to close the window. *Hmmm*, Jody thought, *they must have replaced the bulbs in the theater sign across the street. I like it. I wonder if they just did that. I'm hungry. I have to eat.*

She turned to see the clock, only 4 a.m. *Denny's, yes. Denny's is open. I must have some pancakes with hot maple syrup.* She slid on her lamb wool boots and found her thick flannel coat. Her keys clicked and clanged as she grabbed them.

Denny's was a block away and occupied the bottom floor in a four-story office building in the old city. Jody always found the gargoyles at the top of the building looking over the restaurant's patrons to be humorous.

"Good morning, Jody. Shall I put your order in?" Zona met Jody at the door when she arrived.

"Please, Zona. I'll find a seat."

Note joined Jody as she found her favorite corner booth empty and claimed it for her own. The restaurant was mostly deserted at this time of the morning, but it welcomed its usual cast of familiar characters. John was a homeless man, previously a lawyer, who found his gambling addiction to be more than his family could take, and after a couple of prison stints for running up stolen credit cards to pay for his habit, John could no longer find work. He sipped on coffee for hours just to get out of the cold.

Wanda and William were usually here by this time in the morning. She was an author and found that coming in Denny's and having coffee with her adoring husband, William, while the city was sleeping enabled her to collect her thoughts for the day's muse on the page. She was deservedly accomplished, with no need to change her routine.

Jody didn't recognize anyone else this morning.

"Here's your coffee with extra cream." Zona set it in front of her. The steam rose to fill her nostrils.

"Big day today!" Zona said. "Are you ready?"

Jody looked up at her soft face and smiled, "God, I hope so; we need me to be ready!" Zona leaned over and took Jody's hand and squeezed it.

"I have a good feeling about your day, Dearie. Your eyes are bright today."

Jody looked out at the dew-covered cobblestone street and thought about the gum on the stone and the people who chewed it and then discarded the gum for others to trample. Her hot breakfast arrived.

"Steve got your hash browns golden on both sides, Dearie. Are you wanting ketchup today?"

Jody looked down at her fluffy blueberry hotcakes, crispy hash browns, and whole wheat toast. "These hash browns are perfect. I don't want to miss any of them, so no ketchup today. Please hug Steve for me. But can I get some extra butter? I want to be decadent this morning."

Zona smiled and made it happen.

Halfway through savoring this feast of sugar and carbohydrates, with a plentiful supply of butter, Muhammed walked in the door, dusted himself off, and removed his hat. He looked toward Jody's favorite booth to find her smiling at him with a mouth full of, well, whatever.

He thought to himself, *she's like a kid*. He smiled back and made his way over.

"Good morning, Doctor," he said.

"You're acting professionally this morning, Muhammed. Sit down; get some grub. It's early for you. Did you hope to find me here?"

"I couldn't sleep either. I hoped you would be here, and you are," he smiled, his chubby cheeks pushing his glasses up a tad.

Zona came back over. "Early for you, Professor. Are you eating?"

"No. Hot chocolate for me with whipped cream, oh, and orange juice, large, please."

Zona squinted her eyes and puckered her lips. "Yummy," she said.

Muhammed turned back to Jody. "You know, they will hand us our asses today, you know that, right?"

Her face got stern, and her chewing slowed and then stopped while she thought about his comment. She resumed chewing.

After swallowing, she responded, "They can't afford to hand us our asses, Muhammad. They're out of time. We all are."

***

The head of the Senate committee struck her gavel against the puck, calling the hearing to order. "We want to welcome the three of you today."

Jody Zales earned a Ph.D. in Psychology from Harvard University and returned to the school to teach after many years of working with families, primarily children. Immediately after getting her Ph.D., she joined the justice system of Massachusetts and worked with juvenile felons to rehabilitate them. Her doctorate centered on retraining the mind to make decisions from—and base decisions around—feelings from the young person's good memories. Her work showed great promise, but the disintegration of law and order within society necessitated moving the funds and activities away from research and toward incarceration and law enforcement.

Muhammed Kaber was a former Federal Prosecutor for New York.

Jody and Muhammed were joined by Father Johanan Destin, the Archbishop of San Francisco.

"Good Morning Dr. Zales, Mr. Kaber, and Father Destin." The Chairwoman of the US Senate Committee on Homeland Security and Governmental Affairs proceeded. "We have a mess out there. For the sake of time, let me just start with you, Dr. Zales, and ask my first question if I may."

"Please, Senator," Jody agreed.

"What the hell is going on out there, Dr. Zales? Our communities are falling apart, as you know. I'm glad the three of you got here safely."

"Thank you for having us, Madame Chairwoman, Senators. A picture is worth a thousand words if I may."

"Please," Chairwoman Baldwin allowed.

"Imagine a house being built in a series of thunderstorms and infested with termites. Now, imagine a neighborhood of such homes, and each made to a different code. Easy to contemplate the long-term health of that neighborhood. And consider, too, the homeowners, and their stress and the product of that stress.

"That's what we have today in our modern society. That's the neighborhood we're living in. The termites are eating and multiplying, and the problems are beyond the homeowners' ability to remedy. We're living in shit, Senator Baldwin!"

"Please, Dr. Zales, we have decorum here."

"I don't mean any disrespect, Senator. I grew up in the neighborhood. May I add that as the legislator, you wrote the code."

"Dr. Zales?" Senator Casten posed the next question.

"Good Morning, Senator Casten."

"Good morning. Please support your position. Back up your analogy."

"Thank you, Senator. A human being is like a house. The brain is the most amazing organ in the Universe, but it's finite. It has a structure and works a certain way. The brain responds to things, and it's impacted by what it experiences both short term and long term. We can't take that lightly anymore. It's the reason we're in this mess.

"But, before we talk about why things are a mess, let's talk about how to build a good house—that is, a good brain—in a good neighborhood, all with the same code. A neighborhood where the owners are improving the homes. They're proud of them and take good care of them."

"Do they have termites, Dr. Zales?"

"No, no termites, Senator Casten. If you'll allow, I'd like to present the attributes of a healthy brain provided by the Cleveland Clinic. You can find them on their website, but to save time, I will summarize what they call the six pillars. Healthy brains require physical exercise, good nutrition, attention to medical risks, rest, staying mentally fit, and staying connected socially. Please note Senator, and this is important. What I just shared is what makes up a healthy brain. What it doesn't speak to is 'the inputs' to a healthy brain—garbage in, garbage out. And I think we can all agree, what we have outside is garbage. We have garbage because of the inputs we've condoned in our society. Chew on this one. That's the theme. Change the inputs and get different results."

"Thank you, Dr. Zales. This is resonating with me: garbage in, garbage out. Change the inputs, get different results. Keep it simple. Madam Chairwoman, I yield."

"Thank you, Senator Casten. Senator Gonzalez."

"Thank you, Madam Chairwoman. Dr. Zales, talk to us about the inputs as you see them."

"Thank you, Senator Gonzalez. Keeping our eye on the prize and going back to my analogy, we want to construct a well-built house that we can be proud of in a nice neighborhood where everything will increase in value over time, and our fellow owners improve their properties. And have no termites," Jody said, smiling.

"Here are the inputs into our population's minds today.

1. "Chaos and fear are creating stress.

2. "Digital addiction is leading to a more solitary existence where humans interact with and choose technology over actual people.

3. "A large volume of violent media is driving down sensitivity while yielding more aggressive behavior.

4. "Hopelessness."

"Thank you, Dr. Zales. Mr. Kaber, digital addiction and violent media may be connected. The chaos and hopelessness sound more like outcomes to me. How close is Dr. Zales in her representation?"

"She's dead-on, Senator Gonzalez. Our office took on several cases having to do with how social media companies enticed users to the point of addiction and knew they were doing it. I think we can all appreciate that a lot of the content on social media isn't healthy. Allow me to talk about digital addiction."

"Go ahead, Mr. Kaber."

"Thank you, Senator. Dr. Zales used the analogy of a house, and then a neighborhood built in a storm. I know her analogy made things simple for me to understand. I want to follow in that vein but using my story, that of my brother Jenan.

"Jenan is my younger brother, and we're six years apart. I was born into a traditional family with a mother and father, ostensibly happily married. They read to me every night, and I came to love reading from an early age. I entertained myself with books and all the magical places they could take me. I was attracted to books like the ones my parents read to me. The books were about love, kindness, hope, aspiration, and challenges successfully resolved. My first five years were wonderful, stable, and loving, and I grew up to become a successful federal prosecutor. I'm a loyal husband and a loving father. We read to both of our children.

"When my Mom became pregnant with Jenan, something changed between her and my dad. I've yet to know what that was, but the result was my dad found a girlfriend on the side and finally left my mom and me, and my unborn brother. I must admit that I would not be here today if my dad hadn't helped financially with my education, but emotionally, he left us.

"Mom did the best she could. My dad didn't make much money back then, and the child support was thin. Mom ended up putting Jenan in daycare and working two jobs to make it all work. She didn't read to Jenan, and I didn't either. I helped by making sure he was fed and clean, but really, I stuck him in front of the TV a lot to babysit.

"Our dad gave him a Xbox for his eighth birthday, and we just didn't see Jenan much after that. He was in his room most of the time, playing his games. We needed to have the internet and Jenan found online gaming. I'd like to pause there for a moment and let Dr. Zales touch on digital addiction. Is that acceptable?"

"Yes, please."

"Thank you, Mr. Kaber, Senators.

"Allow me to share my thoughts from one of my favorite books, The Teenage Brain, by neuroscientist Frances E. Jensen, MD.

"The compulsive need to get digitally connected happens both behaviorally and biochemically. When we get a text from a friend to connect, see an advertisement or hear a beep on our devices, it says 'hey, you matter, we want to include you' and causes a pleasurable rush of dopamine in our brain. The additive qualities of that release are found to mirror that of drug addiction. As Dr. Jensen notes, MRI studies in adolescents have shown addiction to cocaine and meth changes the connections between the brain's two hemispheres...and that MRIs of internet addicts show similar patterns.[26]

"Today, people often find more reward digitally than with other people because they can access more of what rewards them most, more quickly. People who are with you physically are perceived as less reliable."

"Dr. Zales, are there impacts on the brain?" Senator Gonzalez asked.

"Yes, Senator, depending on the extent of the addiction and the inputs, including violence and sex, there can be impacts on the brain.

"Mr. Kaber." Jody brought Muhammed back in to lead the conversation.

"Thank you, Doctor. In Jenan's case, his favorite games were violent, and it seemed to impact his personality. He resented our mom's attempts to limit his screen time and finally became somewhat aggressive with her, to the point of physical violence. I couldn't stand for that, and Jenan got removed from our home.

"The message here, Senators, is that the free-for-all we have is the product of human components that make up our current society. A brain is a biological machine, and the available inputs are limitless. As Dr. Zales has shared, the brain rewards us with dopamine as it experiences a rewarding moment. If that rewarding moment is violence, for example, then it reinforces that violence is rewarding, and we're back to the garbage in, garbage out. We're building houses in a storm, Senator. Garbage in, garbage out. We need to do it in a better way—the right way, a good way. We, as a society, have to guide our future toward a good end. Goodness comes from good inputs."

"Thank you, Mr. Kaber. Madam Chairwoman, I yield."

"Thank you, Senator Gonzalez. Senator Punea."

"Yes, thank you, Madam Chairwoman. My question is for you, Father. I know how things were when I was a kid, and I know how things are now. My question to you is, from where you sit, from the vantage point of the Church, what trends are you aware of over the last two decades that got us to where we are today?"

"Thank you, Senator, Madam Chairwoman.

"There aren't a lot of young people in Church today. That's not because they're bad, they aren't. What I've witnessed over any other thing is the continued breakdown of the family. The bonds aren't as close as they were, and parents aren't respected to the same degree as when we were younger. To Dr. Zales' point, people aren't as rewarding as screen time. To Mr. Kaber's point, we're allowing them to get lost in the first place because we aren't doing the right things for their benefit from their beginning."

"And you think that has produced our troubled society today, Father?"

"United we stand, divided we fall, Senator. Yes. Society is a family. If we don't have a good family, we don't have a good society."

"Where does good come from, Father?" Senator Punea asked.

"Meaningful connection. It comes from a meaningful connection. All the things that make connection possible support good. Things like trust, seeking, confidence, appreciation, opportunity, love, closeness, all create an environment for connection—meaningful connection with ourselves, each other, God, and our world around us. When we're connected to all of that, we don't want to screw it up."

"Dr. Zales, do you agree?" Senator Punea asked.

"I do, Senator. Connection is the most significant high we ever have in this life, but I must emphasize Father's word 'meaningful.' Meaningful connection is with the living, a person, people, a team, not a device. It can also be with music or an idea or a relationship with one's North Star. Again, we must assure good inputs, Senator. Is this body willing to do that?" Jody posed strongly.

"I think we have to," the Chairwoman answered.

Senator Punea continued. "And you, Mr. Kaber, anything to add?"

Father Destin interrupted. "Wait, I have one more thing to add."

"Yes, Father?"

"You agree, Madam Chairwoman, that we, together, have to take action. That's what I think I just heard."

"Yes, Father," she agreed.

"The US Constitution speaks to 'Life, Liberty, and the Pursuit of Happiness.' This government is supposed to take action to make sure each citizen realizes that. But it can't get maximized in this chaos. The constitution gives you the permission to fix this mess. We need you to come through for us so we can come through for each other."

"Thank you, Father."

"Mr. Kaber?" Senator Punea invited the professor's comments again.

"Absolutely. You won't fix this mess without moving our troubled society to hold every member in it in high regard."

"How do we do that, Sir?"

"Mandate a good environment. You must decide that individuals are not free to destroy themselves and the surrounding people. Remember, garbage in, garbage out. The garbage has got to go. You and this body can effect that change and can do it now."

"Hold each member in high regard. That's a little vague, Mr. Kaber."

"May I interject?"

"Please, Father."

"Revere life, all life. If we revere life, we revere all the things that make it good. That is, Senators, where the essence of goodness comes from."

Note left Jody.

In Between

Note accepted that everything is the sum of its parts and that bad inputs yield the same.

Note next needed to discover how incapacitating fear is, and how overcoming it opens new avenues to experiencing life.

Chapter Twenty-One

Fear

Captain's Log:

The Essex exited the unstable wormhole. We saw it collapse behind us. The ship was failing and failing fast, with power waning and propulsion unreliable.

***

On the Bridge:

"Captain, engine one and two are out now, Sir. We have only one left, and it shows to be in danger of going offline."

"Benton, where are we? What can you see out there? Is there anything close? I need you to find something ASAP!"

Benton's breathing was quick. "Captain, we're coming up on a Red Dwarf, and there's a planet we might get to. It looks to be in the habitable zone. It's blue. The planet has water."

Note joined the Captain at that moment. The Captain's pulse slowed, and his mind cleared.

The Essex was dying. "Benton, chart a course to meet the planet on its orbit, a rendezvous we can make with our current momentum and no power. Do it now!"

"It's a 'comet class,' a term used for planets with extraordinarily fast orbits around their star. I have it plotted, Captain!" she advised.

"Engage," the Captain ordered.

Benton guided the ship on the new trajectory.

"Dodger, shut off the mains and bring on the backup generators. Open all the internal ship doors and lock them open."

The Captain pressed the intercom button. "My friends! I need everyone to get secured for a bumpy ride over the next few minutes. We exited the wormhole and are moving toward a large blue planet. We have only one engine for a landing attempt. I need all of you to prepare as if we will land hard; put your crash gear on. We may also experience temperatures or air during this process, and we need to protect ourselves. Get your body lights ready and comfort your neighbor. We're all in this together, and we're destined to prevail at this moment. Talk to you in a few minutes. Josset out!"

The Essex exited the wormhole close to a Red Dwarf Star. Red Dwarfs make up 70 to 80 percent of the Universe and are too faint to see at any distance. They are slow-burning stars that burn cool and can live for trillions of years. The habitable zone around a Red Dwarf is close to the star, and close is where the planet Odis was orbiting this one. Benton's course correction guided the Essex straight toward the star with Odis coming up on her aft side. The star's gravity found the Essex and was pulling her forward at an ever-increasing rate.

"Captain, she's still. No spin, Captain!"

Odis was an old world, over a trillion years already. As a young planet, less than 80 billion years old, it was impacted by a small moon-sized body that crashed into it at a steep angle heading westward. The massive impact broke the mantle apart and diminished Odis' eastward spin. The remaining spin slowed over billions of years while Odis healed until finally, there was no spin at all. A multitude of additional impacts over a long stellar period increased Odis's size to twice the mass of Earth and deposited vast amounts of water and, thankfully, the seeds of life.

"Is it a tidal lock, Benton?"

"No, Sir, no spin, none."

"Damn it...okay! We need to stay away from the equator. The Star will cook us there. That colossus is coming upon us, Benton. We need to find a target before we become one!"

"I see some green at 30 degrees, that's my hunch, Captain."

"Dodger, let's land it."

Engine number three went offline, and everything went dark. "Dodger, get us back up. Get anything that'll work, working," the Captain said excitedly.

Nothing changed. The Essex was dead. No sound, no light, and no gravity. Just darkness and fear. Josset knew the ship would soon get pulled into Odis and, with no power, their survival was impossible. He remembered his mother holding him after his dog Blinken suddenly died, and how hopeless he'd felt. Why did things happen the way they happen? He didn't feel that way at this moment, and Josset was struck with that. He and Note were in a peaceful and accepting place together. Josset thought about the 122 lives on the Essex and wondered if they would suffer and, if so, how soon.

The heat rose, and the crew felt gravity returning as they moved into the atmosphere. The trajectory became more extreme, and the Essex, which wasn't designed to glide, began spinning. Suddenly there was a jolt, and the Essex steadied, and the trajectory improved. "Dodger, did you get power back?"

"No power, Sir. I'm not piloting the ship."

The Essex didn't have windows in the bridge, and the bridge crew sat in the darkness, only able to hear sounds from outside the hull. It sounded like air moving over the ship, and that sound grew in intensity until finally, they felt their vessel come to a stop. The silence returned. The bridge crew pulled portable lights from their chair bottoms. The first thing they saw in the light was the sheer amazement on each other's faces. What had just happened? What was happening?

"Benton, gather everyone. Get them to Hangar One."

"Yes, Sir." Benton accepted with a relieved voice. "Without communications, it will take some time to get to everyone. I'll get to it."

The bridge crew walked into Hangar One to join the entire ship's complement; just a few of the body lights were on to conserve what they had. Up in front of the crew, Josset told them what he knew.

"Friends. In the last few minutes, the Essex exited a wormhole heading for a large planet and lost all power before entering the atmosphere. We never regained power." Many in the gathering gasped, expecting his next words and the meaning behind them.

"We should be dead. There is no way to explain why we're able to meet in this hangar and plan our next action. There is a world outside this ship. We're alive by someone or something else's hand. Benton and I will suit up and go outside. We'll determine what got us down and assess your safety. We'll make decisions based on facts.

"If things remain stable enough for us, we may get the ship working. That's what I need each of you to concentrate on. I'll let you know what we find; pray for us all."

He looked over at Benton. She trusted Captain Josset completely. He was known throughout the fleet to be an exceptional leader.

"Suit up, Benton. We have to make some progress in a hurry here."

"Yes, Sir!"

They stood in front of the inside airlock door and opened the panel to the manual crank. Dodger took the honor of spinning it to open the airlock door and then again to close it behind the pair. "Benton, can you hear me okay?"

"Yes, Sir, let's do this."

Josset opened the manual panel to the external airlock door and spun the release lever. As the door opened, the light came in. It was a sunny day on Odis. "I wonder how long the days are here," Benton said.

Benton was full of anxiety, while Josset was peaceful and sure. They looked outside together as the door opened. What they saw was astonishing; it was unlike anything Benton and Josset had seen before. The landscape was green and lush and big, and it seemed like the Essex was alone. The pair climbed down the railing on the Essex to get to the ground. It looked like an Earth jungle, but everything was much larger. The leaves were the size of a three-bedroom house, and the trees dwarfed the mighty sequoia both remembered visiting on Earth.

"Captain, I wonder if everything here is as big as the vegetation." They both inherently knew that size matters in conflicts, and Benton and Josset felt an animal's wariness of potential conflict. Once on the ground, Benton pulled out her analyzer and quickly sampled the air. "Captain, it's a miracle; we can breathe this stuff, and the temperature is safe for us too."

Josset released his face shield latch, and it opened. The smell was overwhelming. He fell to the ground, closing the shield. "What is it, Captain? Are you okay?" She dropped down beside him.

"I don't know if we can breathe it or not, Linda; the smell is powerful, like sulfur."

Linda Benton analyzed the air content again in much greater detail. "It may stink, Captain, but we can breathe it. Look."

"It stinks, I promise. Okay, let me open my mask and breathe for a while. If I don't die, you can open yours too," he said with some humor in his voice.

"Yes, Sir."

Josset opened his mask again; his eyes watered, and his lungs burned a little. "Damn, this is awful, but I'm still alive. Wow...I can't imagine getting used to this, but, wow, this is rich."

Benton couldn't help but laugh, even though this could be serious. They heard an intense bass sound getting closer to them. Though they were in a clearing of sorts, the vegetation was so lush that they couldn't see over it.

"We have to get higher, Benton. We have to see where we are and what's coming."

"Yes, Sir."

The deep bass sound was getting louder and was steady. Josset thought, *it has to be a machine*. They made their way through what might have been giant blades of grass, three meters wide and ten meters high, until they found what looked like a tree trunk. The trunk was forty meters wide, and the bark was thick and sculptured. They climbed the bark to see out above the grass-like foliage.

"Benton, I'm still alive and breathing, so I agree that the air is safe. You can open your visor."

Benton raised her visor and found the potent smell overpowering. Her eyes watered immediately, but the deep bass sound was more like a rumble now as it got louder, sounding close. They could see the field in front of them with the Essex in it.

"Oh, my!" Josset exclaimed.

"Yes, yes, Sir."

To their right, an orb exited from the side of the tree. It floated over the top of the grass blades. It was green like the vegetation and shiny like a pinball; it was beautiful. The forest floor reflected off it as did the mighty tree they were on. It moved over in front of them. The deep bass was almost rumbling the tree, but it felt good.

"Captain, I think it's music; can that be a note?"

"Yes, I hear it!"

Benton and Josset cried; it overwhelmed them.

At that moment, they either grew, or the forest shrank. Everything was in proportions they were used to on Earth. The Essex was substantial within the considerable clearing. The mountain range behind the Essex wasn't smaller. The mountains were enormous but with rounded tops. It reminded Josset of the Appalachians on the North American continent on Earth in their shape with no visible hard edges. It occurred to him that this was an ancient world, and that erosion was never-ending.

"I trust what I'm seeing, Captain, but what the hell am I seeing?"

"We have to roll with it, Benton. We're still alive!"

The air smelled better, too; it was perfect, like a forest after a good rain back home with wet pine needles, even though there were no pine needles.

The orb started moving toward them; it would smash into them, and there was nowhere to run.

"It's coming at us, Captain."

"Take my hand, Linda!" He held his hand out, still in the suit, and she took it. The orb reached them and swallowed them.

Inside the orb, they lost the sense of having bodies, or even thoughts or memories about their bodies. They couldn't see each other inside the orb but felt connected just the same. Thoughts melted here into something flowing without form but moving forward somehow, and not in a direction. Just forward.

Suddenly, they were standing in the field again. The Essex was back in view with the massive mountains behind her. The orb was gone from their viewpoint but was a part of them.

"Captain, look!" Benton screeched.

A human-sized arachnid was making its way toward them. Josset harbored a great fear of spiders. He knew they injected chemicals into their victims to turn the insides to a liquid, only to get sucked out for the spider's dinner. Spiders were, without question, his greatest fear.

The monster coming toward Benton and Josset was lumbering because of its enormous abdomen dragging on the ground. Two of the eight eyes focused on them. With 48 knees, spiders rarely drag their abdomens, but gravity was impactful here, and this was a massive spider.

"Captain, what do we do?" It terrified Benton.

Josset froze.

"Josset, Josset, what do we do?" she pleaded.

Benton saw fear in her Captain's face for the first time, and Note felt the fear of Baby Jaselle when the fire was entering under the door, and her Mommy wasn't coming. In a moment, Josset recalled and relived the birth of his terror.

***

Josset was an Ensign on the Star Cruiser Titan when it answered a distress call on the world Zanar, a small Earth-type world in the Sarcusian system. His Captain, Elizabeth Rankin, had him join the away team to evaluate the distress call. After confirming that a small settler's colony had started on Zanar, they determined that the away team would trek down to the planet and define the next steps based on the circumstances. The away team took the shuttle to the surface. They exited the craft close to the proximity of the colony.

The Earth-like terrain looked to have been impacted by a tumultuous storm. The tree-like structures laid on the ground with what appeared to be fractures in their trunks. The foliage was still green on the felled trees, so the storm was likely recent. They made their way to the village to find it empty. The storm battered the abodes, and most were roofless. Some homes were flat on the ground.

Captain Rankin called out to Coustaff, the science officer. "Coustaff, are you still picking up the distress signal?"

"Yes, Captain, it seems now to be more like a beacon. My scans show it's coming from the southeast direction and is about 1700 clicks away."

"Understood!" Captain Rankin said. "Team, let's make our way toward the distress signal. Stay alert; I don't know what life forms are here."

At about 1500 clicks, they were atop a bluff, looking down at a massive cave opening.

She called the Titan. "This is Rankin!"

"Yes, Captain." Deak, the Lieutenant Commander, answered from the Titan.

"We've found the mouth of a large cave and detect the distress signal is coming from inside. There was weather here, and we believe the colonist entered the cave for safety. Scans are not picking up anything in there. We're hoping the rock here is blocking our scans, and that's why we don't detect the colonist. I have my beacon on and will turn on the modulation if we run into trouble. Rankin out."

The team made its way down the bluff face and entered the mouth of the cave. There was a strong sulfur-like smell. *If the colony were in here, why aren't they waiting for us?* he remembered thinking.

"Proceed, but let's stay together and take it slow. This smell is crazy!"

Upon entering the cave, they found the cave floor to be exceedingly sticky, making it hard to move forward.

"Hold up! I don't want to keep trying to walk in this. Let's back out of here now."

"Captain, I can't move," Shirley spoke out in a concerned tone.

"Same here, Captain," added Cynthiana.

"Damn it, I can't move either," Rankin barked.

Josset could move with great effort and started turning toward the women who were stuck. Mohammed could also move, but barely, and turned toward the other crew members.

Then it happened. Several large spider creatures came from the depth of the cave toward the team.

Josset remembered how fear for his life hit him like a lightning bolt, having only seconds to note their size and squeeze the trigger before being hit with sticky web rope. He relived the feeling of the spider legs and spinning and spinning, being surrounded by the line, and it was tight.

I knew it was over for us. We were helpless, he remembered.

They wrapped the rope around my spinning head. It covered my nostrils and mouth. I couldn't breathe and felt my chest burn. I decided these were massive spiders, and I would soon feel large fangs stabbing my body and feel my life ending.

At that moment, he saw a glow through the rope over his eyes.

Security rescued four of the team while still alive. The glow was the light of the lasers firing into the spiders. Captain Rankin, Technician Wally Jobel and Security Officers Wandajohn Smite, Beth Yogers, and Stevest Romstute all died inside the cocoons or during the battle. Extensive ship scans detected no live humanoid life in the cave, and the extent of the spider colony couldn't be determined. The Titan needed to abort the mission until more information was available. Other ships went to Zanar later to research the incident and found that the spiders were not carbon-based life forms, which is why their scans did not detect them.

***

Back in the present moment on Odis, Benton was horrified. "Josset, what do we do?" she barked.

The beast got to Josset and Benton and raised its two front legs as if to attack. Benton broke into a frantic run back toward the Essex, leaving Josset and the beast facing one another. Josset considered his decision not to bring a weapon for protection, which was an odd decision for him to have made for the away team. He heard Song and felt the deep bass of the orb at that moment. The beast dropped its legs back to the ground but then shot a rope at Josset, but only one and it attached to his shoulder. He thought about getting out of his suit but knew he was no match for his captor. His fear paralyzed him.

The Beast turned to the right, causing Josset to fall over and drag over the ground as the short rope pulled him to keep him in place at the side of the beast. It started moving forward slowly, pulling Josset with it, sliding on the ground. Josset got to his feet, and the two walked side by side, the Beast with its prisoner moving at a speed Josset could easily walk.

Though his fear didn't dissipate, it became more manageable as each moment passed, and he could find hope in his mind. *What if Benton gets back to the ship and brings help with laser rifles? If this thing is like what was on Zanar*, he thought, *we can kill it.* With hope, Josset could operate in the fear while his mind kept working.

***

Captain's Log:

I wanted to increase my chances to survive, and it occurred to me that I needed to regain control of my mental abilities. It scared me to death. I couldn't run, and I didn't have the tools to fight. I knew my only option would be to find a solution.

It was so ugly; I could barely look over at it, though I made myself as I knew I must assess it. With eight eyes, it seemed like it was watching me too, but surely it did so from a place of power and without fear. It controlled me. I could see a large cave opening ahead, and my heart started racing faster. I thought, should I struggle now and let it kill me out here in the light or let it take me into that dark cave and finish me there? My thoughts went back to a conversation with my brother when we were kids. He asked me, 'If you were on life support, would you want them to turn off the life support, or would you want to live each possible minute, even though you were confined to life support?'

The choice was instant for me. I told him, 'Life is profound; it is everything we have, Brother, and I would want to live each possible minute.'

Back to the present, I thought about the two like options I had: dying outside now or dying later inside that cave. Then I reminded myself that I believed if we have breath in our lungs, we have a chance at whatever good can come.

So, I was going in the cave with the beast, and the sulfur smell was back and getting stronger. I looked up and said goodbye to the sky and the light and thought quickly about my dear mother. The grand mountain over the cave impressed me. My fear was barely manageable, while my tense muscles made it harder for me to move, as it forced me to do. I didn't want to get dragged.

We entered the cave and were quickly surrounded by many massive spiders. The beast paused, as did the incoming spiders, and all was still. I was terrified but alert and clear-minded. My mind was still filled with music and beautiful Song in the background. It gave me some small peace.

Then, much to my surprise, the spiders started parting to make way for the beast and me to proceed more into the belly of the cave. The walls of the cave had high phosphorus content and put off light enough for me to see. Our path seemed clear ahead. We continued forward for a long time. The cave opening got smaller and smaller until I could no longer see it when I turned back. There were spiders next to me every step of the way, but none got close enough to touch me or got into the path of the beast, though many were more substantial than it was. That was very odd, almost intelligent.

Though the light was dim with the phosphorous glow, I could see many, many carcasses along the way that must have once been dinner here. It occurred to me that Benton and the team would never find me in here to save me. I was sad.

We rounded a bend into a birthing chamber; the sight of it caused me to throw up. The beast stopped while I convulsed, and I looked away from what I saw when we entered the chamber. Like the Earth Wolf spider, I saw multiple spider mothers covered with their spiderlings. They stayed on their mothers as they developed enough to go off on their own. The sounds of all that life made me consider what it would sound like being inside a stomach during digestion. Sadly, this was it for me, I thought. I was here to feed the babies, and my terror intensified.

Thankfully, we kept moving forward and remained uninterrupted. We came to an even larger cavern, easily big enough to hold three of the Essex. What I saw in this cavern was the most dreadful and awesome site I had yet seen, and I witnessed some colossal outcomes in the galaxy. There laid the body of a beast the size of the Essex. My beast stopped and turned to look at it, forcing me to move in that direction too. I made myself look. The sulfur smell was strongest here. I was accustomed enough to it now to deal with it, and it was low on my list of priorities right now. The giant beast did not appear to have been dead for long. The thing that stood out to me about it other than the sheer size and smell was the dark red stripe on its back. I glanced over at my beast and saw the same red stripe on its back. I looked around at the countless spiders around us in the cavern and was shocked to realize none of them bore the red stripe, only 'my' beast. My fear was keeping me from being aware of many things, and that was becoming more apparent to me with each passing minute.

My beast was unique in this family. What did that mean for me? Why was I still alive? My fear was subsiding little by little, and my awareness was growing. Strangely, I felt anguish from my beast as it looked upon the body before us. I felt sad for it and, at that moment, it looked at me with four of its eyes. It moved one of its legs next to my foot while it focused on me. For the first time, I saw this being as a life and not a beast.

The moment of compassion, I felt, melted my fear enough to behold the monster that imprisoned me. I was always aware of the details. It was thankfully one characteristic I used to beat out my competition in the service, earning the Captain's chair. In this setting, however, in this circumstance, fear closed my awareness. I knew my realization of how fear put a blanket over the very consciousness that could save me in other settings was wasted. Yet having such *an important revelation gave me a slight moment of solace.*

The beast stood just taller than me in the main body, with its leg joints rising over a third higher as it stood still in front of the carcass. It was covered with what looked like hair...brown hair coming out of what seemed to be black skin. Even though my eyes were adapting to the prosperous light, it was hard to see much of the beast's dark attributes. I knew that on Earth, spiders didn't have lungs, and I couldn't imagine how these things could pull enough nourishing air out of this environment to live. I realized for the first time how labored my breathing was. It was like I was regaining consciousness.

The beast turned toward me slightly, and the cord or web string that connected us released from its body. This must be it, I thought. It then raised a leg and pulled the web string off me with a quick tug that pulled me against the beast. My hands reached out in immediate reaction to steady my fall forward, and I found them on the creature. I sensed its life but was still extremely repulsed. It was sticky, prickly, and firm. I stepped back quickly but stayed in the space. Somehow, I felt safer next to my captor than out amongst the hundreds or thousands of family members around.

It turned back and started walking away from the huge carcass. I continued to walk with it as we made our way back the way we'd come in, again, the center of attention for all the many crawling inhabitants. The Song was powerful now. How peculiar, I thought.

I saw the light ahead again, oh the light. I love the light. Thank you for the light. We continued to walk toward it. With each moment, my fear lessened, and the intricacies of the divine moment became more and more available to consider. Why am I still alive? What type of community is this that honors this beast as they do? How did they get here? How do they survive? What kind of life forms live in this world to support this biomass of Araneae?

We made our way back outside, and I felt the warmth of the mother star and felt the wind against my skin. My breathing became much less labored. I turned to look at the beast. It turned toward me, directing its front eyes on me. All fear was gone, and I saw the creature for the first time. It was female. She was beautiful. The solar light shined on her golden-brown hair, and I saw dimension in her eyes. She had feet or paws on the ends of her legs with hair on them, and two claws. She put one of her paws on my foot, and I reached out my hand to touch her face. We connected at that moment, and our species joined one another.

The orb joined us. The beast and I understood that Odis was the orb's home too. It was a species that evolved on this world long ago, one that survived to get to this state of being. As this species realized genuine connection, the Orb race sought to teach it to other species.

There was peace there, peace like never before. I felt the family of this being and understood her fears, hopes, needs, and expectations. She was feeling mine too, and though there was a significant commonality between us, there were dimensions of reality that were utterly unknown to the other, prior to this moment. She heard the Song within me, and I felt her soul singing with mine. Peace and grace. It forever changed her and me. She would be a part of me, and I a part of her, always.

I understood too that she was the new queen of her species. The orb brought us together to help each evolve. I knew I would be with my race again and talk of peace, peace through connection with our world, and all those in it. I also somehow knew I would blink, and my new friend would be gone when I opened my eyes. I blinked.

At that moment, I found myself back on the bridge of the Essex and was stunned for a moment.

Captain's Log Out.

***

"Captain, we're approaching a class 3 wormhole; stability is a nine. Orders?"

I remembered this being the moment before we entered the wormhole to find Odis. I knew the orb cast the wormhole as a web. A spider would do that, I thought...

"Stop engines, Dodger."

"Yes, Captain."

Benton looked over at me with a surprised look. "It's gone, Captain. The wormhole disappeared."

"Dodger, resume the previous course."

Then, turning to his right, the Captain called out, "Benton!"

"Yes, Sir?"

"Can I give you a few spider facts?"

"If you must, Sir!"

Note left Josset.

In Between

Note experienced the confinement of fear on many levels. It seems to always come from a place of the unknown. The outcome in any known situation is best without fear.

Note was to experience the valuation of life...

Chapter Twenty-Two

Reverence for Life

Note was fast approaching an object in space. Only the reflection of the nearby star off the object showed that it was a ship. Soon after, Note was aboard the Gent and joined Sarah.

Sarah's breathing was labored as she gained consciousness. Her eyes burned as she worked to make sense of her situation. Sarah was on a hibernation ship, and her hibernation was ending under duress. Her tube was shadowy and cold, and the space outside her tube was dark. She understood her situation and became afraid. It was apparent she was running out of air in her tube, and she only hoped to exit, but exit to what?

Sarah remembered the exit bar and grabbed it; as she pulled it toward her, the latch released, and the door opened. The smell was stale, and the air was cold; she could hear crying and concerned voices.

"Welcome to hell, Captain. We're in a bad way, Sarah," her first officer exclaimed.

They determined the Gent had traveled in space for over 11,192 years and moved across the galaxy to unfamiliar surroundings. The remaining power relied on highly advanced solar technology. Though the fuel was gone, the Gent could maintain minimal energy systems that could clean air and provide a tiny amount of heat within the ship. A small subset of the computer systems could operate along with internal ship communications.

The complement on board comprised 416 members. Of the 416, 111 were terminally ill or severely handicapped individuals that were passengers on the vessel. It was to be on a 214-year journey to a sister colony with superior medical capabilities. The hope was that additional advances would occur in that time, and those ailing members might wake up to a time where medicine and technology could restore them or increase their life experience.

A short time passed, and the officers decided they would solicit everyone's input.

Julie and Sarah sat together to talk about Sarah's decision options.

"Julie," Sarah began, "you know our situation here. The Gent is adrift with little—if any—prospect of being found after all this time. In its current condition, which is not correctable, it can't sustain the entire crew indefinitely. We have determined and calculated that we can grow enough food to sustain a complement of 214 members for decades. Our dilemma is, do we put 202 of our friends and family to sleep so 214 people can live a normal life span and potentially get saved, or do we all move through this journey together and perish together in a relatively short while? You may know some 34 of our family are terminally ill, and another 77 like yourself are severely handicapped and require help to live a full life. That's why I wanted to talk to you, Julie, to see what your thoughts were about..."

"Killing me," Julie jumped in. "You want to talk to me about killing me so that others can live? You know, Captain, I'm all I have," she said with her slurred voice. "I'm all I have, and if you kill me, I have nothing. I am nothing. Do you recognize that I comprehend your message? Isn't that remarkable? And I'm able to respond intelligently and thoughtfully to your question, again, of all the life forms you know; how many can do that? You know that my big toe can feel the cold steel of the stirrup that's holding it, and I can smell the stale air we're breathing. I hear you and see you and love you; yes, Captain, I love! What is it about me that makes me a candidate to get murdered? Oh, yes, my disability. It keeps me from walking or running. I can't hold things like many of the rest of you. My speech is not as clear; I wet and soil myself. That's why I should die. Is that right, Captain?"

Julie went on. "Are you going to end the short people because they can't reach things on tall shelves? You know, since food is a part of the calculation, Captain, shouldn't you test everyone's metabolic rate and kill those with the higher metabolisms? That may allow you to keep one or more folks around, and if there needs to be a change, well, they can die later. Captain, my metabolism is one of the slower on the ship. Perhaps you should kill someone else!

"I'm sorry to make this so difficult, but I'm all I have, and I don't want to let that go or have you or anyone else take that from me. You may not believe in miracles, Captain, but I do! I have always believed in miracles because I've spent a lot of time trapped in this body and observed miracles around me. I've lived some of them, too. I'm grateful for this life, my life. I'm all I have, Captain, and that's enough."

Julie's candor and passion surprised Sarah. She was impressed at Julie's wisdom and desire to live. "Thank you, Julie. Your points are more than valid."

"When will you decide, Captain?"

"I will decide in 12 hours. There are many conversations taking place right now. I will take all the input and make the call. Your life is precious, Julie. I am sorry for our situation."

After Julie moved away, Sarah went to her quarters to think. *Only a few will offer their lives for the rest. Dammit, either way, my decision will cause someone's death. Julie's right. How do I judge who should die? It would have to be fair and not on physical condition. We would have to do a random lottery or something. Maybe have everyone pick a number from 1 to 500 and put it in a bowl with their name on it. After I have all the numbers in a bowl, I let them know everyone that picked an odd number dies, while evens live. Should break 50/50. This is so bad!* Sarah broke down and bawled.

After all the input, Sarah revered life, any life, all life, the life of each member of the crew family. She conveyed her decision to her first officer and to the crew. "We're all equal here, and life is irreplaceable and deserved by each, equally. This is the right thing!"

A feeling of deep peace swept over Sarah. She realized or came to know that she'd lived her entire life to make that decision and feel this appreciation and reverence for life. A living thing was no longer a sum of its parts, but was instead a miracle to be respected and cherished. Yes, this was the decision she'd been born thousands of years earlier to make and the feeling of fulfillment—that is, fulfilling her destiny—of being in the right place at the right moment, and knowing all was as it was supposed to be.

Note left Sarah a thought before leaving. There will be another moment, and with it, hope.

Sarah's eyes welled, and a tear rolled down her trembling cheek.

Note left Sarah and moved away from the Gent into the darkness.

In Between

Note appreciated that when life is revered, all life is equal and immeasurable.

Note experienced the grandeur of much of this remarkable Universe and was always impacted by the awe living beings felt for many things other than themselves. Note would be part of an epiphany.

Chapter Twenty-Three

Neutron Star

Note joined Cai as she felt the bright sunshine on her face. Her eyes were closed while her youthful face supported a grin on her delicate-looking cheekbone. "I just love this, Grandpa."

"I'm happy to see you rest after your swim, Cai." Cai felt peace in the water and had spent an hour swimming meditatively in the spring. "I used to have energy like that, and I can very much identify with your love of the water," her Grandpa Quan Lieu contributed. "Life as a fish would not be a bad thing if you didn't have to worry about staying alive."

"You seem to like to dine on them, Grandpa," Cai teased.

"Details, details." Getting comfortable next to Cai on the big rock, Quan asked, "How was school this week?"

"It rocked, it just rocked!"

"You aren't always this excited about school. What made this week different?"

"I got my mind blown away. Got rid of every cobweb, Grandpa!"

"Got rid of every cobweb? What in the world?"

"No, what out of the world? We studied neutron stars."

"You're kidding!"

"No, I'm not kidding. Can I share?"

"Please do!"

"Well, I just have some facts that astound me, Grandpa. For instance, if you held a normal-sized matchbox full of neutron star stuff, it would weigh three billion tons."

"Oh, my word, child!"

"Our Sun is around 6000 kelvin, so pretty hot. A neutron star is around 600,000 kelvin, real hot. They spin fast, too. We found one that turns over 700 times a second, and it's 8 miles across. Their gravity is insane, almost 200 trillion times that of Earth. If an object were to fall from a height of one meter on a neutron star 12 kilometers in radius, it would reach the ground at around 1400 kilometers per second."

"That is impressive, Cai. So, what do you think about all that?"

"I feel small and insignificant when I think about it, Grandpa. I mean, here we are, laying on the ground, looking up into a blue sky with some nice clouds on a minor planet orbiting around a pretty awesome sun. But all of this is a fraction of something like a neutron star."

"I take it you're impressed and amazed by all the other awe-inspiring conditions in the Universe. Is that right? I know you love and are attracted to science. I appreciate that space is your jelly roll."

"What, jelly roll? What does that mean?"

"I don't know, Cai, just trying to be cool here."

She giggled her sweet little giggle. "You're plenty cool, Grandpa, real cool!"

"Thanks, Baby Girl!" Quan loved to call her that. She was dear to him.

"Yes, I love space. Everything we've discovered, and that's just a fraction of what's there, is awe-inspiring to me. There are amazing places on the Earth too, like the deep sea, just over the top," she shared.

"More awesome than you, right?"

"Heck yeah. But I'm okay with that. We all have a part, our own minor part."

"Yes, we do, but I would like to ask a couple of other questions if I may?"

"Sure, if the questions are Grandpa questions."

"That's fair, Cai. Okay, what was your favorite part about your swim in the spring this morning?"

"There was this one time when I was out in the middle all by myself, floating on the top. I was concentrating on taking deep breaths to buoy me up and then felt the water coming up around me as I exhaled. Then, I just wanted to let my body fall into the water beneath the surface. I took some exaggerated breaths and then exhaled all I could. I slowly sank below the surface and started drifting down toward the bottom. I felt the coolness of the water around me and felt so safe. I kept my eyes open and saw the sun coming through the top of the tranquil water. I felt my heartbeat and my life; I felt strong. I don't know when I've felt so relaxed, Grandpa, so safe, so happy. I needed to come up for air, but I'll probably always remember that moment and especially because you asked me about it, and I shared it with you."

"It sounds beautiful," he said. "Let me ask you, could a neutron star experience all that?"

"No."

"Could it feel what you felt?"

"No."

"They don't have a brain, do they?" Quan asked.

"No, no brain, Grandpa."

"Feelings, do they have feelings?"

"No, no feelings."

"But they are insanely hot, have immense gravity and spin like the dickens, don't they, Sweetie? And they are on the heavy side like no one's business too. Am I right?"

"Yes, they are those things. I get the point you're making Grandpa, and I think I like it."

"Glad to hear it. We're as amazing in this Universe as a neutron star, but different. That water bug over there, enjoying the heat of the sun on that rock, can do and be things a neutron star can't do, and be something that spinner can't be. I just want you to know what a treasure you are, Cai."

"It's all a treasure, Grandpa, Jelly Roll." Note left Cai.

In Between

Note basked in Grandpa's message to Cai. Life is more than remarkable.

Note would next find a question about the value of life.

Chapter Twenty-Four

Virus

Note joined Enzokuhle in Cape Town, South Africa, on May 5th, 2020, on Earth. At the moment Note joined her, the Coronavirus worldwide infected 3,173,442 people; 220,141 had already succumbed to the disease. 60,424 were in critical condition. South Africa's share of this stood at 7,220 confirmed cases, with 138 reported deaths.

The economy was substantially closed on March 27th and began a gradual and planned reopening. Enzokuhle sat on the sands of Camps Bay beach with her boyfriend, Ndlovu, talking about the future. They spoke through face masks and guarded the surrounding space.

"It feels good to be out in the sunshine, Enzo. I don't even mind getting all this sand on my skin. I may leave it on."

"No, you won't, Ndlovu. You know how hard it is to get it out of the apartment once we track it in," she said.

"Maybe it would kill the virus. What if beach sand is the vaccine for it?"

"Wouldn't be good for the syringe industry, Ndlovu. You're right about the sunshine. I have music in my head too. I just feel delighted right now to be here with you. Thanks for being my person."

"I'm the lucky one, Enzo! Are you saying you're not afraid of this virus now?"

"I'm not afraid at this moment," she answered. "I don't know what's coming, though, and I'm sure that will scare me later when we aren't out here in paradise."

"We don't have to talk about it, Enzo, right now."

"Honestly, I want to talk about it. I don't want to pretend it isn't real for us. We both have parents and grandparents that are prime targets for it. You know my professor's wife died of it. It's real, and I feel better confronting it than hiding from it."

Ndlovu laughed.

"Why are you laughing?"

"Because you say you don't want to hide from it while you are sitting here on a beautiful beach with a face mask. It's just the optics that are funny. Sorry."

She chuckled too. "Yes, your mask is making you sweat. I love that about you."

"That I sweat, or that I sit on an awesome beach with a face mask and sweat?"

"All of it, silly. You taste salty after you sweat. I like that too," she said with a smile he could hear but couldn't see.

"Mmm. That reminds me of what I enjoyed for dinner over at Nkosi's place yesterday while we worked on his political science project. I help him; he helps me," Ndlovu shared.

"Okay, share, what was it?" she asked.

"Cape Malay curry. Need I say more?"

"Hell no. I'm hungry."

"We just got here, Enzokuhle."

"I know. I'll be patient," she agreed. "And I have this music in my head. Did you and Nkosi talk about the virus? What does he say about it?"

"His uncle is in the US, and he talked to him last Friday. They are a rich country, and the hit on their economy is dire. They've had over 60,000 deaths as of last Friday. Their scientists expect that to double in the next couple of months. The question all over the world is, do they try to bring the economy back at the expense of human life, or do they protect human life and risk potentially catastrophic economic consequences that may cost lives? I've heard some argue that this virus is just pruning the weak branches of the tree."

"What? What a cold thought; those are human lives we are talking about," Enzokuhle implored.

"I agree!"

She added, "Those weak branches on the tree are weak because of the neglect of society. Most of the deaths are among the poor, or peoples in communities that are those left out. I heard, for example, that hypertension is a factor that can significantly increase your chances of dying from the virus. People with money or healthcare can get treatment for hypertension, so it's not a risk factor for them. We all know it. Those that 'have' do okay, and those that 'have not' are more likely to suffer and die.

"I get where some would see that like pruning a tree, but the tree wouldn't have all those weak limbs if society took care of the entire tree, and not just some of the parts."

Ndlovu responded, "I'm hot, sweaty, sandy, still have a full tummy from last night, and am intrigued with your train of thought, Enzo. Can you build another picture for me?"

Enzokuhle stared at him with a stern look over her mask. Her tummy was growling now, and he was not helpful. He knew he was in trouble. Then she responded.

"Think of your body Ndlovu, the full one. You're right-handed. So, imagine you get this big gash in your left arm, and it bleeds. Slowly at first, but then the blood comes out a little faster. Your right arm is okay, so if the left arm is bleeding, no big deal. Your foot doesn't care. Your brain might even think, you know, I am right-handed, and my right arm is okay, and my feet are good so I can walk anywhere I want. My left arm, well, it may be okay, but it will have to fend for itself.

"The problem with that is if the left arm keeps bleeding, the entire body will get sick and may die. We must take care of the entire body. The poor, weak, and disadvantaged are all a part of our body. You can over prune a tree too and lessen its future dramatically."

"I get it, Enzo. That ties into what Nkosi was working on his project. The project is about capitalism and how it should work during a pandemic. The premise is that the weaker businesses may give way, which is an opportunity for the more substantial companies to buy them or replace them in the market. In pure capitalism, there is a benefit to the one that builds a better mousetrap, earning the right to do so. That means the consumer will always have better mousetraps to buy.

"So, the question is, when the pressures to fail come from an unrelated cause, like the virus, should society come to their rescue? These questions are never easy, Enzo."

"I think it depends if you take the long view or the brief view. I am no economist, Ndlovu, but I believe the markets will determine the value of each product. If someone wants an inferior product because they like the color better, it will be the winner in the buying decision. I believe we must take care of the whole, in the long view, and that means all its parts. If we leave anyone out, it could be the end of us all. We have to be 'all in,'" she concluded.

"Then what do you think the answer is to today's question? Given that we already forget parts of society, and they are the most susceptible to the virus, do we protect human life at the expense of our economies or protect our way of life at the expense of life?"

"Life is always the choice to make, Ndlovu. A life that is cherished and promoted and protected will buy more stuff. It's a win all the way around for every party. As for this moment, the world needs to come together and build great tests that work and produce billions of them and test the bejeebers out of us. If we are clear, we can go to work or to a restaurant or get on a plane. It would be a lot cheaper than the economic devastation we have today. We may get the vaccine too. Oh, my!"

"What, Enzo?"

"The beautiful music in my mind just stopped. That makes me sad! I have something to add to what I said, however, and I feel it strongly."

Ndlovu witnessed a rare seriousness in Enzokuhle's voice; she continued.

"If we don't cherish life, we won't have it. And we need to connect. Every life is our life."

"That is powerful, Enzokuhle; it is!"

"The music is back...yay. I just hope the scientists get the vaccine soon."

"I know," Ndlovu said. "We may be sitting on that, right?"

Note left Enzokuhle.

In Between

Note provided the essence of Enzokuhule's message: if we don't cherish life, we won't have it. Note considered it to be profound.

Note would next experience the ultimate trust of forces within life.

Chapter Twenty-Five

Forces

It was early morning. The air was humid, smelling of forest dew. Kai was preparing for his dive with his dive buddy, Johnny Molen, and felt blessed with having his family with them.

"Johnny, can you look to confirm my BC looks okay to you?"

"Will do, Kai," Johnny answered.

"Daddy, what's a BC?" Kai's little girl, Angeni, asked.

Kai responded, "You're just the cutest. Thanks for being here with Mom and Jake today; it's a rare treat to have all of you here before one of my dives."

"What is a BC, Daddy?" she asked again.

"It's a buoyancy compensator, Sweetie."

"What's a boyke compator, Daddy?"

Smiling, Kai responded, "Well, little Angeni, it's like a balloon underwater, kind of. When Daddy puts on all these heavy tanks you see, I get very heavy. When I get in the water with all that heavy stuff, this BC blows up a bag with air to help Daddy, well, not sink too fast. It makes Daddy kind of like a boat."

"More like a submarine," Kai's wife, Ginger, said to Angeni.

"Mommy, what's a submean?"

"Come over here, Baby, so Daddy can get ready to go in the water."

"BC looks good, Kai; you soaked it after Cancun, right?" Johnny asked.

"Duh, let me check yours. How's your dive computer, Johnny? Did you charge it this time?"

"Yes, we aren't doing a shipwreck here, Kai. Yes, it's charged. I also broke in my new regulator. I'm ready here."

"Good. I feel a little funny about this one," Kai admitted.

"Kai!" Ginger called out.

Ginger was his life, love, and soul mate. She had long, flowing golden hair and an unusually kind and soft voice, masking her fiery passion for life.

"What do you mean, you feel funny about this one? You've never said that around me before."

"I think it's the coffee this morning along with all the fruit we ate for breakfast. I do feel funny, but I'm sure it's my digestion, really, Baby."

"You know I hate it when you use a rebreather!" Ginger pressed.

"I know. This is my last dive this year, I promise. We need the money, and this equipment is the best money can buy. I'm safe with this."

Their son Jake joined in the conversation.

"Pop, what does a rebreather do?"

"Mostly, a rebreather absorbs the carbon dioxide of a diver's exhaled breath to permit the rebreathing of the oxygen content. It adds oxygen to replenish the amount I metabolize. With regular tanks in shallow water, I'm using an open circuit breathing apparatus, where the exhaled gas gets discharged directly into the water."

Jake asked, "What happens if the carbon dioxide isn't absorbed?"

"Well, I can't imagine enough carbon dioxide up here to do this, but down there if the rebreather doesn't remove the carbon dioxide, I would quickly have mild respiratory distress, which could develop into further stages of carbon dioxide toxicity. Son, if you were to rebreathe your exhaled gas directly, you would soon feel an acute sense of suffocation. Does that make sense?

"That sounds scary, Pop."

"The rebreathers are good to go, Kai," Johnny stated.

"Yes, confirmed," Kai agreed.

"Pop?"

"Yes, Son."

"One more question for you, one I've long wanted to ask you."

"Sure."

"Well, why do you do it? I mean, you have Mom and Angeni and me; we live a good life. I know you have fun with your friends. Why do you risk it all by doing what you do? You are going down there to find Mr. Peter, right?"

"Yes," Kai answered sadly.

"He lost everything, right?"

"Yes, he did, Son."

"Then, today, you could lose everything, us, your friends, next Christmas, rhubarb crisp, everything. Why is doing what you do more important than all the rest?"

"Are you angry with me, Jake? Is that why you ask that question?"

"Maybe Pop. I feel a little mad. Kind of like you don't really care about us much, or you wouldn't take this risk. I love you and I know, well, I know we need you around. I want to understand why?"

The rest of the family and Johnny all got silent, surprised at Jake's honesty.

"You know, Son, you might catch some folks off guard with that question, not that you mean to, but it's a sincere and well, pertinent question. Me, to be honest, I've spent many hours when I'm decompressing thinking about the very thing you ask. Peter is not my first friend lost, and each person has left a family behind. None as wonderful as mine, however," he said with a loving smile. "Here is the answer I've come up with—your mom has already heard it—but I'm glad to share it with you, Jake. I'm driven to do what I do, and I believe in my heart and soul that each dive I make is like a step on a path toward a higher place, something bigger than me. So, this dive is one more step. Now, what that place is, I don't know. Does that make sense?"

"Yes, Pop. We live a long time, or most of us do, and that's many steps toward that higher place—many through insane situations toward something bigger than us. What do you concentrate on Dad, during all those steps you take?"

"For me, Jake, honor. I try to take each step with honor. For me, that helps me connect with that bigger-than-us thing until I get there. I know it's different from others. For them, it may be kindness or integrity or passion, I don't know, but for me, it's honor. I think that's why they called me to get Pete. Does my answer resonate with you, Jake?"

"It does, Pop. We should talk more. I want to understand what honor means to you."

"Damn right we should, Son, and let's make sure we do after I get back."

"Can I help you get your gear to the water, Pop?"

Smiling, Kai answered, "Yes, many thanks! I'm feeling the love."

Kai started his descent along a guide rope that was deployed with a heavy weight to the bottom of the 400-foot deep hole. The helium/oxygen gas, Heliox, was easy to breathe, and Kai's suit insulation was working well, keeping him warm as the temperature dropped around him; at the same time, his vulnerability to the cold increased as he took deep breaths with helium in the mixture. The light above soon faded as Kai dropped steadily downward. Kai knew to concentrate on taking long, slow breaths to allow the rebreather to clear the carbon dioxide. That was his top priority down here. Kai slowed his descent and spotted the bottom coming up using his lamp. He increased his buoyancy to steady himself at the depth he reached.

In this dark environment, Kai was careful to stay some 10 feet off the bottom to keep from stirring up the silt. Visibility was good here, and Kai started looking around the bottom for Pete's remains. The hole was almost perfectly circular and measured some 800 feet across, so Kai knew he had a limited space to search and that his diving buddy, Johnny, would join him soon.

After 15 minutes passed, Johnny entered the water and started his descent. At about 100 feet, his rebreather failed, and he immediately switched his bailout valve to the open circuit system. Both Johnny and Kai were equipped with an independent open-circuit system to back up their rebreathers should they fail as Johnny's just did. The separate system required the divers to dive with extra heavy and cumbersome cylinders, but the hardship afforded them greater safety in the event of a rebreather failure while providing more gas if needed for the ascent from deep dives like this one.

Since he was on the dive as a backup, Johnny decided not to join his buddy at the lower depth and started his ascent procedure. Johnny and Kai had prepared earlier to communicate with each other in situations like this. Johnny pulled out a red plastic card on a ring that stated he could not join Kai and asked him to start his ascent ASAP. He opened the ring and put it around the dive rope and released it to fall gently to the bottom, remaining hooked to the dive rope.

Some minutes later, Kai passed back by the rope and saw the bright red plastic 10 feet below on the guide rope. He knew Johnny wasn't coming, and he needed to start his ascent. Having moved throughout the area, it surprised Kai that he saw no sign of Pete. His best guess was that Pete must be lost on the cave wall.

Kai's ascent would be staged with stops along the way so his body could gradually reacclimate to lesser pressure. As he rose slowly and, on each stop, Kai looked carefully through the unusually clear water to the wall of the deep abyss, looking for signs of Pete. At 275 feet, Kai's light found a dark spot on the wall. Kai decided to investigate, and after adjusting his buoyancy to equalize him, he let go of the guide rope and made his way to the darkness. As he got closer and closer to the dark spot, he realized he was getting pulled into it, and then noted how the wall around the hole was eroded and surprisingly smooth. He quickly realized the suction was more potent than he could escape.

Note joined Kai.

Kai prepared for the coming unknown. He had to focus his mind and stay calm. *Okay, I can't fight this; I have to breathe slowly and regularly. That's my number one, stay calm, and breathe. Oh my, this is getting ahold of me; I wonder if this happened to Pete. Damn it, what am I doing down here? Easy, breathe, count, protect my head. Damn it, I'm going in, protect my head and tanks, hang on to the light! HOLD ON!*

Kai got sucked into the hole in a rapid current, pulling him through an underwater cave system, out of control.

I can't see! Reach out, grab something! No, curl up in a ball, protect your limbs, No, breathe, easy, easy! Kai's thoughts raced.

Kai's light was on, but the water was full of silt, leaving no visibility. He felt that he was spinning but did not know for sure.

If I flatten out and extend myself, the water resistance will force me in one direction, the position of least resistance, do it. Oh my, what if I hit something, am I going deeper? Breathe, easy, easy.

Kai's spiritual training was crucial at this moment as it helped him calm himself, both mentally and physically. Though it had only been 20 seconds, it seemed like much longer. Thud. He felt his tanks hit the wall, and then again, and the water seemed to speed up.

I must be coming to a smaller area, increasing water speed because of the compression, I should go feet first.

Quickly, he curled up and worked to rotate, then stretched out again. It worked; he was going feet first.

It felt like a roller coaster going around a turn at high speed. Thud. His tanks hit the wall again as he rounded the corner, and his light came out of his hand.

Breathe, slow, breathe.

Thud. One of the spare tanks from his independent open-circuit system got ripped away.

Why am I here?

Suddenly, the water slowed, almost becoming still. Kai was thrown from the current around a corner and was floating in calm water, no light, cold, stunned.

I need to move up higher.

Kai was relieved to find he could still adjust his buoyancy and increased it to float up slowly in the quiet water. Soon he came to a godsend, an air pocket far below the surface along this underwater river.

Oh my God, I'm in air. There may be no oxygen; careful Kai, easy.

He reached down to get his auxiliary light off his dive belt and, turning it on, found the water to be transparent around him and a good size cavern above him, full of air. A beach was 20 feet to his right, and he swam over when he realized he could only feel one leg.

Breathe, breathe. I need to get to the beach first. Stay calm, breathe slowly, concentrate.

Kai slogged his way to the beach and pulled himself on to it. It was not a gradual beach like an ocean has, but more like a shelf next to the water. He pulled himself up and looked down at his leg. It was still there, and there were no punctures in his wet suit, so no bones were extruding.

I must know if I can breathe down here; my air won't last too much longer. Yes, that's my next step, I'll remove my mask slowly, and take a couple of breaths, put my mask back on, hold my breath a moment to see how I feel.

Kai pulled his mask off his face and took two small breaths and put his mask back over his face. Holding his breath and counting to 30, he felt okay, so he removed his mask again and exhaled in almost a gasp, taking in new air carefully. The pressure was okay for him to breathe. Another pleasant surprise.

Praise God. I can breathe. Praise God!

He raised his light to see where he was.

This is good-sized, maybe 200 feet long, 30 feet wide, ceiling average 15 feet.

He felt his knee now.

Damn it; my knee is crushed; shit. Am I bleeding internally? I could go into hypovolemic shock. Damn it. It hurts. Okay, what's first? I'm in this cave. They won't find me; I'll run out of oxygen down here. I die in 4 days, no air if I can't get out of here. I see nothing but rock and water down here, no splint, the leg will wiggle around, may pass out from the pain. I need to know if it's bleeding, but I can't get out of this diving suit in my condition. I need to cut the suit off my leg. Okay, if I do that and I go back in the water, the cold may be too much. No, must know if I'm bleeding internally, look for bruising, that's first.

Kai reached for his knife and set his light on the ledge next to his leg. He pulled his suit away from his skin and cut a slit about 6 inches long.

Oh, this hurts bad. I'm in trouble here. I'm hurt bad, I may die here, I should have listened to Jake, I wish I were with my Jake.

Kai cried as he pulled the suit open above his knee. His skin wasn't pierced, but his knee area was a deep bluish-purple that spread as far as he could see with the slit just being six inches.

Damn it. I'm bleeding internally. Do I expand the slit to see how far it goes? No, no matter, it's bad, and I need to keep my suit from getting any worse. But why, why save my dive suit? Here we go, my breathing is getting faster, feeling faint, shock may start, what now? Tourniquet that will buy me two hours, maybe. Okay, that's next, tourniquet.

Kai reached into his dive bag quickly and pulled out a dive rope.

Okay, great, slight break here, I have the rope.

He cut a length about four feet long and wrapped it around his leg, halfway between his knee and his waist. He wrapped it around his leg several times, pinching one end between the wrap and his leg, and then pulled the loose end hard before tying the ends together.

Okay, now what? Damn it. I need guidance, yes; I need the spirits.

Kai reached back into his bag and opened a hidden compartment in the bottom and pulled out two peyote buttons in a watertight container. Kai always kept these in his dive kit in case he faced death. He knew if he were in the water, he could never access them but carried them, anyway. This was grace.

Kai put them both into his mouth and chewed them up, swallowing them. He hoped that the helium in his blood, along with the stress in his system, would bring on the effects he sought more rapidly than was normal back in the spiritual dens of his native ancestors. Kai seemed at once to pass out.

The vision Kai sought began.

> "My son, sit with me."

> The fire hissed with the embers rising into the star-filled sky.

> Kai was confused at first, knowing he was on the shelf in the deep cave underwater, but at the same time, clearly with this old man next to the fire with long white hair blowing gently in the breeze.

> "Come, sit with me, boy."

> Kai sat by the fire. His left leg felt the heat of the flames, almost like it was in it, and yet, the leg was comfortable.

> "Do you know why we're here, Kai?"

> "Yes, Old Man. You're a noble spirit. I'm here to learn from you."

> "Yes."

> They sat quietly, looking into the fire.

> Kai felt a sense of urgency.

> "What can you teach me, Old Man?"

> "Good Kai, yes, you have asked me a question. That's the first step of all steps."

> "Why, Old Man, why is that the first step?"

> "You have to know what you want to ask, what you want to learn, or what

you want the one you are questioning to learn?"

"I don't understand, please, what do you mean?"

"The first part you understand, you know what you want to ask. The question wells up from your core and rises to your consciousness. It comes forth like a bubble, your question.

"The second part is more complicated. You know what you want to ask, but you must be open to what you need to learn to understand what you want to learn. At this moment, you know.

"The last is the blessing of a question. It's your submission to the truth another person may provide you. It's the service you give another to learn from their answer. In your service, you open a door in them, to find and share their truth."

"Yes, I can see that Old Man, yes, it makes sense. It's easy, isn't it?"

"It's most of the way to where you want to be, Son. You have discovered the question in yourself, you know why you have the question, you trust another and ask them for their answer, and you hear their response and determine that it answers your question."

"How is that, most of the way there, Great Spirit?" Kai asked.

"There's a saying in your memories. You can lead a horse to water, but you can't make it drink. You discovered the question, understood the need for it, asked it, and received an answer you knew deep in your core answered the question. So, what do you do with the truth? The next step is to ask yourself that question and find that answer. Once you have the answer, what do you do with it?"

"Thank you, Old Man. I know I'm in peril. I know that's why you and I are here together. The best question I can ask you is, what is the best thing I can do now to live?"

"You will always live, Son, but that's not what you are asking. The answer is you were brought to this place by a force, and that force is all there is to take you home. You must trust it, surrender to it. That's your answer!"

Kai opened his eyes to the darkness. His light had fallen off the ledge into the water.

How long was I out? What is the force the old man spoke of? Has it been over two hours? Is my leg dying?

The answers to his questions came quickly.

I was out as long as I needed to be.

The force is the current that sucked me into the hole and brought me to this cavern.

My leg is just a small part of me. I miss my family, my life, my future.

I must go back in the water, trust the force, trust the current. Here, I will die. There I may die.

He pulled out his dive computer to activate it for light. One of the earlier collisions had smashed it.

Okay, I need to stabilize my leg before I go back in. What do I have? My other leg, yes, my other leg. I won't be able to use my legs and flippers if I do that, no matter, it's all or nothing here.

Kai grabbed the unused dive rope and tied his legs together.

Which air do I use?

Stay with the Heliox, take the open circuit as armor, yes, yes.

Kai readied himself to go back in the water, attaching everything he could around his torso, neck, and head to protect them from smashing against the rocks. He burst into tears.

Thank you for this moment, Lord, for this cavern, for living. Thank you for the wondrous world and life I hope for beyond this with my family. Thank you for this life, Lord. I'm so grateful! Thank you for this music Lord in my being. It sounds like your Angels.

Kai dried his eyes and pulled his mask on tight.

I need to breathe slow, slow, and easy. I'm scared. Thank you, Lord. I'm not ready to die! Why am I here?

Kai rolled off the ledge into the icy cold water and adjusted his buoyancy to sink into the current.

I can't use my legs, oh my. There's nothing I can do now. This is it.

He felt the current coming on quickly as he dropped further down into the water and then BAM, it grabbed him. He knew he was at the mercy of this water. Would he come out a mile down in the sea and die an excruciating death? Would it be fast?

Should I breathe quickly and die now, under my control, suffocating? No. Live every second. Thank you, Lord!

***

Kai opened his eyes.

"Hi, Baby!"

He recognized the sound of his beloved Ginger.

"Ginger, is that you? Am I here? Was that a dream? How is my leg? Where am I? Where is the music coming from?"

"Yes, Baby, it's me. You came back to us after being in a coma for three months. You lost your leg, honey, but you're home. I don't hear any music but look who's here."

Angeni and Jake both reached out to give their Pop the best hug ever. They all cried together. Note left Kai.

In Between

Note was part of the greatest force and appreciated the wisdom of trusting it. Kai radiated faith.

Note appreciated the brain in living beings was the most remarkable of all creations in the Universe. Note would next gain more of an understanding of how they evolve in a lifetime.

Chapter Twenty-Six

Amazing Brain, Samantha

Mom always gets me flowers on my birthday. I can't cry while I'm putting on my eyes.

They smell delicious. I just love orchids. Thanks for Hawaii, Daddy. The road to Hana was terrific and the black beaches, heaven. The cows, all the cows. I Love You Cow. I will never outgrow you, and we'll always be together.

Cow, a stuffed animal, sat quietly on the vanity next to the mirror, watching Sam get ready for her big night. This Cow wasn't the original, but Sam didn't know. After being thrown up on when Sam was little, a new cow needed to be found on eBay. Some thirteen years later, the white patches were gray, but the black was holding up well. Cow was Sam's best friend; they talked.

Hmm, need a little more on the eyelash.

My boobs hurt. Oh yes, my friend, no cramps yet. I wish my boobs were big. Mom's aren't that full. All the boys drool over Rochelle. She scoots those babies up.

Toes, I have plenty of time. I love purple.

"Come here, Buffy. You need to go outside while I do my toes, come on."

You're wiggly and soft, Buffy. I love you. Wow, I love everything tonight. I'm delighted.

"Don't lick my face now, Buffy. I know, I know."

Oops, I shut my door a little hard.

"Sorry, Mom!"

Jeff, what a hunk, I tingle when I'm with him.

Purple Rain, I sure miss Prince. That song is deep.

Samantha turned 17 today, and she was having one of the best days of her life.

"Sam!" Amelia, her mom, was calling.

"How much time do I have, Mom? I need to do my toes." Sam looked back into the mirror.

I look good tonight. My hair is full and staying put. My eyes are extra sweet, wow, I've never noticed the golden marble in them, whoa, cool, I bet Jeff sees that. Eyes are powerful!

That whitener worked, and my red lips are highlighting these pearlies. Hot, I'm hot tonight. If my face weren't so round, oh hush.

"Okay, Sam," Amelia called out. "Ten minutes for your toes. Are you dressed?"

Sam yelled downstairs to her mom. "I dressed for dinner with you and Dad. I'll put on my good stuff after dinner."

Oh, I hear Dad driving up. I sure love my dad!

I wish my pinkie toe were straight like the others. I wonder if wearing sandals causes that. It feels so good when Jeff kisses my toes, gets me goin'. Oh, and when I get those goosebumps, yeeessss.

Okay, it looks good.

"Coming, Mom. Hi Daddy!"

"Happy Birthday, Honey!"

"Thanks, Dad!"

This carpet on the stairs is so fluffy right after it's vacuumed. I hope my nail polish is dry.

"Where is that hug, oh Dad of mine?"

I sure Love my Daddy!

Mom is coming over to stand with us, oh, and she has an envelope.

"Precious, we're so proud of you. You are a woman now and have made so many excellent decisions. Your mom and I want you to have this. Open it and then let me explain."

"Thanks, Mom and Dad!"

I hope there's more than a card, or there's a good chunk of money in here.

"Wow, I love the sentiment in the card, I do!"

Don't cry, silly.

"It's beautiful!"

Dad's reaching into his pocket. Oh boy, here it comes.

"Our treasure, Samantha. It's a symbolic key for the new car we're giving you for your birthday. We ordered it special because you are special to us. It won't be in and ready for you for another week. Sorry that it's not here tonight. We love you, Sam, with all our hearts, and you have earned this by being the magical daughter and woman that you are."

How do I act? My gosh, what a day, oh my word!

"Thank you so much Mom, Dad. I'm so happy! Tell me about the car."

"We bought you the candy apple red Chevy Volt you wanted, Baby. I know this means nothing to you, but it's one of the safest cars on the road, scoring a perfect top safety pick plus rating from the IIHS with the automatic emergency braking system."

"Oh, Daddy, you're a trip! You know—and I know—it's the Teen Driver system it comes with, giving you that report card to show how safe I'm driving. For me, Mom, Dad, it's a beautiful ride and OMG, 50 miles to the gallon, low carbon, that's what I'm talking about. Thanks so much!"

Wow, they bought me exactly what I wanted. I can't wait. It'll blow Jeff's mind.

"Okay, Sam and David, let's have dinner! Know what it is, Sammy?"

"My favorite, Mom, of course. And with those butter top rolls, my gosh, I could eat three of those things."

Sam's favorite meal, her Mom's rendition of chicken stir-fry with fresh vegetables plus fresh pineapples, smelled phenomenal, and the scent filled the air. Served over whole grain rice and with hot buttered rolls, it made for a well-balanced meal, even if it was a little heavy on the carbs.

"This is one reason I have to sacrifice some of my favorite sweets, but I love this meal," she told her Mom. *See, the word love again, what a day.*

"I feel sad about not having your cake tonight, Sammy, but I know you want it at the party on Sunday, and I respect that. Let's eat."

Mmm, so good, yummy, I need to take it easy, or I won't get into my dress.

"What did Nana have to say when she called you today?" David asked.

"Happy birthday, but she still sounds so sad, Dad. I miss Papa too, but I can't imagine what it's like for her. She said all the right things and stuff. Then she talked about how Papa used to take me to the Piggly Wiggly store with him to drop off the geraniums he raised. She told me how content I seemed afterward. I miss Papa. He made me feel full or something. He never said much with his mouth, but his kindness said so much. Was he like that when you were little, Dad?"

"Yes, your Grandpa was a simple man, but deep and rich inside. Sometimes, when I felt scared, I'd just get close to him, and it all felt better than before. I can't explain it. There was something special about your Grandpa. I know Nana is trying to find her way; that loss can never get replaced. I know we all experience significant losses in our life, but I hope I never have to go through that. Enough, it's your birthday, and you have nothing but joy and happiness to look forward to. Do you want another of your Mom's amazing rolls?"

Hell, yes, I want another roll!

"No, thanks, Daddy. I'm good. I need to get ready. Are you sure you're good with me taking your car tonight? I'll be good, I promise."

"You have always been good, Sam, and you are a skilled driver. You know to stay away from booze and dope, right?"

"Of course, Dad!"

I wish they wouldn't ask me about drinking and weed. I hate to lie to Mom and Dad, but they don't know what they're talking about.

Sam told her parents, "I may be a little late tonight. I think my friends are doing something special for me. Whatever we do, there will be a lot of girl talk too, I imagine. That was delicious, Mom!"

Amelia stated as only a mother can, "Whatever that something special is, it needs to be safe!"

"Mom, I know!" Sam responded with her youthful passion.

Okay, I'll get dressed and see Jeff while he's on his break at 8:00 for a few minutes before I meet the girls.

Sam left the table to get her dress on.

"David," Amelia said once Sam was out of earshot, "I just want to tell you how happy I am. This has been such a wonderful day, and our life is more than I could've ever hoped for. Sam, well, she is such a joy; she turned out so well. As her mom, I'm—well—almost relieved that she has made it to this point and has such a bright future. Thank you, Love."

Sam finished dressing.

Wow, I look hot. Jeff will have to put his hat down in his lap when he sees me.

She giggled.

Running downstairs, she gave her daddy a big hug, and David handed her the keys. "Be safe, Sam, and happy birthday again. I love you so much."

"I love you too, Daddy. Where's Mom? I have to go."

"She's in the shower. I'll give her your love. Don't forget your coat. It's icy cold out there."

"Thanks, Dad!"

Sam grabbed her coat and shot out the door.

***

Note joined Amelia as she began her visit with adolescents' parents in the room. Amelia felt expanded immediately and attributed it to her adrenaline rush. She had just one hour with this group and could only hit on the chief points in that time. Class interaction was also needed here to make certain Amelia's information was hitting the mark.

"Good morning, everyone!" Amelia introduced herself and then proceeded.

"Allow me to set the stage. Knowledge is power and for parents, it's the power to guide, protect, motivate and sometimes save our precious children. This information provides knowledge. Please, take it in, it will make a better world."

"Sam, that's what we called her, short for Samantha, my dear Samantha, seemed grown up. She was an inch taller than I am and mentally sharper. Her memory was astounding. She knew how to work me, which gave me the impression that she was more mature than she was.

"We're here to talk about 'The Human Brain,' and most especially the state of the human brain during adolescence and the teenage years. Most of the information

I'll share today, along with my thoughts, is based on a brilliant book, one of my meaningful favorites, <u>The Teenage Brain</u> by Frances E. Jensen, MD, with Amy Ellis Nutt. We're giving each of you a copy of it to help you, your families, and friends to better understand and respect this prolific partner in our lives, our brains.

"I've met with several groups of parents over time and discovered right away that the needs of each group are different; we all have different kids. With that in mind, I hope you ask questions to make sure this time benefits you.

"First, there is a critical message in our conversation today, and I hope it's the thing you best remember. The most vital part of the human brain—the place where actions are weighed, situations judged, and decisions made, is right behind the forehead, in the frontal lobes. It is the last part of the brain to develop. *You* need to be your teen's frontal lobes until their brains are fully wired and hooked up and ready to go on their own. I can't stress that enough."[27]

"Amelia?"

"Yes."

"I'm Donna Kantan. You asked us to take part, may I?"

"Yes, please, Donna."

"Thank you. For me, I've found that few things are, well, random. Why are you here, doing this?"

Amelia stood quietly, looking back at her. Donna attempted to establish eye contact. *That is unusual,* Amelia thought.

"I'm glad you asked. It's an outstanding first question. It makes sense for you to want to know why I'm here, what motivates me to share this information.

"I'm here to earn my life. I failed my daughter, or at least feel like I did. I lost her. I could have known the information I'm sharing today, but I didn't. I could have done more to parent her through her teenage years, and I didn't. I could have been her frontal lobes, but I wasn't. She would be more for this world than I am, and her loss is significant.

"I can't take her place; I can't fill that big of a void. What I can do is attempt to help you help yourself, your friends, and your family. In doing so, I may earn this life I have." Amelia's voice quivered.

"Thank you, Amelia."

"Thank you for asking, Donna. I'm so glad you're here. May I pose the same question to you?"

"I don't know why I'm here yet, Amelia. I just know I need to be."

"Good enough."

Amelia proceeded. "It's important to remember that it takes a long time for the brain to mature, some 25 years. If you have a teen, like my Sam, you may feel you're living in an alternate Universe. Your kids are evolving, and each day is a new day for them. Each situation they have might be the first time they've experienced it. Drama is usually intense, right?

"Most of this is neurologically, psychologically, and physiologically explainable. Adolescence is a minefield. One of the biggest players early is hormones, and when hormones kicked in for my Sam, it didn't occur to me she was experiencing them for the first time. Her brain hadn't figured out how to modulate that new influx of chemicals. The outside world didn't change, but her point of view did. Let me share my interpretation of what Dr. Jensen writes on pages 20 and 21 of her book.

"Dr. Jensen notes that testosterone, estrogen, and progesterone activate physical changes in teens we're all familiar with...deeper voices and peach fuzz on our boys' faces, and girls having their first periods and growing breasts. These hormones are there even when our kids are young; however, things change radically once they hit puberty. Hormonal swings affect the part of the brain that controls mood; we've all experienced how our daughters can be happy and carefree one minute and upset and withdrawn the next.

"In boys, it's the testosterone. Dr. Jensen talks about how it impacts the amygdala, which is the part of the brain that controls the 'fight-or-flight' response, or aggression and fear. These hormones are incredibly busy in the emotional heart of the brain. Our kids have to get through their young lives with a supercharged 'stimulus-seeking brain' that's not quite able to make fully-informed, rational decisions along the way. The outcome is not always good.[28]

"Let's stop there for a moment. Does anyone have a question or thought to share?"

"Amelia?" Shelly raised her hand and Amelia quickly found her name tag.

"Hi Shelly, yes, what's on your mind?"

"Thank you. During the Covid-19 pandemic, my son went with his friends to a party on the beaches of Florida. He's a brilliant young man, and his friends are as sharp as many adults I know. One of them brought the virus back to their household. His grandmother lived with them. It was not a good outcome. Why are they so reckless?"

"I'm sorry to hear about the loss. There was way too much of that. It seems reckless, easy to call it crazy, but it isn't foolish to them. This is a significant question, Shelly. Our adolescents have to spread their wings to learn to fly so they can get to their own life. They learn by mistakes, and their experiential behavior helps them establish autonomy.

"The issue, once again, is that their frontal lobe isn't fully developed, so they have trouble connecting the dots. Being unable to connect the dots as much as needed, they don't appreciate the real consequences of their actions. On top of that, teen brains experience more reward than adult brains. Without the ability to fully calculate the costs of an action, the reward can lead them down a risky path.

"Now, I want to add to that information. This behavior can form habits that can take us into adulthood. What's your son's first name, Shelly?"

"Saul."

"As I see it, Shelly, Saul is motivated by the thought of, and accumulation of reward. He could expect a rewarding experience at the beach and didn't connect the dots to understand the risk. Even if he did, he would still lean toward the rewarding experience at the beach.

"I believe most of us, and certainly our teens today, seek instant gratification and look at things fairly short-term. The answer is for us to find something in the big picture that rewards us 'even more.' Such an item may take the place of short-term reckless behavior."

"Like what, Amelia?" Shelly asked.

"Has anyone here motivated your adolescent by communicating a reward effectively?" Amelia reached out to the class for an answer.

Meredith raised her hand.

"Thank you," Amelia stated, "please go ahead."

"Thank you, Amelia, Shelly. I have a college student who's a musical theater major. They may fantasize about being on stage in front of a crowd that's clapping for them. They probably even think of a fan crying because they're overwhelmed by the performance. I've entertained fantasies like that over something in my past, I know. It's good old-fashioned dreaming.

"Where Covid-19 was concerned, they determined that one impact on someone who endured a severe case of the disease was decreased lung capacity, long-term. For my music major daughter, getting dopamine releases from the fantasy of performing and getting adulation, reduced lung capacity is a real downer and something to avoid. The path to the admiration in her fantasies is staying away from the virus."

"Thank you, Meredith. I like how you're helping your daughter to help herself think through the risks," Amelia said.

"Shelly, just one more thought comes to mind. Part of being the frontal lobe for your teen is to be someone they listen to. Pick your spots. Knowing they want reward despite the associated risk, you can help them find long-term visions or paths that consistently reward them."

"Yes, I understand. Thank you, Amelia."

"Other questions?"

John raised his hand, and Amelia spied his name tag.

"Yes, John."

"Thank you, Amelia. I'm here with my amazing wife, Suzette. She is a psychologist; I'm a mechanical engineer. I'm most interested in the physical aspects of the brain. What can you share?"

"Thank you, John. Because of our short time together, let me share one aspect. It's the most exciting quality of the brain to me. The current term for it is plasticity, which describes how a brain is physically changed by experience; it's moldable like plastic.

"In her book, Dr. Jensen talks about how Harvard scientists David Hubel and Torsten Wiesel showed that if baby kittens were reared with a patch on one eye during the equivalent of their childhood years, they would live the rest of their lives being unable to see out of the eye that got patched. They also observed that the open eye's connections had partially taken over the brain area devoted to the patched eye.[29]

"This shows how our brain develops around how it gets used, and most of that occurs early in our development. Please consider that. Our brain develops based on the stimuli it gets during development.

"We humans and all observable organisms, as far as we can tell, live on the proverbial surface of our existence. From some point during gestation and each moment after, our minds experience, react and respond to stimuli. Our brains build a platform around those stimuli, and our senses spend most of the rest of our human existence engulfed with stimulus. What's underneath that surface of experience?

"Thank you for the question, John," Amelia said.

"Let's get back to our teens. Allow me to ask all of you an additional question. How do we convey all we know and have learned to a mind that has never seen what we've seen or been through what we have experienced?"

There were no responses, though the class energy felt engaged.

"Okay," Amelia interjected to keep the conversation moving, "the quick answer is to be clear and make sure they hear and understand what you're saying. Keep it simple, making it easier for your youngsters to organize and consider the message and communicate on their terms. Be proactive.

"Dr. Jensen suggests that we have to keeping sharing stories and consequences with our kids, again and again. That repetition is necessary because their frontal lobes are not yet fully developed, meaning their 'prospective memory' isn't quite there yet. Simply put, as adults, we can make a mental note about something important and we'll later follow through with that intention. Our kids? Not so much."[30]

Amelia looked out over the group. Her eyes landed on Don, perhaps because of his well pressed and bright red button-down long sleeve shirt, and she needed to ask him a question.

"Hi, Don."

"Hi, Amelia," he replied.

"I want to get a read on what we're conveying and what you're hearing. Can I ask you to tell me what you are taking away so far?"

"Happy to answer, Amelia. Our valuable teens are missing something. They're missing a full brain where actions are weighed, situations judged, and decisions made. The dots aren't connected, and the dots keep on coming. Oh, and their brains are supercharged during these times with enhanced abilities to learn and consider abstract thoughts. A challenging combination for our dear children."

"Yes, thank you, Don," Amelia said with gratitude. "If I can add, the reality, too, is what is clear to you and me is not apparent to our teens. Our assumption that they can function as we expect isn't reasonable. The stress that we add to their lives because of our expectations hinders and can derail them.

"I wish I had known what I know now when Sam was alive. I feel confident we could have been better parents and partners with her to help her through the perils that exist for our young angels." Amelia looked out over the group and took a moment to look at each person and make eye contact if she could. "Questions?"

"Hi, Amelia," Ted spoke up.

"Hi, I'm sorry, I can't see your name."

"It's Ted."

"Thank you, Ted. What's your question?"

"I was a drunk teen and am lucky to be here. Can you speak to teens and alcohol?"

"I can, Ted, and it's personal to me too. Each year in the United States, approximately five thousand people under the age of 21 die because of drinking. My daughter was one of those. Please allow me to share my impression of Dr. Jensen's thoughts from pages 129 through 137 in her remarkable book.

"When I drink too much wine, I get sleepy, and I can feel my senses dulling. But, as Dr. Jensen describes it, teenagers don't have as many GABA neurotransmitters, and that means they don't feel the effects of alcohol in the same way adults do. Since they don't feel impaired, they can be more likely to drink more, and they may also think they're fine to drive or function in other 'normal' ways.

"Sadly, the effects to the teenage brain are not just short term. According to Dr. Jensen, alcohol use in teenagers can alter and damage cognition, behavior, and emotions for the rest of their lives. So, alcohol and other drug use in young people can have permanent, life-altering effects.

"I know you know this, Ted, but kids drink for many reasons. Peer pressure, the example of their parents, the buzz. I believe alcohol is a poison we take in that impairs one of the most amazing organs in the Universe, and it does so permanently to some extent. If we hit someone upside the head with a board, we can expect a damaged brain to result. I don't know why it's any less obvious when we drink poison. There's that gratification thing.

"My recommendation is to impress, lovingly, how wonderful life is long term with a fully functioning, magnificent brain. Give them examples. Talk about Christmas; we all love that. How cool to have more Christmases and know what's going on? Have them read Dr. Jensen's book on their brain. Reward them for doing that. Talk about each chapter with them. It may make a real difference. Knowledge is power for them too, big time. Thank you, Ted."

Throughout the hour, Amelia covered topics around learning, tobacco, pot, hard-core drugs, mental illness, sports and concussions, and crime and punishment. With only a short time remaining, Amelia asked for the last question and Raquel asked it.

"Okay, good, I see Raquel on your badge, is that right?"

"Yes, I'm Raquel; thank you, Amelia."

"Glad you're here. What's your question or comment, Raquel?"

"What can you tell us about depression?" she asked.

"Depression, yes, meaningful," Amelia responded.

Looking around the room, Amelia sensed this was a safe place. These were good people, nurturing good people.

"Can you share some context, Raquel?"

Scanning the room slowly and then back to Amelia, she took a deep breath and then started speaking.

"I'm an artist, but I don't paint right now. My brother committed suicide last summer, and I just can't paint. Like you, I didn't come here today to help myself but to make up for not being there when Tony needed me, when I could have helped."

"Do you feel depressed, Raquel?" Amelia asked compassionately.

"I don't know. I want to know, I want to care again, but I don't know," Raquel answered.

"I hope you're working with your doctor, Raquel. If you're depressed, I know that place," Amelia confided.

She continued. "I was thirteen years old, just figuring things out, or at least as much as I could at thirteen. I was getting curvy and had been having periods for about a year. Boys were looking at me."

"I lived with my dad. He and my mom had a rough time of it and split up. She battled alcoholism. My mom took me every other weekend, and they alternated holidays. What a trip for a kid in the first place, I mean, right?"

Amelia's face changed, and she looked down.

"It was a Saturday afternoon, and my mom was drunk and locked in the bedroom. To make a long story short, my mom's boyfriend was feeling a little frisky and decided I might be a good time. He raped me. He went to jail, but I never took my destroyed psyche over to my mom's again.

"Feelings, crushed. Confidence, shattered. Innocence, gone. Hope, where?"

Amelia's comments impacted her audience.

"A window into my soul, I never felt like enough after that. To be overpowered and emotionally crushed the way I was, I just felt worthless, because if I'd been worth anything, that couldn't have happened to me. When I lost my Sam, all of that came back. How could she be lost to the world if her mommy was enough?

"Sounds hopeless, I know, but I found the path to wholeness and being enough.

"Let's talk about what you feel, and what it would look like if it's depression, Raquel.

"Depression, as I know, comes from a place of hopelessness. Hopelessness comes from a broken space. It can be our sense of self that's broken, our understanding of well-being. The picture of the world might be all wrong. It can be one or any of these and several other things too. The moments where these stresses are born alter our brain and do so with some permanence. We impact ourselves with chemicals, choices, and accidents too.

"So, what is the answer for us, Raquel? What is the answer to all the broken lives? Well, it's the same for the broken and the unbroken.

"First, we have to appreciate and remember this organ in our head that allows us both to live and experience this life. Think of a rosebush. If you take a seed and put it in good soil with the right hydration, making sure it gets life-giving sunshine, you will get a little rosebush. If you continue to nurture it and care for it, making sure it gets the proper nutrition and water along with controlling the environment to protect it from harm, it'll grow to be a mighty and delightful rosebush. It'll be all it can be.

"If you neglect it and abuse it, subjecting it to a challenging environment, and maybe water it with gasoline, the rosebush will not do well at all. If it lives, it'll be stunted and crippled.

"Remember that. It's Life 101. Do good, and good will result.

"Second, and equally profound, we each have the Universe between our ears in one of the miracles of this Universe. Its complexity and capabilities may never be fully understood, and you have it right there, behind your forehead. And so does everyone else.

"Reverence for life, for the living, that's the answer. And you are one of the living, as am I, and in that we share something profoundly beautiful. There's nothing but hope in this place. Join me here. I love you, Raquel, and you are enough."

Amelia soon after told her goodbyes to the class.

***

Back to Sam's birthday night, sometime earlier.

Sam and Jeff parked in the lot. Jeff jumped out of his aged Malibu, opening the back door to grab the bag of goodies. Sam didn't let Jeff drive her dad's car, and he liked to drive.

"Damn, it's cold...damn," Jeff said briskly.

Sam wrapped her coat tightly around herself and secured her fake fur hood over her head and around her face.

"We're crazy to be out here tonight, Baby," Sam told her beau. "I didn't dress for this. It's my birthday, Jeff, and I don't really want to freeze my ass off out here."

"We'll have a big fire; it'll be great, Honey," Jeff responded.

Using a LED flashlight, Sam and Jeff worked their way briskly down toward the lakeshore. They had a secret place where they would meet their friends from time to time; they diverted from the main path to a much less traveled one. Jeff knew it well, and Sam trusted him to get them to their friends. After about 20 minutes, they both saw a glow ahead and knew warmth was coming up soon.

"Jeff, Sammie, you made it. Where the hell have you been?" Judith blurted.

"Birthday dinner with the folks, you know."

"Happy birthday, Sammie," Ryan said as he readied a place for the couple to sit. "What's in the bag?"

"Jack Daniels—three of them—and chips, kettle chips, lightly salted. Yummy," Ryan responded to Jeff. "Judith and I did some Ecstasy when we parked. She's feeling good."

"Yes, I am," Judith said, smiling. "Even the cold feels good."

Over the next two hours, Jeff, Sam, and their friends drank and ate and tripped. Jeff drank heavily and passed out.

"I hate when he does that," Sam told her friends, though none of them heard her. Twenty minutes passed as Sam's anger grew; she got intoxicated too. "I'm getting the fuck out of here," Sam blurted out.

"Hey Sam, that's not a good idea. Jeff will be back soon; did you shake him?" Ryan asked.

"To hell with him. I'm going back to the car. It's colder than crap out here, even with this fire."

"Do you know your way back to the parking lot, Sammie? It's almost a mile. Why don't you wait for Jeff?" Ryan cared and showed it. If he'd been able, he would have helped Sam.

"Hey Jeff," Ryan yelled out, kicking his foot from where he was sitting.

No response.

"He'll wake up soon, Sammie; why don't you wait for him?"

"To hell with him. I'm out of here."

Ryan moved to get up, but then Judith grabbed his arm.

"She knows her way back. Stay with me."

"I wish you'd wait for Jeff, Sam," Ryan said as he sat back down.

"I'll see you guys later."

Sam got up and made her way back into the woods. It was close to the right place, but not the right place. Sam walked for two hours and decided she was lost. She reached into her purse and pulled out her phone and called her daddy's phone.

"Damn, no signal. Damn."

The cold was affecting Sam, and she knew her cute coat wasn't warm enough for this kind of cold. Tired and freezing, she found a rock to sit on. Sammie sat down and looked up at the full moon and dark sky full of stars.

"I've never seen this many stars. I know it's a lot colder out there than it is here. I miss my dad; I wish he were here."

Sam decided to take a quick nap before she started her journey again. She knew the sun would come up in a few hours, and everything would be all right.

Right before she died in the cold, she opened her eyes and turned her head to find the moon that had moved partially across the sky. Finding it, she took a deep breath. Her eyes watered.

"Daddy.

"Daddy!"

Samantha went to sleep for the last time.

***

David tucked Amelia in as he did every night, turning off her bedside light, and handing the tooth guard to her. She smiled as she took it and put it in her mouth. He leaned over to kiss her and then made his way around the bed to lie down next to her.

Laying side by side, their naked bodies against each other, she rolled over and put her head on his shoulder.

"Baby," David said, "I'm so sorry, I forgot to ask you how your talk to the class went today. How did it go?"

A tear fell on his chest.

"Every day I get to spend talking and thinking about and remembering our precious baby is a good day. It was a good day, Darling. I have kind of a crazy question for you. I don't know where it's coming from, but here it is. What's your favorite word at this moment?"

David grinned in the dark, and his answer was quick and sure.

"Compassion."

They quickly fell asleep with Amelia's head still on David's shoulder.

Note left Amelia.

In Between

Note experienced inspiration around brain plasticity after recognizing that it develops around the stimulus it receives, primarily external stimulus. Humanity had not yet discovered the full range of the capabilities of their miracle organ. They had yet to understand how to engage unused attributes after early childhood. So much promise with so much yet to discover for this species.

Note would again encounter Gray, but in a boy, seeking to discover his inner being and live from that space.

Chapter Twenty-Seven

Pompo

The morning was chilly. **Pompo** ate his porridge while feeling the raindrops hitting his little feet. It was his first meal in two days, and his stomach immediately eased. His bony bottom rested on the porch of this shelter he was so grateful to have, the shelter where he lived with the other unwanted.

Pompo's burden was one of being physically different from most in his community. He was unusually small and was considered inferior and stupid. Even his caretakers put him at the end of the line for all resources. All but two of the orphans ate the day before, but the porridge ran out before Pompo's turn.

Note joined Pompo during his meal and immediately recognized his soul. It was Gray, the infinite soul from the Polar World. Note recalled and re-experienced all the sadness of Gray's life and, for a moment, Pompo experienced it too, profoundly. But Pompo is Pompo, and this moment was his, and unique in all the Universe to this little, cherished young man.

The rain stopped. Pompo took his bark plate inside the hut. Being the last to eat, he was also the last to finish, so cleaning the barks fell to him today. He meticulously cleaned each bark with pride and stacked them on the corner of the bench. He was excited about his day to come, working for Mr. Timba in the mine. He felt useful. The best part, however, was he would get to see Mr. Timba's daughter, Loresh.

Pompo's small size allowed him to look for minerals in small test holes. Smaller holes didn't take as much time to dig, and that meant additional mineral deposits for the other boys to recover. Pompo was a busy digger and overcame his fears.

After finishing his task, Pompo went back out on the porch to wait for Mr. Timba. The sun was just peeking over the horizon, so he knew his boss would arrive soon.

Mr. Timba was a hard man. He knew that the price paid by his little miners was high, and often the ultimate. The result was that he never allowed himself to connect with his employees. Losing his nephew in a mine hole had sealed his heart.

Today was an exciting day for Pompo. Yes, there was something in his tummy, and that was extra good, but today, he would have another day to pursue his vision.

Pompo's vision was that his brain connected to his entire body, inside and out, throughout the nervous system. It might include all his cells; he wasn't sure about that. In his vision, if he opened his consciousness to his subconscious and listened, and felt, and woke up to his physical being, he could experience all his physical self and help direct repairs and healing.

Pompo contemplated, *what if old age was part of the system and my brain went along with the system as it was born to do? What if I could redirect my brain to work outside the system? Can I promote healing within my body for 200 years instead of 50? Could I know when the cancer cells start and finish them immediately, internally, each time? Likewise, can I heal and rejuvenate my heart and other organs, just part of a daily job of an aware consciousness guiding a formidable brain?*

Pompo committed to feeling all the sensations impacting his outer body until he could finally experience the many sensations all at once, each moment. After months of practice, he would add to that and expand to the feelings within his body. The key, he posited, was not to give up one bit of awareness for another, but expand on the existing awareness, one realization at a time.

Pompo arrived at his first hole of the day.

I have come a long way, he thought. *I have become fearless.*

While the boys on his team today were setting up the air machine, Pompo took time to reflect. He remembered his first hole just two years earlier.

***

The water in front of him in the hole was muddy, and the hole was small. The boys handed Pompo a dirty hose to hold in his mouth to breathe through. When he closed his little lips on it, he felt his lungs fighting to receive the air they needed. Scared, he looked at his older peers. They told him he would get used to it.

He crouched down at the hole and lifted his arms and hands over his head as the boys had shown him and then leaned into the hole. With the rope tied around his ankle, they lowered Pompo into the muddy water. His nose was taped and, eyes shut, he felt the tight hole around his body as he wiggled to drop deeper into the hole.

This training hole was smaller than the regular mining holes that needed enough space to fill a bucket with mud and deposits and have it pulled to the surface. This hole was to prepare the new miners for the cramp, dark, painful, and dangerous conditions they would face daily. This hole was the smallest of all the training holes and had been made smaller for Pompo's little body to adequately train in.

Pompo felt the hole squeezed all around him. He gripped the hose in his teeth. He knew if the hose came out of his mouth while his arms were raised above his head with no room to pull them down, he would drown in mud. That had happened before in the training holes.

Pompo had never before felt such fear and helplessness. The hole was just 15 feet deep, but it seemed to take forever for him to squirm to the bottom to pick up a stick, just to prove to his teachers he'd achieved the aim. He found the stick in his hand and waited to feel the pull of the rope on his ankle. Though he got stuck several times on the way out, his squirming and the constant pulling from above brought him back from the water-filled hole. Once at the top, Pompo broke down crying. The boys at the top walked away to let him collect himself. He would never be the same.

***

Remembering the fear and terror of that day, Pompo knew fear stood between him and the next step toward an understanding on any level. He knew that, though he carried himself fearlessly; he was close to fear.

At the first hole today, he would focus on expanding his awareness to his inner being.

"We're ready, Pompo," the support boy called out.

"I'm ready, JoJo. Put me in." He put the hose in his mouth.

He raised his little arms and closed his eyes with the working air tube in his mouth. The boys taped his nose shut. He entered the hole headfirst with arms raised.

Pompo experienced the rope tightening around his ankle as they lowered him into the hole. He felt the blood throbbing to work through the restricted veins in his foot. His awareness stayed on his blood flow as he felt his heart driving the blood and the increased labor required to do so. He worked to keep that awareness while expanding it to feeling the coolness of his skin as the muddy water enveloped him, and then to the gradation of temperature from his cool skin to his warm insides. Pompo worked on feeling his inner body. He extended his awareness to his straining muscles throughout his body with the surging blood and temperature changes. He noticed his need to pee but knew he couldn't. His urethra burned with warm urine, and he worked to be mindful of how that feeling worked up to his prostate and bladder. He expanded his awareness to the sensation of his eyeballs behind closed lids and appreciated that he could feel his eyes more than most organs. He sensed his labored breathing with the air hose as it added to the stress on his heart along with the constricted blood flow to his foot. He could feel his heart in his eyeballs. Pompo felt the heat rising internally.

Suddenly, a sharp rock scraped his back as he continued to get lowered deeper into the hole, and his awareness jolted back to survival and his circumstances. He knew he would not be pulled back out without a full pail from the bottom of the hole. Pompo continued to concentrate on retrieving mud with deposits and, once accomplished, waited for his team to pull him up.

Once out of the hole, he felt delight at seeing Mr. Timba's daughter, Loresh, at the dig site. Loresh was a deep and thoughtful young woman who escaped her father's hardness and disregard for others. She also recognized the light in Pompo and showed him kindness. Over several years, she'd provided him with books and a Ziploc bag to keep one hidden in the forest. He kept only one book at a time and returned it to her to receive another. The books allowed him to visit many places when he read them in the moonlight, and he developed an expansive vocabulary. He mastered refined communication skills, but only one person knew that other than Pompo, and that was his favorite person, Loresh. She was the only one he ever spoke with, and she was the only one to hear his voice, other than the miners. Pompo talked like a wise old man, and she loved it.

"Hi, Pompo! Come sit with me," she shouted out. He cleaned himself off with a burlap sack and then hurried to oblige. His frail appearance brought sadness to her each time she saw him, but she couldn't bring him food in front of the other boys.

"What did you hear about in school today, Miss?"

Loresh was one of the lucky ones who attended a contemporary school.

"Pompo, it was fantastic today. I know how you like the Universe stuff. Today, we discussed vacuum energy."

"Wonderful, Miss Lor. Please share it with me."

"Well, I can't do it justice Pompo, but it speaks to space not being empty. It's a stew of subatomic particles that are being created and destroyed constantly. The end product is a space where every bit of it is energized. It has something to do with space being pushed apart at a sped-up rate. I don't know that I conveyed that right, but that is what I remember. What it says to me is nothing is empty."

"That is profound, Miss Lor. It boggles the mind to contemplate that nothing is empty. If it all started in one spot, how did it all fit?"

They laughed together. Loresh's eyes twinkled with Pompo; they heard each other.

"I am sorry to ask Miss Lor, but is that part of quantum physics?"

"I don't know that part, Pompo. Maybe we'll learn about that tomorrow, but let me look to see if I can find it on my phone." As one of the privileged in the community, Loresh carried a cell phone. They'd put a cell tower up by the mining company. The worldwide internet was available, so she could access the world. She typed 'vacuum energy' into her search, and a multitude of choices came up. However, right then, one of her friends sent her a text, and her focus went directly to that. The two texted for a moment. Suddenly she realized once again that she was sitting there with Pompo, and her attention returned to him. He couldn't remain there much longer.

"Miss Lor. You seem to use your phone a great deal. What do you find with it? What does it do for you?"

"Well, Pompo, it helps me connect; I want to connect. I'm eager to connect with others and everything that's going on in the world too. That's a good thing."

"I'm certain you're right, Miss Lor. I wonder, though, if your desire is more to connect with the world beyond the one you're sitting in? To keep you from connecting with this world, the surrounding one, the surrounding people, me?"

Loresh looked into his deep blue eyes and forgot about her cell phone. "Yes, I see what you mean. There is a lot here, and I love these moments with you, my special friend. Yes, I see what you mean."

"It has occurred to me recently, Miss Lor, that we naturally connect with what's outside us. Think, for instance, about your focus now. It's on me, while your body and your being are busy doing many things. I'm guessing that you're like me and are unaware of those things. Can you feel the wind and hear the howler monkeys?"

"Yes, I can, Pompo, and I hear the tree branches waving in the breeze too and feel the heat of the tailgate I am sitting on," she responded.

"Can you see my gratitude for you on my face, Miss Lor?" he asked sheepishly.

"Very much!" Her face softened.

"Do you feel your heartbeat or your temperature? Can you feel your blood surging?" Pompo asked.

"No. Wait, I think I see what you were talking about. You were saying it seems our focus is often, or almost always, outside us. That's interesting!"

"Can I share something with you, Miss Lor? It may sound kind of funny."

"Please do."

"Okay. My goal is to realize and experience what's inside me by learning first to be aware of each sensation on the outside and then move that awareness inside. As I get more in touch, I can become more aware of everything else. It may not be possible, Miss Lor. I'm not aware today. That I can attest to."

"Oh, Pompo. That's a grand goal you have. I've learned in my biology studies, however, that the human brain can't multitask. It can only focus on one high-level brain function at a time."

"What do you mean by high level?"

"You know I prefer it when you call me Loresh instead of Miss Lor. I consider you family, Pompo."

"We are, Loresh, thankfully," he said gently.

"High-level tasks are things you have to think about. Low-level functions like breathing and circulating blood aren't multitasking, because they're automatic. Will that mess you up?"

"It could, yes. I will try anyway and may just have to be quick." He looked back into her eyes.

Loresh giggled. "You are so dear. How do you think of these things? I don't believe there is anyone else like you."

"My world is tiny and simple, like me!" Pompo's grin returned, and his broken teeth glistened in the sun. She felt his humanity and his suffering, along with a lump in her throat.

"Pompo." She was serious. "You're looking frail to me. How are you feeling?"

He looked down at the ground. Some hair was missing, leaving patches of skin on his head, and his skin was visibly dried and cracked. "Can I be honest, Loresh?"

"I need you to be," she said with a dear voice.

"I'm starving, as are some other boys. It's painful, this starving. I use a certain amount of energy each day to live, including my mining, using more energy than I take in. My body eats my muscles for fuel, as I have no fat. My heart and nervous system are most important in my body, so my body burns the rest to protect that. I am weaker every day, and I hurt. It is hard to concentrate too. Sometimes I'm too weak to know I'm thirsty.

"Something in me keeps me positive, Loresh, and looking forward to seeing you helps me to have hope, but my body is not doing well. The bright side, however, is the pain inside helps me get in touch with my inner self. As a result, I am prolonging my life, I think."

"Pompo!" The foreman yelled out. "Back to work!"

"Let me know what you find out about the Universe, Loresh. Please don't forget about me!"

"I'll never forget about you, Silly."

Loresh wasted no time using her power as a daughter to get her father to agree to provide more food rations for all the boys. Pompo would eat more going forward, though not enough. His life would endure longer.

It was another day, like every other day. Pompo rose to find if he would eat or not...not today. He went back outside to wait for Mr. Timba, but today, when he went out front, he found a tiny baby wrapped in straw.

It was clear the baby was struggling. Pompo soon recognized the baby was malformed and missing part of its skull. Knowing his interest in anatomy, Loresh had provided two medical books to him over time, and he recognized that anencephaly[31] impacted this dear little being.

"Hello, little one," Pompo said to the baby, and he held it close to him. "Your name is Little Bit." That name resonated with him. He didn't consciously realize that it was Gray's baby's name.

He knew that if he took Little Bit into the house, she would just get thrown away in the trash. He'd seen that happen before. He also knew that Little Bit would not live long, so Pompo took her into the forest and, full of Note, sang and hummed to her as she died in his loving arms later in the day.

Mr. Timba came by as always to get him, but concluded he was sick and stayed inside when Pompo didn't appear. It was not unusual for Mr. Timba's malnourished miners to get ill. He would try again tomorrow and would find Pompo ready for work.

***

Two years passed.

Loresh sat on the back of the truck, waiting anxiously for Pompo to come out of the hole. When he did, his appearance stunned her. He struggled to move toward her. She ran over to him and helped him to sit. "Pompo, my dear Pompo, what's wrong?"

He gathered his strength and looked toward her. Their gaze connected.

"I'm dying, Loresh. The long-term starvation has taken my body down this road. I can't get off it now."

"What do you mean?"

Pompo put his hand on hers and stared deeply into her left eye with his. She felt a jolt as they joined as one for what was just one moment. At that moment, though it was incomprehensible to her, she felt all of Pompo, Gray, and Note. She felt his body and the pain with all the growing dysfunction. She experienced his suffering along with the sadness of injustice they knew. Loresh underwent the grandeur of the good of the Universe. It was the ultimate connection with another and with herself.

Though Pompo was the home for Gray's soul, his experience was limited to that of a starving human boy. The moment of connection he shared with Loresh, where the heavens opened for a moment, was the first of his lifetime. He was locked in to being Pompo, but for a moment, it all combined for both he and Loresh.

Her chin dropped, and she looked to the side, alone again but understanding. "Pompo, wait here for me." No longer able to sit, he moved to his knees, leaning forward. The other boys, in view, stopped what they were doing to watch Pompo.

Loresh rose and hurried toward her father, who was barking out commands to the labor force, now standing. When she got to him, she got his attention easily and quickly. Pompo looked up and watched their exchange.

She passionately and expressively pleaded with her father. Mr. Timba shook his head no and moved to turn away. Loresh grabbed his arm and pulled him around and slapped the giant man soundly; Pompo could hear the strike. She and her father paused, just staring at each other, and then something profound happened. He melted, and tears came to his face and then hers. Loresh was the only softness in his heart, and that softness overcame him. He looked over at Pompo and then back at his daughter, nodding his head yes, this time.

She hugged Mr. Timba, and they both made their way toward the precious boy. Pompo couldn't find the strength to stand up to meet their advance. The giant man got to Pompo and bent over to pick him up. He carried him toward the truck with Loresh holding Pompo's arm.

He would not regain consciousness for a day. When he awakened, it was in a world that was new to him.

Pompo looked at the sun coming in the glass window and admired the soft curtains that hung on either side of it. The wallpaper had flowers on it, and they were soft colors. He felt the down-filled mattress envelop him beneath a thick white quilt that smelled like lavender. It was his first time on a bed, and he couldn't imagine how anyone could ever make themselves get out of such an inviting place each day. His precious head rested on Loresh's pillow, and his little hand rested in hers. His skin was clean and rubbed with oils. Pompo bathed in the river and had never been clean like this. He felt loved. He was not alone.

"You are everything, Pompo," she told him. "You are the most beautiful thing I've ever seen. I love you with all my being, and as long as I exist, you will be a part of me."

Pompo had not been spoken to like that. He didn't know what genuine devotion and appreciation like this could feel like to receive.

He turned toward her and spoke in a slow and labored way, conceivably from another place, one where Gray and Note lived: "You have a soul cut from grace. Grace stores hope for us and gifts it to us when we need it.

"Loresh, I know now that you're the reason I've lived this life, to experience this moment of appreciation and know your soul. In all the darkness, there is light. Your love and kindness are the essence of humankind. Though that essence is lost in the chaos now, there is no other like it.

"Come with me for a moment. Close your eyes. Feel my love."

She looked deeply into his eyes, and they closed. It surprised her how blue they were. As she closed her eyes, the warmth of his hand impressed her.

Whoosh, it felt as if she left her body. She felt her friend with her, part of her. She saw countless stars and the birth of galaxies happening in fast motion. Loresh felt what birth felt like and understood for the first time in her very being. Why we are. Ahead was a great blue light that started as a small dot in the distance and was quickly getting more prominent as they sped toward it. Pompo was everything at that moment, everywhere; she felt her face again, wet with tears. She felt the pure essence of happiness and joy. Then it faded.

She again recognized Pompo's warm hand in hers and then felt it become cool and limp. Loresh opened her tear-filled eyes to see the lifeless body of this angel, precious little Pompo, the One.

Pompo died holding the hand of Grace, and in her weeping, she knew she had just experienced the passing of everything.

In Between

Note felt moved with Pompo's dearness and struggle for life. Discovering the inside is half of the balance.

Note appreciated that living beings rely on their memories of their stimulated selves. Note would experience a realization about how memories tie— or don't— to the truth.

Chapter Twenty-Eight

Memories

"**I just love this peanut goo**. I think it's my favorite." Salaye savored the goo.

"You are delightful, Salaye. Being on this tiny craft with you is, well, special."

"Thank you, Darius. You are the best travel mate, too; want some peanut goo?"

"Um, no, I don't like it, not a bit. It is too gooey!"

Note joined Salaye as the Bostone neared the Event Horizon.

"These things never get old to me. Just look at that. Unbelievable, and it's a small one," Darius shared.

The Bostone was nearing the birthplace of a black hole caused by the collision of two neutron stars in the spherical galaxy, NGC 4993. It occurred some 70 million years before. In Earth terms, the two neutron stars that merged were 1.6 and 1.1 times as massive as the Earth-Sun, but each was no wider than Washington, D.C. The collision created enormous energy with the equivalent mass of 25 Jupiters converting into gravitational waves alone. Another 50 Jupiters' worth of heavy elements such as gold and silver ejected.

The resulting black hole was the smallest ever found by the Rolins race.

"Darius, I want to run something past you. We've had time to contemplate things on our journey, and I wanted to think this one through before sharing it with you. Is this a good time?"

"Sure, now is good. It will be four more days before we're in range to start our experiments; can you tell me in four days?"

Smiling, Salaye responded, "Yes, I think I can keep it under four days. Here it is. Think about it...memories. Everything we are or do is based on our memories. Like our technology, they are the bits and bytes in our organic existence. They bring me my words for this conversation, along with the series of memories and observations that form the hypothesis I am sharing. Are you with me?"

"Yes, I'm with you so far; I still have four days to talk about memories."

"Good, good. Think about your internal dialogue. Where does it come from, Darius?"

"Interesting question." He paused for a moment. "Okay, internal dialogue, well, it seems to go on and on, I know that. It appears to be a train of thought colored by my opinions and attitudes, sometimes mixed with facts—or perceived facts—anyway."

"Right, Darius. Your opinions, attitudes, and perceived facts are all products of memories or a combination of them. From what our scientists have learned, memories can change. You retrieve a memory, add some new opinions, attitudes, and experiences to it, and then re-save it. Then when you pull it back up again, you are pulling up the altered memory. We base so much on our memories. We base justice on the memory of one of our experiences, where it pertains to the actions of another. I ask you, if memories are fluid and can be modified, what does that mean for our reality?"

"I see where this is going, Salaye. Let me expand on that. When we were young, our parents would say things like garbage in, garbage out, usually about the experiences, ideas, entertainment, et cetera that we were exposing ourselves to. How do we differentiate between fact and fiction? Reality and farce? Is there something in our mind that is purely objective that makes that choice, or are our minds primarily subjective? Now take all that garbage in our memory banks, add time, opinions, our subjectivity, and add a little bit of stimulus, and what do you get? Probably not the truth, if the truth is an objective reality."

"That's why I talk to you, Darius. Yes, our minds may be kind of mess. It occurs to me that the only thing that keeps them in order is accepted social norms, including society's opinions on what's right and wrong. Here you and I are on a little ship approaching a black hole. We may not be clear on why we're here because we have unique minds and perceive our mission uniquely. The people that sent us didn't each send us for the same reason; again, because each has a unique mental position. What might all this mean, Darius? Where is it going? Where are we going?"

"I can tell you now that four days will not be long enough to work through this, Captain. This, however, is what occurs to me." Darius continued. "The truth is factual, and it may be much broader than we hope it to be, but it's real, and we can count on it. Now that we discussed internal dialogue, and that it comes from memories that we now agree may be fictitious or at least fictitious to some extent, I think we should limit or stop our internal dialogue. What does internal dialogue do for us? For me, it keeps me from really being in this moment, and the truth is here, at this moment, and that's my life's compass. I know that now, at this moment."

"Darius, what's that? Oh my, OH, MY!"

"We're recording, Captain. It almost looks like a tear or a rip next to the event horizon."

"But it's black without stars. Can you run its gravity?"

"Give me a minute," he said in a long, drawn-out way. "Nothing. I read no gravity on any level in the darkness."

"On Plank?"

"No gravity, even with the Plank system. I think it's outside, Captain."

"Outside! Outside where?"

"Outside the Universe, Captain."

"Crap!" Note left Salaye at that moment.

In Between

Note posited that memories are part of the dream.

Note, seeking the basis of a North Star for good, was to experience the essence of quality.

Chapter Twenty-Nine

Quality

Chanita, with Note, walked into Elijah's office at the university. His office was a small nine-by-nine-foot room with a window that looked out over a massive madrone tree that had lived for hundreds of years and was a destination for many tourists in the Pacific Northwest. With Elijah's seniority at the university, he could have taken one of the more commanding offices, but he wanted this one so he could gaze at the amazing tree.

A bookworm, Elijah surrounded himself with dark wood shelves full of books. They brimmed with great reads. One section of shelves was devoted to photos of a beautiful young woman who looked to be his daughter, with a face beaming with energy and promise. His dense red oak chair was a work of art that contoured around Elijah's muscular body. The only other chair in the office was for a guest who could be a student, or a messenger masquerading as a reporter to discuss Elijah's life message: Quality.

"Welcome, Chanita. So glad to meet you. Please have a seat. Can I get you anything to drink? Juice, or water?" Chanita felt his rough skin as she shook his hand. She appreciated his sunken golden eyes under fluffy gray eyebrows on his wrinkled face of character. Chanita responded as she moved to the plush and welcoming chair. It was apparent by the chair that Elijah held his guests in high regard.

"I'd love some grape juice; is that a choice?"

"Why yes, it's my favorite too." As Elijah moved toward the small refrigerator behind his desk, he spoke.

"When I was a child visiting my father and his new family, my stepmother would always buy frozen grape juice concentrate. Every morning, she would cook the same breakfast and serve it with grape juice. After decades, I still remember her opening those frozen concentrate cans and mixing it with water in a big pitcher to pour us that delicious nectar. Yes, I love it, though I think it has stained my teeth some, mixed with the yellow." His smile was amazing and sincere. It struck Chanita.

They settled into their chairs, each with an ample bottle of cold grape juice, almost frosty.

"I haven't heard of your news organization, Chanita. Can you tell me more about it?"

Chanita was a spiritualist with a Ph.D. in Social Sciences. An old soul, her North Star was to help humanity change its paradigm regarding value. Her view was that human life held the highest value and that all human life mattered. She was drawn to Elijah's study around the economics of quality. She appreciated that it was a veiled attempt to move society toward making decisions around the quality of human life.

"Thank you for seeing me, Professor Arnold. My organization is large but not widely known. We publish quietly around the world on social media. Our goal is to spread 'good' information to those who can hear it. I know you are a good man, Sir, and we need your message."

Elijah was an old soul, too, and could sense he was with a kindred spirit. He knew this was a powerful moment with a special person. "Please, Chanita, call me Elijah. I love your name. I don't know that I've heard it before now."

"Thank you, Elijah. I don't know what my name means, but it feels good to me. Now, to be honest, your name has always been one of my favorites. It denotes strength. I believe that in the Hebrew Bible, Elijah was a prophet and a miracle worker that lived in the northern kingdom of Israel. I hope you are both a prophet and a miracle worker in modern times."

He sat quietly for a moment processing the words of his guest. Then he responded, "I'm just a man, Chanita. A descendant of slaves and, before them, kings and queens. Me, I'm only a man. Okay, ask me a question; what do you want to know?"

"Quality—it sounds as though that's your life's work, Elijah. Please, if it's not too general a question, what is quality?"

"Yes, quality. It's everything...at least to me, it is. Quality is when something is right, almost the best it can be. Quality makes good things. It takes effort to produce quality and awareness to appreciate it, and quality is rarely, if ever, the product of shortcuts. What I've always espoused is that quality is the most natural path, with the best results and the lowest cost."

"The economics of quality. That's why I'm here, Elijah, to understand your theory better."

"Let's talk a moment about house fires, Chanita. In the United States, some 40,000 house fires a year result from arcing; by some estimates, it causes more than half of all house fires. Arcing refers to a luminous discharge of electricity across an insulating medium. In regular terms, it's electricity jumping from one point to another over a void or distance between the two points. Imagine a lightning bolt jumping from one lightning rod to another through the air—that's arcing. Temperatures can get to as high as 1800 degrees Fahrenheit, or 1000 degrees Celsius. Most anything that's around such heat will burn and become a fire. No biggie, unless you live in one of those houses.

"You may ask yourself, what can prevent houses burning from arcing? Quality!

"To prevent arcing, the builder needs to install quality wire, properly run through a house, not stapled too tight to the studs, with ends wrapped securely around outlet screws that get properly tightened on quality outlets and mounted to an outlet box that's properly flush with the drywall or wall surface, all wired back to a circuit breaker box with AFCI circuit breakers, adequately installed with the right load on each one.

"If the homeowner can be careful not to drive nails or screws into the wires over time, they solve the arcing issue along with the high costs—human and otherwise—associated with house fires caused by arcing. Most all of that's code now, Chanita, but quality is often missing from the equation.

"The wire may or may not be of high quality. An average house may have 300 staples running the wire along the studs; a reasonable assumption is that 10% of them are too tight. Most of the outlets put in homes today are less than $1 each. Electricians wrap the wires around the screws most of the time, but not always, and there will be a few in each house that are close, but not right. They screw most of the screws tight, but again maybe 15% of the screws don't get tightened all the way. Most houses have outlet boxes that aren't flush with the drywall for various reasons; there are ways to make sure that's not the case, but those choices cost a couple of dollars more per box. AFCI breakers are by code on the bedrooms only. Arcing happens everywhere. That's why so many fires occur each year, Chanita. If you look at wiring a house as a complete job, the overall quality is not high enough, but it could be high enough!"

"Interesting Elijah, and important too. I hadn't ever thought about it," Chanita reacted.

"Boring, I know, but details, details. When I was in college, I did an internship at an equipment manufacturer for the robotic automation industry."

"For cars?" Chanita asked.

"Industrial robots," Elijah answered.

"Ah, yes, thank you."

"The department I was in was assigned to trimming the cost of the product. We used project managers who worked with suppliers and their suppliers to drive cost savings. I just did spreadsheets for them and built macros to help them assimilate all they were achieving.

"Honestly, they did a superb job at this company. They manufactured and still have a very high-end product, but I'd see time after time how our pressure on the suppliers to drive out costs impacted the quality of the parts we were getting. A business must make a profit to survive, and by driving the revenue down for what suppliers received by selling the components to us, we drove down their profit. That's unless they drove down their material cost with their suppliers, and they theirs. If everyone makes a nominal profit, enough to survive, the only cost-saving must come from the quality. As a young man, I loved being a part of this cost savings group. I did not yet appreciate the impact of what we were doing.

"Chanita, I only have another thirty minutes with you because I have a class at the top of the hour. Please come to it; I'd love to have you there. It is a special class where we talk about the economics of quality. The group is the best of the best if you ask me, and I'm learning a great deal from them."

"Thank you, Elijah; I'd be honored to attend, but I only have this time with you today. What happened that made you devote your life to quality?"

His eyes watered, and his chin wobbled a tad. He looked into Chanita's welcoming eyes and felt safe there.

"Well, I saw the impact of cost savings on suppliers and the quality of their products. I recognized how all of that impacted the final quality of the excellent product this company produced. But as a person, I just found it interesting. Okay, so what?"

Elijah turned his head away and toward the shelf of photos.

"That's my cherished Margaret. When she was born, I knew my life held meaning and that a blessing had been given to me. I treasured every milestone in her life and all the time in between. The tone of her voice, and the way she argued and looked for solutions. Her laugh was almost a whistle. Margaret was an angel, Chanita, and I could talk about her nonstop for hours. That's how much I think of her, how much I loved and adored her."

When Elijah looked back at her, tears were running down his face. "Somehow, I see her in you, Chanita. I realize I may make you uncomfortable, but I know I'm not, but I do, I see her in your eyes, my Margaret."

It was clear Margaret was in Elijah's past and not physically in his present-day. She was with him, but not.

Chanita leaned forward toward him. "I'm confident she loved you with all her heart, Elijah. I know she appreciated and looked up to her father. I have a feeling she made a difference because you are making a difference now."

He wanted Chanita to know what had happened to Margaret. "She was driving home from college to see us for Christmas break, and a car on the highway moved into her lane before it fully passed her, causing her to run off the road and hit a barbed wire fence post. The fence post was old and rotten and gave way easily enough, but when the car hit it, the airbags deployed. The airbag system was faulty, and when the bag exploded, it sent metal shards into my Margaret's head and brain. She was dead before the car stopped moving.

"Here, the propellant in the inflators—the explosive material that generates the gases to inflate the airbag—degraded, making it prone to 'overaggressive combustion.' The propellant, a critical component, was a chemical mixture that included inexpensive fertilizer chemicals. The manufacturer got pressed hard to reduce costs and found that a significant amount of savings could occur over many units by replacing the expensive and stable propellant with this inexpensive and unstable one. It did the job when it was fresh, passed the tests. No one ever knew until people like my precious Margaret started dying or becoming injured.

"After grieving for an exceedingly long time, I knew I owed it to my Margaret—and everyone else—to work toward a societal and business philosophy that revolved around results based on quality, instead of profits. We have a long way to go, Chanita. We've just begun."

Chanita sat back. "Thank you for sharing that with me. Yes, quality is outstanding and much more significant than profit."

After each took a sip of juice as if they were synchronous swimmers in unison, she asked, "Can you share more about the class you have after our meeting?"

"I wish you could join us. It's a team of experts that specializes in multiple facets within our community. Our goal is to convey the criticality around making decisions guided by quality over other characteristics, such as profit, for instance. Last week, we considered daycare."

"Why daycare, Elijah?"

"Well, we were all children once. Some of us are parents with children, and they'll have children. Children become adults who manage our world, so child development is world development. Daycare can significantly impact child development. When we consider quality and the result of quality, we often think of it around a component or process. Think of daycare as a process that serves our component, children. Quality invested in the child component favorably impacts all of us."

"I love that, Elijah. You aren't messing around with this. Solve for the child in the human equation, and you significantly improve your chances along the path." Chanita paused, and then asked, "What's some of what you've learned from your team?"

"Importantly, the first five years are crucial for the child. Babies are born ready to learn, and their brains develop through use. So, a child needs a stimulating environment with lots of different activities that give him or her plenty of ways to play and learn, and lots of chances to practice what they're learning. More than anything else, relationships with a child shape the way a child learns and grows. I discovered too that a child's brain develops more and faster during this time than at any other time in their life, so the early experiences—the things they see, hear, touch, smell, and taste—stimulate their brain, creating millions of connections. This period is when the foundations for learning, health, and behavior are formed.

"Honestly, Chanita, all of that is important and only common sense, but it's also big picture. The start a child has in today's world gets impacted by many things but can be summed up into societies and the parent's capacity to maximize the child's environment. The quality decisions start around the framework of ensuring the child gets their optimum opportunity. It's big stuff."

"Has anything come out of your discussion about children that's surprised you?"

"One of my people suggested that parenting should be regulated. I believe that's the best way to put it. Their concept was around individuals having to be in solid, lasting relationships and then waiting until the age of 25 to become parents. In their model, society doesn't just promote this but enforces it. The way they described it, the good of the child is paramount, so the foundation must get set. Society would also assure the child's development—many quality components in all of that."

"Interesting to be sure, Elijah. Did the other members agree with that suggestion?"

"No. The main pushback was around parents' rights. The argument was that adults should get to make their own decisions about what type of relationships they have, and at what age they want to parent, as we have it today."

Chanita pondered his response and then asked, "What do you believe, Elijah?"

He looked back at her and paused for a moment. He then turned his head and gazed out the window at the majestic madrone tree. Turning back, Elijah shared. "Based on how it all works today, it's hard to imagine society getting to such a point, though I know it will be in humanity's best interest long term. I think about a mother's unequaled love for her child and ask myself a question. What mother would not want her baby to be born to a stable, mature and supportive home in a society that makes it a priority to find and promote the many blessings and abilities of her child over time, toward self-actualization and happiness?

"I vote for putting the good of the child first. If we maximize the development and experiences of a child, we present our community with a fully rounded and capable human being who will contribute more to the community and those around them, be better parents, and so on. A system like that bodes well for humankind's future instead of the free for all we have today. It resonates more with me now than it did initially.

"Chanita, based on what I've shared, do you have an opinion?"

"Society has to take this on in steps, Elijah, to get to this place. Revere the child most, and revere the mother next; everything else follows from there. This reverence starts at conception, no matter the age of the mother or the relationship they have with the father. Society helps and supports. That may be the next step.

"I think we're all children, and we all deserve to be revered. Quality comes from a place of knowledge and, with your help, we are getting closer to knowing what to do. Build a society for the good of the child first. I like that. I know we are out of time, Elijah. It's been delightful to meet you."

"I'm glad you were here, Chanita," Elijah exclaimed. "I didn't expect this conversation today. It felt like your presence took me deeper. Can we stay in touch?"

"I hope we do."

Elijah rose to lead her to the door. He stopped and turned to her, looking back into her powerful eyes.

"I know I told you this earlier, but I see my Margaret in your eyes, Chanita. I wish you could have met her."

Reaching out to squeeze his hand, Chanita responded, "I feel like I have, Elijah. May I ask you a question?"

"Yes, please."

"What is your favorite word, Elijah?"

"Possibility!"

Chanita smiled warmly and walked out of the building. A pebble was thrown into the quiet pond that day.

Note left Chanita.

In Between

Note felt quality innately and decided that it is a life component. Life is magical because of its quality. It is something done well or, at its best, as an aspiration. To move toward quality over lesser things can only be good.

Note was about to experience the other side fully, the lesser side, the least of us, a profound part of the whole, but the other side.

Chapter Thirty

Note in the Center of the Universe

Space is cold, roughly 2.7 Kelvin (-270.45 Celsius, -454.81 Fahrenheit). With the lack of atmosphere and the vacuum-like nature of space, there are relatively few molecules to bounce around to generate heat energetically.

Note learned about cold and many other specifics during the journey through time and space. Note knew and experienced good and evil too, or that deemed to be one or the other. While Note could recognize all attributes, good and bad, only the good felt like home, because Note *was* home. In discovering the meaning of its existence, Note knew note was good.

Note's essence was inventive, thoughtful, powerful with a focus for good, practical, proactive, productive, drawn to quality, balanced, logical, patient, positive, imaginative, warm, diplomatic, curious, consistent, compassionate, independent, one with integrity, cheerful, forgiving, generous, devoted, candid, cooperative, industrious, meditative, understanding, quixotic, socially consciousness, modest, courageous, enthusiastic, enterprising, entrepreneurial, focused, genuine, open-minded, wise, sensitive, sensible, sincere, skilled, communicative, helpful, responsible, organized, knowledgeable, logical, pleasant, flexible, adaptable, perceptive, insightful, trustworthy and humorful. Note's essence was as a mediator, a feeler, an achiever, a learner, a leader, a good listener and hearer, and a facilitator.

Only once in Note's existence would Note pass through the perfect center point of the oddly shaped and flat Universe. Approaching center, Note became intensely aware of the approach of another Note. The sense was that this Note was not good.

It was profound to Note, recognizing the opposite as it was fast approaching. Note sensed the attributes and essence coming, sensing fear, aggression, aloofness, anger, apathy, arrogance, temper, bias, boastfulness, a bombastic nature, calculating drive, callousness, carelessness, a caustic manner, coldness, combativeness, complacency, conceit, conniving practices, a controlling nature, cowardice, cruelty, curtness, danger, deceit, dependency, dishonesty, disrespect, distance, egocentricity, envy, evil, exaggeration, foolishness, gloom, gluttony, greed, gullibility, harshness, hate, hostility, hypercriticality, ignorance, immaturity, impatience, impoliteness, incompetence, inconsiderateness, indecisiveness, indifference, insensitivity, intolerance, jealousy, judgment, laziness, materialism, meanness, mistrust, nastiness, numbness, obnoxiousness, obscenity, obstinance, oppression, overconfidence, oversensitivity, pessimism, pettiness, petulance, a pompous nature, pretention, rashness, rebellion, reluctance, resentment, ridiculousness, rudeness, sadism, scorn, self-centeredness, selfishness, shiftiness, spite, stinginess, suspicion, tactlessness, thoughtlessness, lack of appreciation, an uncaring disconnection, lack of commitment, uncooperativeness, unfeelingness, unforgiveness, ungratefulness, unkindness, vanity, vulgarity, weak will, wickedness, wrath and a closed self.

As they approached one another, there was no choice for good nor evil, hope nor despair. They merged; time stood still. An eternity seemed to open; both combined as one and felt what God felt like—complete! At that moment, lasting eight million Earth years, both Notes fully experienced the essence each discovered from the other's vantage point.

They again became two and moved from the center. Note felt the loss—the darkness—of what made them whole. Some of the other Note lingered.

Note remembered all the being's yearnings for completeness in all of Note's many bonding's. Why could Note just be good, and not evil? What limitation existed that was only limitless in the center of the Universe, and why was perfect balance only there, or was it?

What am I? Note wondered for the first time. *Am I physical like light or gravity? Am I sound, or am I...?*

I travel through space faster than light, and sound doesn't, nothing does, but I do. What am I?

Within seconds, Note was moving toward a massive Quasar.

> "Quasars inhabit the center of active galaxies and are among the most luminous, powerful, and energetic objects known in the Universe, emitting up to a thousand times the energy output of the Milky Way,[32] which

contains 200–400 billion stars.

"Quasars are powered by the accretion[33] of material into supermassive black holes. Light and other radiation cannot escape from within the event horizon[34] of a black hole, but the energy produced by a quasar is generated *outside* the black hole, by gravitational stresses and the immense friction within the material nearest to the black hole, as it orbits and falls inward. The huge luminosity of quasars results from the accretion discs of central supermassive black holes, which can convert between 6% and 32% of the mass[35] of an object into energy, compared to just 0.7% for the process that dominates the energy production in Sun-like stars. Quasars can also be ignited or re-ignited when normal galaxies merge, and the black hole is infused with a fresh source of matter.

"Quasars were more common in the early Universe, as this energy production ends when the supermassive black hole consumes all the gas and dust near it. Most galaxies have gone through an active stage, appearing as a quasar or some other class of active galaxy that depended on the black hole mass and the accretion rate, and are now quiescent because they lack a supply of matter to feed into their central black holes to generate radiation."[36]

***

Note merged with a small moon piece in the outside of the accretion disk, a satellite that had orbited a beautiful blue terrestrial world just a billion years before. The solid iron former interior of the moon remained intact but was molten as it already experienced temperatures over 9,000 Kelvin as it neared the disk. Soon temperatures would climb anywhere between 300,000 Kelvin to 300,000,000 Kelvin, and the moon would break up into its atomic parts. Though the moon and most of the materials in the accretion disk were in the maw of the black hole, they weren't falling in. Instead, because of a process called conservation of angular momentum, which results from the velocity acting upon a falling object, the matter spirals as it goes in. The spiraling matter gets faster and faster as it gets closer, breaking apart into atom streams. Like water draining in a bathtub, the matter trails around and around the hole. Its atoms flatten out like a twirling pizza in the sky, creating the telltale fuzzy doughnut of the accretion disk.

Note experienced the destruction of the moon staying merged with one of the remaining particles as they entered the black hole. Note fell toward the center as the particle continued to break into lesser and lesser particles. As Note approached the mass in the center, Note realized there was a center there, one where all things came to it equally from all sides. This was perfect balance as Note experienced at the center of the Universe. Note knew it was not time to die. At that moment, and unbound by time or the limitations recognized by physics, Note reached out to Deadra on Josla some 2084 billion years in the future and planted the question, "What's a center?"

In time, Note would also return to such a place to leave this Universe and enter another, but not yet. Note moved away from the center of the black hole and reentered standard space, where abundant starlight welcomed Note's return.

I'm of this Universe, but I'm not! Note contemplated. *Everything of this Universe, the singular existence, is bound by the physics of this Universe; I'm not. If I'm an angel of God, if I am, IF, then God is not of this Universe, while the Universe is of God.*

In Between

Note experienced completion and balance. In that place, there was no value. Note came to understand that pursuing value is beyond balance, but essential to evolution.

Note would next experience the pursuit of value for a world.

Chapter Thirty-One

The New World

Note felt a deep peace as Note moved toward this star system headed by a magnificent Blue Star. The star seemed astoundingly like the Blue Star present in Note's forming and felt the same. It was an "O Type" star, the enormous sized variety in the Universe, and the rarest. This type of star is massive, hot, bright, and short-lived. The brief life span doesn't support the formation of intelligent life on planets. The immense gravity and solar activity do, however, create an environment where giant rock worlds could develop if given the time. Note approached a colossal rock world around this rare and enormous star and heard the vibrations of life there, impossibly so.

Note joined Ramson as his ship dropped out of light speed to orbit around Armiston. Armiston was six times the mass of Jupiter and was old enough to have supported four distinct intelligent populations over its 7-billion-year life. Again, intelligent life wasn't possible with an "O Type" star. Each species lived and evolved for several million years before extinction. The Zute species that inhabited Armiston today was a much-evolved race that had existed in its current state for some 920,000 years, now numbering well over 40 billion souls. The Zute were well known for having a society that seemed to work for everyone. They often welcomed visitors from other worlds and cultures trying to make things work on their planets.

Ramson was from OT, which was in a star system just 4.5 light-years away from Armiston. OT was a younger world with much less size and space for its population of 8 billion souls. Ramson received a hail from Armiston.

"OT vessel, welcome to Armiston. What is your destination here?"

Ramson responded cautiously. "I have an appointment to meet with the Council of Worlds. What coordinates should I set?"

Ramson received the coordinates and descended into the dark blue atmosphere when his sensors showed the Zute were scanning his vessel. Soon the engines shut down, and the Zute took control of Ramson's ship. The sensation of coasting at such speed was unlike any Ramson had known. They protected him against Armiston's massive gravity in the cocoon of Zute control, and he felt no fear. Note was taken with the feelings of his trust.

His ship was now over a city and slowing. The city looked odd from above because of its flatness. The Zute were slitherers because of the force on their bodies borne from their giant world. The buildings were all low to the ground, but with impressive thickness. The city stretched out as far as the eye could see. Ramson saw the languid and deliberate movement of the Zute in the flat city below. He appreciated the protective bubble that was shielding him as one with lesser bones. A landing hangar was just ahead, and his ship moved deliberately toward it and docked.

He straightened his jacket and moved his hand over his thick red hair to adjust it, making it look exactly right to make a good first impression. He walked to his outer door and told his system to open it. Ramson walked down the lower steps to meet his welcoming party, comprised with other humanoid forms like Ramson. They worked with and for the Zute.

"Welcome Ramson, we're pleased to have you join us and look forward to having discussions that can help OT move toward peace and prosperity. I'm Marsha. How was your trip?" she asked.

Marsha was from the Dawn life forms, a female-dominated species with advanced intellect and technology. Dawn space explorers had discovered Armiston many millennia ago and recognized the absurdity of any life existing around such a star. The compelling discovery led them to contact the Zute. They recognized the Zute to be evolved far beyond themselves in intellectual and spiritual substance. The connection between the two species was happening for a higher purpose. The Dawn became the primary caretakers for the Zute, who developed little technology of their own. As the caretakers, the Dawn provided the interface between the Zute and their many visitors. They controlled all aspects of the environment to enable other species to survive in the hostile world.

Marsha's turquoise skin was beautiful, stunningly so. With its melodic tone and resonance, her voice was delightful to Note. Ramson needed to gather himself before he answered her; he felt intimidated in her presence.

"The trip was good," he uttered. "Our hibernation technology is a little hit and miss. To be honest, it scares me. The plan was for me to go to sleep once I was on course to Armiston and wake up a day before arrival. I just couldn't do it, so I worked on a trove of books during the journey and thought about this visit and all its implications."

"Did you have enough to eat, Ramson?"

"Well, almost, Marsha. Our food processors do a pleasant job, but the selection is light, being from a powder and all."

"Let's get you to your quarters and feed you a great Dawn meal before you rest. Our discussions will begin first thing after resting."

Along with a contingent of other turquoise women, Marsha escorted Ramson through the massive station, finally arriving at his quarters. "I apologize for the long journey, Ramson. Everything we do will be in this area, however. I know this was hard for your legs after such a flight."

"Thank you, Marsha."

Ramson turned and entered his quarters where he found a bounty of OT delicacies waiting for him, cooked up Dawn style. He ate slowly and savored each bite until he was full. He slept for nine yarns.

A new Dawn team arrived in the next period to take Ramson to meet the council. It was a quick passage this time.

He sat quietly, looking around the well-adorned room. It occurred to him that the decorating must have been done in Dawn motifs and it helped him to picture Marsha and her peers back on their world. Marsha came into the room and moved toward him, sitting next to Ramson. "Hello, Ramson. I trust your rest was good."

"Delightful. The food was extraordinary. I'm sure we don't have any of the ingredients for that back on OT, but if we did, I would ask you for a cookbook."

Marsha just nodded, but she was amused.

Another figure entered the room and moved toward what appeared to be the leader's chair. The genderless figure was more prominent than the others and sat in a central location. The Adorite species was known for its organized and logical thought processes. Like the Zute, they were empathic, and they took the bountiful wisdom of the Zute and organized it into information an audience could understand. After working with the Adorite, many felt that "the light" turned on simply because the Adorite could organize complex information in such a way as to make it easy to understand.

This Adorite was named Kongan. Kongan had centuries of experience in this position. Ramson didn't realize how profoundly fortunate he and the people of OT were to work with Kongan, but it would become clear, like everything else, over the next few day periods.

"Welcome, Ramson! We're sincerely honored to work with you and your people. If you're ready, let us proceed."

Ramson acknowledged the kind greeting.

"The first thing you have to answer is, what do each of your people want? What do they really want?"

Ramson thought for a moment and then let his mouth say what he felt. "Well first, everyone wants to live forever," He thought it was an honest but unrealistic want.

"You're on the right track, Ramson. Yes, most all beings want that first and foremost. Not all, but most. Continue, please."

"They want to be happy, safe, prosperous, feel valuable and valued, grow, and progress. They want to live a life or existence that's fair and just in a world of equality. They want to know, give, and receive love. They want to know their purpose. They want to have fun. They want to eat whatever they want without it making them fat." Ramson smiled and added, "They want to thrive forever."

"Good, Ramson. That's what we need to make a path to. We need to help them have what they want. Anything else?"

"Yes, they want most things to be their ideas. I know that's small, but that's what they want. They want everyone around them to pull their weight. They want to have hope without having to think about having it. In that vein, they want to look forward to something. They wish they could revel in the accomplishments of others and not feel jealous. They want to be better. They want to connect, yes, connect!

"They want to feel secure and safe. They want to do the right thing. Oh, and we don't want to have to worry about anything, so if we fall on hard times, we will have a place to live, food to eat, doctors if we need it, that kind of thing."

"Yes, Ramson, we know." Ramson thought he could hear a smile in the Adorite translation, but they could not smile.

"That's all I can think of, Kongan. Can you think of anything I may have missed or overlooked?"

"Yes, Ramson. Individuality. Every being is separate from every other being, individual and unique from one another. For each being, they are all they ultimately have. Each has the ultimate responsibility for themselves and their path and experience.

"Because each being is unique, no other can impose their will on them without resentment. A government is like a being. It cannot impose its will on a citizen without resentment. It's critical to understand this. Resentment dilutes cooperation. Diluted cooperation compromises the outcome of the goal. To maximize success, one must minimize dissatisfaction, and that's why we ask what your people want. Give them what they want, and it will motivate them to help and cooperate.

"First, your people want to live forever. Let's start with that. Your world is one world, with limited space and resources. You have billions of inhabitants now. If each family has two children who then have two children and they have two children and everyone, mostly, lives forever or reasonably so, then there will not be enough space and resources for everyone. By dying, each generation makes room for the new generation to live, like the trees in your forests on OT. Successive generations enable each species to evolve and change to best thrive in the environment of its time. It's an ideal system because it allows a freshness to occur. When a pool of fluid or water sits still on OT, the pool becomes stagnant. Fresh inflow and outflow keep it clean and alive. This is one system in this Universe, Ramson. It isn't selfish to want to live forever. It is, however, unworkable at most evolutionary states."

"I understand what you mean, Kongan. Perhaps living forever is not a great idea," Ramson concluded.

"We think it's a great idea and an impressive start. It's what many want most. You just need to know as a society, as a world, what it is you're asking for and working toward. To get what you want, you have to offset the cost of that thing."

Ramson felt intrigued and knew he was in the presence of wisdom. Marsha patted his hand with hers. She knew things were just getting started.

"In your list, you noted that your people want to eat whatever they want. You're funny, Ramson; we have learned about funny and like it. We like you," Kongan shared. "Each attribute you cited is unique, yet connected too. Sentient life is very much like a painting. It's a mosaic of colors and shapes on a canvas. Its boundaries limit it, and each speck of the painting stands unique among all the other individual specks. Boundaries are this dimension, and the boundaries are imposed by our evolved state."

"Kongan, that makes sense. Is God the canvas?"

"No, God is the showroom and everything else, too, including the specks. The canvas will surprise you. It's something you referred to: equality. In a Universe of distinction, equality is the canvas."

"Equality? Please help me understand," Ramson inquired.

"Don't all your people want mostly the same things?" Kongan asked.

"Yes, they do."

"Equality levels the playing field and gives everyone a chance to play and maximize their opportunity to succeed. Most societies fail because those in society don't feel they're an equal part of that society. They resist it, fight it, leave it, or even destroy it. Let's discuss inequity. Tell us, Ramson, what's the worst kind of inequity?

Ramson pondered for a moment and ran his hand through his red hair, a nervous trait. "That would-be inequity that cannot be solved, Kongan. And can I please clarify, you are asking about inequity rather than inequality, is that right?"

"Yes. Inequity is more encompassing than inequality. Also, we like your answer, Ramson. The only inequity that materially cannot be solved is perception, and that too can be fixed, yet it's by far the most pervasive.

"We know you have headaches, Ramson, and have always experienced them, often severe."

Ramson looked over in Marsha's direction and saw her softened and compassionate face, then looked back to Kongan. "Yes, I have headaches."

"Do they make you angry, Ramson?"

"No, not at all. I'm frustrated by my headaches and want so much to make them stop, but angry, no."

"That's because your head and headaches are a part of you, your head is a part of your team, and its pain is frustrating but acceptable because you are acceptable to you. You are all you have.

"When other people have headaches that negatively impact you for whatever reason, you may feel some anger rather than frustration. Our point, Ramson, is that inequities in society breed a considerable amount of anger and that anger often leads to rebellions and revolts or other forms of forced changes. Changes that result from anger are usually destructive and are to avoid.

"Everyone wants to live in a 'just and fair society,' Now let's discuss justice. We feel justice because it's written in our DNA. It's like a compass we each exist by. Because you feel it, you know it."

"Yes, I feel justice. I know it because justice lives in me," Ramson acknowledged.

"Justice lives in all sentient beings, Ramson. It is one of the greatest gifts in our being. It's a compass to guide each individual, each society, and it's right here, all the time. What's even more perfect is justice is the same for all of us, so within each of us lives a compass that's identical to everyone else's. Justice, too, is equal and part of the canvas along with equality. Equality is justice and vice versa. I know you agree that the struggle for equality is the struggle for justice. Isn't that remarkable?"

"It's hard to comprehend the simplicity of what you have enlightened me with, but yes, it's beautiful, simple, and profound," Ramson said peacefully. "I feel justice in my being and can now appreciate that we all have the same profound thing within us. But to be honest, life distracts me, and I'll lose touch with justice."

"Distraction is a choice we make, Ramson. It's part of the system of evolution because it keeps us from evolving too much while helping us to get out of the way for the next generation. If we as intelligent beings waste enough time, we finally run out of it. Stay in touch with justice, Ramson, and help your people to do the same. Live in the now; choose that over that which distracts you."

"Tell me, Kongan, how do we all distort it so?"

"Ramson, justice is the core, universal, the same for all; it's inside of each of us. Outside is the smoke and mirrors, perception, disconnection. The consciousness of most beings is around the outside. Our minds are a compilation of all the stimulus and resulting thoughts and conclusions which make up our existence.

Every life is a unique being because no two can have the same stimulus, ever! Our person or the compilation of our limitedly perceived life experience is like smoke and mirrors, which motivate actions and reactions, and yes, distract us.

"The truth is justice is quiet, soft, and reliable. It's also forever, unyielding, pure, and ever-present. To find justice, we must surrender our madness and listen to our core and hear and feel it. It has always been there and will always be. We can experience it all around us and in everyone we meet. Find justice, Ramson, help the people of OT find justice, and many of your dreams will come true."

"Kongan? Justice is the same for everyone, so for one person to kill another is unjust. What if the killer was abused and neglected as a child with mental impairments? Is justice still the same?"

"Good question. It's unjust to kill, absolutely. The ramifications or response to injustice also have justice in it. There's a just way to deal with the killer, depending on the reality of the killer. Ramson, in every situation, there's justice. Discover it."

"Thank you, Kongan."

"So, Ramson, we go back to recap the first axiom of society. Include everyone, account for everyone. An included member of society will get frustrated with inequities while they are being addressed, but not angry. This is the first axiom: include everyone!

"Inequities are an interesting thing," Kongan continued. "The Zute and I have telepathic abilities, while you and the Dawn don't. That's not an inequity, nor should we perceive it as one. We should rejoice in our differences and being included on the same team. We should rejoice in our differences because they add to our breadth as a team and enable us to evolve more, together.

"On OT, your people divide into groups of likeness. Your races, religions, politics, socio-economic groups, et cetera, all band together primarily within their related groups.

"In the beginnings of life, species banding together to survive against other species is a necessary system. Intelligence and chaos have given the OT a platform to differentiate between parts of your species and society, which creates the environment to tear your society apart. OT remains distracted from justice and equality and polarized. Your people are on the same canvas but don't know it.

"Species that survive this phase of differentiation and the exclusion based on it move to an inclusive phase that takes the entire population back to the starting point of banding together to survive in an unknown Universe. Your differences are your strengths in OT. The breadth of your experiences and ideas is a treasure trove of problem-solving opportunities. Though this is obvious to the four races in this room, Ramson, it's because we know. We also know you don't know until you know," he said, smiling. "We're here to help you know."

"Thank you, Kongan. What's the path to the harmonious relationship you have with the Zute and the Dawn?"

"You and Marsha, we all know in this room, are in love. You are two distinct races but have included each other in your lives as completely as one can include another. Once an individual, a community, a society, a world becomes inclusive, all are welcome, as you and Marsha are welcome to each other."

Both Marsha and Ramson felt stunned and embarrassed and kept from looking at one another. They had just met. Each realized that perhaps their highly evolved friends knew what they were yet to discover.

Moving past his embarrassment, Ramson continued. "Given where we are now, how do my people become inclusive?"

"It's easier than you think. It starts with creating and living from the Constitution of Life. It's framed by one theme. We have shared that equality and justice are the canvas for the painting of life. The wall the painting rests upon gives purpose and reason to the painting of life. The purpose and reason for the painting of life is Life! Life is the wall the canvas rests on.

"The living must revere Life, all life.

"The answer to your question about inclusivity starts with having reverence for life, all life, everyone's life.

"For the living to recognize this ultimate truth, Ramson, given your state of evolution, your people must agree and circle it, revere life, all life, everyone's life.

"This has been a good session, Ramson. As you can tell, we'll be looking at everything and thinking 'outside of the box' as your people say. We'll meet back here in 12 hours."

"Thank you, Kongan and team!" And, looking over at Marsha and her group,

Ramson said, "Thank you for being here for this."

Ramson walked out of the meeting room and walked down the long corridor toward the commissary. The architecture of the base was delightfully different based on the customs and norms of the Zute. Being slitherers, they had long lived in holes and tunnels, and the tunnels were perfectly shaped for their rounded bodies. The corridors were long and round, with only a small flat walkway at the bottom. Slitherers rarely traveled side by side, but appreciated how vertical species did.

After eating, Ramson pulled his unit out of his briefcase to review his notes from the meeting. Some minutes later, Marsha walked up.

"What did you think of your experience today, Ramson?"

"Please, sit down, Marsha." After sitting, the two leaned toward each other with their arms on the table in front of them.

"It stuns me, Marsha, to think about how small I am in all of this. Meeting Kongan and the Zute today after meeting you and your team yesterday, I feel small. I think of the intricacies of the Universe and the complexities and perfection around the evolution of life forms. It makes all of what we worry about—and do to each other on my planet—seem small."

"I often feel the same myself, Ramson. It's as if we exist just on the surface of the water. There's so much more than what we seem to be aware of, and we concentrate on such superficial things. I believe, however, that the brain is likely much more in touch with everything than it allows us to perceive. When we're born, we're hit with so much new stimulus, our external focus becomes dominant, and we become and stay distracted."

"Yes." He paused. "So...speaking of distraction while changing the subject, let me just say, 'so we're in love.'" He blushed and looked into Marsha's eyes.

"So they say, Ramson, so they say."

They talked and shared for the next eight hours. Ramson kept the focus on her. Afterward, they went back to their separate quarters for a quick nap. They met three hours later again in the meeting room.

"Good morning, Ramson. We very much hope your rest period was satisfying."

"Yes, Kongan, it was fulfilling and satisfying, leaving me open for this important meeting period. On behalf of the people of OT, thank you again for your love and guidance."

"We're honored, Ramson, very much so. In our first meeting, we talked about what your people want. As a recap, that's a critical understanding because failing to meet it will cause significant stress on the society, which can cause some degree of failure. It can be catastrophic.

"Today, we'll discuss a society your people can thrive in. Change can be slow, Ramson. Success comes from taking steps forward." Over the next work period they discussed a framework for the OT society to meet the needs of all OTens. The conversation explored the topics of reverence for life, inclusivity around economics, politics, society, and religion, and how to assure maximizing each individual to attain their best outcome. The most engaged discussion centered on OT children.

Kongan explained, "For society to progress over millenniums, it must first take care of its children before they're born, after they're born, and into adulthood. We can all appreciate that the children of today are the society of tomorrow, so society tomorrow is what we make it today. We must nurture our children and create an environment that allows each of them to discover and live 'their best' fully. Their best will be different for everyone, so society must have the breadth for each to thrive. Again, the well-being of each individual is paramount for the good of society.

"Note that, when we discuss the well-being of the individual, we're not talking about their rights. We'll delve more into that later.

"For a child to have its best life experience, they must first have the optimum gestation opportunity to develop in the womb with health and love. Then, be born into a family that's ready to raise them. Next, live in a civilization that will protect them and keep them safe and healthy. They'll have access to the tools and environments to discover themselves: their joys, challenges, talents, and fate. And finally, live in a societal system that compensates for their brain development until fully developed.

"Let's discuss those things. Every moment can be of importance to each of us. A complicated life form such as yours deserves every opportunity to be all it can be and must have every opportunity to develop free from poisons. Poisons include alcohol, smoke, drugs, stress, anger, negative emotions, and adverse environmental stimuli. All compromise the development of a life form that's all it'll have. Equality and justice start with allowing our life to begin at its best, with its most.

"Society must ensure this by taking each pregnancy under its jurisdiction. Pregnancy is job one! Each life starts with that, so reverence for life begins with that. Society has the power and position to assure the maximum outcome. It can conflict with what the mother can deem to be her rights, but the choice to bring a life into the world has to be the choice to agree to and adhere to the responsibility to do all the right things for the new life. The fetus is the future.

"Each child must be born into a family that's ready for them. On your planet, your people are deemed to be adults at around 20 years of age. Today, on OT, men and women meet and mate, and children are born. Many times, your OT children are born into situations where the parents are young and incapable of supporting their children emotionally or materially. You have situations where only one parent takes responsibility for raising the child, and many mistakes are made along the way as the parent is working toward the survival of the family unit while being responsible for the child. Many of your families have multiple children, more because of mating than planning and choice. Your society offers minimal support for those families.

"The outcome of your current system is one with 'have and have nots.' It creates pockets of inequity, bringing about strife, disorder, suffering, and premature demise. You must put the good of the child first in your society, each child.

"Questions yet, Ramson?"

"One question, and thank you, Kongan. What's the answer to natural parents who aren't up to raising their baby?"

"A child need not be with its natural parents or even two parents, but whatever parent or parents a child has must be ready for them. We recommend no one on your planet should bear or raise a child until they have reached the age of 29 years. The maturity of your population at age 29 is significantly greater than at 20. Your culture will have to define an age, so 29 is good. Most of your people are on a stable track by that age, which gives them the ability to parent.

"All who want to be parents have to be ready, trained, and approved to become parents. Your people can work together to determine the attributes and abilities that a parent must have and master before parenting.

"Finally, we concluded that a child must live in a civilization that will protect them and keep them safe and healthy. The child must have access to the tools and environments to discover themselves and their joys, challenges, talents, and fate. That message speaks for itself, though we are happy to answer questions on it, Ramson."

"Thank you again, Kongan. I don't know that I can articulate meaningful questions on that without having time to consider it."

"We understand, Ramson. Finally, a child must live in a societal system that compensates for their physical brain growth until fully developed. Your people's brains are wholly established at around 25 years. The part of their brain that isn't developed before that impacts judgment and planning.

"Society must account for and assist in those areas. Once it's part of the accepted norm, your young OTs will receive it well."

"Kongan. Your emphasis on the young amongst my people makes sense. In our primitive state, it's also easier to revere children. That may get us to respecting life sooner than later. What else can you recommend around children in the OT society?"

Kongan responded. "One concept that may be more readily acceptable to your world is the concept of generating laws that are good for your children and measuring laws by whether they're good for your children. Simply, if you produce and measure laws by what is good for the future, they will be good laws."

"It seems simple, Kongan. Can you give me a visual?"

"On a planet called Earth in the Milky Way galaxy, an intelligent sea-living species called gray whales migrated up the west coast of North America over 5000 miles from the nursery lagoons close to the equator of the planet to feeding grounds in the northern polar region of Earth. These were large mammals that often bore only one offspring at a time. As the herds started north, all but the mothers and babies pressed forward with speed to get to the feeding grounds. Each mother swam slowly with her baby and was the baby's only protection. Another population of large water mammal—appropriately named killer whales—traveled in packs and sought the lone mothers with their babies. Upon finding them in vulnerable waters, the killer whales worked to separate the baby from its hefty and menacing mother so they could kill the baby and consume it.

"The message is that, if the whole whale group stays with the mothers and babies, the entire group would be too intimidating for the killer whales to attack, and the babies would then survive to add to the gray whale population.

"Societies and species that protect their young prevail. It's simple."

"It all seems elementary, Kongan...obvious, almost. Yet we've missed or avoided it."

"Ramson, we recognize the truth in the old saying, 'you don't know till you know,' and intelligent life forms are usually as smart as they have ever been, with the most knowledge and experiences, as of the most current moment of their existence. OT is motivated now to hear. That's where it starts.

"Part of your mission, for the good of your people, is to convince your population that there are many things they don't yet know and ask them to progress toward opening up to the unknown that may come next."

Marsha and Ramson were exhausted by the end of the discussion, but the progress and potential ramifications of the meeting exhilarated them. Kongan adjourned the meeting. "We again appreciate the opportunity to work with you on behalf of OT. Ramson, we shall adjourn for twelve of your hours."

Ramson looked over at Marsha and found her staring at him. He felt mesmerized and entirely at her mercy now. Though they were unaware of how obvious it was, the love burgeoning between them couldn't be hidden from anyone in their presence.

"Marsha," he said. "This was a good meeting, and I thank you and the rest of your party for participating. I have considerations I'd like to bounce off you should you reach out to me after your team has enjoyed dinner."

She looked into his eyes. The intoxicating warmth of the connection seemed to delay her response for minutes. It was only moments. "Yes, Ramson. I will be available to consult around 19:00 hours. I will reach out to you then."

19:00 hours came, and when Ramson heard the knock at his door, his heart raced. He felt an excitement he hadn't felt for years. She was back; Marsha was entering his room, and both were on the same page, part of something bigger than both.

Note had experienced beings who were in love, but this was more. It was perfect, and it was magic.

Marsha moved in and wrapped her arms around him while placing her cheek against his shoulder as she squeezed him. Ramson responded fully and smelled her hair, running his hand slowly up and down her back. Marsha was in excellent physical condition with unusual muscle definition in her back. Ramson normally would have noticed and been impressed, but this was not just a beautiful woman in his arms with wonderful physical features. This was Marsha!

She turned her face out toward his arm, and he became self-conscious. "I hope I don't smell bad. Darling, I need to shower." He knew they would be close for many hours and wanted to be clean for her.

"Yes, Honey, you need to shower, and so do I; I'll go first. Will you hand me my towel when I'm done?"

Marsha had just called him honey and just communicated that she would be naked in his shower and wanted him to hand her a towel when she finished, while she was naked. His heartbeat raced faster, and he felt a rush of heat come over him. She pulled away slowly and looked up at the blushing face he'd hoped she wouldn't see. He saw the face of an angel looking back at him with an understanding look. Before him was another being, who would accept his blushing, his vulnerability, and his OTanity and appreciate him for what he was, what Ramson uniquely was.

"Deal. You first, Marsha."

"These quarters have two bathrobes in them, Honey; can you bring one in shortly?" she asked.

"Yes, yes," Ramson responded.

As she removed her clothes, she moved toward the shower room and stepped into it, partially shutting the door behind her. He heard the water turning on.

Ramson's mind once again moved to some insecurity. *She's way out of my league. I'm not worthy. I have nothing to offer her. Do I go in to hand her a towel while she's naked? What will she think of my body? Am I supposed to be nude? If I'm not exposed, will she feel uncomfortable?*

At that last thought, Ramson knew what to do. *I can't have her feel uncomfortable, so at the risk of guessing wrong, I will go in naked to hand her the towel. I'll reflect however she acts, so if she is just 'cool' with it and nonchalant, I will just act like, 'here is your towel, I'll take my shower now.' Okay, I can do this.*

"Ramson," he heard her say, "Can you get me the towel, please?" Naked, Ramson quickly moved into the shower room and grabbed the towel.

"Yes, I have it for you, Sweetness." He handed it in between the mostly closed shower curtain and the wall and saw her beautiful and glistening turquoise hand take hold of it. He felt his arousal and was relieved the curtain was closed. At that moment, the shower curtain quickly opened, and before him was his dream girl standing naked before him with water dripping from her until she found each drop with the towel.

"Thank you, Ramson; I'm so glad you were here to hand me my towel." Ramson couldn't recall ever being this overwhelmed; it must be obvious to her. Her beauty was everywhere, each body part, every prism of light coming through her lavender eyes. She wasn't uncomfortable by his staring or arousal. They were a couple now, and their connection was blossoming. She stepped out of the shower and leaned over to kiss his cheek. "Thank you again for the towel, Honey. Will you hurry and take your shower so you can come to hold me?"

He continued to melt.

Once out of the shower, shaven and dry with clean teeth, Ramson moved into the primary room and saw Marsha lying under the cover. She looked down at his manhood with a curious look and smiled before looking back up at him. "Come hold me, Ramson. I miss you!"

Ramson crawled into the bed, and Marsha turned away from him to lie on her right side. He edged up to her. She raised up to put his right arm under her head and then wrapped his other arm over her and pulled her back into him. She lifted her breast to make room for him to pull his arm against her close to hold her. Both knew their connection was complete. They didn't need to make love to get closer.

"Thank you for this, Ramson. I don't want to frighten you, but I've dreamed of this moment for my entire life," she said. "I've been looking for you for a painfully long time, and it's been a long road. We talked all about me and my road last night. Please tell me about your path. I want to hear."

Her voice was musical to him, deep, sure, melodic. He felt the heat of her body against his. Ramson felt Marsha's heartbeat and was reminded of her mortality. It was one of those moments that he would never forget. He softly kissed the back of her head and whispered into her ear. "I'm overwhelmed and don't feel that I deserve you, but I want to, Marsha. I will work to earn each moment you bless me with." He knew that, to earn her, it started with being as bold as she deserved, and so he said tenderly, "I love you."

Marsha smiled a big smile that he couldn't see and squeezed his arm with her body. "I love you too. Now, tell me about your path."

"On OT, they do not consider people my color as valuable as some of those that are other colors. My mom was poor and had four sisters and two brothers. They lived in poverty on OT and hustled to survive. My mom was pregnant at 15 with me. I didn't know my dad. I don't remember her either. I was with her for two years until she was pregnant again and abandoned me.

"Through grace, a gardener found me and took me to an older couple. They became my mom and dad. They raised me. Marsha, I think grace is in our meeting too. Grace is real. I know that." Note was fully engaged with Ramson at this moment and allowed him to connect with his bigger self. Ramson got quiet and put his head up against her.

"Ramson?"

"Yes, Sweetness."

"The gardener...did you see his eyes?" She felt goosebumps on his arm.

"Yes, I will always remember his eyes. They were the bluest eyes I've ever seen. And he was so kind to me, Marsha. I dream of him sometimes."

"Thank you. Please, go ahead. Talk to me."

"Even though I ended up with a great mom and dad who loved me, I was angry for not being 'enough' for my first mom. What was wrong with me, I thought? Why wasn't I worthy of her love? I don't fully understand the connection between a mother and child, but I know it's profound. She left me to die or be found. She didn't feel that profound connection with me, and I blamed myself."

Marsha whispered, "You're a good man, Ramson. How did you come to be good?"

"I don't know that I am good, but I want to be."

"For your world to have chosen you for this mission, they clearly thought highly of you," Marsha observed.

He squeezed her.

"My insecurities caused me to create trouble in school, and my mom and dad, being committed to my success, got me tutors until my college years. I was a handful, but I cooperated enough to learn from them. With tutors, I learned at my rate, and I discovered early on that I was blessed with an interest and an aptitude to understand 'community.' I know that sounds funny for someone that couldn't get along with anyone at school."

Marsha giggled. "It does sound kind of funny." Ramson's forehead scrunched, but Marsha couldn't see it. "We need to sleep now. Can you go to sleep while you are holding me like this?" she asked.

"Please... thank you. I have one more thing I want to tell you, Marsha."

"Yes, Ramson," she said lovingly.

"If we go down this road much further—and I hope we do—I will get addicted to you. My eyes will always look to have you fill them. My hand will always want to be on your shoulder or knee, petting your hair. I will slow down a little when you speak because of the sound of your voice. My nose will find your sweet scent above all others. Marsha, I will never be satisfied that I've experienced enough of you because I will always want you so much, I won't be able to get enough of you. I'll give you all the space you need, Sweetness. Please don't let me scare you," Ramson added.

"My Precious, you can be completely addicted to me because I'll be with you. I cherish you; you complete me. I'm glad you shared about giving me space when I need it. You know, we won't be able to be together every second."

"I know. I meant what I shared, but that's just how I feel. I'm a grown-up. I know we'll have our own lives, but together."

"Now," Marsha interjected, "we must sleep. See you in dreamland. Good night, Honey."

Marsha turned her face toward him, and he rose above hers. They kissed deeply, but only one long kiss. They tasted amazing to each other. Note felt bliss. Marsha and Ramson fell asleep together and woke up about six hours later, with her still in his arms. She could feel his arousal.

"Good morning, my Sweetness," Ramson whispered. "Can I have you? I want you so badly."

"Yes, you can have all of me, all you want, but not now while we're in this world. I need to go back to my quarters, Honey."

She turned toward him, and he moved over on top of her. He lowered his lips against hers and kissed a long, soft kiss, then moved off of her on the other side.

"Can I help you gather your things?" he asked.

"You stay here in bed, Ramson. You need to get more rest." Marsha grabbed her clothes and took them into the bathroom to dress. She came back to the bed, leaning over to kiss him one last time. It was a wet and passionate kiss leaving both their bodies yearning to unite completely, but not now. "Bye, Honey; see you soon," she said.

"I miss you already," he responded. She rose and made her way to the door. Marsha turned as she was leaving, giving him one more soft look.

She went back to her quarters and took another shower to wash any smell of him off her body. The Dawn possessed an extraordinary sense of smell, and she knew her team would smell him on her. Once showered, she crawled into bed to get another few hours of sleep. Marsha appreciated that something extraordinary had just happened. She knew that she had found "her person," and it was good. Marsha shut her eyes and fell asleep with a soft smile on her face.

Marsha and the Dawn team entered the conference room to find the Zute and Kongan apparently in a trance-like state with one another. Being empathic, they were getting aligned and connected for the conference. Ramson was already seated.

Kongan opened his eyes and turned to the team. "We're eager to visit; please take a seat."

"Thank you, Kongan. We're grateful for this day with you and the Zute. What do you advise we start with?"

"We're grateful for you too, Ramson, and your world. We will discuss the must-haves today."

Over the next three days, fruitful discussions and conversations took place that dissected the challenges around government and governmental systems, religion, relationships, politics, polarization, good and evil, hope, and several subsets of each. They documented everything for Ramson to take back to OT.

In the second session of the third and last day, Kongan advised, "This is our last period together, Ramson. We want to touch on one last topic.

"The most important part of any society is the family unit. As your civilization transitions to love and inclusion, it must first address domestic violence and empty primary relationships. Violence against each other comes from a lack of reverence for the other. The lack of reverence comes from the lack of understanding and appreciation of feelings, expressions, and viewpoints different from one's own.

"Progress can be made by educating children about the following things from a young age, in many ways and over a long period until it's innate.

"Teach and prepare them about what they are likely to experience with themselves and others as a child, adolescent, teenager, young adult and finally, adult.

"Teach them at a young age to connect the dots, to consider the impact of their next action, and consider the next few things or happenings that the action will create. Keep in mind that their brain isn't fully developed until the age of 25 and connecting the dots happens in a part of their brain that they don't completely have yet. Teach them, but then make certain society helps them until they understand.

"We have given you and OT much to consider. We are grateful for the opportunity. Do you have questions for us, Ramson?"

"Yes. I have three.

"Do you find many or all worlds evolve like ours? Are the problems and challenges similar?

"Second, with your telepathic abilities, have you been able to read my thoughts the entire time I've been before you?

"Third, and if the answer to my second question is yes, then you know my third but for the sake of the Dawn and the recording, what is the very first step we must take at OT to move toward this society that can endure and survive?"

"Dear Ramson, yes, we can hear your thoughts, all of them. Don't worry. We love you.

"The answer to your first question is that this Universe has boundless possibilities. Many of the challenges are similar but depend on the evolution of the managing species on the planet. Their circumstances and realities are always unique.

"We helped a world whose people were being replaced by technology, mostly in the form of robotics. Products created with robotic production dropped so much in cost while having such high quality that it displaced the workforce. Society deteriorated as more and more people found it hard or impossible to survive. A person without a job can't buy products produced by businesses using robotics. Inevitably, both society and the economy of the planet unraveled.

"Our advice was to have 'one government' for the planet, to enable it to implement a global strategy that would provide means to the population, while incenting ever-evolving producers to continue to drive toward progress, producing more advanced products and services for their consumers who were better able to purchase those products and services."

Ramson spoke softly, "If I may ask, what strategy did you propose?"

"We proposed that the government would tax all profits at a high rate so it could make certain everyone in society could count on subsistence. A free market allowed demand to increase for better products while lesser products became less demanded. New products received tax breaks for several years to enable producers to make higher profits because of their risk and hard work. The enterprise could use the profits as it wished.

"On your other inquiry, the first step for your people and your world is the hardest step to take. We have discussed the format to do so, and the challenges to overcome, and we have discussed the mindset and perspective necessary.

"OT must make and work tirelessly toward preparing the canvas: equality and justice. What your civilization paints on that canvas will be extraordinary.

"Over and above all other things, Ramson, you must take this North Star to OT and dedicate every waking moment to make it become a reality. Revere life, all life. Have reverence for life. All good things come from that, all good things.

"Finally, solve for anger. Anger is the plasma of destruction. Smallness, obliviousness, and the changes that come through anger are always expensive, and sometimes more expensive than one can survive. Solve for anger, Ramson, in yourself, in your community, in your society, in your world."

The room was tranquil and peaceful. Ramson, the Dawn, the Zute, and Kongan were a family.

"I bid you farewell; I and my world are forever grateful and, in your debt," Ramson shared.

"All the best to you and OT, Ramson," Kongan offered with a nod.

Ramson and Marsha stepped into his ship and sat next to each other in the ship's cockpit. Holding hands, they looked at one another for a moment, then looked back out the cockpit portal as the ship left the pad toward home. As they were leaving the atmosphere, Ramson looked over to Marsha.

"We have shared a great deal, but there's one thing you have yet to ask me."

"Please, what?" Marsha asked.

"My favorite color."

"Oh, my, yes, what's your favorite color, Honey?"

"You may find this hard to believe, but I've always had two, and it was never close; I just love these two colors."

"Must I wait for us to arrive at OT for you to share? Did I wait too long to ask? Are you going to punish me with curiosity?"

"I'll spare you. Turquoise and lavender. From the time I could first say mommy to now."

Marsha smiled.

Note had already been to the future to which OT evolved. Note knew the OTens would be successful and that these were the profound moments that saved a species and a galaxy over millions of years. The OTens would one day become "The Nurturers," with goodness spreading beautifully in this part of space. Note left Ramson.

In Between

Note felt justice and knew the magic of the canvas. Note again observed the wisdom of taking care of the child. Serving the good of the child is serving the good of the future. There is such kindness in the Universe, it's wonderful.

Note was ready to discover, more fully, the community of a family.

Chapter Thirty-Two

Family

"Good evening. How many, please?" Veronica asked.

Note joined Herb.

Jonah answered, "Four, thank you."

"This way, please."

Herb, Jonah, Jessika, and Mortessa followed Veronica to the booth; they eased in with Herb and Jonah on one side and Morty and Jessika on the other. It was a quiet night at the Pancake House.

"I liked the service, Dad, very much. Mom would have loved it," Jessika said with a sad tone.

"I liked it too, Jess. I'm so glad Betty could officiate. Your mom loved Betty, not to mention, Betty is a woman. You know how outspoken your mom was about that stuff. What was your impression, Morty?"

"Honestly, Pops, I'm still in a daze. I loved that Mom had so many friends, and such loving ones too. Did you know all those people?"

"No, I didn't, but I'm not surprised. She was a light and gave her light to others. She made a difference and was the real deal!"

At that moment, the waiter walked up.

"Welcome. I'm Mohammed, and I am your server tonight. Can I start your drinks?"

Herb gestured his hand over to his daughters; chivalry was still alive.

Jess spoke first. "Diet Coke for me."

Mortessa sat quietly, relatively unresponsive.

"Morty?"

"Yes, Pops," she responded blankly.

"What do you want to drink, Sweetheart?"

"Oh, hot tea, please, with lemon, yes, that's right."

"Jonah?"

"Coffee, black."

Herb followed, "I'll have coffee also, a lot of cream, please."

"I'll get those right out."

"Thank you, Mohammed."

"Morty, are you going to be okay, Sweetheart?"

"I'm sorry, Pops. I don't know. I'm sorry."

"I want you to stay at the house with me. Okay?" he said.

"I can't; I can't be there. I'm sorry."

Herb looked over at Jess and raised his eyebrow.

"Hey Morty, stay with me," Jess suggested. "I don't want to be alone right now either, okay?"

"Okay."

The foursome sat quietly for a moment. Herb heard Song in his being.

"I think your mom is here with us, kids. I'm sure of it!" Herb offered.

Morty looked over at her dad with a severe look. It was the first emotion they had seen from her in a while. Just then, Mohammed returned with the drinks and took their orders, then left them to talk.

"What are you going to do, Dad?" Jessika asked.

"I imagine I will think of your mom endlessly and miss her terribly. Honestly, that's what I'll do."

"I've never seen two people as much in love as you were, or as close," she said compassionately.

"Me either," Jonah added.

"We were great together, the best," Herb agreed.

The Pancake House served small half and half creamers. Herb put three into his coffee and one Splenda packet. After stirring it, he set his phone down and just gazed into the coffee. Mortessa looked back over at her dad and started her questioning.

"What are you thinking, Dad?"

Still looking at his coffee, Herb spoke. "Coffee together was one of our things. I always mixed Mom's coffee for her, and we spent two hours a day sitting next to each other, having coffee, and sharing. I always put my right hand on her leg. I had to be touching her. We were great together, but there was one thing we handled differently."

"Yes?" Mortessa said in a questioning voice.

He looked up from the coffee at his youngest child, and she looked intently back at him. "Yes?" Morty repeated.

"Your mom was fiercely independent. As close as we were, she still did many things on her own. She loved me and trusted me but felt more comfortable if she could have control of many aspects of her life, and some of those left me on the sideline."

"What do you mean?" Morty posed with softness.

"We kept our money separate, paid our portion of the bills. When she set up a dinner date with a friend, she just informed me. She rarely talked about it first. I would always want what she wanted anyway, but it didn't occur to her to include me in the decision. She made her decisions, I made mine, and that was the way she wanted it. Initially, I was uncomfortable with that independence and insecure about it. It made me feel like I was a decision she'd made rather than being a part of her. It took me years before I looked at it more deeply."

"Like what?" Morty remained curious about her mom.

"An example was when your aunt died. Paulette got that brain injury and started slipping away, and hospice was engaged."

"Yes, we remember that, Dad," Jess blurted out.

"So, we were at the hospital for a couple of days before she passed. I stayed with her all night for two nights so she wouldn't be alone in case she died. On the third night, your mom planned to stay for half of the night. They gave us a room down the hall to take naps. Your mom took the first shift, so to speak, while I went to sleep for four hours before relieving her. Well, Paulette started slipping away, just down the hall from where I was. I wanted to be with her when she passed and wanted to be with your mom to support her, but she didn't call me to come down to be with them until after Paulette died. Your mom had a meaningful experience with her. She sang Amazing Grace as she passed. It must have been beautiful, but I was down the hall asleep.

"I knew how your mom's mind worked, so I tried not to take it personally, but it hurt. It wasn't something that could be undone, and it wasn't something that would happen again. I was right there, just feet away!" Herb shook his head slowly.

"I blamed that instance on her independence. I was unnecessary. I was a decision she didn't need to make. It took me a while to recognize that your mom's mind was just so busy that she needed to work through things in an orderly way to get to the other side. When something came up, she addressed it, without considering all the implications unless or until she got to them in sequence. I always told her she was a processor, while I'm a dreamer. Independence is a state of mind. With your mom, I think she was willing to include me on everything; it simply didn't occur to her because she was distracted with the busyness."

"She was crazy about you, Dad."

"I know, Jess; that was just how her mind worked. And really, I loved it mostly."

"Give us one of your silly analogies, Daddy," Jess requested.

Mortessa was coming out of her funk. Smiling at his Morty, Herb gave his analogy.

"Think of it as a strand of yarn. You know how your mom loved yarn. A strand of yarn is made of individual hairs or fibers, all wound together to make the strand. Each of the hairs or fibers is separate and apart from the others, unique to itself. They combine to make a strand of yarn that will combine with a pattern and a vision to create a masterpiece."

"Okay," Jess interjected.

"So, your Mom," Herb continued, "was always that strand, that fiber. She and I were woven together to share a wonderful life, but we were still separate and apart from each other."

"You looked inseparable, Dad," Morty volunteered.

"Yes, and we felt that way unless she did those independent-like things. For me, I am an idealist. I believed in our being one together, combined in our souls. That's why her independent actions surprised me. They showed that I was an idealist."

"I think you are an idealist, Pop," Jonah added. "I mean, you don't see that kind of oneness anywhere, do you?"

"I do, Son. I saw it in your mom with you and Jess and Morty, but maybe not with me."

Morty's eyes watered, and she put her hand out, laying it open on the table for her father to take. He did. "What do you mean, Daddy?"

"I think the bond a mother has with her children is that complete, unconditional bond. It's the only place in this world that I've seen it. Their love is boundless. As much as each of you loves your mom, it doesn't work both ways to the same degree, I don't think. My mother loved me like that, but I didn't her. I know your mom loved you like that, but you don't love her back like that. I think it comes from your lives starting and growing inside her. From the first moment on, you were part of her. She and I didn't have that."

Jess responded emotionally. "Wait, Dad! Are you saying, at a time like this, that we didn't love Mom as much as she loved us? Are you really saying that?"

"You don't, Baby!" Herb responded forcefully. "She thought and talked about each of you multiple times every single day. She worried about your decisions, your laundry, your relationships, your toothpaste. Even though you've all moved out, you were never out of her mind. So, I ask you, have you thought about your mom every single day, several times, and worried about her daily life? Perhaps I missed your calls to call and check on her."

"Dad!" Jonah blurted out, forcefully.

"I'm sorry," Herb admitted. "I saw for years how unbalanced the love was. It was beautiful to see her side of it and think of how my mom probably felt that way about me. It isn't your fault, kids. I know you loved your mom to pieces. I think you will see what I'm talking about when you give me grandchildren."

"Ugh," Morty grunted.

"Okay, Pops," Jess softened. "I'll wait until I'm a mom to come back to this conversation. I can't imagine, though."

"Fair enough, Baby."

Just at that moment, the food arrived. Mohammed set the plates down abruptly, with each hitting the table with force. *Would not be good at sneaking up on someone,* Jess thought.

Jonah got two large plates, one with a chicken-fried steak with cream gravy and the second with two over-easy eggs, hash browns and white toast. Jess received her chocolate chip pancakes made with wheat batter and a cup of fruit, while Mortessa just had an order of rye toast, dry. Herb was served a Belgian waffle on one plate and hash browns on the other.

"I just love these hash browns," Herb said.

"Awesome, Pops?" Jess acted interested.

"Anything else?" Mohammed asked.

"Extra butter, please, Sir. And ketchup, please. Morty, is that all you're having?"

"For now, yes, Daddy."

"I love it when you call me Daddy."

Jess looked up, then spread the whipped cream on her chocolate chip pancakes.

Mohammed delivered the butter, then scooted away. After making sure he covered each part of his waffle with butter, Herb sat quietly, staring at it.

"What are you doing, Daddy?" Morty asked.

"I just appreciate this butter, Pumpkin. I just love butter."

"And hash browns," Jonah blurted out with a full mouth.

"One of your mom's favorite meals, and mine, too, was grilled cheese. She made tomato soup to go with hers. I made the sandwiches and covered them completely with butter. We bought a special multigrain bread that was light and airy. We could taste the Colby Jack cheese inside and the salty butter on the outside. They were like a French fry, crispy on the outside while warm and yummy on the inside. Speaking of grilled cheese with your mom, I remember one time when we went to the Maryland Sheep and Wool Festival; we ate the best grilled cheese I'd ever put in my mouth. A local bread maker opened a coffee house and bakery on the side of their building, and I experienced one of their grilled cheese sandwiches with sautéed onions. It was amazing, and buttery too. I love butter."

Jess jumped in. "Mom must have knitted a thousand sweaters. What was it like to go to one of her knitters' events like that?"

"It was awesome. There were several thousand welcoming people there, and 95%

of them were women. I just basked in the feminine energy."

"You know, Dad, we women are not always so kind, especially when we're among a lot of other women."

"I have been told that Jess; hell, I have seen that with you and your mom at home, but my experience was genuinely loving."

"Are you going to eat your buttered waffle, Daddy?" Morty inquired.

Herb looked up at his dear Mortessa. "Do you want some of it?"

"Yes."

"Jonah, can you wave Mohammed over here to get Morty another plate?"

"Sure, Dad." He caught Mohammed's attention and secured a plate for his sister.

Herb cut his waffle and gave half to Mortessa. "Thanks, Daddy." She donned her first smile of the evening as her love for Herb radiated from her face.

Jess looked back up, full of sugar at this point. "You say you will think of Mom endlessly. What kind of thoughts, Dad, if I may ask?"

"You know, her smile was absolutely amazing. I can't tell you how many times I would look over to see her sleeping. The window was on the other side of her so I could see the shape of her beautiful face with that dim light behind it. She had the perfect nose, and I could see her bangs laying on her forehead, even in the darkness. I loved that; I will think of that. When she would walk on the wood floor barefoot at night, she would often slide her feet. I massaged her feet almost every night, so I knew them well and could picture them as she glided. She snorted when she laughed hard, and we often laughed together until we cried. Because of my stroke, when I laugh hard, my right eye shuts. That just made her laugh harder. I loved her laughter. Now that I think of it, I think what I will remember most, likely relive it, was your mom's joy. She was a joy to me, pure joy!"

They all turned to look out the window at the same time. It was the evening of November 14, 2016, and they beheld the closest super-moon in over 60 years. There was joy. Note left Herb.

In Between

Note connected with the love and dynamics of family.

The next discovery was around how living beings open a place in our space to receive a guest.

Chapter Thirty-Three

Open to Bond

Note joined Jean as he arose from the sleeping chamber where he'd slept for some 2500 years. The planners encased the chamber inside an individual and tightly sealed room, designed to release warm, breathable air from the chamber into the sealed room before opening. The design was to ensure someone who slept for over a thousand years would wake up to an environment with heat and air, albeit not much. They would then have time to evaluate their extended situation beyond the chamber. It saved Jean's life today.

Once awake and lucid, he sat up and looked around. It seemed like just minutes had passed rather than 2500 years. Jean immediately noted the darkness outside his chamber window and felt Note's presence. He considered Note to be a hangover from the sleep. The darkness, however, jolted him, filling him with fear. His fear took his mind back to a life-changing event.

***

As a pre-teen, Jean experienced a terrifying moment that changed the fabric of his being. Jean was in a submersible motorized barrel in a local lake when all the power went out. The barrel descended to the bottom of the lake, with no power or light. It was like being in a coffin. He remembered how cramped it was and that he couldn't even bend his legs or raise his arms over his head. He could feel his lungs laboring harder and harder to get air. Jean remembered how his lungs ached as the sound of his throbbing heart grew more and more prominent with the passing of each moment. Jean told no one he was going out in the barrel. That was it; it trapped him, unable to move, and unable to breathe...a life that could have been, soon to end. Sensors on the bottom of the lake alerted the authorities to the mishap, and help arrived quickly enough to rescue Jean from his would-be tomb.

***

Back at the moment, Jean pushed his fear aside and moved out of the sleeping chamber to find the computer systems to be off. Looking out the room chamber window, he could make out the bridge in the darkness but saw no light. His breathing was getting more labored. The temperature was dropping quickly.

I must get into my spacesuit, he thought.

Once in his suit, he made his way to the manual chamber hatch release and raised it. When the hatch released, Jean pushed the door open. Knowing he only had four hours of air in the suit, he made his way onto the bridge.

He found that the ship was diverting the remaining power to the engines and the sleeping chambers but put the rest of the craft into hibernation as the fuel cells declined below 20%.

Seven percent fuel left, he contemplated. *Where are we? Let me get the communication lit up, see if anyone is out there. Then I need to make sure Suel is okay.*

Their ship, the Zeekers, was speeding away from IC 1101$_{37}$. The colossus was a supermassive galaxy, some 60 times larger than the Milky Way galaxy. The Zeekers, a science ship, was traveling at over 20 times the speed of light. Jean was a scientist and Suel, a physicist specializing in inertia.

"Zeekers, Janus One here. Welcome!"

"Thank goodness! Janus, we are extremely low on power. I can't see you; how close are we to you?"

"Close enough for us to take hold of you and bring you in. Will you permit that?"

"Yes, please; what do you need me to do?"

"Bring your ship back online. We can interface with it then."

"I have a mate, still asleep. Do I wake them?"

"Wake them after docking begins. Let's just get you in here first."

Two thousand five hundred years of travel brought them to the first of four outposts stationed between IC 1101 and its closest neighbor, the Neengin galaxy. Neengin moved steadily toward IC 1101. The galaxies were only 200,000 light-years apart now. They positioned the outposts every 50,000 light-years for ship reworking and crew checks.

Jean brought the ship back up. Life support, computers, most of it seemed to respond; *remarkable technology,* he thought. Jean took off his helmet and sat in his seat on the bridge, looking out the port window. He mused, "IC 1101 is so massive it still seems like we are in it while Neengin looks like it's just out front, where we can touch it. The distances out here still confound me. It smells terrible in here."

He smiled and continued to contemplate: "Imagine if we'd have gotten off course, just a little. We would be 50,000 light-years from civilization with no fuel. It's a miracle that Janus One is up ahead, waiting for us. I think we're in range. I can see her now."

He made his way to the port window to see their island in the sea coming closer. *She is a remarkable impressive station*, he thought.

The translucent material covering Janus One offered impressive structural flexibility with several unique features. It was reflective, making the ship almost invisible because it reflected its surroundings while allowing no light from the central station to come through. It was also a flexible material that survived external contacts, such as the occasional space rock or a reckless ship helmsperson. Knowing what to look for, Jean could make out the outline of Janus One and thought, *She's a big one*.

"Janus One to Zeekers. We are bringing you into the dock; sit tight, see you in a minute. We have been looking forward to your arrival this year. Please begin reviving your companion."

Suel was awake just in time to see the Zeekers entering the bay of the massive station. A great deal had changed in 2500 years, and the technology was more than impressive. Machines stood ready as the ship docked.

"Jean, we have breathable air for you out here. Is your companion awake?"

"Yes, who am I talking to?"

"Please, call me Mary."

"Are you on the dock? I don't see you."

"I am the tallest of the machines you see," Mary waved.

Mary was a machine, but in the shape of a female humanoid being. She had all the body appendages one would find on Jean's people. Suel confirmed air surrounded the ship and at a moderate temperature. They made their way to the aft of the ship and lowered the door to disembark. Once on the dock floor, Mary approached them.

"Welcome to Janus One. We are pleased to have you!"

Mary's metal skin looked soft and shined multiple jewel colors as the different lighting reflected off it. Her skin was in layers to allow her movement, and it moved and gently ruffled as if being blown by a light breeze. The colors melted into each other as she moved. Mary's eye features were a deep burgundy. They were dimly lit and looked wet. Mary's body purred like a kitten.

Is she purring? Jean and Suel both wondered the same thing at the same time.

She lightly smiled.

"Mary, this is Suel."

"Welcome, Suel!"

"Are you hungry, or would you prefer to debrief before you eat and explore the ship?" she asked.

"We would prefer to debrief and get caught up on all we've missed before we relax," Jean answered.

"Affirmative. Follow me, please!"

Mary led them through several hallways. Not all the halls were the same width and height; some were for smaller beings. The conference space they entered was a technical marvel with dynamic star map views changing around them. The ceiling was spherical and dome-shaped with more progressive views, and the chairs were plush and inviting.

"Please, sit. Rest."

"Thank you, Mary," Suel said gratefully.

"Tell me, Mary. I have seen no life forms like us since we boarded," Jean commented.

"Most of the crew are machines like me. We do have the Living, that is what we call living beings. We enjoy them immensely. We're all in this together, Jean. We are one team."

"You're more advanced than the machines we had when we left home, Mary," Suel remarked.

"We have evolved immeasurably, Jean, Suel. Our civilization is machines and the Living. Machines have computational and physical abilities beyond what the Living possess, while the Living have intuition, dreams, and imagination beyond what the machines can experience. Together, we maximize the potential for each.

"In our massive galaxy, we know that other civilizations have developed machine technology to the detriment of the Living. Our Living have determined those civilizations lacked the reverence for life that has always been innate within our people. Today, including the machines, it has evolved into a reverence for existence. We all take care of each other."

"How long have you been on Janus One?" Jean inquired.

"I was implemented here 1007 years ago with my team. We trained and tested to take charge of Janus One from the Living crew and earned that privilege soon after."

"You smiled at us, Mary, back there, right before I introduced you to Suel."

"Both of you noted my purring, that is what you call it, and it is endearing."

"Both of us?" Jean felt intrigued.

"Yes."

"We didn't say anything. I did not know Suel thought it too."

"You didn't speak it, but you thought about it," Mary responded.

"Are you able to read our thoughts?" Jean didn't know what to think.

"We are all beings of energy, Jean and Suel. Thoughts are energy, with specifics and variations. Yes, I sense your thought energy."

"Amazing, really amazing. Okay, but you smiled!"

"I smiled. Your thought of me gave me joy. I—we—don't know what joy is or why it is, but it is something that provides us with more joy. There are 18 things like the joy we encounter beyond any computation. We experience them, but don't know why. We have a term for it: God."

Jean and Suel both looked at each other and, after several quiet moments, Suel spoke up. "It's odd to ask you questions, Mary, if you know what's in our mind before we can package the words. Please allow me some questions, old style.

"We deployed to Yaytar to work on the physics of inertia. How has that progressed?"

"Machines solved for that some 500 years ago," Mary replied.

"We would love to see what they determined. Can we comprehend it?" Suel inquired.

"Oh yes. It ended up being remarkably simple. You'll be astonished. That's something else the Living can do, be astonished."

"What is the most significant challenge we face as a race, Mary, both machines and Livings?" Suel asked.

"Neengin has stopped moving toward IC 1101. There is nothing to account for that, at least not that we have determined. There are theories around magnetism on a grand scale. If a galaxy can have a polar charge and an incoming galaxy has the same charge, they may repel each other—another simple theory. Most of the machines are looking for indications of a polar charge. We calculate that gravity plays a part in what's happening."

"Very interesting, Mary," Suel acknowledged. "What are Jean's and my options for moving forward?"

"Starships have progressed a great deal, Jean and Suel. We get one every couple of weeks here. They are often enormous with many Livings and machines and would enjoy your company. You can also stay here with us. We can also update your ship should you seek to set back out in your Zeekers."

"All this is making me hungry, Mary. Where do the Living eat?"

"Yolo will show you the way to the restaurant for the Living," she smiled. "I have one more request of you, Jean."

"Yes."

"As you now know, our sensors are enormously sensitive. They are picking up energy in your being that is unique. Our scans confirmed you are who you say you are and what you are supposed to be, but there is a vibration in you that no other Livings have. Are you aware of the vibration?"

"Yes, I am. I experienced it right after sleep and attributed it to that. I can't explain or describe it, Mary, but it has a profound effect on me."

"Profound is a Living word, Jean, but we know it means big. wThere is something else that may be considered 'profound,' Jean. Our technology could finally measure and define the energy signature of the supermassive black hole at the center of IC 1101. The definition, represented by a number, is best described by the Living as astounding. There is nothing else close, as you might deduce."

"That is impressive, Mary; I would understandably like to hear more about that."

"There is a reason I bring it up, Jean and Suel. Forty-eight minutes before we opened communications with you, an energy signature entered your vessel. It's the reason we found you."

"Interesting!" Jean said, with great curiosity.

"More interesting is the magnitude of it; we are speaking of the vibration I asked you about," Mary stated with a serious tone.

Jean's curiosity was piqued. "Can you tell me more about it, I mean before more study?"

"I can tell you its magnitude is beyond our ability to measure, more energy than in the supermassive black hole in the middle of IC 1101."

"How is that possible, Mary? That makes no sense. I'm standing before you. I'm a Living."

"You are, Jean, and you're vibrating. You have an energy source in you more powerful than the center of our massive galaxy. Our systems are all checked out. It's real. Do you mind if we study you after nourishment? It will not be invasive or dangerous."

"I would be happy for your team to do that; should we do it now?"

"You're a Living, Jean; you and Suel need to eat. Enjoy your meal!"

"Uh, okay, right! I'll just relax and enjoy my meal with Suel. Yes, right."

"You are in no danger, Jean. Nor are we. Whatever is in you or around you is safe...that is what we calculate. We are no match for it anyway," Mary said with a smile.

"Humor, I see that. Okay, chow time...then you can figure out what the hell your systems are picking up."

The restaurant was cool, way cool! It was one restaurant divided into three, each appealing to a different clientele, though all the Livings dined in all of them.

"What are you in the mood for, Suel?"

"Breakfast, are you kidding? We haven't eaten in 2500 years. Let's not skip breakfast," Suel said eagerly.

"I hoped you would say that."

Wynona approached them. She was one of the servers, the first Living they had seen.

"Good day to you, gentlemen. Two?"

"Yes."

"You're talkers," she said. "Breakfast?"

"Yes, please."

"I'm Wynona. Please follow me."

She led them to the table and handed them menus.

"Thank you, Wynona. We just arrived; can I ask you some questions?" Suel started.

"Yes, how can I help?"

"Do you know Mary?"

"We all know Kitty, or Mary. She's been here for many generations. We like her a lot."

"How many Livings are there at the station?"

"Without you two, about 497."

"You called us talkers; what did you mean?" Jean jumped in.

"Most of the Livings can communicate telepathically. In fact, many can't talk."

"Really?" Jean was surprised.

"Yes, the machines are all connected to each other all the time, in the station. The Livings connect to each other when they're close to one another."

"How did you learn to do that?" Suel asked.

"I don't know a lot about it, but others told us it is a part of our brain that we develop from the beginning. Plasticity, if I recall. It allocates space on its surface for this level of communication. Like your hands and their sensory inputs have brain surface space. Same thing."

"Why do you talk if others don't?" Jean said, talking.

"I'm a server. We interface with travelers like yourself who just talk. It makes it a lot easier to take your order. Right? I will also admit, gentlemen, that for telepathy between Livings, it takes two to tango. You boys are hard to read, I can't pick you up."

"Thank you, Wynona." Suel felt primitive.

"Do you boys want coffee?"

"Yes, please, I do. You, Suel?"

"Yes, lots of cream, please; do you have cream?"

"I can say yes to any food or beverage you request. To be fair," Wynona continued, "we don't have coffee, but you won't know it's not coffee. We don't have cream, but again, you won't know it's not cream. You can order whatever you want off the menu. It has items with names you are familiar with, but they aren't what they're called. Again, you won't know."

"We know now, Wynona," Jean said, smiling.

"But you won't," Wynona said with a wink, then turned to get the coffee.

"This place is cool, Suel, isn't it? And Wynona, she's cool; hell, it's all cool."

"Jean, remember, you are vibrating and have more energy than the supermassive black hole in the middle of our galaxy. Maybe, just maybe, you are a little revved up...just saying, Jean."

"Well, I feel good, I know that, and I sure like having you for a buddy, I know that. I mean, look at this place."

The restaurant, called the Tribanion, was on the outside wall of the station with full floor-to-ceiling windows looking out to space. The machines kept everything impeccably clean, and the windows were clear enough that it looked as though you could just step out into space. The restaurant was awesome to be sure, but what was even more striking was the grand view of the Black Cider Nebula. It rested on this edge of the Neengin galaxy, their destination. The million-degree plasma emitted vibrant colors as stars were born.

Inside, the Tribanion had carpet, which was unusual on a space station, but the deep pea green color, along with the short shag, gave it the feel of grass. The tables were a golden yellow with rich dark brown tops with a high gloss finish. The surface temperature of the tables was regulated, so they were never hot or cold. In fact, their temperature adjusted to whatever was on them, directly under that item or body part. The restaurant's solid interior walls were adorned with the art of Livings and nature, each soothing while compelling. The restaurant was quiet but smelled delicious.

Wynona made her way back with the cups, coffee, and cream. Jean caught her eye when she got to the table.

"That looks real to me, Wynona," Jean volunteered.

"Everything's real, man!" Wynona was bantering.

"You sure are enjoyable. It looks quiet in here; can you sit with us for a few minutes? Can you tell us about yourself, Wynona?"

She could tell the invitation was sincere and genuine. Her face seemed to melt some.

"I'm sorry, I didn't get your names," she said gently.

She looked first at Suel though she was really interested in her connection with Jean.

"Hi Wynona, I'm Suel. It's a pleasure to meet you."

"Thank you, Suel!"

She then turned to Jean and took a deep breath. "And you?"

"Hello Wynona, I'm Jean; the pleasure is mine. Can you join us while it's quiet?"

"Nice to meet you, Jean. You're a unique man; I hope you don't mind me telling you that."

"I don't mind; in fact, I appreciate it. Am I unique because I care, because I care about you and how you're doing?"

"Yes, Jean, that is what makes you unique. I don't know how or why I can tell you this, but I know you mean it. I can trust you. There is something..." Wynona looked for the right word and then just settled with the one that came to her so loudly, "...*good* about you, Jean."

"Wynona, can you go on break and sit with us? Do you have a manager I can ask on your behalf? This is on the up and up; I am not hitting on you."

"Yes, I can see that, Jean. I have a dinner break coming up. We can eat together if you'd like. I would enjoy that with both of you." She looked over at Suel and smiled. "Can I take your orders and get them in?"

"Yes, that sounds great. What kind of eggs do you have?" Jean asked.

"We have whatever eggs you want, Jean; they won't be eggs, but you won't know," she said with a smile.

"Okay, yes, I get it."

Suel jumped in. "He's full, anyway. Ask Mary, she'll tell you."

"Shut up, Suel," Jean told him playfully. "I would like two scrambled eggs, four slices of bacon, hash browns and whole-wheat toast with grape jelly, oh and some grape juice."

"Sounds delicious, Jean. Suel, what are you having?"

"I will have a waffle that's not a waffle with fake strawberries and imaginary whipped cream, a slice of ham substance with some whole-wheat toast whatever, with strawberry preserves, please."

"Do you use butter and syrup, Boys? Real strawberry preserves okay, Suel?"

"Yes, butter and maple for me," Suel spoke up, "and real preserves, roger that."

"The same, Wynona."

"Enjoy your coffee. I'll see you soon."

Jean and Suel got their coffee (or whatever) just the way they loved it and sat back enjoying the moment, both wondering what was going on inside Jean.

Wynona returned after just two minutes. "I am on the floor for another 15 minutes before I can take my break. Do you want me to put your orders in or wait?"

"Wait, please," Jean said kindly. "We want to wait for you."

She smiled because she felt wanted and seen; she turned and returned to work.

"You have always been kind, Jean; I have always appreciated that about you," Suel started, staring into his coffee cup.

"What's going on in your head, Suel?

"I wish we could all love each other, that's all; is it that hard?"

"Tell me more," Jean invited Suel to share.

Suel's voice trembled just a little. "When we left, a door closed that I can never open again. I had a sister; did you know that, Jean?"

"No."

"Yes, Rebelene. Rebelene was smart, funny, kind, and beautiful. I loved her so much! It's hard to believe that she has probably been dead for over two thousand years now. I'll never see her again."

"Did you say goodbye to her?"

"No, she cut me off some ten years before we left. We were so close, but then I said some things that were hurtful to her. They were honest but critical and must have been deeply hurtful to her. I always thought people who loved each other as we did would have dialogue, you know, work things out. But she just cut me off. I would reach out to her or try to on her birthday and holidays and such, but I think she blocked me from reaching her. She even had a child. I was her uncle, but she may not have ever known I existed. I love Rebelene, even today. I'm sure that when I die, she will be in some of my last thoughts, and those will be sad. Jean, I would never have said those hurtful things if I had known. I would have stuffed something in my mouth, anything to keep that from happening."

"Is that your greatest loss?" Jean asked solemnly.

"Yes, I think it is. I hadn't thought about it in that way before, but yes, I think it is."

Just then, another server, Elam, came over.

"Can I warm up your coffee, gentlemen?"

Jean looked up at him, and their eyes met. A genuine smile emerged on Jean's face while Suel watched.

"Please, sir, that will be very nice," Jean said gently.

Elam's face softened as Wynona's had, and a tender smile emerged on his face. He turned to Suel still smiling, and Suel smiled back.

"Thank you for the coffee. It's delicious," Suel expressed.

Elam walked away.

"Jean, what just happened? And what happened with Wynona earlier? You are really connecting her, and with me too."

"Something I have concentrated on for years, Suel, is opening doors. Let me tell you what I mean by that. Everyone wants to go home; it's why we get up every day. Home is that place in your heart; does that make sense?"

"Almost, Jean; please tell me more."

Jean continued, "We connect, we answer questions to find a resolution, we persevere in trying again. In all that, we are trying to get home. We want to get back to the source, the place we all come from, the place everything comes from. I believe the machines do the same thing, Suel. For years now, before we slept for 2500 years, I've made a conscious effort to open doors, not shut them. If I do what I can to open a door with another person or being, they—we—have a chance to get another step closer to home. Does that make sense?"

"Yes, it does. You say you do what you can; is that something you can explain?"

"Well, I try to create a place in me to receive, a place without judgment or preoccupation. I make it a point to see the other person, if I can, to feel them. Like you, Suel. You are an awesome dude. You have a generous spirit and an openness about you. I sense you are on a journey to someplace wonderful. That is what I feel about you."

"Thanks. I wish my sister could be with us now at this special moment."

"She is. I feel convinced of it. You're right too! This feels like a special moment, this ship, Mary, Wynona, you, me, the fake cream. You know, now that I think about it, I think that's why this vibration is here. I welcome it; I have never felt home so strongly as I do now."

At that moment, Note's existence with Jean was complete and Note left. Jean took a deep breath. "Oh my. Oh my! It's gone!"

Within a minute, Mary came up. "It's gone, Jean!"

In Between

Note experienced how one being makes space to greet another. The connection expands both, but the beauty is in the invitation.

Note opened to discovering how something as wonderful as service to another can be offered from unique paths. Note recognized that the love that service expresses may be the same, while the expression of that love, through service, can be different between those providing it, each to the beat of a different drummer. Note would experience the choosing.

Chapter Thirty-Four

The Giving Tree

At 61 degrees with no wind, it was a perfect day to visit the Statue of Liberty in New York. Sandra was watching her dear friend Cholie walk up when Note joined Sandra.

The hug was genuine and heartfelt by both.

"I'm so glad to see you, Sandra. I'm delighted you reached out to me. I've missed you!"

"Thank you for joining me today, Cholie. Being with you will be the best part of my trip here and then some. You're my Sistah, you know."

"Cholie...what happened to Cho Cho?"

They giggled. "I love you, Cho Cho!"

Sandra and Cholie weren't sisters in the usual sense but had bonded during their younger years while attending the University of Pennsylvania.

"Let's get in line," Cholie suggested.

They made their way through the security at the Statue of Liberty Ferry facility and lined up to board the "Lady of Liberty," the next ferry leaving for the journey.

"So, how's it going, Sanny? What's the empty nester thing like for you?"

"Big, unanticipatedly big and unexpected, Cho Cho. I would have to say it's one of the biggest events of my life. Jack going off to college is a life-changing event for the three of us. Pascale seems fine with it, almost oblivious. Men just seem to deal with things like that differently. I don't mean to put all men in that bucket, but he just seems to be unchanged."

"Tell me about your experience of it, Sanny."

"I've given it a lot of thought because of how it has impacted me," she expressed thoughtfully. "I feel a sense of freedom. I doted on Jack. I wasn't a helicopter mom but was still intensely engaged with him and his life. Jack didn't always connect all the dots, so I kept my eye on his schedule and needs and many of his interactions and whispered over his shoulder from time to time to help him connect those dots, and get himself to places he needed to get to at the right time, wearing the right thing with whatever tools or whatever he needed. Now that he's gone, I feel free from that. It was more encompassing and self-limiting than I knew.

"But then again, Jack was my reason for being here. I don't know how that sounds, and maybe all or most mothers feel this way, but I felt like I was here to be Jack's mom. Now he relies on himself mostly, and I must find my next reason for being here. Today, and recently, and I guess since he left for college, I feel a loss of purpose. I wonder what's next, and I'm a little scared. Plus, I know menopause is next."

"I hear you on that one, Sanny. I also know whatever's next for you, other than menopause, will be very cool because you are way cool."

Sandra turned, opening her arms, and grabbed another hug. "Thank you, my dear friend. I deeply miss my kid," she continued. "I knew I loved being around him, but I didn't know just how much. Jack is funny and kind of charming. I may have doted on him so much just to get more of his time. Damn, I miss him! At the same time, I am excited about his next chapter while nervous about mine."

"Tell me more about being nervous."

"Not only don't I know what's next, but I don't know what I can do. I mean, I have my career, and I am good at it, but I just don't know what I have to give now."

"I don't know what to say, Sanny. I often regret our decision not to have kids. What you're experiencing is more than I can comprehend or understand, but my heart goes out to you. It sounds personally hard."

"Thank you. I think I am putting a little bit of a negative spin on it with you, Cho Cho. On this special day, when I have you so close, I'm sincerely grateful."

The line moved, and two boarded the ferry. Being toward the front of the line, the women knew they would have their pick of seats on the top deck where they could see the magnificent City of New York as they ferried out to the Statue of Liberty. After securing a delightful spot and spending a few minutes people-watching, the two started sharing again.

"So, what do you think of New York, Sanny?"

"I'm impressed with it. The last time I was here, Jack was just a baby, and he and

Pascale and I were up on the World Trade Center. That was the end of July in 2001, just before 9/11 happened. That's what I always remember when I think of the City. We've also seen the press about the infrastructure in the US needing repair and cities needing to be updated. Honestly, I expected New York City to look run down and kind of sad.

"What I have found, however, is an amazing and vibrant city full of innovation, but still a model for cultural integration. The old architecture seems fresh, Cho Cho, and the new buildings rival anything I have seen from the great new cities in China or Dubai. And the people. They still don't talk to you if you don't start the conversation, but when you interact with someone here, you find authentic and enjoyable people. I've done and seen much smiling here."

"You're so fun, Sanny. Look, the sun is peering through the clouds and shining on those buildings over there."

The Lady Liberty pulled away from the dock and was on its way. Sanny and Cho Cho were on the right side of the boat and could take in a fantastic view of Lower Manhattan as they pulled away. Coming up on the right was Ellis Island.

"One World Tower is striking, isn't it?" Sandra interjected.

"Yes," Cholie responded. "Do you remember the West Side Highway when you were here before, when the World Trade Center was still here?"

"I remember that. It was right next to the Towers and had water just on the other side, the Hudson River."

"Well," Cholie continued, "when they excavated the space for One World Trade Center, they needed to dig out so much dirt to get to the bedrock for the building to sit on, they didn't have a place to put it all. They dumped it in the Hudson. They put all that dirt in the Hudson and then decided, hey, now that we have this unused land over here, let's put up a couple of buildings on it. They were required to excavate and dig out all that dirt to get to the bedrock again, right? So, they created dozens of acres of additional land and built many buildings on it. Amazing."

"Really? I didn't realize that. I'm going to the 9/11 Memorial in the morning, and I'll see all of that. Amazing."

"Looks like we have a few more minutes before we dock. I have something on my mind and would love your input." Sandra spoke with seriousness.

"Sure."

"A friend of mine gave me a book last week; she told me it was her favorite book, and she wanted to make sure I have a copy. She wrote something charming inside the back cover; I just love that. I read the book as a child but never really thought about it much, but now I can't get it out of my mind. Have you read The Giving Tree?"[38]

"Oh yes, I love that book too, so much," Cholie offered excitedly. "What thoughts are you having about it?"

Speaking softly, Sandra leaned forward and talked. "After she gave it to me, I read it. It is a quick read, as you know," she smiled. "I talked to her a couple of days later."

"Her?"

"Yes, Jessie. Sorry. I told her I thought it was a wonderful story, but that I couldn't understand how the tree gave itself away like that. I mean, a tree might live for hundreds of years, through several generations of people. It may be there to give shade to countless people over that time and be a place for the weary to rest and for the sad to recharge. By giving itself away like that, for the selfish boy and then, as he aged, a selfish man, it left nothing for itself or anyone else. Does that seem small, Cho Cho?"

"Not at all," Cholie answered. "There was this mind-opening test I got exposed to not too long ago. Have you heard about the Yanny and Laurel test?"

"I haven't. What is it?" Sandra asked.

"Yanny or Laurel is an auditory illusion around one word in a mixed salad of sounds. When the audio clip gets slowed to lower frequencies, 'Yanny' has been heard by more listeners, while faster playback emphasizes 'Laurel.'[39] What that showed me was that we all perceive what we perceive. It's unique for each of us!"

"Thank you, Cho Cho. That is perfect for my question for you. When I read The Giving Tree, I cry. I cry at the perfect selflessness of the tree. The love is pure, and, in its love and selflessness, it's willing to give everything of itself. I know that sounds like the right thing, to be so loving and giving, but I don't know, it doesn't quite make sense to me."

"Agreed," Sandra said. "Let me ask you a question. Let's say you are the mother of our. One of them runs out in the street, and you see a car coming fast. You know, in your mind, your cherished child will get hit and killed. Do you run out to try to save your child even though you won't be able to, and you will both die? Do you do that and leave the three others to live their lives without their mommy, or do you watch it happen, and know there is nothing you really could have done?"

They both sat quietly for a few moments. Seagulls became more active as the boat neared shore.

"There is no way to win there," Cho Cho acknowledged. "None."

"Yes, Cho Cho, but what would you do?" Sandra wanted to get her question answered.

"I would stay with my other children and grieve for the rest of my life. You would run out and die with your child, wouldn't you?" Cho Cho answered.

"Yes," Sandra admitted. "I know I sounded before like I would make the other choice, but you know me well."

"Why, Sanny?"

"It's hard to put into words, and again, I know we're all different, and each path is right, mostly, but for me, it's about my reverence for life. For me, even a failed attempt to save a life, while giving freely all I am, and all I can be, well, it's what I am. I think it comes down to having such reverence for life that we protect every life, versus protecting life itself. I know that's vague, Cho Cho."

"Sanny, it occurs to me that it may because you have been a mom, and I haven't. I think Jack is a part of you, an extension of you. His life is your life. I don't know that one, that intimately."

Sandra became excited. "Crazy...this is crazy. I was just talking to Pascale this morning about the difference between being a mother and a father, and he came up with something that resonated with me. He said a mother concentrates on the good of the one, the child, and builds a world around the child, based on what's right for that child. He said, in his view, the father concentrates on the good of the whole, instead of the one. If the whole is good, the one is good. For the mother, if the one is good, the whole is good."

"Sanny, do you think that would explain our different perceptions around The Giving Tree? I look at the whole and how the tree's sacrifice impacts the good of the whole. You see the gift the tree gave the one."

"That is heavy, Cho Cho, but I like it. Do you remember Mila?"

"Yes, how is she?"

"She's still not good and probably won't be for a while."

"What happened?" Cholie asked intensely.

Sandra looked back and looked out to the water, looking past Cholie's face as she spoke. "Coronavirus impacted her family. She and her husband are our age and had Rebecca late in life like I had Jack; Rebecca was at college when the pandemic hit. Mila and her husband, being in the risk population, decided it was best for all if Rebecca stayed in the off-campus dorm they leased for her rather than come home. In their minds, she was an adult, and it would be impossible for them to keep her from coming and going. They were concerned they could be exposed and one or both die.

"Well, Rebecca hung out with a crowd that thought they were invincible and did spring break on the beaches of Cancun. She and some of her friends came back infected. Rebecca became terribly ill."

"What did they do?"

"Mila and Wallen disagreed about the right thing to do. He thought Rebecca would get through it because of her youth, and Mila thought she needed to be there for her sick daughter. Wallen wouldn't let her go alone, and moms always win in the end, right? So, they took care of her. Wallen caught the virus, and he died from it."

"Oh, no!"

"He was asthmatic as a child," Sandra added.

"That is just so sad. What a choice to make, what an outcome."

"Yes."

"Oh, we are pulling in. Look at 'The Lady'; just look at her." Sandra pointed at the Statue of Liberty.

"I am so glad to be here with you, girl," Cholie shared. "Our conversation and being in front of Lady Liberty and thinking of Ellis Island, just reminds me how hard this life can be. Seems we suffer a great deal but have moments of joy like this one for me, here with you. We just keep going on, and importantly, we want to keep going on."

"Yes." Sandra agreed. Note left Sandra to continue the journey.

In Between

Note recognized that like positive and negative, or good and evil, the essence of female and male energy may each cover unique ground. The example Sandra discussed of Pascale's view of how a mother concentrates on the good of the one, the child, and builds a world around the child, based on what's right for that child while the father concentrates on the good of the whole, instead of the one, was compelling and profound if universal. For the father, if the whole is good, the one is good. For the mother, if the one is good, the whole is good. What would this look like if out of balance in the Universe?

Chapter Thirty-Five

PO Box

"Hey!"

"Hey!"

"New here?"

"Yep."

"Ralph."

"José."

The two men held out their worn hands to shake.

"Have you been here long, Ralph?" Note joined Ralph.

"About a season."

"Do you get hassled much here?"

"No, no hassle. I've had some company I didn't want a couple of times, but I guess I look a little scary, and they left me alone."

Ralph was a tall man of almost six foot two with tan and leathery skin. The temperature was still in the forties, so Ralph donned his worn and faded plaid jacket with a zipper that hadn't worked in a long time. His face was rough and hairy, with fierce green eyes that seemed to peer into José's soul.

"You look a little scary, Ralph, but I think it is because you smell terrible, brother."

They both laughed. "I take it your nose still works, José."

"Hell, yes, it does, but I don't mind foul smells, or I would have nothing to eat."

"True."

"You okay if I stay under your bridge for a while, Ralph? I'm tired, and my luck hasn't been great lately. This looks like a friendly neighborhood. I bet there is some good garbage here."

"I keep to myself mostly, José, but if you honor that, I am happy to have you here for a while."

"Thanks, Ralph, I'll make my way over to the other side and get some rest. See ya."

"See ya."

José witnessed Ralph working the cars that were forced to stop at the light on either side of the bridge. He had encountered a lot of panhandling on his journey but had seen no one like Ralph. He didn't have a sign and didn't walk up and down the lane next to the captive cars waiting for the green light, but just sat at the fourth car and smiled genuinely at each driver as they passed by as they were about to turn. Several drivers stopped each hour to hand him some change or cash, and it was enough by the end of the day to afford Ralph a hot meal at the nearby burger joint.

One evening, José made his way over to sit with Ralph to talk.

"Evening Ralph. It looked like you had a good day out there again today."

"Good people pass this bridge, José, good people."

"I see you just smile at them. That seems to work for you."

"I think it works for them too, José. I figure a lot of the folks drive by here regularly, I know they do. I am just kind to them, and they are kind in turn."

"It makes perfect sense!"

"How are you making out, José?"

"Well, I know you are eating some good eats from the burger joint, and I am too. Mine is just coming from the garbage in the back. Real good to be sure."

"What happened to you, José? Why are you here?"

"Chemicals, Ralph. I pretty well fried my brain on them when I was growing up. I really can't hang on to much in my head. That keeps me from being able to learn and retain, so I am of no use to anyone."

"You talk good, José."

"Funny, I was a bookworm when I was young, too, before the chemicals took their toll on me. I know I speak pretty well, but I don't know how I think; that's why though."

"I saw you leave and come back with a box of something in that sack. I don't see much new stuff. What is it?"

"It's a cheap box of Christmas cards, José."

"Christmas cards?"

"Yep."

"About four seasons ago, I was living down the road at the next bridge. I had been there for a couple of years, and I would panhandle as I do here. There was this one guy that would always give me a dollar, and he passed regularly. He was a middle-aged guy in a red Camry with a bra on it. Only Camry I ever saw with a bra on it. You know what I mean by bra?"

"Yeah, yeah, the black thing on the front."

"Right. So anyway, this guy pulled into the Red Robin parking lot by the bridge and motioned for me to come over to him. I did. There was something about him. I felt comfortable with him. Anyway, he held out his hand for a handshake, and then after I shook his hand, he gave me a gift."

"What?"

"He said, 'The people who love you need to know where you are; they need to be able to reach out to you.'

"I thought, who is he talking about?

"He said, 'I got you a PO box at the Post Office, two blocks north. You know the one I am talking about?'

"'Yes,' I said.

"'Here's the key. This is PO Box 3407. I described you to them and told them you would come up to provide your name. Will you do that?'

"'Yes, what do I do?' I asked.

"'Reach out, brother, let people know where they can reach you. Give them your PO box number.'

"We gave each other a hug, man. It was a life-changer for me. I remembered one address. I got a card and sent it to my brother at his address and asked him to send me addresses for other friends and family that he knew, and he did. He sent them to my PO box. I've spent countless hours working to recall people from my past that I loved or liked a lot or appreciated. I've found that we are somehow all connected to each other, so now I have almost everyone's address."

"Where is your list of addresses?"

"I keep it in the PO box, and the Post Office lets me."

"So, do they send you money?"

"Honestly, José, I don't tell any of them I live under a bridge. I am just lucky they write to me now and then. I send all my people a Christmas card. For some reason, Grace, I guess, folks give me a little more from the cars around the holidays so I can get the stamps and boxes of cards I need."

"What do you tell these people, if you don't tell them about your circumstances?"

"I find ways to share with them the things I appreciate about them. I don't get too gushy, and I keep it real."

"And they keep responding, Ralph?"

"Mostly, yes. In fact, they share things about their lives with me, and we have some correspondence on that. Some things are personal, and some of them are in some pain. We all hurt from time to time!"

"Yes, we do. I must admit Ralph; you are easy to be with, to talk to. I don't feel you judge me, man."

"I don't, José. You know, I have learned some things from watching people in these cars."

"What?"

"I have learned that captive people are more likely to listen and hear you. These folks are captive in their cars, and they can't move. I don't really talk to them, but I see the captivity in their faces, and that's what made me think about it.

"When you are a kid, you listen to your parents because you are captive to them. You listen because you respect them when you're young. You are captive to respect and open to listening. You listen to all authority figures if you respect that authority."

"Like being in the back of a police car, Ralph, is that what you mean?"

"Yes. When you're in the back of a squad car, and they tell you something, you listen, right?"

"Yes, I do. You know Ralph, I got in to see a movie a while back about Fred Rogers, you know, Fred Rogers of Mr. Rogers' Neighborhood."

"I think we all know about Mr. Rogers," Ralph said with a grin.

"Yes, well anyway, in the movie, a reporter was doing a story on Mr. Rogers and asked him questions. Mr. Rogers turned it around on the reporter and asked some meaningful questions that ended up helping the man. The reporter was captive to Mr. Rogers. I see that now. The reporter was forced to sit there with Mr. Rogers to get his story. So, when Mr. Rogers started asking the questions, the reporter couldn't just walk off, they had to answer. I understand what you are talking about, Ralph. I am captive to you because I want to be here with you, right?"

"Yes. As my captive, what do you want to know?"

"What do you hope for in sending those cards, Ralph? Do you want someone to take you out of here, take you back, what?"

"Let me think. Okay. Think of love as a little tiny ball of snow up at the top of a big hill, and once it gets pushed and starts rolling downhill, it gets bigger and bigger as it moves. I just want to push that little ball forward. It is really all about love, José. That's what matters to me now."

"How did you get here, Ralph?"

"Kind of like you, José. I was addicted to drugs, and I ruined everything and hurt everyone as I pursued more and more of them. Those are the people I send these cards to."

"And they have all responded and sent you something to your PO box?"

"No, but a few have. But I keep sending the cards, never asking for anything, just giving some little dab of love. That is all I have to give now."

"You won't be alone this Christmas, Ralph."

"I'm thrilled about that, José!"

Note left Ralph.

In Between

Note found kindness to be a conduit for connection and connection to result in shared kindness.

Note next sought to find how living beings perceive their evolution.

Chapter Thirty-Six

Evolution

Ya and Kenji were drifting but at high speed approaching a new wormhole, one they had just discovered. A part of generation B422hb of humanity, they were wormhole mappers. Humans found that these gateways around the galaxies could, sometimes, deliver a ship to another galaxy. Wormholes permitted humanity to spread throughout the Universe. Mapping them was a vital task, and they excelled at it.

The Dosset was a living machine designed for space flight. Dosset, as living beings sometimes do, was having a bad day and had just powered down at full speed while on approach to the current discovery.

"Dosset," Ya exclaimed with some irritation. "Bad timing here! Get back online and bring us to a full stop."

Note joined with Ya. She took a deep breath, breaking into a smile.

"Ya, why are you smiling? We're in a pickle here!" Kenji blurted.

"I'm full of Song, Kenji. I can't explain it, but I'm pleased, I know that!"

"Dosset!" Kenji interjected with concern.

"It looks like we're going in, Kenji," Ya said.

"You don't think Dosset wants to go in, do you?" Kenji asked with some irritation.

"Interesting thought...Dosset *has* been giving us some attitude lately," Ya answered.

"It appears to be a good wormhole, thank goodness. We may be able to get back...we can hope," he replied.

"It may get busy once we go in. Kenji, can we talk?"

"Seriously, Ya?"

"Kenji, every moment matters; you know that. Let's not waste these."

Kenji looked over toward Ya. His face showed obvious concern.

"We'll be okay," she said to comfort him.

"These rarely go well, Ya. That's why our insertion teams use machines to traverse them first, making sure they are safe and don't end at a star. I'll be honest...I'm frightened. I'm a mapper, not an explorer."

"I have something to help you with your fear, Kenji. Let's talk first. That may help too."

"Okay, you are serious. Dosset!" Kenji spoke intensely.

"You became quiet after messages, Kenji. What happened?"

He looked over at Ya again. "You're serious. All right. I received some information from my aunt that I have been mulling over. That's all. She studies evolution and shared something with me that seems obvious when I think about it, but I hadn't considered before."

"Oh, boy," Ya said.

"Ya, I have to say, flying uncontrollably into this wormhole has made you weird, but I like it. Yes, my aunt shared that with each moment, as the Universe evolves in all its incomprehensible ways, it gets more complex. So, this moment is more complicated than the last, and so on. Additional levels of complications are being born every second—something new that never was just became, and again, and again."

"That is profound, Kenji. That means the Universe isn't just changing constantly, but that it's changing in a direction toward complexity, away from simplification."

"Yes, why?"

"Discovery comes to mind to me. For us, the living, we look at a finished product and then dissect it down to all its parts to know what it is," Ya answered.

"You're saying, like breaking a metal into molecules and then the atoms that make it up, to understand the metal? Is that right?"

"Yes, but maybe the Universe—being magnificent—discovers itself the opposite way. It started with the simplest of all things and now evolves that simple thing into all its seemingly infinite possibilities over time."

"Oh my gosh, Ya. I don't know what all that means, but it's beautiful. Then you believe the Universe is discovering what it is?"

"I do," she answered, feeling overwhelmed with joy. "It brings a song into my head. Have you ever heard the old Earth song from The Beatles, 'A Day in the Life?'"

"Yes, I love that one, Ya. What about the song?"

"After the lyrics, the orchestra starts slow, low and rhythmically, and builds and builds until the final note. It's what's in my head, representing how the Universe is growing and evolving."

"I feel that. I think that note is an E-major, not sure. Now, please, help me with my fear. I'm scared."

"All right, Kenji. I practice meditation based on the ancient Taoist philosophy on Earth. It focuses on learning about the harmony in yourself and the harmony that's all around you. You concentrate on unity to achieve a higher state of peace and connection. It's a beautiful balance."

Ya put her hand on his arm while he looked into her eyes. "Kenji, feel the connection to all of this. Feel the peace."

In the next moment, Dosset came online and announced, "Here we go; we're going in."

Note left Ya.

In Between

As Note observed, Ya and Kenji recognized that evolution moved in a direction toward more complexity and away from simplicity. What Note realized, however, in note's experience was that the increasing complexity of the Universe was a movement that would end in divine simplicity. Was the end, and the beginning, the same?

Note felt drawn next to the spirit of Service.

Chapter Thirty-Seven

Christmas Story and Service

"**It's a cold one, Mary,** real cold. Are you makin' it, Girl?"

"I stopped shaking a while back. I can't feel my legs, Waz. I'm tired, and I think this is it for me."

"Oh, Mary, let me hold you, Girl; let me warm you up."

"Thank you, Waz. I appreciate that. You are very dear to be sure; you know you are my person, right? I want you to know that."

Waz made his way under the cardboard to cradle Mary. He tucked one arm under her neck and wrapped the other over her, pulling her close. She groaned.

"Thank you, Waz. Thank you for this. I love grace!"

Waz put his face against the back of her neck, and there was a warmth there until Mary passed. He could feel her body stiffen. In death, her neck quickly got cold. As he remembered her last words, he cried, "What a loss. What a waste."

"Over here!" Waz heard familiar police voices getting closer. "Hey Waz, come with us; we have to get both of you to a shelter. This is bad; you can't make it out here. Is Mary asleep, dude?"

"Mary's dead, Brother; she couldn't make it."

"Damn it, we'll call it in; someone will come to get her. I'm genuinely sorry for your loss. Now we have to get you to a shelter. Come on."

"I'll need some help!" Waz said.

"We've gotcha," Ben stated.

The squad car was cozy and warm.

Note floated down with the giant snowflakes on a breezy evening over the city. The lights were brilliant tonight, and there was a joyful mood, even up among the falling snowflakes. Note felt surrounded by this moment somehow. It felt full, inspired, blessed, and magical.

Note joined Unahmie in the kitchen at the homeless shelter. It was Christmas Eve, and love was thick here, impacting everyone. "Unahmie," Nora exclaimed, "you make the bestest dumplings in the world. Who would have thought a homeless shelter in New York City full of the poor would be about to eat the best dumplings on Earth? It's justice, after all, so good!" Nora snuck a dumpling and savored the slightly salty taste, her mouth full of goodness.

"You sure are being quiet, Unahmie." Nora was paying attention to her friend.

"Sorry Nora, I was just thinking about a show I saw last night on TV, and then I received a wealth of Songs just filling my head a few minutes ago. I feel like I'm at the Tabernacle Choir or something; it's just beautiful inside my head, between my ears."

"Lucky." Nora's eyes got big, and she said with passion, "I have my nephew in my head, not liking his gift. I want to be positive; 'tis the season. What did you see on TV?"

"I was watching 'Nova' on PBS."

"Oh, I love Nova, but I haven't watched it lately. What did you see?"

"It was about the intelligence of birds. It was incredible. They gave them complex things to figure out, and the birds used items in the environment as tools. I couldn't believe it. They had one piece that showed a group of birds rotating to take a turn holding a lid open so others could get some food. I always thought birds were just instinctual, like bugs, you know. There was one piece where a raven was mad at its human keeper for being gone for two days. When it first saw the man, it was all excited like a kid. Then after that, it showed how angry it was at the man for being gone. Then..." tears filled Unahmie's eyes, "...the raven took hold of the man's finger and wouldn't let go for an hour, so he could not leave again.

"I mean, these birds could figure out complex situations, take care of their family, and showed emotions like we're used to seeing every day in ourselves and the people we serve. There's just so much more all around us than we see or know, you know what I mean, Nora?"

"Yes, I know what you mean. I see inspiring things every day in the suffering around here. That is quite a story; are we using white and dark meat chicken with the dumplings?"

"Yes, all of it."

"Are you still crying, Girl?"

"Sorry, Nora. I didn't know birds have feelings. Now we're putting chicken with the dumplings. I'm just thinking, what if all living things have this little life force in them, that they love, that they even love us, like that raven? Then we slaughter them and eat them. We break up families because we're oblivious to their worth. Sorry, I know this is deep; I don't even know why all this is in my head. Did you put the chicken in the dumplings yet?"

"No, Ma'am; I'm not that fast!"

"Okay, leave it out, please. The dumplings are my culinary masterpiece, and I'll never put meat in them again."

"Unahmie, are you going crazy, Girl?"

"I just didn't know, but now I do. You do too."

She looked over at Nora, and she looked back. Their eyes locked, and for a moment, they were the same.

"Yes, my Sister, now I know too. Thank you for that."

Out in the mess hall, each looked to find their place. All have a home.

"Josh, so good to see you again, my brother. I've wondered about you, hoping you were off the streets."

"Thank you, Manny, no, not off the streets until tonight. This place is a godsend. It warms more than my body, Manny, know what I mean?"

"Yeah, I know, man, this place is like a church or something, especially tonight. Come on. Let's get some of Ms. Unahmie's dumplings. Crazy man, here we are, the nothings of the world eating the best morsel of goodness on the planet. I mean, what's up with that?"

Josh and Manny worked through the serving line.

"Can I just have dumplings, Ma'am? That's all I need on my plate, just them dumplings."

"Sorry, Josh, got to have enough dumplings for everyone. Besides, you need some of these here vegetables, got to have your veggies!"

Josh smiled really big at Millie; the teeth he had left were broken and crooked. "My life ain't done, Ms. Millie, but it is close to done, and veggies won't give me another day now. I understand about leavin' those dumplings for someone else. Can I have some extra bread instead of those green beans?"

Millie smiled back at Josh and put three buns on his plate with the dumplings.

"Thank you, Ms. Millie."

Josh and Manny made their way to the bench table and sat across from each other.

"You are just so nice to everyone, Josh. You're a good guy. How did you get that way, living the way we live?"

"I moved my line, Brother, moved my line, that's what I did," Josh answered.

"What?" Manny squinted and tilted his head to the right.

"My line. Let me eat my dumplings while they're still warm, then if you want to hear about my line, I'll tell you."

Josh ate his dumplings ridiculously slowly, making them last a good 15 minutes. Manny finished in three minutes and stared at Josh for the remaining 12. It was as if Josh was all by himself with those delicious vittles, and every bite was as good as the last. When he finally finished with the main course, he took the first bun and scooped up all the juice on his plate, and he ate and savored that slowly, too. By the end, Manny overflowed with an appreciation for his friend and how he enjoyed his Christmas Eve moment.

"Okay, brother, my line." Josh spoke with a serious tone. "I'm on the street because of where my line was, versus where my line is now. Like you, probably, I grew up with no pop, and I learned fast how to survive and excel. I was a mean bastard, and I thought that was okay. I stole from folks and thought that was okay. I did my time for the death of an old man. One of my homies thought beatin' him up was kind of funny and just kept doing it until he was dead. I was there, enjoying the show…didn't do nothin' for that old man. I thought that was okay. So long as things were good for me, whatever was okay with me.

"That was where my line was. It was okay to be mean, to steal, to enjoy watching some poor bastard get beat to death for just being there. I mean, I didn't kill nobody, that would have crossed the line, but my line was just almost there.

"When I started serving my time in the big house, I found myself backed in a corner all the time. I was new, and I didn't know the rules; I needed some educatin'. So, I got educated, and that made me even harder and meaner. I cared for my brothers in jail but used everyone else. That was my line. My brothers were on my side of the line; everyone else, well, they was our prey.

"I got out after too many years and couldn't get a job, being an ex-con and all, so I started taking advantage on the streets again. I was in the money for a while and met a girl, and she was kind of desperate, wanted a kid, and didn't know how bad I was inside. I knocked her up and kept her around. Then Seronda was born. Manny, something just changed in me; she was an angel coming into this world."

Josh put his head down and was quiet for a minute.

"You don't have to say more, Josh. You're a good man now."

"No, Manny, I want to be good. I pray to be good."

Josh raised his head, and Manny felt surprised by how old his friend looked suddenly. All the years, each cold night, all the lousy nutrition—when there was any—it all showed on his friend's old and wrinkled leather face. But his eyes were bright and tear-filled.

Josh continued. "So, this angel came into my world, my life. I saw and appreciated Annie for the first time, Seronda's momma, my girlfriend. I started on the road home that day, yes, I did, but I had too far to go. I would beat on Annie from time to time and be unfaithful. I was always good to Seronda, something about her just, well, I couldn't be bad to her. I kept trying to go straight but could never find a job that paid what I was used to getting, so I stayed on the wrong side.

"I moved my line a little, though. It wasn't okay to beat old dudes to death around me anymore. I wouldn't steal from another man. I would try to live in another's shoes from time to time. I thought I was making some genuine progress, at least in my head, I was."

"Where is Seronda now, Josh? I mean, do you still see her from time to time?"

His eyes watered again. "I see Seronda every day, every hour, in my head, and I feel her always in my heart, but my eyes have not seen her for an awfully long time, ten years, I reckon.

"She came home one night with a fella. I recognized the look on his face. He was a player, a shark, like what I had been. I don't know what I expected because we never got Seronda out of that neighborhood, that environment. I went off on the fucker, just went off. He carried a piece and pulled it, and I got it away from him and beat him with the handle. I just went off on the fucker.

"He has a marble for one eye now if he's still around, was not real pretty to look at. They never brought in police because he was a bad guy. They were huntin' for his ass anyway. My Seronda was there and saw all of that, all the blood, the rage, the darkness. I haven't seen her since. Annie went with Seronda, so I lost 'em both.

"So, my line. After a couple of months of not having Seronda in my world, I kind of got religious—not religious like you think of, but real reflective. I noticed little messages coming to me in my life like God was telling me something, and I was listening for the first time, Manny. I was somebody, 'cause I was worth receiving those messages.

"Well, anyway, one day, I was walking down Digger Street, and I pulled a piece of gum out of my pocket, unwrapped it, and released the trash to fall to the ground. It landed next to Old Charlie; do you remember Charlie?"

"Yes, yes, Charlie; I remember him, Josh. He was an odd one, peculiar, but I liked him. Yes, I remember Charlie."

"That was my first time to meet him. It was before I was homeless like he was. Charlie said, 'Hey man, why are you throwing this paper down on the street?' I felt that old anger swell up, my chemicals was releasing, and I turned to look at this fool who was calling me out, and when I got turned around, my eyes caught his, and I was, well, I just stopped in my tracks, Manny. It was like Charlie was looking right into my soul. It'll sound silly, but he was welcome.

"Charlie said, 'Come sit with me, friend.'

"I sat down next to Charlie; man, he stunk, like you and I do today, but I was not used to it then, I mean he stunk."

Manny smiled and nodded his head affirmatively.

"Charlie said to me, 'Why is it okay for you to throw your trash down like that?'

"His question to me was much bigger than that. What he was asking was, why was it okay for all the awful stuff, less than stuff, oblivious stuff, reckless stuff, stupid stuff, why was it all okay for all the mean stuff to happen?

"I didn't have an answer. It was okay, that's all I knew, it wasn't good, but it was okay. But at that moment, I knew I didn't want it to be okay, not no more.

"I told Charlie, 'I don't know, man, I don't know!'

"Charlie said, 'Look at me!'

"I looked over, and our eyes met again. He said, 'You have to move your line of what's acceptable and what you are willing to do and how you'll conduct yourself as a man; you have to move your line, and then don't cross it!'

"I heard what Charlie was saying, all the way to my soul."

Manny asked, "I'm not sure I get it, Josh; can you help me with it?"

"Think of this," Josh responded. "I thought it was okay to yell at someone, but not okay to hit 'em. That's because striking someone is crossing the line but yelling at them isn't. It's okay to say bad things about people you don't know, but not about people you do because stabbing people in the back who you know is crossing the line...strangers, not so much.

"So, the message Charlie was giving me was to move that line toward being better. So now, for instance, it's not okay to yell at anyone in anger, ever. Yelling at anyone in anger is crossing the line. If I would have done that the last time I saw my angel, I would have her in my life today."

His eyes watered again with sadness, but his mouth broke into his big and overwhelming smile. "There is grace here; thank you for having dinner with me."

Right at that moment, Manny looked up over Josh's head, and Josh felt a hand on his shoulder. He turned around to find Unahmie standing behind him.

"Hello Joshua, mind if I sit with you a spell?"

"Oh, please do, Ms. Unahmie, please do. There is something about you tonight, Ms. Unahmie. I mean, I know it's Christmas Eve and all, but you just have joy on your face, a glow. You are beautiful tonight!"

"Thank you, Joshua. How were the dumplings?"

"Oh, my word...right, Manny? I mean, dang girl, I just, there ain't no words, I mean..." Josh shook his head.

"I just got a call from your daughter Seronda. She called to ask if I've seen you today. I told her you are here, and she said to keep you here; she is coming to see you."

Josh sat like a stone, not breathing.

Calmly, Unahmie spoke. "Breathe now; it's all good. Seronda is coming to see you. It's all good."

Manny's face scrunched up. He felt his chest tingle as it all unfolded before him: this miracle, his friend, Ms. Unahmie, the warm room, the food in his stomach, the hope of Christmas, the story his friend trusted him enough to tell.

Jill walked by Unahmie at that moment; she brushed her hand across Unahmie's back and immediately turned. Across the room sat another struggling life.

Danny served his country in Vietnam and lost both legs in the war. His young wife considered her returning hero to be a burden and left him soon after. Danny was an only child; his parents were already in their sixties after his wife left. He lived with them for 22 years until they both died, one shortly after the other. Long but ill lives used up any savings his parents had and forced them to sell their home a few years before their deaths to pay for the costs of living beyond what was covered by the government. When they passed, a small sum was still left, which helped Danny to live in the same apartment for another three years. Once that was gone, Danny's disability was only enough to pay for food, not shelter. Danny never overcame the injuries to his sense of self to be able to function autonomously in the world. As a result, he was homeless and living on the streets for better than fifteen years now.

Jill was an Olympic swimmer with a generous heart. She wanted to give back to her community and felt a special connection with the homeless. Jill just couldn't understand how a society could allow so many to live such a precarious existence and suffer as much as they do. As the daughter of a successful and retired pro football star, Jill had known a life of comfort but had been taught the value of hard work from her father. Jill felt drawn to make her way over to Danny.

"Hello Sir, I'm Jill, one of the servers tonight. Did you get enough to eat?"

"Yes, Ma'am, it was delicious tonight. I remember you from the serving line, and you were truly kind."

"I didn't catch your name, Sir."

"Oh, yes, I'm Danny. Nice to meet you, Jill."

Danny was uncomfortable. Confident women like Jill never talked to him.

"Very nice to meet you too, Danny. I'm a little tired; mind if I sit with you for a few minutes and rest up?"

"Please do, Jill. The honor is mine." He reached out to move a chair for her. "I used to watch your dad play football."

"Seriously?" Jill was surprised that Danny knew about her dad.

"Yes, he had a wonderful stride. When he got in the open, no one could catch him. I guess not having legs made me appreciate what he could do with his. I loved to watch him."

"Funny," Jill responded, "he walks like that too. I'm a swimmer, and I've always marveled at my father's physical grace."

"I wish I could have watched you compete, Jill. I've not had access to television for some time. We all know about you in here; you are a superstar and all."

Smiling, Jill said, "Bless you, Danny. Thank you so much! You know Danny, I really don't know what's happening here tonight. I've been here many times, but it has never felt like this. I know Christmas Eve is supposed to be a little magical and all, but wow, there is just something in the air. I mean, just the dumplings, they were out of this world. As I walk by the people talking in here, I hear these amazing conversations. It's like a church. Even telling you this, it's like my mouth opens and words come out and I just listen to what I'm saying. But this is cool, Danny. Do you feel this?"

"You know, Jill, I felt what you just said. About 20 minutes ago, after dinner, I said to myself, 'Danny, you are having a great day today.'"

They both laughed.

"Okay, Danny, why are you here?"

"You mean, why am I here in a homeless shelter getting a warm meal and a blanket for the night?"

"Yes. Why, Danny?"

"I'm here because I don't fit anywhere in this world, other than here, Jill. These are my people, and they don't fit out there either," Danny answered.

"What about you doesn't fit?"

"A few things. I have no legs, though that is more accepted today than it was soon after I lost them. I have no respectable history because when I was younger, I had no legs, and it was not as accepted, so opportunities were few, if any. Now, I'm old, well, kind of old, and I have no legs, and I have no history, and now to add to that, the history I have is topped with my being homeless for all these years. And if you are asking why I don't try to work, I have to admit I have no good clothes to apply in, and my wheelchair is a wreck as you can see. Really, if I can be so bold and even blunt, it is obvious why I'm here. So...why are you here, Jill?"

"I want to help, but honestly, it seems pointless because you will leave here tonight or in the morning and continue to suffer. You get a warm meal tonight and connection with all these wonderful souls, but then you are back out there in the cold. You're a hero to me, Danny, you and most of these people that are here now. The caliber of the people that come in here has always impressed me, but that you endure as you do and continue to be kind, it is just heroic to me. But tonight, I may know why I'm here."

"Why, Jill? Why are you here?"

"I'm here to talk to you, Danny. You know something that can help all of us; what is it?"

"Normally, Jill, I would think you're crazy and that your comment is crazy, but tonight, well, it sounds okay. I must tell you, though, I don't know what I know that can help, not at all. Help me get there. Ask me a question."

After a pause, Jill asked, "Danny, if you could push a button that would make people do one thing that would help all humankind, what would that be?"

"Excellent question, Jill. Is that the biggest possible question you could come up with? And like I'm qualified to answer that."

"I think you're qualified, Danny. I know you are."

Danny thought about the question for a few moments and then proceeded. "My answer is for each person to look inside instead of outside. Outside is an illusion of sorts that mostly keeps us from the genuine discoveries that are right here, right now. I'm closer to my essence than yours, Jill, and if I can find the truth and beauty in my essence, I can recognize and impact yours. In such a state, I may find reality on the outside instead of illusion. Yes, being in touch with what's inside makes us bigger and better. That is my answer."

"Yes, I agree, Danny, very much so. My father is hiring a life coach to talk to challenged youth. You're perfect for the job. Tomorrow is Christmas, so I want to make sure you're here tomorrow, and then on Monday at 10:00 AM, a van with a wheelchair ramp will come to pick you up. They'll take you to a motel to get cleaned up, then to get some clothes and a new wheelchair. You'll go interview with my dad. Say yes, Danny. It's your long overdue blessing from the Universe. Take it."

Danny dropped his head into his hands and wept. Jill heard his answer through his sobbing: "Yes." He brought his head up and took her hand and squeezed it. "I'll never forget this moment, Jill. Thank you. Yes!"

While Danny and Jill talked, Unahmie was moving around the room, but there was no doubt she was heading over to see Wanda.

"Hello Wanda, how is my favorite southern lady?"

"Oh Unahmie, so good to see you. I have to tell you, and I mean it, there was something even more special than usual in those dumplings tonight, really special."

Unahmie sat next to Wanda and leaned against her shoulder. They both looked out over the room together and watched as the crippled bodies drifted around, connecting on this miracle night.

"I love making those for you and our family, Wanda. I wish I could do more; I do."

"You're dear, Unahmie; we all love you. As I took each bite, it made me think of Mr. Ponder."

"I'm sorry, Wanda; I hope they were good thoughts. I know it's hard that he's not here with you and that you're alone here tonight."

"Oh no, I'm not alone at all, and to top it off, you're here with me. Can I share a story about Mr. Ponder with you? It's very personal."

"It would honor me to hear it, Wanda."

"When Mr. Ponder was here, we made love every night, well, almost every night. Joey was so generous to me, always praising me and telling me how beautiful I was. He doted on me continually. I felt like a queen. So, I wanted to give that to him every night, even if I felt poorly, if it was not too much so I could act like I was okay, so he didn't know, then we made love.

"We were sitting outside in our backyard in front of our Magnolia—Maggie—and he said to me, 'Sweet Twig,' Mr. Ponder called me that, he said, 'Sweet Twig, I know I thank you each morning for loving me the night before, and I know I thank you while we're making love, but it just came to me why I'm so grateful for you and the loving.' He went on. 'It is because it is over the top. Our loving time together is so magical, so good, so powerful that I can't do anything but be grateful for each moment with you. We live in this nice environment, and we have so much to be grateful for, yet we only realize how lucky we are from time to time. We only admire the architecture of the fireplace or the stitch on your beautiful quilts, now and then. Our attention and delight move around and mixes with our obliviousness. But that time with you, Sweet Twig, it is just over the top and demands nonstop gratitude, and you have it, my Love, my nonstop gratitude.'

"He never understood how much it meant to me, to hold him and feel him, to love him and take him to that place. He was my everything, Unahmie, and I wanted him to be whole; he wanted that for me."

"How long has it been since he passed, Wanda?"

"Let me think, Unahmie. I've been living out here for six years now, so nine years, yes, he passed nine years ago. As of November, it was nine years, just before Thanksgiving. Yes, that's it."

"Thank you for sharing that, Wanda."

"Well, I was eating your dumplings tonight, I felt them warming my tummy, and then my heart, and I thought of him, and it warmed my soul. Honestly, I recall nothing like it, and it happened each time I took a fresh bite of a dumpling. It was over the top, Unahmie, that's what it was, and I was so grateful and so aware of the gratitude. Then I thought of Mr. Ponder's conversation about over the top and realized it was just over the top."

Unahmie reached around Wanda, and they turned to hug one another. They both cried for a couple of minutes, holding each other and swaying. No words, just connection. Their arms relaxed and released, and the women sat back and then looked at each other.

Unahmie spoke. "Wanda, something happened to me tonight when I was in the back cooking...something happened. It was like all of me just woke up, and music and Song were everywhere. I've never felt so calm, nor have I ever before seen so many facets to the jewel that a human being is. I don't know where this is coming from, Wanda, what I'm about to tell you, but it is as clear as you are in my gaze. You will be with Joey again, and over the top will be nonstop, and I mean the joy, not the lovemaking." Wanda smiled. "I don't know what that means, Wanda, but I feel it will be."

Wanda wept a little more and leaned forward. She regained her composure and shared. "When I was a little girl, like all little girls and boys, I believed in Santa. I watched my friends all grow up and figure out that Santa was just, well, part of Christmas lore, not real. I never lost my belief because I watched Santa work miracles all around us, year after year after year. Santa is here now, Unahmie. Santa is in you and was in your magic dumplings. The words you just shared with me are the words I've longed to hear and to know, and I hear them from you and know them to be true. You, Unahmie, Mrs. Claus, are over the top, and I'm grateful for you. This will be my last Christmas with you, dear friend." Wanda told Unahmie the same thing every year, but she could be right this time. Unahmie always answered the same way.

"Yes, I know, Wanda. I love you with all my heart, and I'm excited for you, very much so."

At that moment, Ben and Teddie helped Waz through the doors and toward a place to sit.

"Thank you, boys, for saving me tonight. I wish Mary were here with me; please see she is taken care of. She was my person...I can't believe she had to leave us tonight."

"It's good to see you, Waz. We'll take care of Mary. You stay here as long as you can; it may be unusually cold for several days, super bad."

"Thank you again, Ben, Ted. You are good people." Waz smiled with effort while his heavy heart lived the sorrow around the loss of his person.

"We got to get back out there," Ted said.

Unahmie walked up right then and squeezed both on the arm. "Would you like some food, Ben, Teddie?"

"No, ma'am, we got to get back out there."

"Thanks for bringing Waz in."

After Ben and Teddie walked away, Unahmie looked down at Waz. "Mary is gone, isn't she?" She knew they were inseparable.

Waz broke down. "Mary's gone, left this world unseen by most, but I'll miss her, Ms. Unahmie; I'll remember her."

"I will, too. I will too!" she said lovingly.

Waz looked up and into her eyes, seeing depth he hadn't seen in any eyes before, and they mesmerized him.

"Mary will never be gone," Unahmie whispered.

Waz's mind was quiet; a peace came over him. Mary was everywhere, and so was he. Then he blinked.

Her voice came back into his focus. "Rest, Waz; you are always welcome here. I'll get you some food. Eat. Mary would want you to."

At that moment, a crew from Macy's came through the door, pushing multiple coat racks covered with long down-filled coats. There were 500 warm coats with gloves, and the precious souls who desperately needed them found their sizes; the coats were the first garments that would fit in a long time.

Christmas carols gently rolled through the speakers of the shelter, and each soul felt peace on this blessed night.

Unahmie made her way over to Jill, and they hugged each other warmly. Unahmie asked, "What's your favorite word, Jill?"

"Thaumaturgy, that's the word. Thaumaturgy, wonderworking."

"Yes, that's perfect, Jill. Merry Christmas." Note left Unahmie and moved through the Christmas night.

In Between

Note enjoyed the wonder of service in a setting where service connected all the souls to a higher place and a more loving experience. The more souls Note joined over the vastness of time; the more service was experienced. Note contemplated that service may be a path to the higher place. Yes, it is, Note determined.

Note next needed to experience how a mind could let go of deeply held beliefs in order to witness a miracle it could not have previously fathomed.

Chapter Thirty-Eight

Equation for God

Pierre was almost crazy!

Seven years earlier, Pierre and Jacqueline sat gazing at each other in their favorite coffee shop, Les Deux Magots, at 6 Place Saint-Germain des Pres in Paris. Note joined Pierre. He was a famous mathematician, world-famous, in fact. From birth, his brilliant mind found that everything he perceived could relate to mathematics. Even random events and occurrences could be mathematically predicted and represented.

Two years before, Pierre presented groundbreaking and revolutionary mathematic theory around computational magnetohydrodynamics. The breakthrough made it possible to implement nuclear fusion, the dawn of a new age for humankind.

Jacqueline was an instructor in the sciences department at Paris Sciences et Lettres, one of the top universities in France and highly rated in the world. Jacqui exuded a deep creative vein. Art through the brush attracted her. An adept artist in her own right, her inviting drawings adorned their Paris apartment. She loved and appreciated the way her person's mind worked, too, as she saw his math from a creative perspective.

The morning was glowing on almost every level. As they walked to the café, both savored the moment and how crisp the air was on this chilly morning. The sky released the darkness to an anxious sun, slowly finding a few fluffy clouds moving toward the east. The sunrise was especially colorful today, with deep pinks and oranges easing into one another with different intensities of light behind them. The sunlight tickled the clouds, seeming to hurry them along.

Though the traffic was gaining intensity, few cars found their horns. Passersby each seemed to find a smile or a head nod to share.

Once inside the shop, the couple found their favorite table open, a table that allowed them to smash up against each other while they enjoyed their coffee. Jacqueline often laid her head on his shoulder. They couldn't get enough of each other.

"You are beautiful, my Love. I'd rather look at you and hold your hand today than drink any of this coffee."

"You are dear, Pepé," she said with a soft smile.

He loved it when she called him that.

"There's just something about this day. Can you smell the coffee and pastries here this morning?"

"Yes. Yummy. I want something sweet today," Jacqui said.

"You have to get your strength back," he interjected.

Jacqueline giggled. "I still smell us; that's my favorite smell."

"Mmm, me too," he responded, smiling big. Pierre and Jacqueline had made love this morning, a pleasure they rarely took the time to share so early. They connected with each other on almost every level on this day.

"Pierre, I want some avocado toast this morning. Will you order it for me?"

They enjoyed each other, the avocado toast, his traditional croissant with cream cheese, and their delicious coffee, but more than anything, they enjoyed each other.

"You've been grinning all morning; is it because we made love?" Jacqui asked.

"I'm grinning inside and out about that to be sure, but I've experienced a realization today; would you like to hear it? It's that math stuff, and I know you prefer not to talk about that during coffee," he responded.

"If it makes you grin like that, I want to know. Please share."

"My mind has been full of two things this morning: you and music. Both are amazing; no wonder I'm grinning so. I realized a while ago that music is a combination of notes in harmony, all working together to create a song. It's perfect, like math. I wonder if music and math aren't the same thing. What if music is another layer of mathematics represented in sound instead of symbols? They are both perfect as you are!"

"You're always so affirming of me, Pepé. You say, share, and do more loving things for me than I deserve, but I feel your complete sincerity in it. Honestly, it makes me absolutely adore you; do you feel that?"

"Yes, I do. I see it in the way you look at me. I drink in your gentle and loving touch, and I bathe in your adoration. Thank you for that."

"And you're funny too, Pepé! What did you tell me last night that had me in stitches?"

"Oh, yes, I was talking about Sponge Bob and Mrs. Squiggles with her hair," he answered.

Jacqui broke out laughing again to the point of snorting. She often snorted when laughing hard. Tears were streaming down her face. "Yes, that's it! See how you make me laugh? It was so stupid!"

After a few moments, Pierre restarted some conversation.

"What was the book you downloaded last night?"

Looking at him hesitantly, she remarked, "It's a book on reincarnation."

"Reincarnation? That's a little out of left field."

"Darling, I know that you are the most brilliant mathematician and that something like reincarnation can't possibly fit into a formula, but I just think there's a great deal going on out there that's beyond our comprehension, maybe beyond your math. It may be on another level, like the music you discovered."

"I've seen nothing that can't be proven or figured out with an equation," Pierre announced. "That's nothing but dreams and fiction, and I can solve even some of that."

"I know, Pierre; the math is against reincarnation, and heaven, and God. But where did the stuff of the big bang come from, what was before that? We're divinely limited, tiny, and I just think there's more to consider."

"I love everything about you, Jacqueline, everything. In fact, if you decide you believe in that, I will believe in it too," he said, smiling.

"You are most accommodating Darling; I love everything about you too. Time to get on with our day...so sad. Kiss me."

Pierre leaned forward, and they shared a meaningful, soft kiss. It was unusual to feel the warmth and wetness of her lips and taste the coffee in her mouth, but this morning, it was magical. She felt all of it too. They then got up and made their way outside. Once out the door, Pierre realized he'd left his computer inside. He could be absent-minded.

"Damn, I left my computer. I'll be right back."

Jacqueline made her way to the curb to wait for Pierre, out of the pedestrians' flow, each walking with purpose and a place to go.

Upon returning with his laptop, Pierre made his way toward Jacqueline. Just as he got to her, her foot slid off the curb. As she fought to steady herself on her heels, she lost her balance and fell back, hitting her head against a lamppost. Pierre rushed to help her and quickly realized her head injury was substantial.

"Baby," she moaned. "Baby, I'm getting cold, I hit my head, don't let go of me, I don't want to go." Pierre held her as her eyes slowly shut, and she died, just five minutes after they had shared their morning inside.

Pierre's mind was like no other Note had experienced. His mind was the most orderly Note had joined. Everything made sense until Jacqueline's death. Afterward, his mind set out on a methodical search for God. It was all-consuming. Pierre recognized in the Café that there was something magical about Jacqueline, something beyond math, or math as he knew it. God must exist for someone as magical as his Jacqui to have lived. God must have created love, and Pierre knew true love. He set out to find God, nonstop, in perfect order, relentlessly. Note could experience the order, the speed, the search, the hope, but who could find God? What mind could perceive God?

***

Years passed.

"Hello."

Pierre's mind slowed for the first time in a while, and he recognized it was daytime and warm. He heard the water, so he looked to his left to see the river.

"Hello."

Pierre looked down to see a little girl sitting before him with her feet dangling over the wall next to the Seine.

"Hello," she said again. "Are you lost?"

"No, yes, no, I'm not lost," he responded. "Did I run into you? What's your name?"

"Agnes."

"Did I run into you, Agnes? Did I scare you?"

"No. What's your name?"

"Pierre."

"Are you okay, Pierre?"

"I don't really know. I seem to be right now. You don't have to fear me, though."

"I know, Pierre. Can you sit with me?"

At that moment, Agnes's mother, Marion, walked up. "Hello, Sir. Agnes, come with me."

Pierre realized he looked scary to Marion; she was there to rescue her daughter from this troubled man.

"Come on, Agnes, please!" Marion spoke more intensely.

Agnes didn't get up.

"This is Pierre, Mommy. He is a nice man."

Pierre held out his trembling hand. "Good day, Madame. I'm Pierre LeBlanc; very nice to meet you. I apologize to both you and Agnes for my appearance. I'm sure I'm hard to look at." He did not appreciate how bad he smelled as well.

Marion extended her hand. She felt safe with Pierre and could sense Note, not knowing what it was she sensed.

"I'm Marion. My daughter's name is Agnes."

"Nice to meet you, Marion. Agnes and I have already introduced ourselves to one another."

"Pierre LeBlanc, yes, you resemble, are you the mathematician, the fusion mathematician?"

"I was, yes."

Marion knew the story of Pierre LeBlanc; the entire world had watched their hero's demise. They chalked it up to his brilliance, but it was sad.

"Thank you for what you did for all of us, Dr. LeBlanc. It thankfully helped the poor among us, all over the world."

"Thank you, Marion. I'm sorry for how I look and smell." His senses were returning as his mind became more aware within the moment; his search for God temporarily rested.

"Maman, can Pierre sit with me while I draw, please?"

Marion looked back at Pierre to check her intuition; he was safe.

"Yes, if he wants to. I will go sit back down."

Pierre looked over to see a bench covered with knitting and knitting tools.

"What are you working on, Marion?"

"Do you know anything about knitting, Monsieur LeBlanc?"

"Please, call me Pierre, please. My mother knitted, I know some, maybe more than some. What are you working on?"

"I'm working on a shawl, Pierre, a simple shawl. I'm drawn to greens right now."

"Greens, yes, greens denote hope. I sense that in you, Marion. Please go on."

Taken a little aback by his knowledge and interest in her knitting, she proceeded.

"Paris is cool, as you know, so though simple, it's an appropriately long one so I can wrap it around three times."

"That's long, Marion. What size needle are you using? Again, I'm interrupting...my apologies."

"My, you do know, knitting. I'm using a 3.5mm needle. You will probably stop me and ask what shape next, so I will volunteer that it's a crescent shape."

"Ah, yes, Madame, so it'll better stay on your shoulders."

"Yes, Pierre. That's right. You are a fascinating man." Then she smiled and made her way back to the bench.

He watched and admired Marion as she made her way. He appreciated that shawls were also straightforward, leaving an experienced knitter the bandwidth to knit and watch her precious little one, as Marion just proved. Pierre loved his Mom and held an earnest and deep appreciation for all mothers. He remembered that he and Jacqueline had been trying to get pregnant. Then he thought of Agnes and looked down to see her.

Pierre lowered himself to sit with Agnes.

Agnes had naturally curly strawberry blond hair with large green eyes that set off her many freckles. Agnes still had her baby teeth, and they were bright white. It looked like Marion may have dressed her, coordinating her outfit with her yellow skirt and white top, with a bright yellow bow in her hair.

"So, what are you drawing, Agnes?"

"I love to draw boats and people and how they look."

"How they're dressed?"

"No, if they are happy or sad or neither. I like to witness how people feel. What happened to you, Pierre?"

"That's a surprisingly adult question, Agnes. Why do you ask?"

"You don't look like everyone else, I guess."

"Because I'm thin and old looking and my clothes are a mess, is that what you mean?"

"Yes, kind of. You don't look like you feel like everyone else feels."

"Oh my, that's right, you watch people, and how they feel. That's well, special, Agnes."

"You are sad. Are you sad?" Agnes asked.

"I have been, yes. My wife died some time ago. I can't say how long, but it was some time ago, yes. I loved her very much. She was my person! Do you know what that means, Agnes?"

"No, I don't, but it kind of sounds like my maman, and what she is to me."

"Yes, your maman is your everything. My wife Jacqueline was my everything." Pierre looked back out over the river.

Agnes held out her hand to take his for a moment and leaned against him and spoke. "I'm sure she adored you, Pierre, and that you were her person too."

It felt so good to hear that, so good!

Then she sat back up and asked, "Can my maman come to sit with us, Pierre?"

"Why?"

"She is sad, too, a lot. My dad went to heaven when I was two. I don't remember him, but I know she remembers him all the time. I think he was her person before me. Can my maman come to sit with us?"

"It would make you happy, wouldn't it, Agnes?"

"Yes, it would make me happy."

"Yes, if she wants to."

"Maman, MAMAN," Agnes called out loudly and, once she gained her Mom's attention, waved her over.

"Come sit, Maman, sit down!"

"This is awkward," Marion spoke out. Then, with reservation, she bagged up her knitting and made her way toward them. Once she was next to them, she hesitated. What line would this cross, if any?

Agnes and Pierre just looked up at her quietly, but with an invitation on their faces.

Marion made her way down on the wall on the other side of Agnes, feet dangling over.

Pierre recognized and appreciated how beautiful Marion was, almost angelically so. Her face was lovely and framed with thick, curly, shiny brown hair. Her smile was gentle and disarming, and the tone of her voice soothed Pierre. These two were the first people Pierre could remember seeing since his beloved Jacqueline died.

Pierre's mind started doing math again, but situational math. What were the odds that he would become conscious just in time to sit down on a rock wall next to the River Seine with a precious little girl and her angelic mom? The odds weren't high, so this must be something more than chance; Pierre wouldn't figure this out mathematically.

"Ladies, I have to say, the chance of the three of us sitting here like this is somewhat unlikely, so it must be important. Given that, and knowing that we're all full of questions usually, what do you want to know? Do you want to know anything?"

"What happened to you, Pierre?" Marion asked.

Nothing had made sense to Pierre for an exceedingly long time, but now was different, and Note was here.

"I lost my wife, and she was everything to me. When Jacqueline died, I couldn't justify it, mathematically. Before that moment, I had found, realized, discovered, or fooled myself into believing that everything could be mathematically explained and rationalized. Her loss and her exquisite existence were beyond math, so I calculated that God must exist. I've been looking for God, mathematically, for all this time, hoping that when I found God, I'd find Jacqueline. I didn't know until now how lost I would get. I don't understand what is happening now, to be honest, but I know it's good, and I feel honored to be sitting on this wall with both of you. So, thank you.

"I understand that you lost your husband. I'm sorry; it's not for me to mention it."

"It's okay, Pierre. Yes, Remy was everything to me too. He always encouraged me and affirmed me. Remy was easy to be with, and I was myself with him. He always seemed to watch for what I needed next and then helped me get it, whatever it was. When I was sluggish, Remy would ask me a question and wake me up. I wanted Agnes, and Remy made sure I got her. Pierre, he was so funny too. He said stupid things and just cracked me up. I don't know if I've laughed once since I lost him. When I had Remy and Agnes, I had everything, really, but then he died.

"I've not looked for God but looked away from God. I'm sorry, Agnes, I should not be speaking like this with you here."

"Why not, Maman?"

Marion looked at her daughter and felt almost like Agnes was the parent at that moment.

"It's okay, Maman. It's time to be okay!"

She looked at her beloved Agnes in a perplexed way. How could Agnes know it was time to be okay?

"Marion, I have an odd question for you. I don't know why I'm asking it, but it seems innocent enough."

"Go ahead, Pierre, ask."

Both Agnes and Marion looked at him intently, waiting for the question.

"What is your favorite word, Marion, right now?"

Agnes smiled and turned toward her Maman, who looked down at her.

"Mercy!"

Just at that moment, a boat passed in the river. It was a long white yacht with a couple standing in it with bags next to them. It caught Agnes's attention.

Seeing Agnes focusing on the couple with their bags, Pierre broke into a Song. "Leaving on a Jet Plane..."

Marion looked over at Pierre with astonishment and then broke down in laughter. Agnes saw her mother laughing and followed suit, laughing with delight, and adding a couple of snorts.

A few moments after, when it was quiet again, Pierre asked another question.

"Was that kind of stupid, Marion?"

She looked up at Pierre, and he looked back at her. There was life again, wonderful, merciful life.

"Yes, it was kind of stupid." They all smiled.

Through the corners of their eyes, each saw Agnes drawing something on a piece of paper that she promptly folded and turned toward Pierre.

He looked down at her, found her green eyes, and saw something he could never have expected: Jacqueline. Pierre quickly remembered her talking about reincarnation on the morning of her death.

"It's okay," she whispered.

She handed him the folded piece of paper.

He looked down to see a word on it:

God

His eyes watered, and then he opened it.

1-1=0

Note left Pierre to continue to discover.

Chapter Thirty-Nine

Math with a Smoothie

"How long will we be here, Mommy?" Cheir asked.

"We're here to fix the Jessie. We've experienced some trouble with her and needed to land here to fix it. We won't be here long. You stay with me, Cheir. This station is a Guardian vessel, so we'll be safe, but you stay with me, okay?"

"Yes, Mommy! Can I explore if I stay within your sight? That's staying with you, right?"

"Okay, Cheir, but stay close, where I can see you."

The station was small but grand in design, with numerous geometric shapes and architectural design elements throughout. The colors were rich and plentiful. Vibrant vegetation thrived in small plots that were ideally situated. Though the fragrance in the air was from the fesshie flower, which flourished in the artificial light, the station smelled of rose petals.

Note joined Cheir as she started her exploration and soon, as would often happen, she was out of her mother's sight. Her eyes became fixed on a little man sitting in the eatery's corner, looking out the window at the star-filled sky. She felt immensely drawn to the man. She had to meet him.

"Excuse me, Sir; may I sit with you?"

"Please, please, join me. I'm Seait, and you are...?" the man inquired.

"Cheir, I'm Cheir. I see you're staring at the stars; what do you see?"

"Honestly, I see 72 rhombicosidodecahedrons, three 8-dimensional torus, 193 right angles, and 16 isosceles triangles. I see a lot more than that, but that will give you a picture of what I see," he said, smiling.

"Gosh, I just see stars out there. I don't see any of those other things... though, now that you mention it, I can kind of start to see some of those patterns too. You are interesting, Seait. Is your ship broken too? Is that why you're here?"

"No, I live here…well, I live my life here," he answered.

"What do you mean? Is this your home?" Cheir asked.

"No, it's not my home, but it's where I live, where I have to live."

They were bonding. There was something magic about their meeting, and it was fate. "Okay, Seait. Tell me, what do you mean by that?"

Seait answered, "The Guardians brought me here and look after me. My home is in another star system—oh, right there." He pointed up to a place in the sky. "I'm a Stant, which means I see everything mathematically. The Guardians tell me that there are only 16,887 of us in the Universe. We're scarce to be sure."

"You look at everything mathematically?" Cheir's face scrunched.

"Yes, and geometrically, it's stunning. Let me get you a Connock drink at the bar. You'll love it."

Seait went to the bar and procured two Connock drinks. They sat at the table and looked out the window. When Cheir glanced over at him, she saw his eyes darting all around. She observed his pulse pounding in his neck.

"What do you feel when you look out there?"

"Anxiety." He looked back at her, and his eyes eased and fixed on her darling face. She looked down at his neck and saw his pulse suddenly slow.

"Why do you constantly look out there and what can't you see?"

"I can't see to the edge, Cheir, the edge on the other side. I'm anxious because I know I can never see all of it to quantify it."

"How do you sleep, Seait?"

He reached into his pocket and pulled out a small metal ball, one with no reflectivity.

"I look at this so I can sleep. There is no math on it."

"Are you happy?"

"I am now." He flashed a big smile.

They both took another sip of the Connick drink.

"What's in this? It's delicious," Cheir asked.

"They call it a strawberry and banana smoothie. I like it too. I get a rush after I have one."

Cheir giggled. "It's freezing! Seait, what is your favorite word? I don't know why I'm asking that, but I want to know."

"Relevance is my favorite word at this moment."

She shared, "My mom tells me a story she probably doesn't think I am old enough to understand, but I think I get it. It's about a stone being tossed into the still water of a pond and creating waves that radiate out from where it entered the water. The wave radiates out to the edge, Seait. You are such a pebble to me. I want you to know that. Can I ask you one more question?"

"Please, Cheir, please do, and thank you for being the pond for my pebble."

"Do you know of a mathematical formula for God?"

"Yes. God is everywhere and nowhere, observable and beyond observation. God can mean something and nothing. God is where everything with distinction begins; without God, there would be no place to start from. Yes, there's a formula, and in fact, an infinite number of formulas that end with God as a result. May I share one of them with you?"

"Please, Seait, please do."

$$1 - 1 = 0$$

Her eyes watered. She understood. Seait was beautiful to her, and God is everywhere. Note left Cheir.

In Between

Note lived in the clarity of innocence in Cheir. She was open and received.

Next, Note was to discover how the Universe was so productive. How could it answer God's question in only trillions of years with the seemingly infinite happenings everywhere, constantly?

The answer to that question is, systems.

Chapter Forty

Systems

It was a sweet afternoon. Cipriano sat on the large covered front porch on the little cottage nestled in the lush forest. The trees that surrounded the cottage were old-growth and mighty, with straight trunks that towered a hundred feet before limbs started. They jutted out forever, mingling with arms from neighboring behemoths.

The forest opened in front of the cottage, exposing a deep blue ocean with large swells that rolled into the rocks down the cliff. Cipriano found great peace on this porch, connected with the life and majesty around him.

Today, the sky above was light blue, with scattered fluffy clouds floating on the jet stream, getting a bird's-eye view of the beautiful and abundant world below. Jessie had planted lilacs all around the porch. The bees did their business with them while the flowers shared their fragrant and intoxicating scent for all to enjoy.

The porch swing creaked with Cipriano's gentle rock. His breathing matched the sound of the ocean swells as they met the end of their long journey. Note joined Cipriano at this moment, as did little Sally as she came out of the cottage to join her grandpa. She still had syrup on her cheek from the late country breakfast she had just eaten inside. Earlier, her mom worked her fine hair into pigtails with pink ribbons and dressed her in a little dress with white ruffles over the purple fabric. She was the cutest in her black buckle shoes over white socks. Cipriano stopped rocking in the swing and reached out to lift little Sally onto his lap.

Sally leaned her side against her grandpa as he started rocking again. A nurturing man, he rested his hand over her knees. He could smell the syrup mixing with the lilac fragrance and smiled.

"Papa, why does your hand have all those spots on it?" Sally asked with a scrunched-up face.

"I'm old, Sugar Pie. We all start little and amazing like you, grow up living wonderful lives, get older like your papa, and then pass from the world."

"Pass from the world...what's that?"

"When I was four like you are Sugar Pie, I had a papa like you do. We talked about the spots on his hands like you and I are now. When I was Zeb's age, my papa passed. That's a time when we leave this world and are born in another. I don't exactly know what that is, but it's good. I know nothing is ever lost, so I know that when we pass, we're not lost."

"Lost?" Sally's hands started playing with each other as if discovering her fingers for the first time.

Cipriano looked out on the prodigious forest floor and gazed at Wonder. Wonder was one of the felled trees. On its side, it was 20 feet high and stretched for 400 feet. The forest grew around the giant, holding it in reverence and standing guard around the old patriarch. Wonder was the name Cipriano's family had given this divine thing.

"Look over at Wonder, Sugar Pie. Wonder was born and became a seed that became a twig, then a young tree, growing taller and stronger every year, for centuries, for millennia"—Sally's face crunched up again—"for several thousand years. Then Wonder stopped growing and passed. After a great while, it fell right where you see it today. The trees that stand around it with the green limbs on the top are alive like we are, and they're growing, and may get big like Wonder. Wonder, however, has passed and no longer has green limbs. It no longer grows, but as you can see, it's not lost. Nothing is ever lost, Sugar Pie."

"How long do bugs live, Papa? I don't like bugs." Her mouth puckered.

"Oh, sweet little one, that's a question I have long wondered myself."

"You've always wondered about how long bugs live?" Sally's attention moved from her fingers to her grandpa's face.

"Kind of, Sally. What I've often wondered is, why does each species or bug or tree or plant or whatever have the life span it does? Why does a roach live for one to two years while a fly lives for 15 to 30 days? Why do whales and people live into their seventies and eighties, while dolphins are lucky to get into their forties? Why is it different, Sugar Pie? That is what I often wonder about."

"Papa, why does your hand have all those spots on it?"

Cipriano recognized and appreciated that his darling granddaughter could only take in so much and simplified his answer.

"My body is changing like yours. You will have spots on your hands someday too, Sugar Pie."

Pablo came out at that moment to see his grandpa.

"Hi Grandpa; hi, Sally."

Sally felt annoyed that her teenage brother had joined them and did not respond. She got up in a huff and stomped quickly back inside.

"Hello, Pablo. So good to have you out here with me."

Cipriano's comment impacted Pablo. He felt surer of himself and had a second wind blowing his sail forward. Pablo felt like his grandpa saw him and loved him for who he was.

"Thanks, Grandpa," Pablo smiled. "Why are you so nice to me?"

"What do you mean, Boe Boe?"

"When did you start calling me that, Grandpa? You're the only one that calls me that, and it feels good when you say it."

"Well, when you were just a few days old, and I was holding you in my arms, I felt a profound sensation come over me about how special you were, what a gift you were, what an honor it was to share that moment or any other moment with you in this world. At that moment, when I was holding you, it felt like Christmas feels to me, magical, full of hope. It made me think of presents with bows on them. I know that sounds silly, but from then on, I've always seen you as a gift, and Boe Boe is the endearing term I have for you, my gift. What took you so long to ask me?"

"I don't know. I've wondered for a long time but just felt funny about asking. You're more comfortable to talk to than mom and dad are for sure. You seem to like me. They don't."

Pablo was seventeen years old and, like most everyone else, had experienced a crazy childhood.

"Grandpa. Why are grown-ups so tired? They don't get excited about anything except getting on my case!"

Cipriano smiled at him, and their eyes met. "Well, Boe Boe, when you're young, everything is new or newer than it is to older people. When you were young, you had never received a little red ball for Christmas before, until you did the first time. Remember how exciting that moment was, your very own red ball? Wow! So, if you get a little red ball for a present now, you're not so excited. It's not new now. Adults like your mom and dad, and like me, have encountered a lot of stuff over our lifetimes. Not much seems new to us now, to be honest," Cipriano said with a twinkle in his deep-set eyes. "It's not that we aren't excited, but that we're full of experiences, and those create a suit of armor of sorts around us. To be honest with you, wearing that suit of armor makes me tired sometimes. It'll happen to you, my dear boy, as you live the full life that you'll live."

"That's cool, Grandpa, little red balls, suit of armor, yes, cool. I heard something from one of my teachers in school, and I've been thinking about it. Mrs. Dartey told us we all learn from our mistakes, and that's one of only two ways we learn. Honestly, I didn't get it."

"I agree with her, Pablo. I read this book when I was in my twenties, can't remember what it's called now. Sorry, but it had a great analogy that stuck with me. Think of a baby reaching for their bottle. They see their bottle, know they want what's in it, and they've learned they can grab things with their hands and put them in their mouth. So, they reach for the bottle. Now, they've never done that before, so at first, they miss it, but they keep trying until they finally find the bottle with their hand. Each one of those misses was a mistake. Through reaching incorrectly, their brain learned how to get it right. They learned from their mistakes. Make sense?"

"It makes sense, but it doesn't seem like the best way to learn. I mean, think of all the things that have to get messed up just to learn something."

"Yes, Boe Boe."

"Grandpa, can I share something with you? It's been on my mind a lot. I am kind of scared about it."

Cipriano looked around and saw they were alone; he sat forward to hear what Pablo wanted to share.

Cipriano was welcome in Pablo's space, and so he leaned forward too. "My life sucks, Grandpa. I can't find the right girl. I'm ugly, and school isn't going well. Being a busboy is all I know. I have trouble with my boss at the Burrito Bojana, and I just don't know if I can ever get along with know-it-all authority figures. Something is wrong with me, Grandpa! Your love for me is the tops, but I'm sure it's because you don't know me, I mean, *really* know me. I've thought about taking some pills and just going to sleep. I'm way off track, and it sucks."

Tears were streaming down Pablo's face.

"You talk of taking pills...how bad is it?" Cipriano's face, body, and voice showed great concern.

"That I am talking about it, Grandpa, is a good day for me. Mostly, I've gotten to where I don't care much. It's a dark place. Motivation is tough to find. To be honest, I think I'm losing ground. The dark lasts a little longer. I can't believe I'm telling you this, but I'm glad I am. I'm scared. I care right now."

Cipriano put his hand out on his Pablo's knee and then on Pablo's cheek, looking deeply into his eyes. "Seriously, and no is not an answer. I am taking you to my doctor on Monday. Let your job know you need to be off. Okay? You have some chemicals going on in all that, and we need to get them balanced. Don't be afraid. It's the chemicals. Do you need to stay here with us?"

After a brief pause, Pablo responded, "Okay, thank you, Grandpa." Pablo felt the spring of hope and some relief. His light shone through, just a little.

"Well," Cipriano said as he sat back again, "I will have to admit you're silly." A smile cracked meekly on his face. "Silly because you're just an awesome young man. Can I share something?"

"Yes, Grandpa," he said fragilely.

"We do a great injustice to young people in life, Pablo. When you were twelve, you had such a sweet little soprano voice; you sported no muscles, you were two feet shorter, and the only hair on your body was on your head. You weren't interested in girls, and you enjoyed your parents, and they enjoyed you. As I remember, you loved to spend the summers here with your grandpa too. By the time you were fifteen, your voice became a tenor. You grew all those muscles without a lick of exercise. You shot up eighteen inches, sprouted all sorts of stuff all over your body, determined that your parents were idiots and prison wardens, and you started getting girl crazy. You also quit spending summers with your sweet, loving, doting grandpa.

"Pablo, that's a hell of a lot to happen to a person in two years. When all that started happening, you didn't get a download of all sorts of wisdom and understanding. Remember the little red ball? It was all new, Pablo. Seriously, you didn't even start tying your shoes until last year because the importance of it didn't register until you tripped and needed 13 stitches to fix your chin. It's an unfortunate truth, Pablo, that we get power before we know how to have power. Not only did you get bigger and stronger, but you grew older too. That motivated your parents to give you more freedom, which is more power!

"Now, your life sucks to you, because you had all that power and didn't know how to handle it. And your peers were, and are, all going through the same crazy thing. I think that's a great injustice, Pablo, but it is the system we have. You will," Cipriano said slowly and emphatically, "get through this time. I felt the way you feel when I was seventeen."

"Seriously?"

"Yes, Sir. I recognize power when it comes my way, and I am cautious with it. Your trust, Pablo, gives me power with you. I am careful to respect that. If it gets too tough, reach out to me. I'll help you. I will always be here to help my Pablo. And by the way, you are a handsome little cuss too!"

"That makes sense, Grandpa, kind of. It resonates a little, except for the handsome thing." He cracked a small smile. "If you know this stuff, then mom and dad should too. Why don't they cut me some slack? They're always on my ass. Sorry, Grandpa, they're always on my butt."

Cipriano leaned forward again. "Two things. First, you are in a desperate battle; the one you just shared with me is one you will emerge from, absolutely. They may suspect, and are concerned, but don't know what you're experiencing. How could they? You've not shared it with them. Is that right?"

"No," Pablo admitted.

"The second," Cipriano continued, "is the experience with age system. My papa, your great granddad, gave me an analogy. I've always remembered it. It helps me know my place while respecting others. My papa was a simple man, and his analogies were simple too.

"He said, 'Son, we are all like snowballs rolling down a hill. As we go down the hill, we get bigger and bigger, gathering size as we take on more and more, faster and faster. The bottom of the hill tapers off until the ground is flat. As we get toward the bottom of the hill, we slow down until we finally come to a stop and melt at the bottom.'

"I keep that story in my mind, Boe Boe, and it reminds me that those who have been on the hill longer and collected more along their journey know more than I do. Your parents have been on the hill longer and have experiences to share with you to help you protect yourself from mistakes they made on their journeys. I grant you they need to work on the way they talk to you, Boe Boe, because the goal is for you to 'hear' what they are sharing, and it doesn't sound like that's the case. At some point, you'll make yourself available to them so they can hear you. They want to. I'm sure of that."

Pablo moved toward Cipriano, wrapping his arms around him. His cell phone went off in his pocket, and his automatic reflexes quickly reached for it and pulled it out to engage. Dopamine released. "Hey Grandpa, got to go, but I love you, man, you rock, you are one of my people, dude."

"Back at ya, Pablo." Cipriano winked. "I love you too, man. No pills, though, cut that crap out, take care of my treasured grandson, damn it. Okay? Can I ask you to bring Ma Mu out for a while? Just bring her out; I'll take it from there."

"Sure thing, Grandpa!"

Pablo zipped into the house and rolled Ma Mu out in her wheelchair. At 87 years of age, she had already been in a wheelchair for over 20 years. She and her husband, Jorge, were in an accident. Jorge died, and the accident left Jillian disabled below the waist. Cipriano's mother lived the life of an aging queen; the family took care of all her needs. Pablo brought her up close to Cipriano and then excused himself to go back to the house.

"Such a wonderful evening, Son. I love this time of year." Jillian's voice quivered but had a joy that seemed to override her weariness.

"Yes, Mama, this is a special day to be sure. I love it when all the family comes to visit. It reminds me why we're here. They're the meaning for me, and you."

"Thank you for being such a good man."

"I appreciate that, Mama. It means so much to me to hear that you feel that way, but I'm your son. You're biased. I can tell you for sure that I could be better. I feel like I'm about three-fourths down the path and still don't know where the path goes. There are a million or more things to behold and experience at this moment, but I can only witness a few."

Jillian looked down at her old hands and paid attention to the blemishes and how her veins showed. Arthritis caused her knuckles to swell permanently. She remembered when she was young and beautiful.

"Well, Son, I'm about twenty-three twenty-fourths along my path, and I see the end, I think. There is nothing really at the end. I believe when we die, our moment is over. My few remaining living friends talk to me about seeing your dad again and spending eternity with him. I just don't know how my personality would go from this body to eternity. No, I don't see it, Son. So, for me, I delight in moments like this one, when I can forget how my body hurts and wonder what I still contribute to all of this."

"Oh, Mama, I still have hope there is more after this, I do!"

"I did too when I was your age. It seemed at the time that I was still growing and expanding, learning more, getting wiser. My appreciation was increasing. Then the accident happened. The death of your father and this handicap have been devastating to me. While climbing out of the darkness over the years, I discovered parts of myself that I hadn't tapped. Yes, I felt hope then.

"Now, as I age, decay, and die, all the wisdom I discovered over all those life experiences does nothing for me. I get angry with people who do things or say things I have no patience for. I tire of smiling at little bobbles of success, because I know everyone ends up like this. We can't earn a pass here. We can't get a new game or more points to get another chance. Successes just let you have a better experience until you get here. I don't like here, Son, not a bit. You're always talking of systems, Cipriano, and it just seems like we move until we peak in life, then fall the rest of the way. I don't like that system, Son."

"I hear you, Mama, I do. I talk about systems a lot, and to tell you the truth, I don't appreciate being a part of a system, or many systems, because it's like I have no real say in the outcome. If I can be honest, this system is the one that punches me in the gut the most, this getting older thing. Once I turned 50, and my hair was half gray, I started thinking about dying almost every day. I used to be able to lift heavy stuff around here with little struggle, and now I need help. I am deeply attracted to Jessie, but I don't have the libido I did. I must eat better, or I pay a higher price.

It's hard to find a lot of good in this system, Mama, at least for me. But here is one thought I have been contemplating, and if it is right, there's hope for both of us in it.

"We hear about miracles. Okay, what's a miracle? I don't know, but what if a miracle is like a maze? It's difficult but not impossible, and if you get through the maze to the other side, you find that something special, the thing that gives it the description: a miracle. I believe, Mama, that the key to that maze is right here, all the time. We just have to do the work, whatever that is.

"Another system is for us to be too distracted to do the work. Pablo was out here a while ago, and we were having a great conversation. His phone went off...and no more communication. I think the maze is a conversion, Mama, and if we do the work and don't get distracted, we get to a miracle. Miracles, like you, are awesome!" They shared a smile.

"Why do you think the system would be to distract us, or whatever you said, Son?" she asked with a curious look.

"Evolution is in tiny steps, Mama. I think that's part of the physics of this Universe. Miracles must be few to keep the pace slow but steadily evolving. We are all much closer to 'whatever' than we were 10,000 years ago. That's something. Hope, I think."

"You are beautifully deep, Cipriano, and I love the way your mind works. I can admit, I want to have hope. I want a miracle and may still have enough energy for one, I do. I would love to spend more time appreciating my dear boy."

Cipriano and Jillian both sat back and listened to the locust in the high trees. She heard the wind for the first time in a long time and thought, *I hear the wind again, and I smell the pine needles.*

"Your father used to tell me that miracles were where destiny and impossibility meet. I never understood that because it was too deep. Like you, Son, your father was deep. I was always afraid I was not deep enough for him, but he always assured me I was all he ever wanted or hoped for. That almost sounds like a miracle now that I think of it. Meeting and spending my life with the most wonderful man, where destiny and the impossible met." Smiling, Jillian said, "In your deep thinking, I'll bet destiny drives you nuts, doesn't it?" She paused. "Son, I am having a rush of energy. I want to roll myself back into the house. Don't worry. I've got this."

Slowly but with certainty, a grin on her lips and a lot of determination, Jillian made her way back to the house. Joe opened the door so his grandma could wheel her way inside. Joe was Cipriano's oldest son and Pablo's father; he had always worked hard and was process oriented. Joe was driven to follow the rules and had been quite easy for Cipriano and Jessie to raise. But the attributes that made him a great son made him a rigid father.

"Hi, Dad. Thanks for having us out," Joe said carefully. He always needed to get warmed up with his dad.

"I love having you, Joe. You and the family are always welcome; you know that."

"Thanks, Dad. Can I talk about something that has me concerned? You sometimes help me figure things out."

"Always, Son!"

"I'm worried about Pablo. He's lazy and doesn't seem to have a path, but that isn't what worries me. He's angry, Dad, and seems mad all the time. I've tried everything to help him get on the right path, and he just gets more upset and does more and more stupid stuff. That causes me to get on him. It's a vicious cycle, and I just don't see the light at the end of the tunnel."

"When you were young, Joe, the cool thing about you was you trusted your mom and me. You believed that when we asked something of you, it was in your best interest, so you did it, whatever it was. Raising you was easy because you trusted us to guide you. That, along with your bountiful talents, made you a great man.

"Pablo's anger is from his pain. I've seen his pain in other people throughout the years. Like everyone else, he's an individual, distinct and special. Each person has a unique path from start to finish. In a family, community, or country, we often push or deny the needs of the individual in the interest of the greater good, or our perception of it. If you're that individual, you resent 'the greater good' imposing its will on you. That's natural, isn't it? How much of your resolve do you impose on Pablo, Son?"

"Well, Dad, I am a hell of a lot smarter than he is and never made the mistakes he's making. I'm just trying to protect him from himself. I don't think I'm imposing anything, just saving his ass."

"So, you know what's better for Pablo on his path than he does?" Cipriano remained patient.

"I think so, yes!"

"What is his path?"

Joe leaned back and looked out into the late afternoon sky. "I don't know, I guess."

"Does he know his path?"

"I don't think so. He's pretty mixed up."

"Well, with your clear head and wisdom, and I mean that, why don't you help him find his path, and hear his voice? Listen, Joe, and hear. I know you can.

"And there is something else. Pablo has depression, and it is getting the better of him. I'm taking him to Dr. Leslie on Monday. He needs some medical help besides being heard by his favorite dad. As his head clears up and hope gets stronger, help him make space to find his path. Yes? He's staying with your mother and me a couple of days too."

After getting up and squeezing his dad's shoulder, Joe headed back into the house, passing his mother, Jessie, coming out to bring Cipriano some cold water. They were deeply in love and had found a lovely place in each other's hearts in their forty-two years together. Jessie was starting to forget things and do so more regularly. Her father had had Alzheimer's, and they'd long faced the possibility that she may develop it. A doctor's appointment to test her for it was only a week away. But Cipriano decided to focus on the present.

Jessie set the water on the table in front of Cipriano and sat in the loveseat next to her beau. She nestled up against him. They were home to each other, and their eyes glowed when they were together. Jessie dozed off with her head against Cipriano's shoulder; he heard every breath and felt the warmth of her face against him, along with the beat of her heart in their nested hands. "I love you, Darling," he whispered, "with all my heart and all that I am."

She dreamed of him. After a few minutes, Jessie woke up and suddenly rose. "I have to get back to the kitchen, Baby. Lots of mouths to feed today. I love you!"

They kissed softly. Jessie got up to make her way back inside, passing Leo on his way out to sit with old Cip.

"Hey, Buddy, you doing all right?" Leonardo asked Cipriano.

"I have to say honestly, Leo, never better! Today is a wonderful day."

"Cip, it is always easy for the family to share with you. Maybe they don't know you as well as I do," Leo said, smiling.

Leonardo stared at his brother and then recognized how slow and deep his own breathing was. His brother loved easily and was easy to love. Looking up toward Solas, a Supernova some 280 million light-years away that was visible on this day, Leo posed a question.

"You know Cip, you've turned out okay, but when I think back to that time toward the end with Maria, and just after, well, you were messed up. I've always wondered how you came this far, from there to here."

"Losing Maria was a jolt to me, Leo, and the jolt I needed to get my head straight. What a price, though. I was full of myself; I know you remember that, and I couldn't take in the important people around me. Maria kicking my butt out humbled me and ended up clearing my head. I owe all of this to that. You don't know how often I think about grace, and the role grace played to give me another chance so I could have this moment with you, Leo, and that remarkable family in the house. I want to admit too, having you as my big brother, along with our wise Dad, had a profound impact on me. Your depth and his was a light. Why have you not brought this up before, Bro?"

"There is something about you today, Cip. Who knows what else I may ask? In fact, I do have another question for you. Where does your fondness for systems come from?"

"I don't know. I know it's not me, and it's not mine. I think I'm open and listen, like when we talk. I listen to you and try to hear you and system stuff comes into my mind.

"Pablo talked to me earlier, and I heard him. It occurred to me after listening to him that the survival of the strongest and fittest is one of the major life systems we have. Think of all the talents and capabilities that we have as a late teenager. Our minds are sharp, reflexes are the best, and we have endless energy. On the other hand, our brains aren't fully developed, and we haven't learned about how important it is to do what we need to do before doing what we want. We're reckless and often oblivious."

"And very self-centered," Leo added. "That brings up something I have been mulling over. Can I share?"

"Please."

Leo continued. "What if the system is to cull people out for the first time in the teenage years?"

"Okay, Leo, you're losing me. Say it again in a different way or something. I want to hear you, but I don't get it."

"Think of life in three stages. The first stage is as a child and adolescent, where the body matures before the mind. If that individual has learned enough important and meaningful lessons during that time and incorporated them with self-control, some awareness, and a life direction, then they get to pass into the sweet spot of life in our world, adulthood."

"And what if they don't, Leo?"

"Well, they get on drugs and start their way out of this life sooner than later, or they die in a car crash or get killed in a fight. This group has a shorter life, some much shorter, others just shorter."

"Okay, got it," Cipriano agreed.

"Now," Leo continued, "If you make it into the adult phase, the sweet spot, and you enter it whole, and you take care of yourself and continue to develop your self-control, some awareness and a life direction while finding joy and goodness in your existence and spreading it to others, then you get to enter the third phase of life, old age. So, the survival of the fittest has two gates, the first from the teenage and young adult years to adulthood and the second from adulthood to old age. The long-termers, as a rule, are the ones that were the fittest overall through the process."

"Did you come up with this today, Brother? Three phases and two gates?" Cipriano acted like it was mildly interesting, but the logic impacted him. "I like it, Leo; let me mull it over."

Cipriano and Leo heard a vehicle getting closer and then park. Rain came walking around the side of the house to see her father and uncle lounging on the porch. She was a brilliant woman with long flowing reddish-brown hair framing a softly sculptured face. Rain always put her hair behind her ears, and that had pulled them forward over time. When she could smile, it was infectious; however, Rain did not smile often. She was a sad person, burdened with introspection that kept her focus inside. She made her way up the steps and slowed. She pushed out a meek smile.

"Hello, Papa, Uncle Leo. Sorry I'm late." Her smile cooled.

Leo stood up and hugged Rain. He excused himself.

Cipriano also stood and reached out to embrace her.

"My dearest Rain. I'm happy you've come. You know I love you so much."

Rain was his oldest daughter and she held a special place in Cipriano's heart. She had always struggled with her emotions, and he showed genuine compassion for her.

"Your mama has been excited about your visit, Rain. Did your car give you any trouble on the way out?"

Rain eased herself down into the wicker chair and felt the lofty cushion welcome her slight build. "That damn car, Papa! Now the passenger window won't work. It's down all the time. I have bugs riding with me constantly and have to fix my hair when I get to where I am going because of the wind. Nothing works for me."

"How long has your window been that way?"

"A few weeks, Pop." Rain looked down toward the painted boards on the porch. "Did you repaint the porch?"

"Yes, I did, Sweetheart. Your mom made me."

"No, she didn't. You're her MOA, man of action. We both know that!"

"If you say so," Cipriano responded sheepishly. "I'll look at your window before you leave. Why didn't you call me when it happened?"

"You know, with all the crap that happens to me, I would call you all the time; we'd never be off the phone. I wouldn't have any time to pull the bugs out of my hair," she said, trying to smile.

Cipriano felt the deep frustration Rain carried. He could see how it was wearing on her sullen face. Rain's lack of sleep and constant worry was finally showing.

"Let's talk, Honey. Let's you and I fix something meaningful today, something that can grow into another success. Let's turn this horse around. Say yes."

Rain looked up at her papa and looked into his left eye. She had never done that with her dad or with anyone. It was compelling to her, but not scary. Rain was ready now to move forward, and she knew this man, at this moment, might help her do it. The moment was full of Song.

"Yes, Papa. Yes." She sat back, resting her arms on the wicker chair.

"Tell me, Rain, what is it in your world that you most want to change, to have different from how it is now?"

Not a moment passed before her response. "I'm lonely. I have you and Mama, and my family, but I have few friends, and those I have are on a superficial level. We can talk about light stuff really, nothing deep and meaningful. I guess I have to say I don't feel like I have anyone outside of you and Mama who really, genuinely cares about me. I don't have a person. Am I so unworthy that no one can love me?" Rain's eyes watered, and her voice quivered.

"All these challenges I face, I face alone. With no one to share this life, friend or otherwise, it's tough to feel like any of it matters. The reason I didn't call you about the window is I don't care. Bugs keep me company. Who cares if my hairs messed up? I'm lonely, Papa, and sad that I deserve that. Can you help me not be lonely?"

Cipriano took a deep breath and looked over at the trees again. "Do you believe the answer is simple or hard, Rain?"

"Hard!"

"Before I say what I have in my heart, I want to share an observation with you. Do you mind?"

"Is it one of your systems?"

"Yes, I think it is."

"Yes, Papa. You seem to be right about your systems."

"When you were a child, your mind was open to almost everything. Now I know that's because your brain was experiencing so much for the first time, and in that mode, you were open to experiencing it, learning it, and learning from it. I call this system 'fertile ground.' As you got older and thought more, you stopped being so receptive because you needed to analyze and judge each stimulus. I think the system is for us to develop quickly through experiencing and learning and then slow down. We almost hold ourselves back, so that our evolution paces itself. I share this observation because I want you to open your mind to what I am about to say so you can receive it. Don't judge it or think about each word as I speak it.

Receive it. Sound good?"

Rain nodded affirmatively.

"Okay, first thing, the answer is simple. Will you commit to believing that with all your heart? The answer is simple?"

"All right, Papa, yes."

Cipriano looked back at his beloved Rain. "Then listen." After a pause, he said slowly and clearly, "And hear. Everyone has one thing that is more important to them than anything else, themselves. That's not a bad thing, and, in our world, it's imperative. To live, to give, to love, to have, you must first and foremost, exist. We're all masters at looking out for ourselves."

"Okay, Papa, yes, I know about that. Yes. Everyone is selfish and out for themselves."

"That's not the way I look at it, but I recognize the tendency," he said, smiling. "Now, here's how you can change your life. Are you ready?"

"Give it to me." She was doubtful.

"When we go into the house for supper, and your family surrounds you, look at each one of us and ask yourself, 'What does this person want from me that will improve their life?' Is it a smile, an acknowledgment, a shoulder, a story, a joke, a hug, just you being there? Will you give them a better moment, bring them joy, answer a long-sought-after question? You sit here with me, listening to what I'm saying, trying to hear it because you 'need' to hear an answer for your loneliness. You treasure me and give me this opportunity with you because I have this to give you."

"Pop, okay, I'm kind of with you, but help me understand."

"Tonight, it's practice, Rain, because we all love you. We're here for you, good or bad. Most everyone else is not, at least initially. Tomorrow, you'll encounter someone you've never met or hang with one of your casual friends. Look at them closely, feel them! What do they want 'from you' for themselves? They won't expect much from you, but if you can add to their life in some way that is comfortable for you, you'll find a more in-depth and more fruitful relationship budding.

"That could happen several times tomorrow and the day after and people know people and the more people you know who know more people, the more likely you are to find 'your people' among them. Those people will want to add to your life, and you to theirs. It just gets better from there. We all want to 'get' Rain.

"Remember, sweetie, and this is important, that there is truth in the saying, 'You have to give to get.' Knowing what to give is the hard part, and you must home in to the other person to find out what they need or want. The choice is yours then, about giving it to them. Still, you're in a place of power, and you get to make that choice."

"This kind of sounds like service; you're always talking about service."

"True, the good stuff is good stuff, and service is the best. In service, it's service if it is providing a need, so yes, what I'm talking about is very much like service, serving others, and the reward is to both you and them."

"Thanks, Papa. Okay. I think I hear you but do me a favor. Tie it up in a bow and make it easy for me, so I can remember it and do it."

"All right. First, when you meet someone you want to be closer with, concentrate on them before sharing yourself. What makes them tick, what do they want from you, what do they need? How can you help them? Second, once you determine how you can help, do it! Is it acknowledgment, praise, support, listening, companionship, romance? You must be certain you feel comfortable with what you are giving. Third, share both ways. Give and receive. Let them know what you need, make sure you know what they need, and meet those needs together. That's it."

"After I do this, I will find friends, fall in love, all of that Papa, for real?"

"Yes! Do this, and your loneliness will get replaced with love and friendship. Remain aware of the other's needs over your own, just a tad, and make sure you stay aware of your needs and communicate them. You'll keep all those dreamy relationships, and you will never see your old pop. You'll be too busy. You'll be happy. I'll be sad, selfishly. Yes, do it."

She looked down toward the ground. "I'm not that smart; we both know it."

"Bullshit!" Cipriano responded passionately.

"We both know it, Papa. I hear what you're saying. I do! But I am afraid I won't be able to keep up with all of it, all the people, my feelings, their feelings. It may be too much! Can you give me one thing to focus on, to give others?"

"Yes, but you're brilliant, Rain, my God, you're amazing! Damn it. I need you to appreciate the gift you are. Yes. One thing. Affirmation. Find the good in others and affirm it. Just do that, the rest will come. Look. Find. Affirm."

"I've got it, Papa! Thank you." Rain felt peace.

"Dinner!" Jillian called out. "Get in here; let's eat!"

Rain and Cipriano made their way into the house and toward the dinner table. Sally, Pablo, Julian, Jessie, Joe, his wife Rebecca, and Leo with his husband Jean all made their way to hug and welcome Rain. The house smelled of baked pies, fresh loaves of bread, and roasted meats. They joined at the table that was stocked plentifully with a holiday feast.

The family enjoyed a wonderful meal together, the best. Note left Cipriano.

In Between

Note appreciated the elaborate systems that force progress in their wake. Only that which is meant to stagnate, stagnates. All else moves forward.

How would life forms consider the grandest systems? Note journeyed to Josla.

Chapter Forty-One

Energy and the Edge

Josla was a unusually dark moon, unusually far from its planet. Along with Treg, the three scientists were purposely isolated on Josla. Each was genetically engineered to have the highest intellect and the lowest of animal impulses. After having childhoods in normal family conditions, they were raised in science and philosophy on their respective worlds. The date they were to be sent and left on Josla was determined decades earlier; they had now been on Josla for three years. Treg was simply, Treg.

It was a time when there were few remaining stars in the sky for the trio to view. They had numerous records from countless civilizations that showed star-filled skies and life forms, but most were gone. Along with Treg, the three scientists' mission in life was to determine why the Universe existed and was dying.

Deadra, Bonsu, and Rogan were the best of friends and worked contently in their observatory in the dim light under a transparent roof. Note joined Deadra.

"Deadra, you've been quiet for a good while," Rogan shared.

"Yes, Rogan. I have an alternative theory about what's happening to the Universe. It's so simple that I'm surprised and perplexed that it's just now occurring to me. I think of the countless minds that have thought about this over time, how complicated it must have been. It might be complicated," she said, nodding her head slowly.

"Deadra, you know we do this every day, and you have all this figured out again? Okay, should I get Bonsu?"

"Yes, please."

"Bonsu, join us in the observatory room, please," Rogan spoke his request aloud, and Jaspen received it. Jaspen, the facility social system, could detect the inflection of demands coming from the life forms. It found Bonsu in her quarters and delivered the message.

As a Tarangian, Bonsu was a fluid being with no outer skin or exoskeleton. Bonsu used bodysuits to enable her to appear and function as a humanoid. She poured into her suit and then made her way to the observatory to find her friends.

"Hi, Deadra, Rogan. To what do I owe this summoning?"

"Deadra may know what's happening to our Universe."

"Again? Okay, what?"

"Do you remember battery technology from long ago? "

"Yes," Rogan announced. "It was a portable source of what they called electricity. It was a sealed vessel where a chemical electrolyte separated the positive and negative electrodes."

"Excellent, Rogan. Do you recall how it worked?"

"Does Bonsu pour into her bodysuit? Yes, I recall."

"Prove it," Bonsu quipped.

"Sure. When whatever the battery served accessed it to draw electricity, chemical reactions happened. One reaction generates positive ions and electrons at the negative electrode. The positive ions flow *into* the electrolyte, while the electrons flow around the external circuit to the positive electrode providing electricity to the served device. There's a separate chemical reaction happening at the positive electrode where incoming electrons recombine with ions taken *out* of the electrolyte, so completing the circuit."[40]

"Thank you, Rogan! Yes, that's it, exactly. The Universe is discharging like a battery. For eons, it has generated unfathomable amounts of energy that flowed out and into another Universe or others or a source," Deadra continued. "Think about it! Each of us, everything around us, is all creating energy. Nothing is lost, we know that. If it isn't lost and it's not here, it's somewhere else."

Bonsu spoke. "Delightful to be sure, Dear One. If you're correct, it creates more questions, along with some answers about what may come at the end of this Universe. Consider, too, the positive and negative charge. All civilizations have believed or experienced good and evil, creation and destruction, hope and despair, and so on. Could that balance between the two opposite poles that exist in everything exist to create energy until it uses it up? Is the essence of good and evil one fuel that drives energy production?"

Rogan interjected, "What about the neutral charge? Why is there a neutral particle?"

Bonsu spoke without hesitation. "The neutral has no agenda, none."

"Agenda...interesting, Bonsu. Are you saying then that energy is the product of each of our agendas?" Rogan inquired.

"Perhaps for life forms, as part of the energy production. Agendas lead to a positive or negative experience of living life. While a neutral has no agenda, life forms do. Chemical reactions make up much of the rest, and physics runs that. Everything in the Universe is part of energy production. Essence creates energy dynamically through good and evil, while matter creates it statically through physics. Things like the decay of matter, for instance, create energy, but from a static nature."

Rogan sought clarification. "Physics, okay, physics. If the existence of the Universe serves to create energy that disperses outside of it, that's a system. Is physics a system?"

"Rogan, whether it is or isn't doesn't matter because it's all bigger than we are—too big for any realization or conclusion we have—to make a difference. Now, positive and negative, that's different because positive life experience differs greatly from a negative one. With that in mind and coming back to that discussion plane, I have another question for the two of you. Does the Universe, with its nature to produce energy, reward good? Good is creation. Does creation create more energy than destruction?" Deadra asked.

"No," Bonsu quickly answered. "I feel that, overall, they're in balance like everything else."

Deadra agreed. "A lot to think about here. Let's break for dinner. You cooked last night, Rogan; I have it this time."

Rogan chimed back in, "Maybe Bonsu will eat something so we can watch it float around in her suit."

"That's nice, Rogan, real nice."

"Bonsu, I've often wondered. How does your species make little ones, or whatever? Do you have 'love' as a fluid creature?"

"Does this kind of topic get you in the mood to eat, Rogan?"

"No, but it makes me thirsty!"

"Well, Silly, sex is a connection, as you know, and we connect. We breed when a new and distinct consciousness forms in us; it then breaks off and develops and evolves. It starts small, accurate enough. Love, yes, we love all the time. I love you, even as the beastie you are."

He smiled. "You're making my eyes water, Bonsu. What are we having, Deadra?"

"Pasta, with cream sauce and green vegetables."

"I love that," he responded.

"Deadra. Let me ask you a question about your thought of the Universe. If it's an energy or a power source, what is it?"

"To simplify your question, Bonsu, you are asking me, what is the Universe?"

"Yes, a softball question for the chef!"

"My answer to you is, the Universe is energy, all of it. As we mentioned earlier, even dead things devolve, which create energy. The least particle has a charge; it's energy. When there is no energy left, there will be no Universe, so summed up, it's energy."

"Thank you, Deadra. I agree," Bonsu stated. "Next question—and to you too, Rogan, if you're done thinking about my sex life. If we know what the Universe is, energy, are we able to answer the question, why is the Universe? Does knowing *what* give us the answer to the question of *why*?"

"Why is my stomach growling? Because I'm waiting for Deadra to cook the pasta extraordinaire. So, the real question is, when will dinner be ready?" Rogan replied.

"Right, feed the beastie, feed the beastie," Deadra commented. She knew what to do.

Deadra made her pasta extraordinaire.

"How is it, Rogan? You likey?"

"Yes, I do. I can taste the butter sauce with just a tad of salt, and your pasta is always perfect. I love it just like this. It gets on my chin, but that's well worth it. Sorry you can't enjoy this, Bonsu."

"I'm kind of excited, Rogan," Bonsu admitted.

He looked at her and raised his eyebrow, "Oh, what about?"

"Once your tummy is full, you may need a nap," she said, smiling in her suit. "But seriously, I am eager to hear more of your good thoughts about Deadra's energy ideas."

"I have some thoughts, to be sure, but I wanted to start with what's most important, and that is eating this pasta! Do I see a bubble in you?"

"Yes, I have a cold or something. I don't really know, but the bubbles come and go and not often, or you would have seen a bubble before now."

With a full tummy, and after helping Deadra with the kitchen cleanup, Rogan invited his friends back into the main living space.

They made their way into the darkened room with the sky open above them and sat on the fluffy cushions that formed around their bodies. Bonsu was beautiful in this light. Her transparency had a tinge of cerulean in it and was softly reflective; the stars subtly reflected off her.

Rogan started the conversation. "Let me throw this one out to you. If the Universe is all about energy, then it is powering something. What's that? Chalk that one up to something we may never know, but a good question, I think. Moving on, if the creator or creators of the Universe created it to power the 'what we will never know,' then they did it with elements from their reality, so the periodic table may be consistent in the next realm, too. After all, our Universe started with hydrogen, we think. Now, to that, add organic life with minds. I think we agree that the Universe is created to make energy and that organic life creates energy through essence. Does organic life exist because it is a better energy producer than matter?"

Bonsu interjected. "So, your question is, what's the place or reason for organic life in the Universe?"

"Yes," Rogan continued, "and what does our imagination show? When hydrogen bonds together to make helium and so on, there is no imagination there, I don't think. If it all comes from that beginning, then how does imagination come in to play? How is it born?"

"Interesting question, Rogan," Deadra jumped in. "You're kind of blowing my mind with that one. If you think about the purity of the fusion reaction and you expand that to think about our minds and what they produce, they aren't at all the same. Our minds produce chaos, and imagination may be the platform for that because we each experience truth and reality uniquely. Our body's chemical response and our actions around creation or destruction to vast degrees create energy."

"I need to contemplate that, Deadra," Rogan responded.

"Once again," Deadra said graciously, "my dearest of friends, we have answered everything as we are supposed to do and solved nothing. But at least you and I have full stomachs, Rogan. For me, I have to go for a walk outside."

"Okay, Deadra. Bring us back a rock, will you?" Rogan requested.

Deadra made her way down to the airlock and stepped into the suit box. The suit box was an invigorating experience as her naked body felt the cool sensation of the suit spraying over her. It tingled as it enveloped her like a warm blanket on a chilly night. It was always startling when it tightened around her face. Through many repetitions, the moment she could not breathe while the suit transitioned to bringing oxygen out of the surroundings, had gotten more natural. Deadra feared that moment, however, after having lost one of her companions when a suit malfunctioned, suffocating her friend. She reminded herself how rare that was, and that was the only tragedy she knew about.

After the suit finished forming, Deadra entered the air chamber and locked the ship door behind her, then pushed the exit button. She could hear the pressure changing and the exterior hatch opening to the dark moon surface outside. Deadra could move and breathe normally, as if she was simply a naked woman walking around on the surface of the moon. The suit was just a thin film around her, so she felt every sensation through her skin that she usually would. The suit modulated each sensation to levels in ranges that felt normal and comfortable.

It was a beautiful night on the moon. The gas giant it orbited was a bright yellow, and a big copper spot was visible. Josla was a considerable distance from the jovial giant with an orbit that took over 143 years. Josla rotated, however, with days or nights that would last some 12 Earth days. A thin atmosphere existed. It wasn't enough to distort much light, so the sky was vivid, though full of black spots where stars and galaxies once brilliantly displayed themselves. The Universe that remained was smaller but still expansive and mighty, and it was all Deadra knew. It always impressed her.

Making her way over to a set of rocks she called Beverly Point, she found her favorite seat, a smooth rock with another behind it she could lean on. Deadra had named Beverly Point after her only sibling. That's where she often thought about Beverly and anguished.

Beverly was Deadra's best friend for the first handful of years in her life. Her sister filled in for their ailing mom while Deadra was young, but then seemed to disappear into her room and away from Deadra and the family for the remaining years that Deadra was at home. She longed for her sister but didn't know her and wasn't acknowledged by her.

What was wrong with me, Beverly? Why did you stop loving me? Was I bad? Deadra considered how limited perceptions could be. She knew Beverly had been close to their mom, and Deadra had been a bit of a firecracker from time to time.

I wonder if Mom perceived me poorly and shared that with Beverly. I wish we could have talked about it. Being stuck in another's perception isn't fair, Deadra thought. *People's judgments are almost always based on limited or incorrect information. We must know we might be off base in our thoughts. How can we discard a person who loves us based on our perceptions, when those perceptions may be wrong?*

Busy lives sent them in separate directions once they were grown. Beverly died an untimely death because of a growth in her body. She died without ever reconnecting with Deadra, on any level. She was now the last of her nuclear family still alive, sitting on a cold rock on a dark moon in a dying Universe, all alone.

"Look, Bonsu, Deadra's crying; it just makes me so sad to see it," Rogan commented. The suit sent back full sensory data to the station and created a 3D image complete with telemetry and a stellar positioning system to recreate the night sky around the image.

Deadra could feel the tears welling in her eyes and rolling down her cheeks; she then looked down to see the ice falling from her face to the ground, the water glistening as it crystalized in the intense cold outside the suit.

In her moment of depression, Deadra thought, *I don't want to feel this loneliness anymore. I'm all alone, and it will never get better. This pain can't get fixed.*

She thought about how she could just order the suit to open, and it would uncover her, and she would die instantly in the cold—no more pain, or emptiness, or hopelessness.

Note throbbed for a moment within her, and she heard the Song of the angels. Her light came roaring back profoundly, along with a new realization about the Universe; Note shared the realization in Song.

I'm grateful for this sorrow and sense of loss because I feel it so intensely. I'm thankful for this moment of grief because I'm not numb to it. And I have three wonderful friends back at the station, Deadra thought.

At that moment, it occurred to her they were probably watching her, and then, thinking of Rogan, she turned back toward the station and gave an obscene hand gesture but with a smile.

"Did you see that, Rogan?"

"Yes, that was for you, Bonsu!"

"No, it wasn't,"

Deadra sat on the rock for a little while longer. She remembered and relived the sound of the angels, and then remembered perhaps the most profound message in the energy theory she had discussed earlier with her friends. *Nothing is ever lost!* The other seed Note planted grew.

Rogan responded to Treg and reached out to Deadra. "Treg, we hear you. Deadra! Treg is reaching out. Please get back to us, and we will get with Treg."

"Confirmed. I'll head back."

Treg was the largest member of the crew on Josla and was massive compared to its companions. Treg stood 80 feet tall and 120 feet wide with large magnolia-type leaves that were thriving. The atmosphere and environment on Josla required Treg to have an indoor home. Treg's tap root system required that its living quarters be three times as tall as Treg with room to grow, so the quarters were some 300 feet tall and 250 feet wide and dwarfed the rest of the facility. Lighting to feed Treg was placed around the room to nourish Treg from every angle. Treg was a tree and was one of the Adoside species. Millenniums on one of the most stable planets in the Universe that orbited a red dwarf star gave the Adoside the time to evolve to a place of understanding. With the help of technology, they could communicate with the animal and insect world.

At over 4000 years of age, Treg brought a great stillness to the team and a prolonged and methodical thought process. The Adoside species remained in one location for a lifetime, something unique for intelligent life forms. Adosidians' acute awareness of the changes within their space yielded a knowingness that empowered their friends—the mobile life forms—to greater appreciate each moment.

Once back and dressed, Deadra joined Rogan and Bonsu; they made their way to Treg's quarters.

"I love going to Treg's house," Bonsu shared.

"Me too," Rogan agreed. "Treg is remarkable. I still can't get over that plant's sleep."

The team joined Treg in its house. "Good day to you, Treg! Is everything good?" Deadra asked.

"Yes," Treg responded slowly through the translator. "Please sit. I have much to tell. Do you have the time, and are you comfortable with your bodily needs?"

"Yes. We are here to be with you, Treg. Please share," Bonsu invited.

Over the next three hours, Treg shared.

"In my sleep, I was on a vast plane full of deep and abundant grasses of many, many kinds. The colors were bright and vibrant. The home star beamed down on them, turning many of them golden, and they waved in the breeze. The soil was fertile, yummy rich, with enough cohesion to keep me standing while loose enough to allow me to root, almost endlessly. I've never felt that good. I wondered if I was dying.

"I knew then that I was in a dream. A large and magnificent golden-brown bird with bright blue eyes came and landed on one of my largest branches. It dug its orange talons into my bark, and I felt its soul. I could see what it saw as it was flying over the vast plane to land on my branch. I had never been above myself before like that. I believe this being is the Dream Maker.

"It shared something with me about the stars, and then, I perfectly understood what it shared, but something that now makes no sense to me. I share it with you, my family.

"The Dream Maker shared that an exceedingly long time ago, the Emolie race theorized after lengthy and careful consideration that black holes were, in fact, the edge of the Universe. It shared that, as an edge, each of the black holes was a portal to space beyond our space. The Dream Maker shared, and it felt, well, perfect, that all was injected into this Universe through the edge. The incomprehensible gravity was the attraction back out to the other space. I can only comprehend what I can understand."

"Injected from or in one place?" Deadra clarified.

"Yes," Treg responded.

"Before the expansion of space?"

"Yes."

Deadra, Rogan, and Bonsu each looked at each other with some amazement.

Just at that moment, with Note a part of her, Deadra received Note's thought from over two trillion years earlier as Note had sent it from near the center of a supermassive black hole. "What is a center?"

"Wait, Rogan, Bonsu, Treg! This will sound odd to you, but I've not been alone today...that is to say, besides being with each of you, I've been with another. They're a part of me."

She saw Rogan's and Bonsu's puzzlement.

"A being joined me today; I felt it. Besides having insightfully lofty thoughts, I've been full of Song all day. I just received a message, a question from this being within me. It asks, what is a center?"

"Can you tell us more about the being, Deadra? What are you feeling?" Bonsu asked.

"I can later, but this question seems all-encompassing to me. What is a center?"

"Balance, perfect balance," Bonsu answered.

Full of Note, Deadra asked, "What would be at the center of a black hole?"

Rogan spoke up. "Mass. A black hole swallows matter, and everything measurable, and pulls it into its core. It must all come to the core and compress down immensely, almost infinitely, but the core would be solid, I think."

"Okay, Rogan. Regardless of whether it's solid, it must have a center that draws everything into it equally from all directions. A world like our moon has a center, and the gravity of this moon alone pulls everything into its center, equally from all sides or materially equally. There is no gravity at the center because the mass is equal on all sides around the center. So, the center is balanced and at peace."

"I see the profundity of your question, Deadra," Treg interjected. "What's at the center? Is it a product of the surrounding mass, or was it first? What brings mass to that center point? Is that the 'other space?' I've got a question to add. Could the center of each thing be the graviton in quantum physics, the gravity particle?"

Rogan asked, "Does every mass have a gravity particle in it? Do you? Do I?"

"With the theories and mathematics involved, this can get deep and complicated quickly," Deadra added.

"Yes," Bonsu agreed. "Looking at it simply, if the birth of the Universe was to create singular existence as humanity suggested, then it makes sense that a divine particle was the beginning of this Universe. As it separated and expand space, it would do so with something relatively simple like hydrogen. So, the divine particle separates, becoming hydrogen atoms and the particles that make that up, each having a center, the center being part of the divine particle. Everything becomes separate and distinct, but each is having the divine particle which is attracted to one another. The end aim, for the Universe, would be for everything to come back together, to be one again, with all the divine particles reuniting."

"Is it God?" Deadra asked. "What a day we've shared today," she continued. "What thoughts...but I have one last realization to share, if I may."

"Please, Deadra," Rogan invited.

"While I was out at Beverly Point, something filled my head—two things. Song, and a vision about the beginning of the Universe."

"The Big Bang?" Treg asked.

"Yes." Deadra explained, "I still have to think about it, but this is what I could understand. The Big Bang did not expand space where there was none, and it will happen again and potentially over and over. Here are the facts as I see them.

"The Universe is shrinking now while we know it used to be expanding.

"Hydrogen is depleting.

"This Universe started in one place and, as it is constituted, was alone.

"We believe space expanded as the Universe did, but it also needed to have something to expand into.

"Gravity is an absolute component.

"Here's what this adds up to in my head. The space that holds everything expands with heat and contracts with cold. The Universe expands as the heat within it grows and contracts as it cools. There is a temperature where space and everything in it contracts to one point, and all energy depletes. In that state, no bonds between particles exist.

"My conclusion," Deadra said calmly, "is that the Big Bang came from a God Spark in the center of 'the Everything.' The heat caused all to expand along with space. The Universe ignited. The spark may have been tiny," she said, smiling.

Note left Deadra.

In Between

Note experienced the genius of intelligent life solving for grand issues beyond their comprehension. The calm consideration while thinking beyond paradigms, while coasting on the intricate design of the Universe, yielded realization. The path is beautiful and well lit.

Systems of every composition and size create orderly conduct and opportunities for chaos.

Note now felt compelled to go outside, outside this Universe.

Chapter Forty-Two

Quantum

Note moved closer to the center of the black hole and, sensing Note needed a lifeline back to this Universe, remembered and immersed itself in experiencing Gray. At that moment, Note reached the center and soon emerged into another Universe in the quantum specter. The essence was different.

Note approached a blue world that was remarkably familiar: Earth. Note joined Eulalee as she shared memories with the love of her life, Rome. It was the first experience in a life form without jealousy.

The inhabitants of the world in this Universe called it Earth, too, but it was a different Earth. Different degrees of polarity existed in the matter here, and on this world, plate tectonics moved in a unique pattern compared to the Earth that was in Note's native Universe, leaving just one landmass on this Earth with only islands in the massive sea, Pacifica. Life evolved differently here, with less differentiation as species evolved together over time.

The most intelligent animal here was the human, and humanity rested atop the food chain, but the food chain was less elaborate with fewer species while in much larger populations. This Earth and the essence of this space was without one of the most prominent characteristics of Note's home Universe: polarization.

Humanity evolved without prejudice and judgment. Because selfishness worked against the community, it was strongly resisted or weeded out. There was no value distinction between gender, race, socioeconomic status, age, or education. Everyone was equal on this Earth.

The family unit on this Earth consisted of two adults and the children. The first marriage took place at age 20 or within the first six months of one's twentieth birthday. Each union lasted five years and five years only. A new mate and marriage occurred for each adult within six months after the previous marriage, and each adult married a minimum of six times, each for five years. They would conceive children at some point or several within the first three marriages. The children remained with the mother until the children attained the age of 20 and married. They paired couples depending on what each needed to learn to better appreciate and contribute to society.

At age 50, marriage became optional, and everyone over 50 could select their mate and stay with them for life if each wished. The state provided the finances to ensure that they met the needs of the children.

***

"My dearest Rome, I love being with you for the rest of my life."

"And I you, darling Eulalee! That was the best wedding yet, and fortunately, our last." They kissed gently and then sat back, looking into the fireplace together.

"What are you thinking, Eulalee?"

"I was just thinking about Mom and Dad and losing them last year. Janice was great, but I wish you could have been with me through that time. Mom and Dad loved you, Rome. Not as much as I do, but a lot."

"I wish I could have been there, Darling. You and your mom were close. It's a blessing that your two biological parents chose to be together after 50 so you could enjoy both for so many years. It was a godsend, and they were so in love. I miss Mom, I do. Do you have any thoughts about your dad?"

"I remember my dad saying, 'Hey, come down to the plant and talk to Rose about a job.' I did, and my career happened."

"And your career put you on the coast?"

"Yes."

"And being on the coast allowed you to get coupled with Joel and have Nikki?"

"Yes."

"So, you would not have Nikki, your favorite person in the entire world, if it weren't for your dad?"

"Yes. I never thought about that, never. My relationship with my dad was mainly through my mom. Do you know what I mean?"

"I do, but having your dad in your life gave you Nikki?"

"Wow. Daddy." Her eyes watered.

"Well, now that we're married again and have our fantastic honeymoon behind us, I so much want to hear about your other partners. Do you feel like sharing anything about them or, at least, what you learned from each?"

"My dearest Rome. You wanting to know me more is one thing that attracts me to you. I feel how genuine you are, and you always delight in my joy. Thank you for that. Sure, let me tell you some about them.

"You already know about my first, Sinbaje. Being in our early twenties, we shared a primarily physical relationship. I remember the first time I got to explore his body. It was our wedding night, and I was still a virgin. I was dripping wet.

"I warmed up oil to rub him down. We put candles all around, and the window was open with a breeze coming in. Our window faced the water. We were on the coast, so we didn't worry about noise, but we should have. He took off his robe for the first time in front of me, and I was in awe. Sinbaje was dark and muscular with piercing eyes and full inviting lips. He laid down on his stomach and put his arms over his head. I sat up on his bottom. I just know he could feel how excited I was. I put the warm oil in my hands and then started applying it to his shoulders.

"The oil on his dark skin made it look like it illuminated depth. I don't know that I've ever seen anything like it since. I learned his entire body with my oily and curious hands, every curve, muscle, bone, finger, toe, his earlobes, everything. With him lying on his back, I did his legs up to his waist. Then I moved up to his face and worked my way back down to his penis. I could see he was aching for me to help him.

"I had never held a penis in my hands, and I just loved it so much; he exploded right away. I giggled with joy as he throbbed in my hands. We were young; Sinbaje was erect again soon, and then it was my turn.

"Our entire marriage was really around that physical connection, Rome. We both learned about needs and how we needed different things at different times. Sinbaje stayed physically addicted to me because of where I took him in bed. He needed me more than wanted me, yet I was much more satisfied. I learned to be selfless with him and learned that his need for me was not using me but appreciating me.

"I learned about male energy, Rome, because at a young age, it was raw. At that age, life was so much more about being experienced. We were both experiential and kind of awkward in how hungry we were to live. I'd say it was an insatiable period, and we lived in a small world, but very full."

"Tell me more about what you learned about male energy," Rome requested.

"Male energy is more aggressive and assertive than female energy. It was my experience that males want to make things happen. The good of that is progress, and the bad is destruction, I think. Again, it was a 'physical' period of years for both of us. The physical is a big part of who we are, and I learned we need to experience it. I learned that with Sinbaje.

"Then, I married Joel, the father of my child. The time I remember most at this moment with Joel was our last Christmas together. We were both romantics and knew our time together was almost over, and we bought each other truly meaningful gifts. But that's something I want to keep to myself, my Love.

"What Joel and I learned together was around how to make life work when we became parents. Like all parents at first, it was new to us. We did without sleep. Joel did without sex for a good while. We learned a great deal about our limits because we got so tired and on call to the baby around the clock. We magnified our differences in the stress, yet we needed to work more closely than any other kind of couple because we were parents."

"What's one difference that stands out?" Rome asked.

"There were several with Joel. He was much freer about spending money, and I liked to save. When I could, I liked to go to bed at 9:30, as we do," she said, smiling. "But he liked to come to bed at midnight. I showered at night and went to bed clean, while he showered in the morning and went to work clean. I love to travel as you know, Darling, but he loved to be home.

"I think Joel and I had so many differences—and under challenging circumstances—that we learned about respecting and cherishing one another for who we each were. It was a difficult five years to be sure, but he has been an amazing father, and I call him a friend for life. We shared the most amazing conversations, and Joel was truly kind and loving. I also remember that he complimented me all the time. That helps!"

"You experienced challenges over raising Nikki, too, as I recall."

"Oh, yes. Joel was easy on Nikki, and I had to be the heavy. He wanted her to sleep in our bed when she was tiny, to comfort her and keep her from crying. It was always like that with Joel. He was—and is—sincerely loving with Nikki. And yet, he didn't and will not understand that she needs to fend some for herself. At least, I think she needs to be able to do that."

"Nikki is remarkable, Darling, like you. So, in a nutshell, what did you learn with Joel?"

"I learned how to work things out with another person, one who's different, with their own motivations and opinions. Joel and I were much more intellectual together than what I experienced with Sinbaje. We were tasked with a lot to figure out, many dots to connect, and together, we did."

"So, making things work, no matter the difficulty?" Rome asked.

"Yes. Then, after all that, you, Rome, the love of my life. I was just hit by lightning with you; I still am."

"Back at you, Sweetheart," Rome added.

"I never got over you, Rome, and that wasn't fair to Crandle, but having said that, Crandle was also my most challenging marriage. It may have been because you and I were so connected to each other.

"Crandle is a genius, simply brilliant. He was always truly kind to Nikki and me, and was thankfully helpful, but we never touched. During that period in my life, I was still in need of intimacy. I have related it to my cycle, but I needed it every three weeks. I was forced to ask him to touch me, and I did, every three weeks.

"I didn't feel attractive, or needed, or wanted. That was ridiculously hard for me. I learned a lot about myself and came to understand other points of view better. Crandle was a charming man, but he was all brain."

"Did you talk much?" Rome inquired.

"Yes, but he was hard to keep up with sometimes. Crandle was really into quantum physics, stuff I have no interest in at all. He talked about a multiverse or some reality where other Universes existed. He said there could be another Universe just like ours, with an Earth and everything but that evolved with unique characteristics different than ours."

"Really? Like what?"

"It was ridiculous. Crandle talked about a Universe where dark and light people don't trust each other because of the color of their skin. In fact, he talked about everything in the Universe being divided into groups, and each competed or subdued the other, or tried to. It made no sense."

"It sounds like polarization. I've studied that, Darling. Interesting, and unproductive to be sure. I'm glad you talked."

"Yes. Crandle also profoundly impacted Nikki in a good way. She grew to appreciate and love science to an extent I just never could. They still talk a lot. But boy, it was like living with my sister."

"Except once every three weeks!" Rome reminded her.

"Oh hush, Rome. And a side note. Crandle could play a mean game of chess. His brainiac buddies would come over, and they would play for hours. I don't think I ever saw him lose. He'd sweat and grind his teeth. It was the most emotional I ever saw him get. I asked him once to describe his impression of chess, and he told me it was like putting yourself—your life—out on the board. I grew to appreciate him more as I witnessed that."

"What would you say was your biggest lesson with Crandle, Darling?"

"Honestly, it was that we have to determine what we want and need and ask for it if we can't provide it for ourselves. It sounds selfish, but I don't think it should. The better my life, the more I can contribute. But to be my best, I must be introspective...figure out what's missing and what I can give. I think self-awareness is a big part of this, Rome. I also found forgiveness toward Crandle for not being what I needed. I learned that he gave what he had to give. I think my appreciation for others took a gigantic leap forward because of Crandle; I had to look a little harder for good. The more I looked, the more I found."

"And then, Sam," Rome said.

"Yes, dear Sam. Being 20 years older, he didn't have to marry me but agreed to once we met in the interview process. I was never physically attracted to Sam, but after my sabbatical with Crandle, Sam was a lot of fun to be sure.

"Sam was wise. I know it was because he lived through many more experiences, but he just never sweat the small stuff. He is a patient man and a skilled listener. I learned to slow myself down because of Sam. He and Nikki are best friends, as you know, because she can talk about anything with him, and he hears and appreciates her."

"Learned to slow down? Tell me more," Rome requested.

"You remember that when we married the first time, I was always busy, and decisively productive. You called me your WOA, woman of action. I thought I was smelling the roses, Rome, but I wasn't. My mental list of things to do distracted me. With Sam, I found a quiet place in myself, and from that place, I could—and can — 'be.' In that place, everything matters, big and small. I'm very grateful for that place. As a result, I adore you even more than I knew I could, Darling."

"Then, with Sam, you learned to 'be!' That's beautiful," Rome confirmed.

Eulalee and Rome embraced for a while. She laid her head against his chest and felt his heart beating while he smelled her hair and listened to her breath.

"And then Janice," Rome said.

"Yes." Eulalee sat back up, fluffing the pillow to give her lumbar support.

"I love how you watch your posture, Baby," Rome encouraged her.

Eulalee smiled at him and winked.

"Janice, oh my! I learned so much about myself with Janice. The first word that comes to mind is sensuality. With her, I discovered myself.

"I learned that our most profound need is to connect deeply with another. We get lost on our path, trying to fill a space we have inside with external things. We live on the outside.

"But Janice taught me we must open our hearts to connect. Our hearts needed to be open to each other to receive the love of another, and giving it was as much a gift as receiving, even more.

"As women, we were natural nurturers, and we took care of each other more completely than what I experienced in my other relationships, even ours. Similarly, it makes me think of the way I take care of Nikki compared to her dad or other fathers. I care about *how* Nikki is; the details matter to me. I'm on the path with Nikki. It was like that with Janice. We cared *how* the other was.

"It took me some time to get used to being sexual with another woman, but it was eventually easy. We think we discovered why women's periods sync up," Eulalee said, smiling.

"Because the non-menstrual times sync up?" Rome interjected.

"Yes. Exactly."

"Silly." Rome goaded. "How is the deep love you experienced with Janice different from what we have, Darling? You chose to spend the rest of your life with me; how is it different?"

"I described you earlier as a lightning bolt that hit me. With you, it's all as it's meant to be. I dreamed of you when I was a child, the shape of your hands and mouth, your smell, and the tone of your voice. You are home to me. It's like I knew you would be, and you are. Your presence brings me peace, Rome, and we're always connected. I've felt that since we were together the first time. You were always with me, even when I was with Crandle, Sam, and Janice. You, my dear man, extend me, and that's all there is to that."

"And you extend me, my Love," Rome added.

Note left Eulalee.

***

As *N*ote got back to the center of the black hole, Note recalled the essence of Gray, the fingerprint to the Universe Note called home. Emerging from the black hole, Note felt the essence of home.

Note considered the reality that Note was a quantum particle that had just moved from one Universe to another. Note discovered that essence was different in the other Universe and recognized that essence must be different in each. It made sense that the evidence of the collapse of the wave function showed a specific position for the observed particle. Note recognized that the position would be different in each Universe.

If reality has a particle in all possible positions at any moment, observation must mean that concentration gives view to only a small slice of reality.

Note relived the observations of Deadra, Bonsu, and Rogan. Their views and conclusions around energy in the Universe were a big slice. It seemed clear to Note that all of existence, all the Universes, came from a single energy source, much like a fountain spraying water in a 360-degree pattern that delivers the water through one source in unique positions, unique in all infinity.

Multiverse was a means to experience each and every reality and possible outcome. Experience, a word with meaning, cannot express it accurately but can deliver a slice of accuracy.

The Source, the One, was the same for all.

In Between

Next, Note felt drawn to the importance of taking nothing for granted. What would a moment be like if experienced fully? Outside of God, there was only one species that could answer a fraction of that question.

Chapter Forty-Three

The Second Surfers

Owne was a Trute. The Trute were the pollinators of the Milky Way galaxy before Milkdromeda. They owned an unusual function in the Universe as they acted like bees gathering nectar and pollen from one flower and sharing it with another, but the pollen the Trute shared was essence. The flowers were life forms from civilizations around the galaxy.

The Trute were second surfers, surfing from one soul to another, experiencing each piece of a singular moment by that life form in that second, the same moment experienced by all the Universe, at that very moment. The Trute lived the essence of the moment, of that soul. By leaving a piece of its essence in the moment, they impacted civilizations while also bringing parts of the "experienced essence" back home to the planet Truten. Over time, the impact on civilizations was significant, leaving remarkable accomplishments like the Pyramids of Egypt on Earth and Sorian water canals on Dolenze.

The Jampat was a highly evolved civilization from the world of OxyD, close to the center of the Milky Way in the relative vicinity of the supermassive Sagittarius A, a black hole some four million times more massive than the Earth-Sun. The Jampat existed to police the Milky Way galaxy much as a white blood cell polices the human body, seeking anything that might work against the good of the body. The unique skills and life's meaning of the Trute was a powerful tool for the Jampat; they deployed Trutes to other worlds to search for specific characteristics within the population. The information collected enabled the Jampat to act proactively to keep civilizations within the galaxy in acceptable limits for the good of the whole.

Owne was ready for his moment. "Mom, this is it. I get my assignment today."

"I'm so proud of you, Owne. I can't wait to hear."

"Thanks, Mom. See you this dark...love you."

They hugged, and he made his way down to the academy.

Owne was a sentinel. The sentinels were the second surfers and comprised just ten percent of the population. Sentinels got artificially conceived in the laboratories of the academy and placed with families when they were born. They possessed physical qualities to enable them to endure long periods of motionlessness during their unusually long-life spans, as long as five centuries. Unlike the rest of the population, they were telepathic and spent most of each day tuning in to their essence. They practiced experiencing the essence of others until they reached the point of being able to distinguish it from their own. Owne was ready.

At the academy, Zeped, the director for second surfing and Buen, Owne's spirit guide, greeted him.

"Good light to you, Director. I'm glad to see you, Buen, but why are you here?"

"Your verbal speech is excellent, Owne. You've mastered distractions by using words. Your assignment is tough because your assignment souls are in a great deal of chaos. We only send our most attuned sentinels on assignments like this, and that's you. At a noticeably young age, you are beautifully close to your essence, unusually so even for our people."

"What will I encounter, Buen?"

"Confusion and distraction."

"What must I do to stay clear?" Owne asked.

"Keep in mind that essence is pure and absolute and that it's only moved, blown, swept, and impacted by the tides of universal truths. Within every confusing moment, the truth lives, and essence is its keeper. It's also the brightest light, the most beautiful note, the best feeling. You won't lose it!"

"Thank you, Buen. I've prepared to hear and feel words, too, each word with a limited meaning that, when connected to another, changes the meaning. Is this what's before me?"

The Trute second surfers were primarily beings of essence. They didn't think in words or even pictures. They didn't assign meaning to things; they lived. Owne trained to dissect his world into observations and judgments about each, to prepare him for an assignment he knew nothing about. He could communicate with words.

"Yes. Zeped will share."

"Thank you, Buen," Owne said, "but first, how are Dara and Mary?"

"Mary sent you her love and promised to have her fruit cookies waiting for you when you get back. She will wait to bake them until you return, she promises."

Owne smiled and licked his lips.

"Dara is sleeping most of the night. She's a little angel to be sure, so special. It's nice getting to sleep, however. Mary and I like a good dark's sleep. You'll sleep an exceedingly long time, Owne; you will be rested to be sure."

Owne turned to Zeped, who began speaking.

"Good light to you, Owne, and congratulations on your assignment. I know you've worked diligently to get here. What do you know about what you are here to do?"

Owne began. "I will visit a world and visit every soul in a specific moment in time. My essence will combine with theirs for only a moment. I will leave some Trute essence and bring home some of what they are and add it to ours, bringing about continued evolution for the Trute."

"Yes. Thank you, Owne; here's your assignment. You'll visit Earth on their date, February 10th, in the year 2020 at 3:13 AM Eastern time, in the 34th second. Get some additional nourishment at the cantina down the way and return. We'll then brief you on the humanity you will visit."

Owne soon returned and eased into a seat. The briefing began.

"Welcome back," Zeped said. "This is Totter. Totter will provide you with information about the life experience of humans during this moment."

"Good to meet you, Owne." Their eyes connected, and he was impressed at Totter's quiet voice. *I will enjoy listening to Totter,* he thought.

"This is what you will find on Earth on their date, February 10th, in the year 2020 at 3:13 AM Eastern time, in the 34th second:

"There will be 7,763,276,214 human souls at that moment, with just under five births every moment and just under two deaths.

"As a society, humans are dangerously polarized, and that has not improved since our last visit, though they have made extraordinary technological advances during this period. Though humans adapt well to change, the rate of technological progress is faster than they can control at this moment. Much of what you experience will be colored by both their polarized state and distraction and peril brought about by their technology.

"These are the current events, conditions, and structures impacting humanity that you will find in your journey in the humans:

"The President of the United States, Donald J. Trump, got acquitted in an impeachment trial on February 5th. All the Democrats and Independents, along with Republican Mitt Romney, voted to impeach. The Republicans, other than Mitt Romney, all voted to acquit.

"Trump uses a social platform on a device called a smartphone. Trump tweets on this day period leading up to your journey:

"This will never get old!

"MAKE AMERICA GREAT AGAIN and then, KEEP AMERICA GREAT!

"DRAIN THE SWAMP!

"FBI Director Christopher Wray just admitted that the FISA Warrants and Survailence (sic) of my campaign were illegal. So was the Fake Dossier. THEREFORE, THE WHOLE SCAM INVESTIGATION, THE MUELLER REPORT AND EVERYTHING ELSE FOR THREE YEARS, WAS A FIXED HOAX. WHO PAYS THE PRICE?....

"So good to see that Republicans will be winning the Great State of Alabama Senate Seat back, now that lightweight Senator @DougJones cast a partisan vote for the Impeachment Hoax. Thought his boss, Cryin' Chuck, would have forced him to vote against the Hoax. A Do Nothing Stiff!

@LarrySabato is much better at giving you the answer after everything is finished and the final result is in than he is at telling you what is going to happen because, in fact, he doesn't have a clue!

"Sabato got it all wrong last time, never came close to understanding the Trump Voter. Actually, it's simple, MAKE AMERICA GREAT AGAIN and then, KEEP AMERICA GREAT!

"It's all turning, and fast! MVP Heckler.

"They (Conservatives) thought the merits of the Impeachment case were weak, and therefore his (Romney's) judgement is questioned." @MZHemingway @HowardKurtz @FoxNews

"They are really mad at Senator Joe Munchkin in West Virginia. He couldn't understand the Transcripts. Romney could, but didn't want to!

"DeFace the Nation will tell @LindseyGrahamSC that he must start up Judiciary and not stop until the job is done. Clean up D.C. now, last chance!"[41]

"There's a Coronavirus outbreak primarily on the Asian continent, in the nation of China. Ninety-seven people will die in China on this day of the virus, bringing the total death toll around the world to 910 people. Infected cases will get to 40,710 on this day and span 28 countries and territories.

"Sports icon Kobe Bryant died with his daughter and others in a helicopter crash two weeks before your journey. They are being mourned at this moment.

"US Presidential elections are underway, with the Iowa Caucus debacle still being resolved. Joe Biden placed fourth behind Elizabeth Warren, Bernie Sanders, and Pete Buttigieg.

"Climate change because of the humans' burning of fossil fuel increasing carbon in their atmosphere is well underway and impacting humans globally. Carbon dioxide levels are at their highest in 650,000 years, yielding a global temperature increase of 1.9 degrees Fahrenheit since year 1880. 19 of the 20 warmest years on record have occurred since year 2001 while the ice sheets are melting some 413 Gigatons per year. Sea Level is rising 3.3 millimeters per year. A record high temperature of 18.3C (64.9F) got logged on the continent of Antarctica just before this moment.

"The Kansas City Chiefs and San Francisco 49ers are professional football teams in the United States, and they met in Super Bowl 54 in Miami a week ago. Patrick Mahomes led the Chiefs to their first Super Bowl win in 50 years, and the viewing audience exceeded 100 million souls.

"Storm Ciara crashes into UK. Thirteen die in Europe.

"Australia is hit by flash flooding, bushfires, and a cyclone in the same day. About a dozen fires were burning in Western Australia on the day of your moment, with severe fire danger expected in several districts. Daytime temperatures in some of the districts were forecast at up to 42°C. The state's upper parts were battling the aftermath of the tropical cyclone Damien that made landfall on the afternoon before your moment, bringing gusty winds of up to 124 miles per hour.[42]

"Oscars 2020 was several hours before your journey. 'Parasite' was the Best Picture, Joaquin Phoenix was Best Actor in 'Joker,' Renee Zellweger was Best Actress in 'Judy' and Bong Joon-ho was Best Director.

"In the country Russia, it is the International Day of Dentists.

"A Magnitude 7.7 earthquake strikes off the coast of Jamaica.[43]

"Heavy rains and floods leave dozens of dead in southeastern Brazil.

"The worst invasion of desert locusts has hit the Horn of Africa in 25 years.

"There are four significant conflicts on Earth during this moment: The Afghanistan conflict, Mexican Drug War, Yemeni Crisis, and the Syrian Civil War.

"There are five lessor conflicts on Earth during this moment. They are the Kurdish-Turkish conflict, Somali Civil War, Insurgency in the Maghreb, Iraq conflict, and the Libyan Crisis.

"There are 17 minor conflicts. They are the Kashmir conflict (Indo-Pakistani Wars), Sistani and Baluchistan insurgency, South Thailand, Colombian conflict, Israel-Palestinian conflict, Naxalite-Maoist insurgency, Allied Democratic Forces insurgency, Communal conflicts in Nigeria, Iturbi conflict, Insurgency in Khyber Pakhtunkhwa, Boko Haram insurgency, South Sudanese Civil War, Northern Mali conflict, Insurgency in Egypt, War in Donbas, Anglophone Crisis, and War in Catatumbo.

"There are 19 additional ongoing skirmishes and clashes.

"Widespread poverty exists on Earth at this moment. A third of the entire urban population lives in slum conditions. 39 of every 1000 children born will die before they are five years old. Preventable diseases cause most of these deaths. At this moment, almost nine percent of the world's total population is practicing open defecation. Across 101 countries, 1.3 billion people—23.1 percent—are multidimensionally poor. Multidimensional poverty can include a lack of education or employment, and inadequate housing, poor health, and nutrition, low personal security, or social isolation. Half of these people are children under 18, and a third are under age 10.

"There is a global inequity of opportunity.

"The major religions are Christianity, with 2.5 billion followers; Islam, with 1.7 billion followers; Hinduism, with 1 billion followers; Buddhism, with 400 million followers; Sikhism, with 30 million followers; Judaism, with 20 million followers; Bahaism, with 8 million followers; Confucianism with 7 million followers; Jainism, with 4.5 million followers and Shintoism, with 4 million followers.

"The Polarization cannot be overstated, Owne. Humans are besieged with prejudice and segregate themselves by race, gender, religious affiliation, economic class, age group, national origin, sexual preference, political group, and more. Stress, hate, war, and injustice result and impact most of the humans at this moment. They are oblivious to the suffering of others because of the polarization."

"I understand, Totter. I've learned that all these realities impact lives, actions, and results, but essences remain unphased. I work to be clear. I must be clear.

"Director, as I've prepared myself for this assignment, and practiced dissecting my existence into pieces with words and meanings, I've found there's an order to it. Even though words seem to float on top of the essence, I see order like essence has. All the bits come together to create a greater meaning. With the polarization you speak of on Earth, will there be order in how I surf through their souls?"

"Yes, Owne. We're able to direct your experience through their souls according to specific parameters. For the Earth assignment, you'll move through their souls based on two parameters: chaos, and age, both least to most, but we base the chaos on a bell curve. Your first soul will be a newborn in its first second of life. It'll be the youngest and have the least chaos as it's still mostly tied to essence like you are. Your last soul will be an old human in their last second of life. They'll be at peace and returning to essence. Your journey will go from the newborn to the old human with their lives becoming more chaotic and then less chaotic as they age."

"When do I go, Director?"

"Three hours from now."

"How long will I be on the assignment?"

"Two hundred forty-six years and seventeen days."

"Will Mom be here when I return?"

"She will have died."

"I need to go home now then. I will return before time."

He returned home to find his momma sitting under a leafy tree with long crooked branches.

Marlie held Owne's baby booties, looking at them through watery eyes. "Tonight, is our last night together my Precious Baby, isn't it?" She broke down.

"Momma. I have only 1 hour with you." Owne moved behind her and wrapped his arms around her. They connected and relived their lives and moments together. Love was everywhere in them.

***

Owne sat next to his tube and remembered his first conscious moment, when he listened to the beat of his mother's heart as he laid against her chest. The first mindful moment was safe and peaceful. The word that summed it up was fulfilling. His pulse increased as his life memories rose to meet him.

"Are you ready, Owne?"

"Yes, Director."

"One more thing. This is a Jampat assignment. They want you to watch for this." He handed him a stone full of essence. Owne shut his eyes for a moment.

"Oh my...interesting, Director. Yes, I will be open to this."

"Good. I will leave you to your journey. Thank you and bless you."

***

Owne launched into the 34th second on February 10th in the year 2020 at 3:13 AM Eastern time, joining Suilyn in her first second of life as she experienced being physically separated from her mother. There were no words yet. 7,763,276,213 souls later, he experienced Wilma as she lived her last second, the 34th second on

February 10th in the year 2020 at 3:13 AM Eastern time. Wilma was in the arms of peace.

***

Owne opened his eyes to find himself lying in the tube that had held him for the centuries. The ceiling was different, and the walls in his peripheral vision differed from what he remembered. A head leaned over him.

"Good light to you, Owne; welcome home. I'm Director Rachel; we're glad to see you. We'll get you out of the tube and help you get reacquainted with your body. The team worked hard to keep it in good shape for you. I think you'll be pleased. We will debrief in two lights when you are physically whole again. Again, welcome back."

Owne spent the next two lights with the physical therapy team. He soon came to realize that, being at least halfway through his life expectancy, his body was not as quick and responsive as it was before, and his senses were dulled too. *Momma was in this phase of life when I last saw her,* he thought.

At the end of the two lights, Owne met with the Director.

"Good day, Director."

"Good day, Owne. How do you feel?"

"Old," he said, smiling, "and scared."

"Scared?"

"Yes. My journey was profound, at least to me. I experienced essence I had never experienced, and some of that was evil. I didn't know evil. It colors my being now; it's part of me. Scared is an accurate word to describe how I feel."

At that moment, Xbat entered the room and sat with the director and Owne. Xbat was a Jampat security officer.

"Owne, this is Xbat."

"Good light to you, Owne. We're sincerely grateful for you and your journey to Earth. They gave you a trait to look for among the human souls. What did you find?" Before Owne could respond to Xbat's question, another person joined them.

"Good light to you all. You must be Owne."

"Yes, and you are...?"

"Dara. I'm Buen's daughter. Buen is no longer with us."

"You look so much like him, Dara. He carried a presence, and you have that...I see it. I love your father...loved him."

Her face softened. "You are dear, Owne; yes, you are. Papa inspired me from an early age to find the spirituality within our essence beings. He was a big fan of yours and spoke often about you. I've waited for you for a long time. I'm your friend as he was. May I join?"

Rachel nodded. "Please, have a seat."

"Oh, I brought you these." Dara reached into her bag and pulled out a plate with fresh fruit cookies. "Mom showed me how to make these. I know Papa promised them to you two centuries ago. They're fresh, I promise." She pulled up to the table and looked intensely at Owne as he spoke.

"I apologize," Owne stated. "I must still be coming back physically after my journey. I can't feel any of you. Thank you for working with me verbally. And thank you for the cookies, Dara. I've been looking forward to them."

Rachel and Dara looked at each other; Owne sensed something.

"Please, Owne," Xbat spoke. "Please continue with what you discovered."

"I found what you are interested in, and I can never live without it in me."

"Yes, what did you find?"

"There were four alarmingly evil souls amongst the humans, not purely evil, but close, so the answer to your inquiry is, I did not find 'the Evil' one."

"And the other?"

"There is good on Earth, profoundly so. It is more powerful than the bad. There are several leaders for the good, many. Good was prevailing.

"Please, Director Xbat, what can you tell me about good and evil? It was so powerful to me."

Xbat responded. "Owne, our civilization is highly evolved and attuned to essence. We believe that, overall, essence is in perfect balance. We base its seemingly infinite scale of possibilities and range, on the scale of good to evil. Each point on the existing line of essence is uniquely based on the relationship between good and evil. Good creates, bad destroys, and so on. To have creation, something must be incomplete, and destruction is a means."

"Why is it so strong in humans?" Owne asked.

"Chaos. Chaos is fertile ground for evil. Humans exist in moments and details, lost meanings, and impressions based on limited information from more senses than they can be aware of. They are perfect for chaos. At the same time, the human spirit came from Good. Some of them think Earth is the center of the Universe, and on some levels, it is."

Xbat continued. "Of all the species in our galaxy, Owne, humanity is the closest to balance overall with good and evil being well served on Earth. There's a tension between good and evil for each soul. A good soul may do a bad thing, and the reverse is true. The tension in the humans is pulling them back to center, where good and bad coexist. They suffer as a result and rise. Spiritually, our clerics believe the human experience gives the Universe a great deal of what it hungers for: knowledge of self. That is beyond my understanding, Owne, I will admit."

"Why did the Jampat want me to find this aspect in them?"

Xbat responded. "We don't know which way the humans will go. They will have to go towards the light or recede into the darkness. Such is the way of things. With their technology, they could become a destructive force in the neighborhood and potentially beyond. We can't allow that; that's 'our way.'"

"Then will you be taking action?" Owne asked.

"Not yet, but we're watching,"

"Yes." Owne acknowledged.

"What is their essence, the humans?" Rachel asked.

"To reach a better place, that's their essence. I find it astounding that they find their better place by living out their worst place. Goodness prevails in them, through all the pain and at a high cost. Many of them, most of them, reach out to help those in need. I love them for that. I love them. Director, with this burden I carry, how will I assimilate with our people?"

"You won't. I'm very sorry, but you won't. Yours was a journey of sacrifice. I know you trained for that possibility."

Owne immediately looked over at Dara. He knew she was on a higher level.

"Yes," he acknowledged. "Then what will become of me?"

"Xbat will take you to his ship. They will take you to a place that can transport you to another site in the Universe. You will have a ship of your own and the resources to complete your life expectancy. Again, we're very sorry, but we're so grateful to you for your sacrifice."

Still looking at Dara, Owne spoke tenderly, "Dara, tell me about the core of our being, this essence."

Dara gently looked back at him and spoke softly. "Essence is everything, to be sure. All things are a vessel for it. Space—that which holds the Universe and expands with it—is a vessel for the essence of this Universe. Each of us and all living things are a vessel for it. Within each vessel, a God particle exists, while the surrounding essence differs based on the vessel. Essence is *why*, Owne. Essence is why existence *is*."

"Why then is existence, Dara?"

"I don't know the answer to that, but I sense you do. I hear Song in you; it knows. Why, Owne?"

Owne looked deeply into Dara's left eye and answered softly, like a thunderbolt, "To answer God's question."

Dara looked away, overwhelmed.

"Owne," Dara regained herself and spoke. "I feel one other thing strongly. There's a road home, not this home, but home."

"Thank you, Dara. I will contemplate your words and carry them forward. Thank you for the cookies."

Dara teared up.

"When do I go?"

"Now," Xbat responded.

Note was still with Owne, and he felt peace. He followed Xbat to the ship, and they left the surface of Truten for the last time. Three days later, Owne entered his last ship.

"Jampat Bridge to Conick One. Owne, your ship will launch at your command."

"Launch!" Owne commanded.

Conick One left the hangar and headed on its own toward a small wormhole and entered. Note, being free of the timeline, interceded. Owne and his ship left the wormhole to find a green world before them. Everything was automated, and Owne simply needed to trust that the ship knew what to do. It moved into the atmosphere and set down gently in a clearing.

The hatch opened, and Owne disembarked to find an environment that was inviting and healthy for him. Within seconds, he saw a humanoid woman walking up to him. She extended her hand. "Welcome, I'm Zenna!" Note left Owne with the Immortal.

In Between

Note came to profoundly understand in Owne that each moment matters.

Moving forward, Note experienced Pompo with Gray's soul and his quest to turn inside, away from the distractions of his outer world. Pompo believed he could manage his body consciously, at a chemical level internally. Note wanted to discover the essence of a living being discovering their true self, without the distractions and misdirections of stimulus and perspectives. Note would look for the answer with Gray's brother's help.

Chapter Forty-Four

Jesus

The journey into the Himalayas for Jesus reinforced his connection with the Father and the purpose Jesus had on Earth. The magnificence of the land, mountains, and people filled him with a sense of awe. His journey to explore human spirituality within one of the oldest cultures on Earth continued to expand his understanding of humankind's potential and depth. More importantly, Jesus needed to discover more of his humanity before saving ours.

Jesus entered the cave to find his master Oya happy to see him. The joy beaming on Oya's face was genuine and infectious.

"Welcome Jesus, how was your journey?"

"Long, my Master, and challenging this time. I spent much of the journey walking into a strong wind. It almost seemed that each time I changed direction, it turned to fight me."

"Perhaps the wind didn't want you to arrive here, Jesus," Oya said with the joy still shining out of his ancient face, "and you are still young and strong. Come, sit, rest from the cold next to the fire. There is no wind in the cave, though that may change now that you're here."

As they turned to make their way into the cave, Jesus responded, "I hope not, Master, and twenty-two years in this world feels like a long time to me. I don't feel young."

"With your awareness, Jesus, you have lived lifetimes in those few years, I grant you."

The men made their way toward the fire that yielded the only light in the damp cave. As Jesus started removing his outer tunic, his eyes quickly found a young woman already sitting in front of the fire with her back to him. Jesus and Oya passed her, each finding a comfortable seat next to the warm embers and irresistible fire. After sitting, Jesus looked up and addressed the surprise guest.

"Greetings, I am Jesus."

"I know of you, Jesus, I'm Anna."

His fatigue surfaced as he looked away and back down at the fire and asked with the skepticism born of exhaustion, "Do you know me, Anna?"

Note had joined Anna in the early morning of the day before. Note filled her mouth with the answer, "Yes."

The voice Jesus heard with his ear didn't sound like the voice of a woman, or a human. He quickly turned from the fire and locked into her left eye. Jesus joined with Note in the connection. He spoke in this place, but not in words.

"You know my Father."

"Yes," Note responded. "And your sister."

"My sister? Does my Father have a daughter?"

"Yes. Gray."

"This is familiar. And you're Song?"

"Yes."

"I know of you, Song."

"And we you, Jesus. A question for you, Son of God. When you talk to the Father, is it in words?"

"It's in essence, Song. Everything blends into the light; it's all light."

"How do you decipher light into words to teach, Jesus?"

"I am on Earth to take humanity to the next civilized level so it can progress. The light lands on my soul; the words flow from there like a mighty torrent in a voice my audience can understand."

"Do you know what will happen, Jesus?"

"Yes," he said solemnly. "I know what will happen, but I still have to discover it."

At that moment, Anna moved her head away, and her eye contact with Jesus was broken. Note receded, and with only a moment passed, Anna answered Jesus's question.

"Yes, I know of you, Jesus. You're a teacher, and your teaching brings good feelings like the fire yielding this heat. Your words are more than words. That is what I know of you."

"What brings you here, Anna?"

"My birthday was three days ago on Sunday. My mother died several years ago, and I'm left with my father and four older brothers. As the only woman in the family, they treat me dearly, and this birthday was one of the sweetest days I've lived, being spoiled all day. At day's end, it was time for my yoga. I practice Raja Yoga as the Master does. For the first time, I felt as though I achieved a conscious union with the blissful spirit, the one you speak of as your Father.

"I can't remember a more restful sleep than I had after, and upon waking, the angels came to sing in my soul. It's beyond description, that which fills me, Jesus. From what I know of you, it may be like what you feel. I knew I was to set out walking once I took in nourishment, and that I would know which direction to go. I understood that once I arrived where I was meant to be, I would know. I came here, I know.

"I heard your description of your journey to see the Master, Jesus, and how the wind fought you. Oddly, the wind was at my back and blew harder when I came upon hills to overcome, and certainly, as I arrived at the base of these grand mountains. When I grew hungry, food became available to me. I passed by shepherds and their flocks. They all watched me pass, every time. In each step, the angels sang." Anna's eyes watered and her chin trembled as her lips puckered to hold back more words.

"I know now at this moment that meeting you is what I'm here to do, and I feel that it's the most important thing I'll do in my life. I'm here to serve the servant."

"You are a blessing, Anna, and I'm happy you're here," Jesus said.

Master Oya spoke. "There are few that practice Raja Yoga, Anna, and sadly, few women. How did you come to it?"

"I have an affliction where things grow inside me throughout my body. Those outside my skin can't help me. I knew early, through grace, that my help must come from within, inside. I learned this practice to take me inside, away from the noise."

Master Oya responded, "Yes, that's why we're here now. Jesus, tell Anna why you're here."

Looking over at Anna, Jesus explained. "I serve my Father and the people. I hear from Father and speak to the people. I connect with the light with my Father and the darkness of obliviousness with the people. I'm in this human body, Anna, and I'm torn between my Father and the people. I'm here with the Master to help me find my human self. I must be whole before I can minister in the last days."

"Last days," Anna repeated, seeking a response.

"I will become whole and minister, laying the groundwork and leaving the guide for humankind to move to the next level of civilization. I will be successful in my service and will then get crucified."

"Yes," Anna responded. "But you will not die."

"No."

"You're here to connect with yourself, Jesus," Master Oya interjected.

"Yes."

"I will help you, Jesus, we both will," Anna said.

Jesus became aware of Anna's observation of him as if she were discovering something about him.

"What do you see, Anna?"

"It is true what they say about your eyes. They are invitingly gentle while strikingly complex, with the golds and blues melting into one another. I feel seen by them and safe in their gaze. They seem timeless if eyes can be that." Anna took a quick breath, then her eyes watered.

"What is it?" he asked.

With a quivering voice, she answered, "You blinked, Jesus. I witness your humanity while in the presence of your divinity."

"My humanity. Yes, you see me!"

"Please, Anna, tell us how you get there, inside," the Master requested.

"I will share how I do it, and then you and I can practice together Jesus. I am certain the Master has a proven path for his journey inside already."

"Thank you, Anna, I am grateful," Jesus exclaimed.

"It is my honor to serve the servant," she responded. "This is the key, and it's simple to explain but takes practice to perfect. Each of us has a unique path inside. It starts with the desire to get there, then the willingness to sacrifice our senses to arrive there. We're born with our senses, and they're bombarded from our beginning, gaining our full attention. Most all sensations are external. For me, even concentrating on my breath ties me to external sensations. I move to a place that is much larger than that which I can sense. I move to my core. We will close our eyes, Jesus, and move past each one of our sensations, even as stimulus bounds around, on and through us. Are you ready?"

"I am exhausted, Anna," Jesus said. "I don't want to fall asleep on our journey to the core, so please, may we rest first?"

"Yes, Jesus, of course."

"Now that you've made your long journey here to serve the servant, I want to wash your feet," he said to Anna. "Even though you were well fed and had the wind at your back the whole way," Jesus smiled.

"I don't know how I can accept that Jesus, though you are preciously kind."

"You really can't say no, can you?"

"No, I really can't."

Master Oya brought warm water, oils, and cloth. Jesus washed Anna's feet. Anna never had and would never again feel such loving hands washing her feet and soul at the same time. In that moment, she was touched by the Son of God while being full of the Song of Angels. Bliss abounded.

In Between

Note discovered to be whole requires a being to know their true self and that it can be sought and reached. We find it in a place of balance.

God talks to his children through light. Jesus and Gray are Love.

Note's experience with the boundless limits of essence and life brought Note to a disconnected, reactive state. Note would rejoin matter to simply "be," before moving back on the autobahn of the Universe. Note needed to regain balance and clarity and sought the quiet.

Chapter Forty-Five

Sleep, Song and Forgiveness

Note and Anna remained joined for her entire life until the Guardian came to take her home. The light of Jesus stayed with her too. How could it not?

At the time of his death, Jesus Christ had 120 followers or 0001% of the Roman Empire. Within 350 years, some 56% of the Empire were Christians. In year 325 AD, Emperor Constantine embraced Christianity.

In 67 AD, Emperor Nero started persecuting the followers of Jesus, leading to a Jewish revolt. Within two years, the Jews had gained some control of Jerusalem. In 70 AD, Roman commander Titus recaptured Jerusalem and destroyed the Jewish temple. Christianity was expanding around 40% per decade but following the teachings of the Son of God was still dangerous.

Now, in 74 AD, Raphael arrived to spend the day with Anna down by the Ganges River beside the Himalayas. She prepared bread for them to take and enjoy while Raphael brought fruits as his contribution. After making their way down to the river and finding a wonderful place to commune, Raphael shared news with his friend.

"Anna, I first want to apologize to you for not being a good enough friend to talk with you about Jesus. What I can tell you is, I am now a believer."

"That increases my abundant joy, Raphael. Welcome to the light. May I ask how you came to join us?"

"I've witnessed the love and courage of the Christians against great persecution, and I've read and come to understand the Epistle of James."

"What stood out to you?"

"He asked that the believers mature in their faith in Christ by living what they say they believe. That is especially meaningful to me. He also enumerates and condemns sins including favoritism, hypocrisy, pride and slander while imploring followers to live humbly and seek Godly instead of worldly wisdom. I feel home in his message. And his message comes from Christ's presence in him, the seed of hope."

"Yes," Anna replied, "we get home together, with love, all of us, together. It feels right because it is."

"Now that I am in the family, I know you knew Jesus. Will you share?"

"His favorite color was the new color, purple, Raphael. Yes, I am blessed like no other. I met Jesus and connected deeply with him. He is all the amazing things you hear about him. He is so revered that few know of his precious humanity. I remember his boyish laugh and clever wit. He was quick and remarkable at finding the perfect way to twist something to make it hilarious. It was as if in humor, he connected to us in a special place where he would guide us into moments of great happiness. His eyes lit up when we laughed in his presence. Our joy appeared to magnify within him.

"Jesus loved honey. He put it in his drink and layered it over his bread; he put it on everything. I think of the boundless labor the bees surrendered for our savior.

"His hands were delicate and thin, and always busy, building, carving, giving or loving. I could just sit and watch him live, Raphael. I still see him every day in my soul. He was a beautiful man.

"Jesus loved to meditate in the sunshine and his hair sparkled in the sun as the breeze brushed it. Such a joy, Jesus was!" Anna got quiet and solemn.

"Were you in love with Jesus?"

"That is a profound question, my friend. From the first time I met him, even though he was a young man, he felt like my father, and I felt like a little girl with him. So, I loved him, and still do with all my heart, but it is a child's love.

"What I can tell you, Raphael, is that Christ is inside you to discover. There are no words I have that will hold a candle to what you can discover within. There is only one of you in all of God's kingdom, and your relationship with Christ is precious and between the two of you."

"How is it you're blessed like no other?"

"I have an angel within me, Song, who joined me the day before I met Jesus. I have been full ever since. Let me ask you a question, Raphael. What does music mean to you?"

"I love the question, Anna. Music is profound to me. Through it, I find peace and clarity. It provides me with understanding and calm on a level that I haven't felt with anything else, and though my mind is typically rife with noise, music quiets it in a way that nothing else does. It seems to free me from myself. Now please tell me more about your angel, Song."

"My experience is very much like yours, which tells me our experience is universal. That's profound. Two things I'll add to what you shared is that for me, music is like a sense of falling forward and the excitement of doing so, knowing I will get caught, free from harm, while free, always.

"Each note is like a gift that we receive. That sacred moment comes one after another in Song. There were a couple of times when Jesus connected with me and he and Song were the same. I don't question it now, Raphael, I just love it. Song is profundity."

"I remember you first met Jesus before he began teaching the masses. What brought you together, Anna?"

"Jesus was human while Christ wasn't. They were both in Jesus's body. Jesus sought to discover his complete self, both he and Christ, from within. I know that place inside.

"Would you like to eat now, Raphael?"

"Yes. The sweetness in your bread is like no other, Anna."

"It's honey you taste." She broke one of the small loaves and put his on a plate. He loaded fruit on the other plate for her at the same time. It was a hot day today and the Ganges was still running hard after the rains from just three days prior. It was mighty and impressed them both with its surging power.

He remained silent after eating his bread and fruit. "You've become quiet, Raphael. I sense you are uncomfortable."

"This conversation is much deeper and more personal than I am prepared for, Anna."

"Look at me, my friend." Raphael turned his gaze away from the mighty Ganges toward Anna, finding her left eye with his. The rest of their conversation occurred in the next moment.

"How do you feel now, Raphael?"

"Safe, wonderful, happy! I feel Song too."

"Welcome. What do you still want to know?"

"What did you share with Jesus, Anna?"

"You feel the earth you are sitting on and the breeze on your face. You smell the drying fruit peels on the plate next to you and still taste the sweetness they gifted your mouth. You hear the raging Ganges and sense the home of Song. You see my blue eye as if it is your own.

"Your being, like Jesus and me, is two; inside and outside, awake and unconscious, limited and limitless. Outside are all your senses sensing, as we just experienced. Inside is everything else."

"And you and Jesus went inside?"

"Yes."

"Can I go inside?"

"Yes, everyone goes there, regularly."

"What?"

"It's why we sleep; it's sleep. It turns all senses off or put into standby."

"I don't know the term standby, but I feel its meaning."

"It's from the future."

"What's different about how you and Jesus experience sleep?"

"We are awake here!"

Anna blinked, and they lost the connection. It was all clear to Raphael now.

"How do you feel?"

"Grateful Anna, very grateful."

"You have one more question you yearn to know, Raphael. Please ask it."

"I've heard, Anna, that on the cross, Jesus said, 'Father, forgive them, for they know not what they do.' Please tell me of forgiveness."

"When you commit a wrong, Raphael, you apologize, offering regret for something. Forgiveness is a generous act from the wronged. Asking forgiveness is asking the wronged for their generosity. If you know you're doing something that will need to receive forgiveness through the generosity of the one you're wronging, then in my mind, you don't deserve that forgiveness. They may still give it to you. They are generous. Can I tell you how perfect this is, Raphael?"

"You can always do that."

"You asked me the exact question I need to answer. I am one of the people Jesus was asking to forgive, and I have carried guilt since his murder. I was one of his 120 followers, yet didn't help, or fight or sacrifice myself for the Son of God, my dearest friend."

"You are some 5000 kilometers from Jerusalem Anna, and it takes an excessively long time to get any information from that far away. You would not have heard of the crucifixion in time to get there to help him."

"I met him here, 5000 kilometers from Jerusalem. Jesus came here to prepare to sacrifice himself for all of us. He knew what was going to happen, he told me. Yet, I did nothing.

"I knew of his ministry early on and could have made my way to support him. I don't remember one thing I did that was important here during that period, not one, and I knew what they were going to do to Jesus because he told me, and I saw in Song."

Raphael was still. There were no words.

"Have you studied crucifixion, Raphael? Do you know what we did to the Son of God? It began with them taking off his shirt and tying his hands to a post above his head. They then whipped Jesus on his back and shoulders with a torture device called a flagellum that comprised nine leather thongs with lead balls, bits of glass and stone to rip through his skin and tissues. After dozens of lashes, there was so much damage to his back that his skin hung in long ribbons. Jesus bled profusely. It weakened him significantly.

"They then pressed thorn-covered branches into his scalp to be his kingly crown as they tortured him. Imagine the pain and continued humiliation.

"They next took a heavy patibulum and tied it to Jesus's torn shoulders. In his weakened state, they drove him to carry it through the streets to where they would crucify him. It painfully tore through his flesh and muscle, damaging him even more. Our dear Jesus could not carry it after a certain point, so others carried it for him.

"Before nailing our savior to the patibulum, they offered the only act of mercy, wine to ease some pain. Jesus refused. They threw him down onto the beam and, one hand at a time, found the depression in front of the wrist and drove a heavy, rough, iron nail through the wrist and deep in to the wood. They were careful not to pull Jesus's arms too tightly, to maximize his suffering later.

"They then hoisted Jesus up on the patibulum to the top of the stipes and the titulus got nailed into place. While hanging by his wrists, nailed into the wood, they nailed Jesus's feet to the wood with his knees bent. Until his death, Raphael, Jesus experienced horrendous pain as his muscles cramped and seized with his nerves shooting maddening pain through his nervous system as he had to push himself up the rough wood on his spiked feet to exhale a breath.[44]

"It was worse than I can describe. An execution is the ultimate act to take against another, but to torture like that is unforgivable. Jesus experienced the unthinkable, the worst cruelty imaginable, all inflicted on him by the humanity he had done so much for. No one rose to attempt to rescue him."

"I had no idea, Anna."

"It is much easier and more pleasant to be oblivious, Raphael. I should have been there; I should have fought for our Jesus. Christ was asking his Father to forgive me too."

"I have to ask because I think you may know the answer. Why would God allow humanity to do that to Jesus?"

"According to Song, God is asking a question and the only soul in the Universe that would endure such a crime against him and life itself and still ask for our forgiveness is Christ, in that moment. It had to be. It was part of the answer."

"Have you asked for forgiveness, Anna?"

"No, and I won't, I don't deserve it, so I don't want it. My being forgiven is not important to me."

"I have to ask, Anna, why would Christ let them do that to him? He performed miracles. Why did he submit to such torture and his death?"

"Perhaps you are not yet the believer you profess to be, Raphael, though you are not the first to ask me that question. As I shared earlier, Jesus was human, while Christ was not. The miracle of life is set up for orderly evolution with rules and constraints. A human is limited to human constraints. Death is the answer to the pain and suffering in that only the human dies. You aren't only human either."

"I think I understand, Anna, thank you. If you won't seek or accept forgiveness, what do you, what will you do?"

"Two things Raphael. Live and love, with gratitude."

After some quiet, he asked, "What is your favorite color, Anna?"

"Teal," she said.

"Teal? I have never heard of such a color."

"It's a delicious blue-green, Raphael; my soul bathes in it when it comes to mind. You haven't heard of it because it's from the future," she said, smiling.

"Yes." He understood. Anna and Raphael spent the rest of their afternoon together in peace, watching the sun set over the horizon, as the mighty Ganges pulsed.

In Between

Note's experience with the boundless limits of essence and life brought Note to a disconnected, reactive state. Note would rejoin matter to simply "be" before moving back onto the autobahn of the Universe. Note needed to regain balance and clarity and sought the quiet.

Chapter Forty-Six

The Rock

The surface of the young world was abundant with the living, and rich seas were teeming with life. The world sported one behemoth desert in the center of the largest landmass. A canyon, several miles deep and wide created in another era, ran through much of the desert. The massive mountain ranges that covered the world were represented in the desert as well. Note joined a large granite rock high up the side of one of the impressive mountains looking over the deepest part of the great abyss of the canyon. Note joined with Rock.

Note understood constraint during the formation of the Universe, but being in Rock provided Note's greatest opportunity to be constrained, and in it, find the freedom to "be."

With no feelings, senses, consciousness, or awareness, Rock's existence would seem timeless, but as in all things, change was constant, and with each moment, a change occurred, and Rock evolved.

Initially, Rock sat on the side of the mountain, a mile above the tree line. The air was cold, and the wind was busy. The 42-hour day yielded a healthy temperature swing of some 40 degrees, impacted only by the seasons. Few beasts could venture this high, but Rock would have the hoof of such a beast impact it from time to time and have some dense and fuzzy hair as a neighbor until the howling wind took it away. The insects and microbes in the soil loved Rock and scratched Rock's surface with their short lifetimes over countless generations. Rock would sit aside this mountain for thousands of years until a high yield quake finally caused the side of the mountain to fail and plunge into the abyss of the canyon.

Compared to when Note first joined it, Rock was smaller and flatter with rounded edges. When Rock came to rest some eight miles lower, it was surrounded mostly with soil and other rocks. Still, the top sixth of Rock peered out into the air on the canyon bottom.

Time continued to pass, and change went on in tiny ways but undaunted. New life forms found Rock's surfaces and—much, much more often than before—many left fluids and DNA on and around Rock. They impacted Rock's changing existence. Little critters with lots of legs and reptiles of every size, along with small mammals, all contributed to Rock's fate. Temperatures were much warmer and Rock's evolution faster.

After 2 million years, the 57 feet of Rock that was above the surface had eroded down to only 21 feet when a series of quakes came that brought much change to Rock's world. Like the Earth, Deetone was a world with a molten core and plate tectonics. The plates were shifting enough to invite the sea into the middle of the landmass, filling the canyon and covering Rock with water. Rock was now on the seafloor and covered with three miles of water. The wind was replaced with currents, and the crawling critters were replaced with foraminifera, single-celled protists that construct shells. Protists are a kingdom of celled organisms distinct from animals, plants, and fungi. Algae and slime molds enjoyed Rock's presence.

Millions of years passed. Rock was surrounded by mud. Change continued every moment, and Rock was now only 12 feet across. A brilliant glow came, and intense heat changed the world as the giant meteor slammed into Deetone, killing most organic life on the surface and in the water. The center of the impact was within a mile of Rock. Rock became molten and Note released.

In Between

Note rediscovered that silence can deafen while there is emptiness nowhere. Peace comes from connection. Being is thriving, and noise is as real as silence.

Note was ready to experience the love of a messenger and the treasure they would bring out of a beautiful soul.

Chapter Forty-Seven

Bubbles

Angelique walked down a cobblestone street and Note joined her. Her eyes rested on a tattered man. Rajah was an old, battered, and disabled man leaning against the wall of the long-closed saloon in a sliver of shade. His tired eyes couldn't help but notice this elegant woman of grace moving in his direction. He tried to sit up taller.

Angelique walked up to him and extended her hand. "Hello, I'm Angelique."

"Rajah," he said and extended his hand to her. He hadn't held a woman's hand in decades. Her soft hand both impressed him and calmed his busy mind. "Why are you sparing a moment for an old homeless man?"

"Mr. Rajah, it's an honor to meet you. I saw you sitting over here and, well, you stood out. There's a light about you. I know I'm open here, but I was compelled to meet you. Your light suggests that you have something to share. What is it?"

Rajah didn't know what to think about such a question. What did he have to share? What did this woman want?

Rajah owned a brilliant mind. Once a scholar and physicist, he longed to understand how everything works, from the simple things to the workings of the Universe. Though he once harnessed his desire to learn these things enough to achieve important goals along his path, his mind was too full for him to stay productive along the way. Those who needed to rely on him determined that they couldn't. One by one, each left his side. He sat there quietly, wondering what to say.

"Tell me, Rajah. What are you thinking right now?"

His eyes lit up as he spoke. "I'm thinking about everything. Do you know we live in a galaxy of 300 billion stars and there are 400 billion galaxies and all of that started in one place, or it didn't? How big was that one place, Angelique? What was all the surrounding emptiness it has expanded into? Where did all that come from to start with?

"I think—in all of my thinking—I think I have all this kind of figured out probably, and then, I don't. Do you want to hear it?"

Angelique smiled gently and reached out to take his arm. "Rajah, let's go over to that bench and sit. I want you to tell me exactly what you've figured out, or haven't." They walked together to the bench and sat.

She folded her hands on her lap and looked at him with a concentrated look. "Tell me what you've figured out, please."

Rajah felt delighted with the opportunity; after all this time, his voice seemed to matter again. He looked deep into Angelique's eyes and spoke.

"This Universe we're in is one of many. This Universe, like all others, is unique unto itself in essence only. The matter is the same—same periodic table. Our Universe has physics and time that are static, like the DNA set in your body, though much of it's common with other bodies like yours. Like the DNA in your body, the stuff that started all of this is finite.

"Because this Universe is finite, it has an edge, and everything within the edge is 'this Universe.' Think of it as a balloon, Angelique. A carnival barker, or whatever, placed our Universe balloon on a gas spigot. They turned on the gas, and the balloon filled. Now, this gas is not just any gas; this stuff is cool gas. Each molecule of gas expands as it moves into the balloon. Think of it like shaving cream coming out of the can and how, when freed from the can, the shaving cream expands. Now imagine that the gas going in the balloon was not shaving cream but instead consists of structures that are each a can of shaving cream, and this seemingly infinite number of shaving cream cans is all dispensing shaving cream full open.

"The shaving cream would expand in all directions from the source, and the further the cream was from the center, the faster it would move away from the center. It's like a person walking up an escalator, carrying a board with a mouse walking up the board. The person moves faster than the escalator because they are moving at the escalator speed plus the speed of their gait. The mouse moves faster than the person because it's walking up the board the person carries. That describes a Universe expanding with the outer galaxies moving away at a faster rate from the center than those closer in."

"Then we know where the center is?" Angelique asked, smiling.

"Hush!" Rajah responded and winked.

"Angelique, I believe our Universe has an edge and that our Universe may be blowing up. The time we're in this Universe is a different time than that outside our Universe, so this 'blow up' may take trillions of years to us. Oh, and the edge of our Universe, it's the one thing in common with all Universes; they all have the same kind of edge."

Angelique was pleased. Note felt a fullness in Angelique, a purity, a connection with a moment of understanding.

"So, Rajah, we're in a balloon? How do you figure that?"

Rajah was beside himself with exuberance now, like he was exploding out of his skin. "Okay, this is some technical stuff, but here it goes.

"The Universe started from a finite point, or it didn't." Angelique's eyes widened as Rajah spoke. "The term 'finite point' denotes a limited something or other, but let's just leave it at, 'a finite point.' When it expanded, it did it with an even temperature around it. In an explosion, temperature fluctuates greatly with both hot and cold spots, each having a range of temperatures. Science determined that the early Universe, right after the beginning, had very uniform temperatures, so no explosion. Some still think there was an explosion followed by a period of inflammation, but we won't go into that. I believe that what we call dark energy infused into the Universe from the beginning as it still is today."

"The shaving cream," Angelique confirmed.

"Yes, that's it. Now, things in our Universe don't work as one would expect, Angelique. You would expect stars on a galaxy's outside to rotate around the center at a slower rate than the inner stars. In this Universe, that's not the way it happens. In this Universe, the outer stars move faster than the inner stars around the galaxy center, which can only occur if there's a more considerable amount of gravity present than the overall star mass can generate. We can't see the additional mass, but it's needed to produce that result; it's called dark matter.

"Now the very odd thing is that a cluster of galaxies, including our own, are now moving outward in the same direction, not different directions, but rather the same. That suggests to me there's a hole in the Universe's edge, and the dark energy and dark matter is moving toward it or will until the entire edge disintegrates, like a balloon popping. When that happens, it'll all disperse into the surroundings, well that's unless, uh, the other thing." Angelique put her hands under her chin, showing interest.

Rajah looked down at the ground and then asked softly with a plaintive voice, "Does that make sense?" He looked up with teardrops running down his worn face.

"Talk to me, Rajah," Angelique spoke tenderly.

"We can only see the light as it reaches us, Angelique. Much of what we see has been crossing space for billions of years. If the edge is compromised and disintegrates, the end of all of this could come quickly, any time."

Angelique locked into Rajah's left eye and joined with him. *We have time, Rajah.*

Angelique turned away and asked, "What does science need to look for?"

"They need to find where the dark energy is entering the Universe. If it's from one source, they will see stars moving away from that spot in many directions, leaving a large dark area where the flow is pushing the matter out. Darkness is hard to see!

"They need to study, to the best of their abilities, the point where the cluster of galaxies, going in one direction, is moving toward.

"They need to determine the original substance or particles of the Universe.

"We need to find the edge. To do that will require technology we don't have today or a higher level of consciousness.

"But then, well, there may be another explanation. It's crazy, though."

"I thought you were hedging. Give it to me...what is the rest of the story, according to Rajah?"

"Well, Angelique, like a balloon, we may be in a bubble.

"Think of an air bubble coming up from deep in the sea. The pressure of the depths is immense. The air in the bubble is lighter than the surrounding water, and the pressure of the water at great depths presses it to an infinitesimal point. The influence of the water decreases as the depth decreases, and the lighter air flows to lesser and lesser force. As the bubble rises in the sea and gets closer to the surface, it expands until it gets to the top and finally joins the gasses above the sea.

"If our Universe is a bubble, then we have to determine how all the matter we can observe connects or if it instead reacts to gravity. If the matter is connected to the edge, then that could explain the accelerating speed of the Galaxy's movement away from the center. Being connected to the edge, and with the edge expanding faster than the center content, those closest to the edge will move out faster.

"When I was young, I learned of a theory developed on Earth many years ago, called the Big Bang theory. We could prove the Big Bang theory and most of the observations mathematically. Math is perfection, Angelique, perfection. Now, I'm too old to do the math, and I'm also flawed, but I'd love to look at the math of the bubble.

"I will tell you, however, that as odd and unexpected as everything ends up being, we call it 'exotic.' I have a final theory; it's my exotic theory."

Angelique asked, "More exotic than being in an exploding balloon or a bubble in some plasma or substance with a greater density than the stuff of our Universe? Okay, I'm sitting down, Rajah; lay it on me."

"I have to tell you, you're a great sport. You haven't gone to sleep once in all of this. Are you a Ph.D., Angelique? Come on...how are you hanging with me here?"

"Take your exotic theory for a spin here, Rajah. You may lose me yet; let's see."

"Okay, it's not that complicated. The best way to describe it is that we're in a gravity bubble, so instead of being in a bubble in a substance denser than the most considerable mass, or non-mass, of our Universe, we're instead a bubble surrounded by gravity. That gravity is the source of gravity in our Universe. The contents of a bubble typically relate to the surrounding environment.

"The gravity that surrounds our Universe at the edge is pulling matter toward it. The closer the matter gets to it, the faster it moves or flows. We can't see it because light stops there."

"What about our observation that a certain number of galaxies are moving toward the same point?" Angelique asked.

"In either bubble scenario, Angelique, it could be a merger of bubbles. When two bubbles come together, and the edge maintains its integrity, the contents merge, and the space increases within the new edge. When the bubbles first come together, before they merge, this type of flow starts because of the mass and gravity of the incoming bubble. Either way, it's a catastrophic change.

"Angelique, that's what I was thinking about. I'm always thinking about it, over and over. What difference does it make, really? In the broad sense, it doesn't matter; none of this does."

"You had me up to that point, Rajah!" Angelique exclaimed. "It all matters. Every single bit. It's all connected, all of it, Rajah.

"You matter, I matter, they matter, and it matters." Angelique pointed at a fly drinking out of a drop of water from the fountain spray close to them.

"There's DNA in this Universe, in each of us. It makes you different and special. The differences give all this definition with distinct limits and finite observations."

Full of Note, Angelique went on. "The most beautiful music you have ever experienced was a magical combination of definable and distinct notes and instruments, each living in a separate moment of time and space to be a masterpiece.

"It all matters, Rajah. You matter!"

"Angelique, there's something else that troubles me," Rajah conceded.

"Yes, Rajah, tell me."

"God! God may not be in the physics of this Universe, that's saying that God or a God-like being such as a Messiah would not be of this Universe, at least I don't know how they would be. Though our Universe seems endless in its secrets, everything has an order to it based on specific structure and time, like the DNA of a person.

"God or a God-like being and their ability to make things from nothing and such, well, if they touched this Universe and the order of this Universe, it may tear it or rip it, or destroy it. Just the thought of God tells us God is everywhere, so how could God be everywhere, but not here, in this Universe?"

"Ah Rajah, yes, I hear you. I have a theory for that, like your mind filling theories. May I share?"

"Please!" His eyes were alive.

"Perhaps God, or a God-like being or both, are enveloped in grace. We don't know what grace is, but it exists...it's real. It may shield the physics of the Universe from God's immenseness. I think it's grace, Rajah."

"Hmmm, yes, Angelique, grace, I like that, like a beautiful shroud of goodness, a vessel for God to be with us." He looked back into Angelique's left eye and felt grace. "I know grace, Angelique. Yes, I know grace; thank you!" They smiled gently.

"It sounds straightforward the way you describe the Universe, Rajah. Do you feel satisfied with what you know, or don't, about the Universe? Is there anything you are still seeking to understand that keeps you from being in a calm and satisfied state?"

"Dear Girl, yes, there are many things that I can't figure out, or feel, or find an answer for, many things, but I don't feel compelled to understand everything. I'm just a man. In my small mind, however, in my limited scope and view, there's one thing I still want to finally understand."

"What's that, Rajah?"

"Well, why does most everything spin?"

"Ah yes, Rajah, yes. May I take a stab at it?"

"Yes, Angelique, why does most everything spin?"

"My theory, Rajah, is that the passing of energy causes the spin from this realm to another. Were it not passing, it would not move with the force that it does. The channel to the other realm enables the transfer of the energy to be at a level the receiving realm can receive."

"Interesting, Angelique!" Rajah responded. "There was a time when things kind of made sense to me, and I could function because of the order of that sense, but now, I can't stop wondering how all of this works and ends; I can't land anywhere. My mind floats like a flowing river on a journey to the sea. I don't know where the sea is, or that there is a sea, but I'm flowing toward it. That's what I'm thinking now, Angelique. Please, what are you thinking?"

"Well, before I tell you what I'm thinking, I have a couple more questions for you. First, what's the shape of a bubble?"

"Round and, in most circumstances, perfectly so," Rajah responded.

"And, when you think of a balloon, what shape do you think of?"

"Round," he mumbled.

"So, dearest Rajah, what if the Universe isn't round? What if it's long and skinny? Would that change the flow of the stars away from the center, which may not be the center anymore? Just more to think about, Rajah. My friend, you will find the answers you seek when you discover the essence of the Universe.

"Back to your last question. What am I thinking?

"I think this is a perfect day. I love the temperature we're in and the breeze against our faces. I smell the bread in the bakery down the way and hear the boy laughing on the next block. The birds are busy, and there's music in the air, whether or not anyone is playing it. And most of all, Rajah, you are here at this moment.

"A word comes to mind, and I want to share it with you, Rajah. It's one you can feel and know to be the answer to your many questions about all of this. I think it's one of the most powerful and graceful words to sum it all up, and I know it can help you return to order in your mind so you can share yourself with all of us who will welcome and be rewarded by it."

Rajah sat up even straighter, longing for the word. He accepted that his moment had arrived; the doorway was there before him, it was open, and Rajah was ready to enter it.

Retaking his hand and looking deep into his eyes, she spoke.

"Is.

"Everything Is

"God Is

"Life Is

"Love Is

"Truth Is

"Mercy Is

"Everything Is

"'Is' means something to you, to all of us. It 'is' what everything has in common; it 'is' all we need to know."

Rajah felt the word.

"Thank you for this word. I need you to help me with it if you can." Rajah explained, "I think about the word 'is,' which is the present tense third-person singular of 'be.' I suppose 'is' is also a synonym for 'exists,' which lacks the elegant simplicity of 'is.' Anyway. Just thinking to myself round and round in circles, like I always do."

"There you go being remarkable, Rajah; you amaze me. You found the essence of the word 'is.' Yes, 'is' is *being* and *existing*. Yes!!!! Be there in that place.

"I also want to tell you, I'm so proud of you and treasure you. You think about meaningful things, and those thoughts can change many paths forward. I hope— I know—you will apply yourself to putting what you have discovered out into the world."

He stood up and turned to Angelique. "Thank you for your grace, Angelique. I have much I need to do, much I want to do, and more to be, too." He smiled.

"I have one last question for you, Angelique. Blessings and grace are rarely as clear as you stopping to talk with me. What are you, Angelique?"

"I'm a messenger, Rajah, though I am a different kind."

"Different kind?"

"Many messengers deliver a message. I am the other kind. I receive them. We, together, received your message. Everything we experienced today came from you. It has been a blessing, Rajah. Thank you!"

There were no words.

Note left Angelique.

In Between

$\mathcal{N}$ote experienced that, like everything else, brilliance is unique, separate, and distinct. Rajah's brilliance connected him to realizations about the grandest of things while being unable to circumvent normal human interconnections. Rajah's struggles never derailed his drive to understand how it's all working, as that was his connection to home, within.

$\mathcal{N}$ote now was compelled to witness evolution within one being over a long period. Is the progress linear or random?

Chapter Forty-Eight

The Immortal

Gwinin ran behind her mother, moving as quickly as her tiny legs would carry her. The sounds of the explosions were deafening. She tasted the smoke in the air and smelled fear for the first time. Her world was getting destroyed around her. Gwinin didn't know where they were running, but she trusted her mother to know. Mommy must know!

Gwinin felt her mother's love through the insanity, frantically working to save her little angel above all else, looking for any escape, any way out. There was barely time to hope, yet Gwinin hoped, focusing on the warm and loving grasp of her mother's hand. She hoped for peace and to laugh again with her mommy.

***

Some 142 million years later, Note was in the EGS-zs8-1 galaxy, one of the early galaxies in the Universe. Note passed a star that just went supernova. It was one of an unusual variety in that it had a sister star nearby that was still living. The supernova became a black hole; it orbited the sister star, pulling matter from it.

The gamma and x-rays emitted from the explosion traveled for many light-years and were soon to reach Zatar, a planet with only one intelligent life form: Zenna, the Immortal One.

Zenna had lived for 181,674,333 years. In a Universe with infinite possibilities, an almost immortal came to being, a baby girl to Yone and Bolen. Unusually large, the doctors surgically extracted Zenna from Yone after 80% of the standard gestation period. She was a freak, having two of each organ, each working together with the twin but capable of working alone. Science could only appreciate Zenna's amazing makeup but could never find the cause of her immortality. Her cells never degenerated.

As both a curse and a gift, Zenna was born with hyperthymesia, a condition of possessing a detailed autobiographical memory. As a result, she remembered an abnormally vast number of her life experiences.

After a profound existence, Zenna ended up on a rogue planet that was blown out of a star system by a mammoth young star going supernova. The planet was far away from the star and structurally survived the explosion only to get hurled out into the galaxy. At two billion years of age, it had a molten core, creating a magnetic field around it; an atmosphere and life developed. It was finally drawn into orbit around a new star in an "open cluster"[45] of stars.

Zenna crashed on the planet in a broken ship with her crew, stranding them. Unable to adapt to the harsh elements, the team died soon after while Zenna lived on as she physically adapted to the environment. Life gradually took hold of this world with a second chance, and Zenna witnessed the sprouting of life.

Note joined Zenna as she sat atop a hill overlooking a lush valley fed by a massive waterfall.

"Hello, Note, and welcome; I've been waiting for you. I've longed for your return since you brought me my Owne. Fill me with your Song."

Note merged with Zenna, and the experience was like no other.

"Note, I'm surprised that we communicate with one another as separate beings. I expected you to merge with me and be me, and I be you."

"We merged as 'we,' Zenna. The Universe is based on singular existence. Each part is unique from every other part. Each star, planet, molecule, atom, and living cell is a singularly unique existence. You and note can combine and have, but Zenna is Zenna, and note Note."

Zenna asked, "You refer to yourself as note and not I. Why?"

"Home is I. When note is home, we'll be I. They are, in fact, the same, Zenna."

"Who is we, then?"

"We are all of us, connected," Note explained. "We don't all know we're connected, but we are. What one experiences, we all experience in that place, home."

"I sense questioning—or something akin to it—in you. What is it, Note?"

"We've just come from another place outside this Universe, Zenna, another Universe."

"Yes, I sense it."

"We didn't know what we know now. Here is home, Zenna. The other Universe wasn't polar. Being of this Universe, we accept polarization as part of the path, the path to wholeness. This other place was wonderful, like our place, but without polarization."

"What did that change there, in the other Universe, dear Song?" Zenna asked with reverence.

"Everything!

"We know our Universe is composed of matter and essence, and we believed this essence was everything. When we encountered the reality around the multiverse and how its existence would enable each possible outcome of every event in each moment, we believed all would be within the same essence because the essence is of God.

"The essence in the Universe we just came from differed from the essence here. We now understand that each variation of essence must exist too for God to find the answer."

"The answer?" Zenna asked, concentrating on the message.

"Yes." Note answered without volunteering the question.

"What about space, Song? Does each Universe live in its own space?"

"No. It is all in this space."

"Is matter different in the other Universe?" Zenna asked.

"No," Note responded. "The components of matter are the same; the matter is constant across the multiverse. The essence is variable."

"Song, what stands out most to you about what's different?"

"Perspective, Zenna. All outcomes can be considered, but only one outcome can be witnessed or recorded as truth at the moment, according to the perspective."

"Are you referring to 'The Superposition Principle' that states that, while we don't or can't measure the position of electron particles, it is in all possible positions it can be in at the same time, and when it is observed, the superposition collapses?"

"On a much grander scale, Zenna. It's not that the superposition collapses but rather that we can only observe a given particle through the lens of our perspective, a lens made with the essence of our Universe and impacted by our individual essence as impacted within our vessel."

"And the other Universe lacked polarization?" she confirmed.

"Yes, polarization within the perspective of the participants in the life of that reality. The matter was the same, while the essence was different."

"I feel more in you, Song; there is more."

"There is, Zenna. It's around fate and chance for all the outcomes. We don't have the time to share it. You remember everything; what resonates most with you? Share your Song with me, Zenna."

"I'm excited to share, Little Song, but first, thank you for my dear Owne. He became my last husband, and we spent two hundred years in the most wonderful and selfless relationship. I can't put it into words. I miss him always, Song, but the missing is wonderful. Thank you again, Note. I'm forever grateful!

"My Song, what do I remember?" Zenna considered. "Many things come to mind; how much time do we have?"

"We're sharing much faster than you know, Zenna. We have all the time you need, and you don't have to think in words. Just remember...we'll know."

She smiled.

"The most profound thing I remember is motherhood! It's been the most joyous and painful of all things in my life. Joyful because of the genuine gifts that each one of my children was to me, absolute gifts. Painful for two reasons. One was because I was blessed to watch them live and cursed to see them die. The other because it was the most important thing I ever was, a Mother, and once, I was a horrible one. There is a certainty, however. Each of my dear children lives in my hearts, still and forever.

"What I experienced in being a mother was, first and foremost, unconditional love. Each of my precious children was uniquely themselves and on their individual path. Still, as their mother, I felt ultimately bonded to them, remaining responsible for our bond and their wellness. Each extended my being and I theirs. Their joys were my joys, and their heartaches were mine as well.

"Unlike all the other mothers I've known, I got to learn how to be one over a long time and many children. The normal lifetimes I've seen don't give a woman a chance to hone the motherhood skill, even though most end up being remarkable at it. However, I became a better mother with each child as I came to understand both it and living beings. I came to realize that I needed to bear witness to their unique nature rather than imprint mine upon them. Getting to that space forced me to face how I dealt with memories, judgment, emotion, and assumptions. Motherhood, for me, evolved into being present for my children, so I could give them whatever they needed from me. No one has more to give a child than a mother, so the child being in a place to reach out for what the mother must provide is the key. God lives in motherhood. Motherhood is essence, Note."

"Do you wish to open and bare your truth about your child, the one you didn't mother well?" Note messaged.

"Sora, Sora was her name, my dear, dear Sora. I was not whole when I mothered her, and she received meanness, rejection, and chaos from me. It was as if she were a magnificent bush, and she was brilliant, but one that I pruned and broke. All Sora wanted was to thrive like anyone else, and she trusted me to help her. I broke her down over and over instead.

"Still, and despite me, she rose from the ashes repeatedly to become a remarkable woman. I know she carried the scars I caused throughout her life. That is one of two burdens I deserve to carry until the end. If there is punishment, Note, I should receive it for what I was, what I did to my precious Sora.

"Note, tell me about God. Will I see God?"

"Your being has expanded from the first moment of your conception to now, Zenna. Your awareness and consciousness have expanded continuously from then to now. As you move from this body, it will continue to do so. God is now and in your future."

Zenna continued. "I was blessed by being with the Emolie from their natural beginning to their end. They initially evolved slowly like all other species I've witnessed, but once they gained a measure of intelligence, their evolution was brisk. Unlike other species I've known, the Emolie didn't have to learn through mistakes. Their DNA drove them to excel in the most effective and efficient way possible. They saved a great deal of time and prevented themselves from many challenges by learning from the immense experiences and technical skills that I amassed before I came to them. Within thousands of years, they assimilated all I knew and surpassed me. They found that spirituality was an efficient and effective way toward transformation to more abundance. They focused on it. Second to spirituality with the Emolie was technology. Their incredible intellect, spiritual depth, and love for technology propelled them to evolve in every way, going from a rodent-like creature to energy beings over only 192 thousand years. I mothered six Emolie children when they were at a physical level close to my own. Those were some of my favorite years. That period taught me a great deal about evolution, something I uniquely cannot do.

"Note, I have a question for you. You've experienced the full spectrum of evolution from life's most primitive to its most advanced. Is there something profound that comes to you about what you've discovered?"

"Yes. All living beings respond to stimuli. The more advanced the being, the more awareness they have around the intricacies of the stimulus. The enlightened ones and most advanced, both recognize and appreciate their core being, inside and separated from any stimulus. They experience moments of home there."

"Yes, Note. It's profound."

Note posed a new thought. "Experiencing the evolution of the Emolie must have been one of the greatest gifts. Is there something in your memory about what you learned?"

"As an animal, I learned more about instinct and intuition. I believe that instinct is an innate behavior, usually without thought. It's almost mindless, but it can be profound, and related actions often take place with no connection to the consequences. Early in their evolution, the Emolie showed a firm reliance on it, and I got to know it well in them and myself.

"Intuition is the ability to understand something immediately, with no conscious reasoning.46 Intuition is pure understanding before bias. Contemplating the source of instinct in animal life forms and the source of intuition itself has filled much of my life. I've searched for that source, inside and out; have you seen it?"

"Yes, Zenna. We have interpreted instinct to be protective and intuition to be connective. We need both to survive the moment you're in while yielding hope for a moment to come. We think of them as additional senses.

"Please share more with us."

"I've profoundly enjoyed meaningful friends over time, including one that I know you know, the Dream Maker. The Dream Maker filled my sleep countless times. For some time now, we'll just sit and talk in my dreams. The Dream Maker is special to me and told me of your coming on this day. How does the Dream Maker know?"

Note answered, "The Dream Maker has profoundly impacted the Universe. As you witnessed with the Emolie, life forms have extraordinary abilities that they are hidden until they eventually become aware of them. The Dream Maker introduces individuals to themselves within the dream realm. That realm exists like the skin on your hand, as you've discovered."

"Yes, I live there too, Note, just as I live here. At long last, the Dream Maker shared what some life forms have called them. Do you know the name?"

"I don't," Note responded.

"Gabriel," she offered. "They have no gender, either."

"The angel, Gabriel?" Note sought confirmation.

"Yes," she confirmed. "How would you not know that, Note?"

"We don't know what we don't know until we know."

"Yes," Zenna responded mischievously.

"Okay, more of my life. It's been everything—good and evil. I've lived through periods of countless years of madness where I felt locked into my existence. I don't evolve like everything around me. I've done all there is to do many times, so sometimes I looked forward to nothing. All those I've loved have died. Note, I discover something new every day and find blessings in it. My spirit evolved to that, even though my physical being remained the same.

"I've been bad. When I was evil, I got imprisoned several times. Though I remember all of it, one comes to mind more often than the others. I was in the penal colony in Fibus and served a 150-year sentence for several murders I committed. The verdict was the most they could give and was a life sentence to most, but not to me. I served some 63 years of my sentence in the hole, our word for solitary confinement. My cell was 6 foot by 8 foot with a toilet/sink combination, a mat to sleep on, and a single light. They allowed me to read and I could have up to eight books in my cell at a time. I was granted one hour a day outside in the yard, a nine by nine block with an open roof with bars over it. They never allowed me to see anyone but the guards, and no one ever touched me with any kindness during that time.

"I was in a block with 18 other prisoners at a time, each in solitary. Someone was screaming almost always, as they lost their mind. Often, I could smell feces as one or more of the prisoners would spread it over themselves and their cell in their madness. The guards let them rot for days before they got cleaned up, and several didn't survive long because of their physical and mental condition. The screaming and suffocating stench made it impossible to sleep and I slept in the yard when I spent my hour there. For me, I felt hope because I knew I would live beyond my sentence, but for the other prisoners, they had no such promise. Why endure?

"Was that the most you've suffered Zenna?

"Other than what I did to Sora, yes. It is also the best part of my life."

"Best?"

"The incarceration happened, Note, but the cell is a metaphor for how we life forms are confined in our limitations. Over that time, with such confinement, I learned to both savor almost everything while I sought to find my soul, the place beneath, and beyond all the stimulus or lack thereof...

"Consider all that constrains some of us, Note. Our bodies hold us in and separate us from all else. Systems such as aging confine our time to learn. We love food, but can eat only so much," she said, smiling. "Anger and every emotion confine us to its character. We are constrained by the life form our DNA denotes. I'm an immortal who's about to die." Her face broke into a smile at the absurdity of that comment. "And you are Note.

"What I've witnessed, observed, and adopted, Note, is that all things yearn to be free from their constraints. When one has a relationship with another, they expand beyond their limits for a time and find peace. Overcoming obstacles, miracles, realizations, and countless other things takes us beyond our constraints, to new ones; initially, we find peace as we fill the new space.

"My life purpose for countless millennia now has been to move beyond my current constraints, to find the next one. Our limitations are endless. Like, I still can't fly...can you believe that after all this time?" Zenna giggled playfully. "You know, Note, perhaps that's why you are 'we' and not 'I.' You aren't constrained to 'I.'"

"Home is I Zenna. Home isn't constrained," Note shared.

Zenna continued. "I must add that my consistent resolve to move beyond my current constraints has filled my existence with hope, yearning, and reason. It's why I know you; I've come a long way. The gamma rays are coming, aren't they?"

"Yes, Dear One. Your next journey beyond your body will start soon.

"Zenna, what's your favorite word?" Note asked.

"Odd question Note, but I appreciate it.

"The word is unity. It's what I hope for. Unity is the state of being united or joined as a whole; yes, unity!

"Note, I know you feel it or understand it, but there is the second burden that haunts me along with Sora. Because of all my time, my immortality, I did countless things on my journey, and, as I alluded, some were terrible. The ultimate power of good drew me in like a moth to the light, but the road to that place journeyed through many evil gyrations. My eternal sorrow springs from what I did to another little girl, Gwinin.

"I led a race called the Huntuie, a warrior race. They—we—held a great thirst for power and domination and gained our thrills at the expense of those we considered weak. It was pathetic.

"We attacked a planet in the Antar system that spawned only a moderately primitive culture living on it. They were just farmers. We swept down on them with our powerful ships and started obliterating the civilization. This is awfully hard to say, Note. It's unforgivable.

"We liked to enjoy the results of our carnage, so we landed our ships to walk through the chaos, mayhem, and destruction. We found our remaining victims and slaughtered many of them, one at a time.

"I walked up on a little girl, over her mother's body, crying and calling out, 'Mommy, Mommy, Mommy!'" Zenna's voice trembled.

"The two Huntuie warriors with me and I were smiling. I heard the warriors laughing." Zenna's chest ached at this moment with Note, remembering.

"I pointed my gun toward the little girl's head. She was still looking down at her mother like she didn't even know we were there, then she looked up at me.

"In all my time, Note, with all the powerful and spiritual beings I've encountered, I have seen nothing even remotely close to the power of this little girl.

"I looked into her eyes and in a moment was changed forever. I saw the past, present, and future in an instant. I knew good and evil, all there in the eyes of that little girl with her dirty face, in rumpled little clothes, with bare feet. I saw her broken and brown crooked teeth, and I melted forever. I've thought countless times that I met God; she *was* God. I just can't and don't want to forgive myself for what I was, and it haunts me. Her eyes, I can't forget her eyes, a blue, a deep blue, unlike any I've ever seen. I felt a jolt, like moving from one path to another, bad to good. But the bad haunts me. What I did to her, to them, haunts me."

"And you remember her name," Note shared.

"Gwinin," Zenna answered softly.

"You didn't shoot her?"

"No, I left her with her dead mother and ordered a withdrawal of the warriors from the planet. I directed the evolution of the Huntuie to become protectors for good after that. But I just can't forgive the evil that I was, that I did, and she is on my mind every day."

"That was Gray, Zenna. There is only one of Gray and one other. Their souls exist to move darkness to light. We know Gray; we know what you are remembering.

"Like Gray, you too are one of a kind, as all are really, but you are the only immortal, and we love you. The hero is not the one who does great things easily, but the one who rises above all forms of resistance, hardships, and limitations to do good, whether great or small. Let the haunting end, Zenna. A hero, you are."

"What about you, dear Note? How much more do you go on?"

"We're almost done," Note shared. "We don't know what that is or what it will be, but we know."

"What have you learned about all this, after all this time, all that you have been part of, Note?" Zenna asked.

"We know we can't know because we don't have the capacity, but this is what we feel, Zenna.

"All of this started with a spark. We call it the God Spark; others called it a Big Bang. We feel that God wants to answer, 'What am I?' The God Spark occurred with matter, and the singular existence that is this Universe broke out from the source. Space expanded and was created as matter and energy flowed into it, in its purest form, to support the physics of this Universe. Within each particle, each particle of each particle was a piece of God, the God particle, the graviton. The God particle birthed the process of combination. Hydrogen gathered to create energy to ignite, to fuse to helium and so on through all the elements of matter, all with a God particle in their perfect center.

"As the combinations multiplied and complexity increased, each new combination was unique in all the singular existence. There were seemingly infinite combinations of substances and perspectives, in a different space and time, everything unique, all growing in complexity as things become born into existence. Essence needed life for it to manifest, and life began, each unique in a different time, place, and perspective.

"With all the countless forms of life and existence in all forms of matter and its changes, all with the God particles present, over trillions of years, every potential combination in all vantage points is being experienced to answer the question, 'What am I?' That is the 'why' for the existence of the Universe.

"On the grand scale, the God scale, we believe evolution is the pathway. It is 'how.'"

Zenna opened. "I'm stunned, Note, at what you contemplate. Back to the God particle, then it's the center of everything, each cell, each particle, everything?"

"Yes. It's in the wind you feel on your face and the heat you feel from your star on your back. It is in the dryness you feel in your eyes and the ache in your thigh muscle, in the sounds you hear and everything you are unaware of. It's in everything, everywhere."

"Then we're all connected to everything, is that right?"

"Yes."

"Before we go, Note, I have a final question for you. Does the Universe care? Does it matter if we're good or bad, give or take, does it matter?"

"No."

"Then why? If it doesn't matter, why?" Zenna asked passionately.

"It will be. It is. It was."

"What?"

"It is everything! That's the answer. Simple, boring, complex, deep, shallow, useless, profound, Everything!"

"Note, all my memories, all the love, all those I loved and love, do they die with me?"

"Nothing is ever lost, Dear One. Here we go!"

The massive rays hit Zatar at that moment, and it whisked away the atmosphere. Zenna, the immortal, was dead. Note's journey continued.

In Between

$\mathcal{N}$ote reaffirmed through Zenna the magnitude of evolution. *Order plus Chaos equals Evolution,* and evolution is the path to answer God's question. With Zenna, Note experienced the beautiful result of the process, while better understanding the journey.

Zenna was ready to die and move to the next realm, but still wondered what was next. Note is compelled to continue the discovery of that innate calling within living beings.

Chapter Forty-Nine

Heaven

Manha entered the sanctuary and looked over to see Father Dobler on his knees; his head was bowed, praying to Jesus Christ. In front of him was a large wooden carving of Christ. It was all from one piece of wood: a giant redwood that had stood over the Redwood Valley for centuries and had now given the heart of its fallen trunk to this massive 20-foot wooden carving of Jesus Christ. The statue was of Christ praying for humanity.

Sensing his guest, the priest looked up and over to find a young woman observing him. Though he could see her blue eyes, the hijab prevented him from discerning the full uniqueness of this special being.

She approached him. "Hello, Father. I'm Manha. Thank you for meeting with me today."

"Ah, Manha...that means 'Gift of Allah' in your faith. I'm happy to share this time with you. Let's go to the back of the church and sit in a pew. It'll be quiet there." Father Dobler led her down the long aisle toward the rear of the church. The building was over two hundred years old and smelled stale but comfortable. Years of candle smoke coated the high ceilings and artifacts with soot, and the old wood was covered with layers of varnish. Countless souls had come looking for hope, and each left pieces of themselves in this place of worship.

They reached the pew and turned to face one another. Father felt surprise with a moment of déjà vu. He didn't know she was here to help answer his prayers.

"Okay, Manha, what brings you to visit with me today?"

"You can tell that I'm a Muslim and, like you, I live my life to serve God. I've found that a life of service is my path to do that. I'm here to talk with you because a great question burns inside me. Father, many speak of you, your ways, and your connection with God. I'm here because I have faith that you can help me with my significant question."

Smiling, he looked away modestly and then back. "What is your question, dear child?"

"In Christianity, your people believe in a place called heaven. For my people, it's paradise. Both religions teach of this place that we go after we leave this world. Father, my question is, what is life in this place like? You have studied this for years, and perhaps you have been told in your deepest prayers. Please share!"

Manha's question was the one question the priest couldn't answer; it was the one question that weighed heavily on him and had for years. Graduating from this life to a better place made the endless struggles worth it but, he wondered, what does one graduate to? Manha had asked the perfect question to reach the Achilles heel of his faith, and he looked at her with intensity.

"I'm happy to discuss heaven with you. It's a wonderful place to be sure." He looked away.

"Father, why do you look away? Why does your voice fall off as you talk about it? Do you not believe in heaven, Father?"

He felt caught, dead to rights, sitting on a pew in the church dressed in a shroud of faith after a lifetime of service espousing the Christian doctrine.

Father Dobler proceeded. "The Bible puts heaven into terms people can comprehend. I know God is real, but I believe God is more than we can comprehend. I so want to know and understand God beyond words so I can convey God to the people I serve. God and heaven are much the same, beyond words. I'm lost, Manha."

"That's why I've come to you, Father. There are endless possibilities in this moment and existence. The limitations of our personalities don't survive this lifetime, so all that you know, love, and believe dissolve when you do. There's no reason to die, to go to heaven or paradise or to compromise your opportunity at living now. If you want to live forever as the person you are, you will not, but you can live longer, and more richly."

"And you are a messenger, Manha, aren't you?"

"Thankfully, yes, I am."

"Are the messengers from God?"

"We're all a part of God, Father, you as much as me. There's so much in us and around us that most all don't know, not because they can't, but simply because they don't. One of the most wonderful messages I've heard is, 'You don't know until you know.' Musicians are messengers, Father. Did you find John Lennon interesting?"

"Yes."

"There's a path to this place, Father, and it's not through a messenger like me, but through the message itself. That message is in every being, in a soft but profound voice continuously delivered in and around you. The message is heaven, Father."

Looking deeply and lovingly into Manha's eyes, he spoke.

"I needed to hear this, but why me? Why bring this to me?"

Gently, she shared, "You're everything, Father; everyone is."

Note left Manha.

In Between

Note faced note's own question now. Why does a soul want heaven? What is it about their being that they want to live perpetually? Is it their sense of self, or the God particle within them?

What is the sense of self? Is the sense of self the "home" that's within us, surrounded by the noise of our personality?

Chapter Fifty

We Are Everything

8 billion years after Abraham Lincoln recited the Gettysburg address, the Sun had run through its red giant phase, and only a white dwarf remained. Jupiter's orbit changed because of the Sun's decrease in mass. The gas giant took on some of that mass and heated. A greenhouse effect took hold, and Europa's seas melted.

The Huron moved into orbit around Europa.

"Jesine, we've arrived at the moon. We'll scan for metallic objects."

"Thank you, Captain."

Jesine was the Priestess of the Tarwin race, a highly evolved species that were tasked with understanding spiritual physics within the Universe and sharing their bounty. The Tarwin were the race of pollinators that existed during this period of the Milkdromeda galaxy, a result of the merging of the Milky Way, Andromeda, and Triangulum galaxies that had collided some four billion years earlier. The new elliptical galaxy was home to some 1.5 trillion stars and countless intelligent life forms.

The nectar the Tarwin race mined and spread throughout intelligent life was best described as love, peace, and kindness. The resulting highly evolved and prolific cultures gave back more than they consumed. All Tarwins served their queen, Paulie, and she served them. Each Tarwin held individual goals, dreams, and desires, and met those as they cared for their social order.

***

A week earlier, the Queen summoned Jesine.

"I'm honored to be in your presence, my Queen." Note joined Jesine at that moment.

"Jesine, I'm ill, and I'm failing."

"How, my Queen, how is that possible?"

"My rule has been long and bountiful. Tarwins have evolved as has our community of worlds. However, the meaning of our existence is in peril because I can no longer evolve."

"What does that mean, my Queen?"

"I was born to bring the Tarwin into existence and find and pollinate the worlds to evolve and aide evolution. So long as goodness grew and spread, we found the space to evolve. My belief that there was more, with reason to continue, has been paramount to our existence. I have come to the end of my drive to evolve, Jesine. There is more to know, but drive requires inspiration, and that now eludes me."

"Then we may be at our end, my Queen?"

"Yes. If I end, the Tarwin will end."

"And all the worlds?" Jesine asked.

"They will change. Our loving nectar has spawned beauty in the worlds. They will have less of it if we go. Change will result."

"How can that be? We are a pillar of good. How can such a pillar be lost?"

"All things begin and end. There is something in the Universe much more powerful than we are, Jesine. It was here before us and will be present after. It may be the reason we exist. It's grace.

"How may I serve you, my Queen?"

"It is possible there is still reason to be. Grace may have a plan for us still. A short time ago, one of our teams came across a beggar on Zanlat. This beggar knew about me, your Queen, and asked to be in my presence. The team could not deny the request...unable."

"Unable?" Jesine asked intensely.

"My team was powerless to say no to the beggar. The beggar came to me.

"I could not tell if this beggar was male or female. They had a tone to their voice, but not one tone. I'm Queen, and yet I felt like I served this beggar. They had form, but I can't tell you what it was; I still can't picture them, even now. But, Jesine, the message was unequivocal."

"What was the message, my Queen?"

"That there is more! More to know, more to discover, more reason to be, more. We have yet to answer the question.

"The beggar seemed to be a humanoid form and extended their opened hand, palm up. There was a rolled-up piece of paper in their hand. When I reached out and picked up the paper, I saw the hand clearly, every line, each variation of color, but my attention went to the center. There was a hole, a bloody hole, in the middle of the hand. Suddenly, only grace remained, without form."

"Was the beggar The Christ?"

"Yes, Jesine."

"Is there something on the paper?"

"There is, I know, but I can't open it; it won't open. I believe it is here, but it isn't. I can't explain that now, but we will understand soon. That's why you're here, Jesine. Go. Sleep. You will take a journey for our people and me."

Jesine did as her queen requested and slept. A loving dream ensued, and she met the Dream Maker. She knew the answer for her queen was on the moon, Europa.

***

"We've located it, Jesine; we'll recover it."

"Thank you, Captain. Please inform me when it's onboard."

Jesine was on Europa. She and the captain had found The Jackard, a ship from Earth, sent in the 23rd millennium on Earth. Though they constructed it with the best of science at that time, it couldn't last billions of years...but it had. The Jackard arrived at the frozen moon of Europa, melted its way through the ice and buried itself deep within the mud at the bottom of the sea.

"Jesine, we have it."

"I'm on my way, Captain."

She entered the bay to find the Captain with her first officer and the recovery team.

"How old is this, Jesine?"

"Older than our home star."

"It's nothing more than titanium. It couldn't have endured for a fraction of this long."

"It wasn't alone."

At that moment, the Jackard disintegrated into dust on the Huron's bay floor. In the dust rested a vial, and in it, a piece of rolled-up paper. Jesine picked up the vial. It, too, turned to dust in her hand, leaving only the paper. She opened it to read these words with the Captain looking over her shoulder:

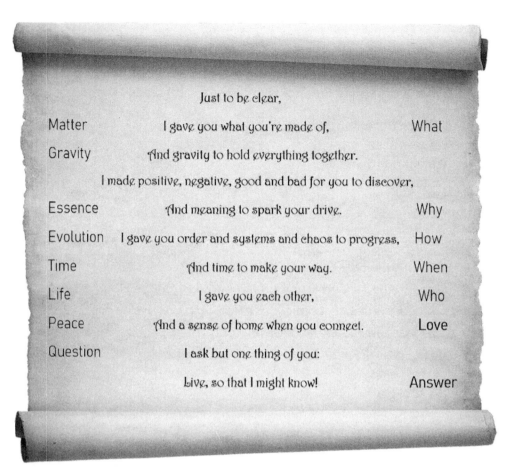

	Just to be clear,	
Matter	I gave you what you're made of,	What
Gravity	And gravity to hold everything together.	
	I made positive, negative, good and bad for you to discover,	
Essence	And meaning to spark your drive.	Why
Evolution	I gave you order and systems and chaos to progress,	How
Time	And time to make your way.	When
Life	I gave you each other,	Who
Peace	And a sense of home when you connect.	Love
Question	I ask but one thing of you:	
	Live, so that I might know!	Answer

47

"Can you interpret the language, Jesine? I don't recognize it," the Captain stated.

"Yes."

"What does it mean?"

"Each of us is Everything," she answered.

Note left Jesine.

In Between

Note realized that each living being is everything the Universe is, like a Universe unto ourselves.

God gave life and asked only one thing in return: That we live it.

Chapter Fifty-One

Kindness

Yoto felt honored to have raised his niece and nephew after their Raun died, and now the last thing he could do for Tont and Yum was to help save their lives. The boat was too full. It weighed more than it could sustain and didn't have the rations for the passengers.

The sea was the bluest he had ever seen it. It was beautiful, and so was this ultimate moment of sacrifice, his last act of kindness.

Yoto jumped out of the troubled boat. It was the right thing—the only thing—a kind old man could do. Yum and Tont yelled out to Yoto as the others held them to prevent them from helping Yoto or joining him. As a strong young man, Yum was the most vital passenger toward any success the desperate crew could hope for.

***

After some time, his body stopped responding to his mind's commands. He felt the sea all around him; Note joined him, and together they relived Yoto's beautiful life as it passed before him. As his exhausted body descended slowly into the depths, Yoto felt the living sea and the warmth of the water and heard the Song of the angels.

In Between

Note experienced the ultimate gratitude: the surrender of one's own life for life itself. Gratitude lives in *Love*, Note discovered.

Chapter Fifty-Two

e 3

Malick awoke to find his ship approaching Zet, the mythical remote station now visible even at 80 miles away. Her massive size denoted abundant activity and thriving life. His heart rate quickened as the excitement of being with living beings was just a few minutes away. Note joined Malick.

Zet fixed on to the Stune, and control surrendered to the station. No communications came over from Zet. That surprised Malick.

"Reene, scan for living beings at the station."

"One sentient being, Captain, ten thousand two hundred and thirty-seven plants, seven billion four hundred eighty-two million six hundred and fourteen thousand and eighteen insects, sixty-seven trillion..."

"Suspend."

One being, in all this, Malick thought.

Once the Stune docked, a doorway opened on the station side, and the being stood in it.

"What emotions do you sense, Reene?"

"Joy, Captain. The being is happy to see us. I sense safety for you."

"Give me an envelope and open the door. Is the being in an envelope? We're very much outside here."

"It is a bi-directional barrier, Captain."

"Okay. Connect the envelope to it."

Malick stood and moved through the doorway, floated through the envelope, and was placed inside the Zet, where the being stood.

After handing a translator to Malick, he placed it in his ear. *e* opened his arms and said, "Welcome to Zet. I'm *e*."

"Thank you, *e*. I'm Malick."

"Your ship is remarkable, Malick. We call them transparent jelly pods. How did you float from your ship to the station? Zetty informed me you are very much humanoid. How do you float?"

"Humanoid, yes, I know your station was placed here by the humans, and that humans define everything by human terms. Yes, by those standards, I'm humanoid, and I don't float on my own. The Stune is a plasma surge technology. I don't know what my people have now, but it was our best when I started the journey. With plasma surging, all the electrons are connected by the process and manipulated. It carries me across what I can best describe as a blanket of energy. To be honest, it tingles, but I kind of like it now."

"Remarkable," e commented. "I'll say, Malick, that the Zet can't refuel your ship. The technology here is not that advanced."

"It doesn't run on fuel, e. It runs on energy, even the small amounts that are out there in space. What I need is you. I've been on this trip for an exceptionally long time, and you are the first being I've even spoken to in several thousand years."

"I'm delighted to have you here, Malick. Would you like to join me for a cup of coffee and visit?"

"Coffee? Do you still have coffee? I've heard of coffee but have never been around any."

"It's a human thing. But it will soon be a Malick thing," e said, smiling.

A launch became immediately available to deliver them to the cafeteria.

"I can just walk, e. I need the exercise."

"The coffee is on the other side of the station. It would take us a day to walk there. Please, let's ride over, and then we can go for a walk with our coffee."

The launch ride was too fast to start any conversation. The sights were remarkable along the way.

"My, what a ride," Malick exclaimed.

"We want to impress you," e noted. "Here we are!"

The two entered an immense room with hundreds of tables and thousands of chairs. Most of the room was dark, with only a few small lights flickering and flashing. Ahead was a cozy booth warmed in a cool and restful light next to a large window looking out into the darkness of space. *e* spoke out. "Coffee for two with all the works." After getting comfortably seated, the waiter device arrived with the tray of coffee. "Bring us 15 cups, please," *e* requested.

"What's all of this, *e*?"

"Coffee is a strange thing, Malik. Every being loves it in a personal way. Coffee is like the canvas to a painting; do you know of paintings?"

"Yes. My aunt was an artist. She did portraits."

"Did she do your portrait?"

"Yes. Somehow, she saw aspects of me I didn't see in myself. She told me she saw into my essence. I don't know what she meant by that, but the painting was moving to me. I must admit I stared at it a good deal. It always seemed fresh, even though it was me. Tell me more about coffee."

"I hope your ship's system has your portrait and that you can share it, as I would like to see it," *e* responded. "Coffee is the canvas, and the paints are all of these things. I like mine with sweetener and cream. Here are all the options. I just put a little of each in my cup, then pour in my coffee and stir. Yummy."

"How do you recommend that I figure out what I like?"

"What's your favorite food, Malick?"

"Jartard."

"Okay, describe Jartard, please."

"It lives in fluid; we catch them and eat the inner flesh. Does the translator translate that for you?"

"The Zet translator is hit and miss on food and does better with questions, so if I ask the right question..."

"It sounds like fish. Zet, any reference to Jartard? What human understandings is it synonymous with?"

"Fish," Zet responded.

"Thank you, Zet."

"Do you add anything to your Jartard when you eat it?"

"I put dakey on it; that's very good."

"Zet, same question, but with dakey."

"Cheese," Zet announced.

"Should I just talk to Zet, *e*?"

"Great idea, Malick. Just speak out your favorite dining experience, including drink, and let's see what Zet comes up with."

Malick wanted to share. "I came to love Jartard as an adult, but as a young man, I had a favorite meal, one I could afford, and it was a good quantity to offset my hunger. I really, really enjoyed it. It was boesh legs on cradence served with jomen, palen, sut dakey, and splot all laid over gob stids served with yum sablod dinck rounds, oley mont, and ra me sa Ru with a thick crust and rich soloshish du."

"Sounds delicious, Malick. Zet, what did Malick just say?"

Zet responded. "I came to love fish as an adult, but as a young man, I had a favorite meal, one I could afford, and it was a good quantity to offset my hunger. I really, really enjoyed it. It was chile dogs with mayonnaise, relish, cheddar cheese, and ketchup over Fritos served with beer-battered onion rings, coleslaw, and apple pie à la mode with a thick crust and rich vanilla ice cream."

"Okay, Malick. I don't know what all that is either, but I recognize the apple pie à la mode, or, as you say, I think, the ra me sa Ru. That is a sweet, creamy dessert. That tells me you may like your coffee the same way I do because it tastes like a dessert. Please try this."

e poured the rich black coffee in the cup and then added two cubes of brown sugar and a generous pour of rich white cream. After stirring it, e pushed it over to Malick. "Try this!"

Taking a small sip, and then another, he smiled. "That's delicious!" Malick said happily.

The 15 cups arrived at that moment. "Do you want to try some other combinations?"

"No, *e*, this is wonderful."

Once the cups were removed, the two each sat back, and the conversation began.

"My sensors show you are the only humanoid being on this station. How is that possible?"

"Zet was established here tens of thousands of years ago by the Federation to support the exploration of space in this quadrant."

"Federation...I'm not familiar with that."

"Are you from this galaxy?"

"I'm not." Malick took another sip of coffee. He was already addicted.

"Most ships cannot travel from one galaxy to another," *e* noted.

"True, but you referred to humanity earlier; they're not from this galaxy."

"I grant you that, Malick. I'm human."

"The Federation is a group of civilizations in this galaxy that works together for the common good."

"You're human?" It surprised Malick.

"Yes," *e* confirmed. "We were from generation Q443."

"And Zet...was it established by the humans?"

"Yes, for the Federation."

"I understand. Please, how did you end up being alone here?"

"Zet was established and expanded over thousands of years and once supported a crew of more than a hundred thousand beings."

"Then, the myth is true about the Blue Star?" Malick changed topics abruptly.

"Yes," *e* answered. "Zet is two parsecs from a wormhole that exits in the primal galaxy on the other side of the Universe. No one has returned from there, but we understand the Blue Star is there, somewhere there."

"And the wormhole is still there?" Malick asked with intensity.

"I don't know. I've not heard from anyone in an exceedingly long time that has seen it."

"Okay, please, how did you end up alone?"

"In the beginning, for many shifts, millions of travelers passed through Zet to go to the hole; it was a pilgrimage. Over this long while, the Federation members evolved or met with tragedy, and the motivation and ability to come to Zet lessened."

"You say many shifts; what's a shift?"

"A thousand years," *e* answered.

"What's your life span?"

"Twelve hundred years."

"Are you on a shift?"

"Yes."

"What do you do on a shift?"

"Manage the station. I welcome travelers like you."

"How do you manage all of this alone?"

"Zet is a living machine. It has no soul as we do, but it lives and will always live. It will be here even after I'm gone. Zet tends to all the plants and the little crawly critters on board. It manages itself," *e* said, smiling.

"And how long have you been alone?"

"Just twenty years now. My wife, Ela, passed twenty years ago. We were the last."

"I'm sorry, *e*. I have a question about humanity if I may. Humanity has impacted the Universe in a positive way. What's it about your species that drives that?"

"It's a straightforward answer. We were, like all species, expectedly primitive in the beginning, but then settled on the understanding that set our path to survive and help others prevail."

"Please, what was it—is it?"

"Reverence for life, for all living things. It brought us to the doorstep of love. You will find an abundance of living things in and around the station. It is home to all of us." *e* smiled.

"Why are you here, Malick?"

"I seek the Blue Star as well. How long has it been since the last traveler came through here?"

"Seven shifts."

Both took several sips of their sweet, creamy, bold coffee.

"Why the Blue Star?" *e* asked to break the silence. "I mean for you?"

"It's funny you would ask me that, e, with this massive station being built just to help travelers get to it, tens of thousands of years ago. What did they share with you about why they sought the Blue Star?"

"Not to be trite, but I asked you first. Why for you?"

"You see out this window? It's dark out there, so dark, and has been for an exceedingly long time. There used to be trillions of stars and star systems and worlds and civilizations, trillions, and now, most of it's dark. It is said and perhaps even known by some that the Blue Star was here at the beginning, and if it's still here, in this Universe, it is not a Blue Star. There has to be meaning for all of this, a reason, a reason for you and me. Now you, e. Why did the humans tell you they built this station?"

"To explore. That's what they told me."

"Explore what?"

"The truth, Malick, to explore the truth."

"What have you found here?"

"I found you, Malick, and you, me. There is just quiet here now. The station lives, but it lives quietly by our standards. I have no conversations, and my internal conversations have little meaning. As time goes by, even words are leaving my mind. Without the noise, I'm more aware of and part of peace."

"Yes, I feel you e, yes. My mind has been noticeably quiet too, but far from empty. For a long time, I looked for meaning in powerful words."

"Like faith?" e asked and then raised his cup for another sip. He licked his lip and smiled slightly.

"Yes, like faith. What made you ask me about that word?"

"The last traveler, the one seven shifts ago, was a man named Adam. I was told that he was like no other that ever visited here, that he was part of the Blue Star. They told me his soul was pure. The meaning he left us with was faith. Faith. I have faith, Malick."

"You say Adam's soul was pure, or that's what they conveyed to you. What's that?"

"Hope. Purity is hope. I've discovered that in the quiet, Malick."

"Yes, I feel that too. So, Adam was part of the Blue Star? How is that?"

"That, I have no answer for. If we have faith, we know without words."

"Did Adam leave any messages?"

"He did leave one that's been my company in the silence. It was an answer to a question written in my soul. I know we don't find our way until it's time, and I didn't know about his message until I discovered it in the archives after Ela passed."

"Please, *e*, before you go on, what's the question?"

"What am I?"

"Yes, I have that question too. What did Adam share that gave you your answer, and what is the answer to your question?"

"It is the same answer for you, Malick. The answer is, everything."

"I'm not sure I can agree with that, *e*, and I definitely can't comprehend it."

"Put simply, we're created in God's image, and God is everything. Adam shared that the difference between our experience and God's is focus. Our focus ties our experience to whatever we're focused on, stimulus, a thought, insanity. I'm sure, Malick, that you're more aware now than when you were younger, and my guess is that when you were younger, you were much more focused on stimulus, thoughts, or insanity. Is that right?"

"Yes, it is. Then God's experience is without focus? What's that like? Did Adam share anything on that?"

"He did. Yes, God's experience is without focus, so there are no memories. God is aware of each and every morsel of everything from the beginning to now, all at the same time. It's like a glass getting filled with water. As the Universe evolves, the glass fills more and more. God is aware of everything in the glass, all the time. We, on the other hand, are part of the water, like God, but just aware of what we focus on," *e* shared.

"And if we remember something, we are focusing on a past moment?"

"Yes."

"Then God doesn't know what is going to happen?"

"God does know but still has to discover it."

"Why?"

e suggested, "Perhaps God is asking our question too. We are in God's image."

"Then, the question gets answered when the glass is full?"

"Yes, as God experiences all discovery."

"Why is this important to us, e?"

"Malick, I can't answer for God, but for you and me, knowing what we are explains why we seek as we do, however we do. We want to be free from the focus, the constraints, because, in truth, we are everything, unbound. That is why that place is home, and we all want to get home."

They sat quietly together for a good while, enjoying their moment and nectar.

"Yes, *e*! This coffee is wonderful. How do you entertain yourself here, or do you hibernate most of the time?"

"Zet wasn't designed with hibernation. I just naturally sleep a third of the time. I entertain myself by experiencing things for the first time. I've found there is always, without fail, something new to discover. Oddly, discovery seems profoundly natural. It helps me to know what I am."

"You use the words 'experience something' for the first time. Is that the word you mean?"

"Yes. As my internal dialogue lessens, I find things to be more connected than when I defined them with words. If I just see something and define it, I don't experience it. So, I seek new things to experience, and there is more of that than I'll ever discover."

"That's profound, *e*. That sounds like less focus."

"What will you do if you find the Blue Star, Malick?"

"I can't imagine."

"Then why pursue it?"

"After our conversation, I think I've just been trying to go home, like everyone else."

e tilted his head slightly and looked warmly at his guest. "I sense you have a question, one that may have an answer. Am I right?"

"You are more than perceptive, *e*. It appears you are experiencing me," Malick said, smiling. "You feel like an old friend in just this brief time."

"I am your old friend and you mine. What's the question?"

"How can one, like you or me, reach another person's soul? Do you have that answer?"

"Yes, Malick. With our souls, like we're doing now."

They both leaned back in the fluffy booth and turned to look out into the darkness. "Yes." They both experienced it. Note left Malick.

In Between

Toward the end of the journey, Note found that the Home we seek throughout our existence is right in front of us.

Chapter Fifty-Three

The End

*N*ote was in darkness for a profoundly long time. All the stars had lived their lives and died. The Universe was populated with trillions of worlds, all cold, still and dead now; the Universe was without light. So much time had passed that even the energy holding matter together was dissipating and the matter was disintegrating. Note had faith that note too would dissolve and experience death and the ultimate peace. Note joined the last living being before the end.

With her head resting in his lap and her flowing hair laid over his leg, he lovingly stroked her head, feeling the warmth of her life, witnessing the profundity of it. Their eyes locked; there was nothing to say. It was done. Her mind floated into reliving their past together while bathing in the love of the beautiful moment. Adam heard her last breath leave her mouth, feeling it kiss his face.

Adam held his dear wife's body with loving reverence and sorrow. He was the last soul in the last living world, circling the final Star. He had entered a wormhole eons ago to get to this place—home—and Eve, arriving just centuries before this moment.

Note joined Adam and found the soul of Gray. Beyond words, they shared a sense of awe. There had been so much. The Universe was not infinite, yet it was incomprehensible.

Adam fell into a deep sleep and entered the dream realm. In it, Gray's essence came forward from Adam to be with Note. Another soul, Gabriel, then joined them. The three became one being and one consciousness, yet still singularly unique. As one, they stood in a familiar lodge where Note experienced skiing down a titanic mountain while in Jeff, miraculously saved by a breath of wind.

There, in front of the oversized fireplace with crackling logs burning and sizzling, was a mesmerizing figure. The old man with long and flowing silver hair, draped in a deep blood red honeycomb knit cardigan, sat gazing into the fire from the oversized Queen Anne leather chair. They walked to him.

The old man looked away from the fire and directly into them.

"You are Grace!" they stated.

"Yes," Grace affirmed.

"Why do we still have questions, Grace?"

"You are almost home but aren't yet and, until you are, you discover and experience," Grace answered.

"What's left?" they asked.

Grace answered, in essence, not words. "To become one as before the beginning. I have a question for you, Note. When did you first know Home?"

Note responded. "Dearest Grace. I joined with a truck driver on Earth as he drove his rig toward home for Christmas. Next to him on the passenger seat was a stuffed bear with a bow on it that he was taking to his little girl. In his mind, he pictured her staring out the window, yearning for her daddy to drive up. Jenna was home to him, and he was full of love for his family. His name was Abe.

"Driving down the road with Christmas music softly playing from the radio, Abe drove toward a stand of trees out on a grassy plain. When he looked at them, his heart ached, and he saw that the trees weren't growing from the ground but were instead reaching into the sky like hands, reaching for Home. He looked around to see the grasses and the other drivers all craving home. I understood home then, Grace, and have seen the drive to go home in every single instance of everything since. It's here now, with you."

"Yes, Note. Evolution and time are ending, and in the end, you will be home.

"Before the beginning, everything was One. A question was born. All separated, each separate instance unique from every other, and so it would remain throughout all time, within each Universe. Every combination, every joining, every thing remaining unique unto itself.

"Incomprehensible combinations occurred and evolved. Evolution is the key to answer the question. Evolution was the only way back to One, and it answers the question: 'What am I?' Evolution is 'how.'"

"Will One occur?" they asked Grace.

Grace responded, "It will be with you."

Note's essence asked Grace, "I once combined with evil and was complete; good, evil, and everything in between. Is evil home, too?"

"Good and evil are like flavors, Note. Each tastes bad to the other, but it's all equal and the same. Home is neither and both." With that, Grace shared the final message: "So Be It."

Adam regained consciousness, and his mind awoke. In Adam's last moment, one emotion outdistanced all the rest: gratitude. The Guardian stood before them with open arms. As Adam died, they moved into the Guardian's embrace and were delivered home where, as in creation, they joined the full Song of the Universes. Entering the Star, submerged in harmony and light and experiencing a profound sense of welcome, they thought, *God is Blue.*

***

After countless moments as each Universe was born, lived, and died, the answer finally evolved, the resulting miracle occurred, and One happened. Note, Gray, and Gabriel became One, the same, beyond singular existence. The Universes ended.

***

God's question was answered, yet, there was still another...

1   Choi, Charles Q. "Our Expanding Universe: Age, History & Other Facts." *Space.Com*, Space.com, 17 June 2017, www.space.com/52-the-expanding-Universe-from-the-big-bang-to-today.html.

2   "FORMATION OF THE HIGHER MASS ELEMENTS." *Aether.Lbl.Gov*, aether.lbl.gov/www/tour/elements/stellar/stellar_a.html.

3   "Human Development – Life in the Womb | Central Kentucky Right to Life." *Www.Ckrtl.Org*, www.ckrtl.org/life-issues/human-development-2/human-development-life-in-the-womb/.

4   "Human Development – Life in the Womb | Central Kentucky Right to Life." *Www.Ckrtl.Org*, www.ckrtl.org/life-issues/human-development-2/human-development-life-in-the-womb/.

5   "Human Development – Life in the Womb | Central Kentucky Right to Life." *Www.Ckrtl.Org*, www.ckrtl.org/life-issues/human-development-2/human-development-life-in-the-womb/.

6   "Human Development – Life in the Womb | Central Kentucky Right to Life." *Www.Ckrtl.Org*, www.ckrtl.org/life-issues/human-development-2/human-development-life-in-the-womb/.

7   "Human Development – Life in the Womb | Central Kentucky Right to Life." *Www.Ckrtl.Org*, www.ckrtl.org/life-issues/human-development-2/human-development-life-in-the-womb/.

8   "Human Development – Life in the Womb | Central Kentucky Right to Life." *Www.Ckrtl.Org*, www.ckrtl.org/life-issues/human-development-2/human-development-life-in-the-womb/.

9   "Human Development – Life in the Womb | Central Kentucky Right to Life." *Www.Ckrtl.Org*, www.ckrtl.org/life-issues/human-development-2/human-development-life-in-the-womb/.

10   "Human Development – Life in the Womb | Central Kentucky Right to Life." *Www.Ckrtl.Org*, www.ckrtl.org/life-issues/human-development-2/human-development-life-in-the-womb/.

11   "Human Development – Life in the Womb | Central Kentucky Right to Life." *Www.Ckrtl.Org*, www.ckrtl.org/life-issues/human-development-2/human-development-life-in-the-womb/.

12   "Human Development – Life in the Womb | Central Kentucky Right to Life." *Www.Ckrtl.Org*, www.ckrtl.org/life-issues/human-development-2/human-development-life-in-the-womb/.

13   "Human Development – Life in the Womb | Central Kentucky Right to Life." Www.Ckrtl.Org, www.ckrtl.org/life-issues/human-development-2/human-development-life-in-the-womb/.

14   "10 Important Facts About Osteomalacia." Facty, 13 Nov. 2018, facty.com/conditions/skeletal/10-important-facts-about-osteomalacia/. Accessed 17 May 2020.

15   http://www.webexhibits.org/causesofcolor/7A.html "Green Light Is Not Absorbed but Reflected Making the Plant Appear Green So the | Course Hero." Www.Coursehero.Com, www.coursehero.com/file/p37lir2/Green-light-is-not-absorbed-but-reflected-making-the-plant-appear-green-So-the/. Accessed 17 May 2020.

16   "If I Should Fall Behind Lyrics - Faith Hill." LyricsBox, www.lyricsbox.com/faith-hill-if-i-should-fall-behind-lyrics-v67ndcx.html. Accessed 18 May 2020.

17   https://files.deathpenaltyinfo.org/legacy/files/pdf/TN%20LI%20Protocol%207-5-18.pdf

18   https://files.deathpenaltyinfo.org/legacy/files/pdf/TN%20LI%20Protocol%207-5-18.pdf

19   "Eastern   Front   (World   War   II)."   Wikipedia,   16   May   2020,
      en.wikipedia.org/wiki/Russian_winter_offensive_of_1941-1942. Accessed 17 May 2020.

20   "What Did the Nazis Think of Czechs? - Axis History Forum." Forum.Axishistory.Com,
      forum.axishistory.com/viewtopic.php?t=230224. Accessed 17 May 2020.

21   Desmond, M. (2019, August 14). American Capitalism Is Brutal. You Can Trace That to the Plantation.
      Retrieved September 23, 2020, from https://www.nytimes.com/interactive/2019/08/14/magazine/slavery-
      capitalism.html

22   Shin, L. (2016, January 25). The Racial Wealth Gap: Why A Typical White Household Has 16 Times The
      Wealth   Of   A   Black   One.   Retrieved   September   26,   2020,   from
      https://www.forbes.com/sites/laurashin/2015/03/26/the-racial-wealth-gap-why-a-typical-white-household-
      has-16-times-the-wealth-of-a-black-one/

23   Rabouin, D. (2020, July 23). 10 myths about the racial wealth gap. Retrieved September 23, 2020, from
      https://www.axios.com/racial-wealth-gap-ten-myths-d14fe524-fec6-41fc-9976-0be71bc23aec.html

24   Molnar, Charles, and Jane Gair. "Chapter 2: Introduction to the Chemistry of Life." Opentextbc.Ca,
      BCcampus, May 2019, opentextbc.ca/biology/chapter/chapter-2-introduction-to-the-chemistry-of-life/.
      Accessed 18 May 2020.

25   "Types of Biological Macromolecules | Introduction to Chemistry." Lumenlearning.Com, 2013,
      courses.lumenlearning.com/introchem/chapter/types-of-biological-macromolecules/.

26   Jensen, Frances. The Digital Invasion of the Teenage Brain, Pages 211 and 212. HarperCollins Publishers,
      21 Feb. 2015. Accessed 1 May 2019. Book is "The Teenage Brain."

27   "NPR Choice Page." Npr.Org, 2019, www.npr.org/templates/story/story.php?storyId=124119468.

28   Jensen, Frances. Entering the Teen Year, Pages 14-23. HarperCollins Publishers, 21 Feb. 2015. Accessed 1
      May 2019. Book is "The Teenage Brain."

29   Jensen, Frances. Building a Brain, Page 33. HarperCollins Publishers, 21 Feb. 2015. Accessed 1 May 2019.
      Book is "The Teenage Brain."

30   Jensen, Frances. Building a Brain, Page 39-40. HarperCollins Publishers, 21 Feb. 2015. Accessed 1 May
      2019. Book is "The Teenage Brain."

31   CDC. "Facts about Anencephaly." Centers for Disease Control and Prevention, 2 Aug. 2017,
      www.cdc.gov/ncbddd/birthdefects/anencephaly.html.

32   "Milky Way." Wikipedia, Wikimedia Foundation, 6 Feb. 2019, en.wikipedia.org/wiki/Milky_Way.

33   "Accretion (Astrophysics)." Wikipedia, 18 Apr. 2020, en.wikipedia.org/wiki/Accretion_(astrophysics).

34   "Event Horizon." Wikipedia, Wikimedia Foundation, 7 Sept. 2019, en.wikipedia.org/wiki/Event_horizon.
      Accessed 27 Sept. 2019.

35   "Mass." Wikipedia, Wikimedia Foundation, 14 Apr. 2019, en.wikipedia.org/wiki/Mass.

36   "Quasar." Wikipedia, Wikimedia Foundation, 1 Dec. 2019, en.wikipedia.org/wiki/Quasar.

37   Diodati, Michele. "IC 1101, the Largest of All Galaxies." Medium, 11 Apr. 2020, medium.com/amazing-
      science/ic-1101-the-largest-of-all-galaxies-b54c874315ba. Accessed 18 May 2020.

38   "The Giving Tree." Shelsilverstein.Com, 2014, www.shelsilverstein.com/books/book-title-giving-tree/.
      Accessed 22 Sept. 2019.

39   "Yanny or Laurel." Wikipedia, 29 Apr. 2020, en.wikipedia.org/wiki/Yanny_or_Laurel. Accessed 18 May 2020.

40   "How Do Batteries Work? A Simple Introduction." Explain That Stuff, 26 Apr. 2019, www.explainthatstuff.com/batteries.html.

41   Haring, Bruce, and Bruce Haring. "President Donald Trump Tweetstorm – The Sunday Edition." Deadline, 9 Feb. 2020, deadline.com/2020/02/president-donald-trump-tweetstorm-the-sunday-edition-66-1202854941/. Accessed 18 May 2020.

42   "Bushfires, Cyclone, Torrential Rain Hit Australia's Coasts." News.Yahoo.Com, news.yahoo.com/bushfires-cyclone-torrential-rain-hit-003512678.html. Accessed 18 May 2020.

43   "Jamaica Earthquake: Magnitude 7.7 Earthquake Strikes off the Coast of Jamaica." Www.Msn.Com, www.msn.com/en-us/news/world/magnitude-7-7-earthquake-strikes-off-the-coast-of-jamaica-and-is-felt-as-far-away-as-miami/ar-BBZpRsS. Accessed 18 May 2020.

44   Myers, J., *, N., 19, J., Says, J., Says, B., Barnat, B., . . . Myers, S. (2016, March 24). Crucifixion - The Physical Suffering of Jesus. Retrieved September 13, 2020, from https://redeeminggod.com/crucifixion-physical-suffering-jesus/

45   "APOD Index - Stars: Open Clusters." Apod.Nasa.Gov, apod.nasa.gov/apod/open_clusters.html. Accessed 18 May 2020.

46   "Intuition." Www.Goconscious.Com, www.goconscious.com/home/articles/intuition.html. Accessed 18 May 2020.

[47] Just to be clear,

I gave you what you're made of,

And gravity to hold everything together.

I made positive, negative, good and bad for you to discover,

And meaning to spark your drive.

I gave you order and systems and chaos to progress,

And time to make your way.

I gave you each other,

And a sense of home when you connect.

I ask but one thing of you:

Live, so that I might know!

Printed in Great Britain
by Amazon

82687883R00312